RESEARCH HANDBOOK ON THE INTERPRETATION AND ENFORCEMENT OF INTELLECTUAL PROPERTY UNDER WTO RULES

RESEARCH HANDBOOKS ON THE WTO

This timely series of *Research Handbooks* analyses the interface between international economic law and other disciplines at the centre of current debate about the role and impact of the WTO. Each volume is edited by a prominent expert at the heart of this debate and brings together original contributions from an internationally recognisable cast of leading scholars and practitioners.

These *Handbooks* will be essential reference tools for academic researchers and doctoral students as well as for policy-makers and practising lawyers.

Future titles will include:

Research Handbook on Environment, Health and the WTO
Edited by Geert Van Calster

Research Handbook on the WTO Agriculture Agreement
Edited by Joseph McMahon and Melaku Desta

Research Handbook on the Interpretation and Enforcement of Intellectual Property under WTO Rules

Intellectual Property in the WTO
Volume II

Edited by

Carlos M. Correa

Director, Center for Interdisciplinary Studies of Industrial Property and Economics, University of Buenos Aires, Argentina

RESEARCH HANDBOOKS ON THE WTO

Edward Elgar
Cheltenham, UK • Northampton, MA, USA

Published by
Edward Elgar Publishing Limited
The Lypiatts
15 Lansdown Road
Cheltenham
Glos GL50 2JA
UK

Edward Elgar Publishing, Inc.
William Pratt House
9 Dewey Court
Northampton
Massachusetts 01060
USA

A catalogue record for this book
is available from the British Library

Library of Congress Control Number: 2009941281

FSC
Mixed Sources
Product group from well-managed
forests and other controlled sources
www.fsc.org Cert no. SA-COC-1565
© 1996 Forest Stewardship Council

ISBN 978 1 84980 107 2 (cased)

Printed and bound by MPG Books Group, UK

Contents

Contributors

Ermias Tekeste Biadgleng is a legal expert at the United Nations Conference on Trade and Development (UNCTAD).

Christophe Charlier is economist and Maître de Conférences at Nice – Sophia Antipolis University.

Susy Frankel is Professor of Law at Victoria University of Wellington, New Zealand.

Xuan Li is a legal expert at the Secretariat of the International Treaty on Plant Genetic Resources for Food and Agriculture, Rome.

Viviana Muñoz Tellez is Programme Officer at the South Centre, Geneva, Switzerland, and a PhD student at the Ecole Polytechnique Federale de Lausanne, Switzerland in the field of economics of innovation.

María Julia Oliva is Senior Adviser on Access and Benefit Sharing at the Union for Ethical BioTrade.

Pedro Roffe is Senior Fellow at the International Centre for Trade and Sustainable Development (ICTSD), Project on Intellectual Property and Sustainable Development.

Maximiliano Santa Cruz is Director of the National Institute of Industrial Property of Chile.

Joshua D. Sarnoff is Associate Professor at DePaul University College of Law.

Dalindyebo Shabalala is Assistant Professor at the University of Maastricht Faculty of Law.

Christoph Spennemann is a Legal Expert in the Intellectual Property Team, Policy Implementation Section, Division on Investment and Enterprise, UNCTAD.

David Vivas-Eugui is Deputy Programmes Director at the International Centre for Trade and Sustainable Development (ICTSD).

Preface

Carlos M. Correa

The Ministerial Conference that launched the GATT Uruguay Round in 1986 adopted an ambiguous mandate to initiate negotiations on intellectual property rights (IPRs), one of the 'new issues' to be addressed by the Contracting Parties. The proponents of such negotiations advocated the adoption of a comprehensive instrument that would supplement pre-existing international conventions on IPRs. They stressed that new international standards on the matter should not only ensure the availability but also the means to enforce conferred rights. An innovative feature of the proposed instrument was, hence, a detailed set of provisions on the enforcement of IPRs.

The relationship of the provisions of the Agreement on Trade-related Aspects of Intellectual Property Rights (TRIPS) with the international conventions it is based on, as well as its relationship with other components of the World Trade Organization (WTO), has raised a number of specific interpretive issues. Panels and the Appellate Body were called on to provide interpretations of century-old conventions, and to decide on the extent to which prior GATT jurisprudence (elaborated in relation to the trade in goods) could be applied to the protection of intangible property.

While the task of the WTO dispute settlement body in dealing with TRIPS issues has been challenging, Members bound to implement the TRIPS obligations at the national level faced a considerable burden. The broad coverage of the Agreement, in terms of both substantive and enforcement standards, required a complete overhauling of IPRs legislation in many countries. Moreover, as a result of strong divergences during the negotiations, the Agreement ended up with a number of ambiguities, often the price paid to reach a compromise, that required proper interpretations for the incorporation of the TRIPS obligations into national laws.

This *Handbook* offers studies, elaborated by a group of distinguished academics and IPRs experts, on the main issues raised by the interpretation and enforcement of some of the key TRIPS obligations. This volume provides an indispensable complement to the *Research Handbook on the Protection of Intellectual Property under WTO Rules: Intellectual Property in the WTO Volume I*, which addresses the origins, history and substantive provisions of the Agreement. As with Volume I, a basic objective of this *Handbook* is to provide a source of high quality original reference for research, teaching and professional practice on WTO-related issues concerning intellectual property protection. It is intended to offer a state-of-the-art overview in this complex area. Although it is not intended to be used as a textbook, it would be useful for advanced and postgraduate students as reference points, as well as for scholars and policy-makers.

This volume starts with a much-needed analysis of the applicability of GATT jurisprudence to the interpretation of the obligations contained in the TRIPS Agreement. It then offers a detailed discussion about the implementation of two of the main enforcement measures mandated by the Agreement: injunctions and border measures. A subsequent chapter is devoted to the conditions (concerning IPRs) under which new WTO members have been admitted since its creation in 1995. The remainder of the book consists of detailed analyses of the main rulings adopted under the Dispute Settlement Understanding concerning the TRIPS Agreement. Cases involving geographical indications, copyright, patents and test data are examined.

I am immensely thankful to the authors for their contributions. I am sure the readers will also appreciate their effort and the quality of the materials presented in this volume.

Carlos M. Correa

INTERPRETATION, ENFORCEMENT AND IMPLEMENTATION

1 The applicability of GATT jurisprudence to the interpretation of the TRIPS Agreement

Susy Frankel

1. Introduction

To assess the applicability of interpretations of GATT[1] to the TRIPS Agreement[2] it is necessary to examine the relationship between those agreements. The relationship between the TRIPS Agreement and other WTO agreements is complex. Structurally, the relationship is that the GATT, GATS[3] and the TRIPS Agreement are the main annexes of the WTO Agreement.[4] The TRIPS Agreement preamble, among other broad statements of intention, says that the members recognised the 'need for new rules and disciplines concerning . . . the applicability of the basic principles of GATT 1994' to the TRIPS Agreement. When the TRIPS Agreement was first in force, this preamble made sense as there were established practices and understandings about the operation of GATT 1947. The new WTO Agreement, including TRIPS, was established to develop and change the original GATT 1947, particularly the process of dispute settlement. However, GATT disputes were the known source of discussion of trade principles and WTO panels and the Appellate Body referred to them, particularly in the earlier disputes brought to the WTO.[5]

---

[1] General Agreement on Tariffs and Trade 1994, Marrakesh Agreement Establishing the World Trade Organization ('WTO Agreement'), Annex 1A, Article XX, 15 April 1994, 1867 UNTS 187, 33 ILM 1153 (1994) ('GATT').

[2] Agreement on Trade-related Aspects of Intellectual Property Rights, 15 April 1994, Marrakesh Agreement Establishing the World Trade Organization ('WTO Agreement'), Annex 1C, 33 ILM 1197, 1198 (1994) ('TRIPS Agreement').

[3] General Agreement on Trade in Services, WTO Agreement, Marrakesh Agreement Establishing the World Trade Organization ('WTO Agreement'), Annex 1B, 1869 UNTS 183, HR Doc. No. 103–316, at 1588 ('GATS').

[4] Marrakesh Agreement Establishing the World Trade Organization ('WTO Agreement').

[5] In *Japan – Taxes on Alcoholic Beverages*, the Appellate Body said, 'Article XVI:1 of the WTO Agreement and paragraph 1(b)(iv) of the language of Annex 1A incorporating the GATT 1994 into the WTO Agreement bring the legal history and experience under the GATT 1947 into the new realm of the WTO in a way

The same preamble passage refers to the relevance of international intellectual property agreements or conventions relating to the operation of the TRIPS Agreement. International intellectual property agreements fall into two broad categories. The first is agreements that set out substantive law standards and the second is harmonisation of certain principles relating to international registration of trademarks and patents. The TRIPS Agreement preamble reference, to international intellectual property agreements, is directed to substantive law agreements and most particularly to those that are incorporated into the TRIPS Agreement. The incorporated agreements are the Berne Convention,[6] Paris Convention,[7] Rome Convention[8] and the Treaty in Intellectual Property in Respect of Integrated Circuits.[9]

The Paris Convention and Berne Convention have been in force since the late 19th century and provide substantive law minimums in the fields of trademarks, patents, designs and copyright. Thus, at the time of the negotiation and entering into force of the TRIPS Agreement, intellectual international property law was well established. However, the creation of the WTO led to significant changes regarding the internationalisation of intellectual property. Prior to the WTO, the linkage between trade and intellectual property was not the subject of international agreement in the same direct way. The involvement of the WTO in dispute settlement over the TRIPS Agreement and ongoing negotiations about intellectual property rights has changed the international face of intellectual property. The TRIPS Agreement minimum standards are higher standards and the flexibilities are more stringently confined than in previous international agreements. Compliance with the agreement is subject to dispute settlement and

---

Footnote 5 (*cont.*)
that ensures continuity and consistency in a smooth transition from the GATT 1947 system. This affirms the importance to the Members of the WTO of the experience acquired by the CONTRACTING PARTIES to the GATT 1947 – and acknowledges the continuing relevance of that experience to the new trading system served by the WTO. Adopted panel reports are an important part of the GATT acquis.22'.

6 Berne Convention for the Protection of Literary and Artistic Works, 24 July 1971 (Paris text), 1161 UNTS 3, 102 Stat. 2852, ('Berne Convention').

7 Paris Convention for the Protection of Industrial Property (Stockholm text 1967), 828 UNTS 305, 308 ('Paris Convention').

8 International Convention for the Protection of Performers, Producers of Phonograms and Broadcasting Organizations, 26 October 1961, 496 UNTS 43 ('Rome Convention').

9 Treaty in Intellectual Property in Respect of Integrated Circuits, 26 May 1989.

possibly trade retaliation if any dispute settlement recommendations are not complied with.[10] This chapter examines those changes in the context of the relationship between the TRIPS Agreement and the GATT and specifically the applicability of GATT jurisprudence to the interpretation of the TRIPS Agreement.

It has been almost 15 years since the TRIPS Agreement came into force and its relationship with the GATT has developed in that time.[11] The relationship between the agreements has been discussed in dispute settlement and in negotiations in the TRIPS Council. As the role of TRIPS has become more widely understood, it has become clear that its relationship with other trade agreements may not be what it should be. While the GATT and GATS agreements have as their overall goal the liberalisation of trade, the protection of intellectual property is a different goal that sometimes works as a trade barrier, rather than as a liberalising tool. This feature of intellectual property was known when the TRIPS Agreement was completed, but the rhetoric that intellectual property protection, within the WTO, was necessary to prevent counterfeiting in the global world won the day.[12] Also, there continue to be concerns over the impact of the TRIPS Agreement on innovation and technology transfer, particularly in developing countries. The flexibilities in the TRIPS Agreement have not produced results that really assist in development of local innovation and technology transfer. It seems likely that the exceptions to exclusive intellectual property rights are not strong enough to achieve those goals. A comparison can be made with exception in the GATT and GATS. However, there are many more GATT decisions where the flexibilities have not been successfully invoked compared with its successful applications.[13] The real difficulty is that the protection of intellectual property, in the form of the TRIPS Agreement, creates some barriers to trade and that as those protections increase, the barriers to trade and technology transfer, and even innovation, become greater. Members of the WTO have agreed

---

[10] Panels and a standing Appellate Body and the rules of dispute settlement and enforcement were established by the Understanding on Rules and Procedures Governing the Settlement of Disputes, 15 April 1994, WTO Agreement Annex 2 (1994), 1869 UNTS 401, HR Doc. No. 103-315, at 1654 ('DSU').

[11] The TRIPS Agreement came into force on 1 January 1995 along with all of the WTO agreements.

[12] See generally Susan Sell, *Private Power, Public Law: The Globalization of Intellectual Property Rights* (Cambridge, UK: Cambridge University Press, 2003), ('*Globalization of Intellectual Property Rights*') pp. 75–94.

[13] Of course, statistics of outcomes of disputes don't reveal the cases that are not brought because of the likelihood that the criteria of flexibility have been met and the measure at issue will stand up before a tribunal.

that the TRIPS Agreement minimums are a kind of acceptable barrier.[14] Under the GATT Agreement, members agree that tariffs are an acceptable trade barrier as long as they are progressively lowered.

When the TRIPS Agreement was negotiated, its critics questioned the linkage between trade and the protection of intellectual property rights.[15] At the heart of the linkage question is that intellectual property rights can be a barrier to international trade because the assertion of an intellectual property right can stop the free flow of goods or services. This function of intellectual property is fundamentally in conflict with the WTO aim of the liberalisation of trade. Intellectual property protection is important, but excess intellectual property standards are often a form of protection of domestic industries. Additionally, the TRIPS Agreement is a fundamentally different type of Agreement from both GATT and GATS. TRIPS is an agreement that requires members to implement its minimum standards of legal protection, as compared to GATT, which is primarily directed at converting non-tariff barriers to tariff barriers and then progressively negotiating the reduction of tariffs. Both GATT and GATS are market access agreements because they prohibit certain types of restrictions on market access. In contrast, the TRIPS Agreement requires countries to enact intellectual property laws to control the market in products, such that intellectual property rights protect rather than liberalise access to it. These core differences may mean that in some situations GATT jurisprudence seems fundamentally unsuitable to interpretation of the TRIPS Agreement. However, as the TRIPS Agreement is part of the WTO, the interpretation of the agreement ought to be consistent with the WTO trade-liberalising goal.

Section 2 discusses some core differences in structure and object and purpose of the TRIPS Agreement compared with GATT and GATS. That part discusses the use of GATT jurisprudence in the interpretation of the core non-discrimination principles: national treatment and most-favoured-nation ('MFN'). Section 3 discusses the way in which the relationship between the agreements has been handled in the jurisprudence of the dispute settlement body. Section 4 discusses the potential use of GATT jurisprudence in interpreting the flexibilities in the TRIPS Agreement

---

[14] Although whether there was true 'acceptance' or consent is hotly debated because some countries clearly signed up to the agreement in order to obtain other trade benefits, particularly under GATT, and became members of TRIPS because it is part of the WTO single undertaking. See generally, Peter Drahos, 'When the Weak Bargain with the Strong: Negotiations in the World Trade Organization', [2003] 8(1) *International Negotiation* 79.

[15] See generally *Globalization of Intellectual Property Rights*, above n. 12.

and in interpreting whether the prevention of parallel importing of copyright and trademarked goods is WTO consistent.[16] Section 4 offers some conclusions.

2. Structure of the TRIPS Agreement compared with GATT and GATS

2.1 Minimum standards, increased standards compared with market access

Fundamentally, the TRIPS Agreement is an agreement that sets out minimum standards of intellectual property protection and related flexibilities. Members of the agreement must enact domestic laws that meet the minimum standards set out in the Agreement. The exceptions are optional, but they are governed by certain rules. The reason why the minimum standards structure was chosen for the TRIPS Agreement is primarily because this is the main methodology adopted in international intellectual property law outside of the WTO arena. In particular, it is the structure of both the Berne and Paris Conventions, which are administered by the World Intellectual Property Organisation ('WIPO').[17]

When the TRIPS Agreement was entered into, many of the future members of the WTO had, and continue to have, intellectual property standards in excess of the TRIPS negotiated minimums. Other members had standards lower than those minimums and the TRIPS Agreement required them to increase levels of protection in their domestic law. The level of intellectual property protection in a country's law, before the TRIPS Agreement, was a reflection of what it had agreed to internationally, combined with what was economically appropriate for a country. Broadly, developing countries were likely to have less protective standards of intellectual property than countries with developed economies. The TRIPS Agreement standards have caused many countries to have standards of intellectual property in excess of what is necessarily economically appropriate or likely to assist innovation in their country.[18]

---

16 The TRIPS Agreement, above n. 2, does not govern parallel importation of copyright and trademark goods. Article 6 provides, 'For the purposes of dispute settlement under this Agreement, subject to the provisions of Articles 3 and 4 nothing in this Agreement shall be used to address the issue of the exhaustion of intellectual property rights'.

17 The preamble of the TRIPS Agreement states 'Desiring to Establish a Mutually supportive relationship between the WTO and the World Intellectual Property Organization . . . as well as other international organizations'.

18 For a general discussion, see Daniel Gervais (ed.), *Intellectual Property Trade and Development: Strategies to Optimize Economic Development in a TRIPS-Plus Era* (Oxford: Oxford University Press, 2007).

The debate between the developing countries and developed countries over the scope of the TRIPS Agreement continues. Another factor that keeps intellectual property standards a dynamic issue is a split in approaches between the developed countries. Since the formation of the Berne and Paris Conventions, Europe and the United States have been in dispute over the scope of some fundamental aspects of intellectual property rights. The United States did not join the Berne Convention until the late 1980s. Additionally, although both Europe and the United States have, in many areas, levels of protection that are greater than what TRIPS requires, there remains disharmony. There is still no Transatlantic agreement over the protection of databases,[19] the protection of geographical indications, the patentability of certain types of subject matter and many aspects of the protection of audiovisual works in copyright. The most significant effect of the European and United States differing approaches to aspects of intellectual property in the TRIPS Agreement arena seems to be the alliance of some developing countries with the European Communities, in the WTO, on issues such as geographical indications. This alliance over increasing geographical indications seems to be based on the developing country view that geographical indications will benefit them and because in exchange the European Communities have agreed to support a limited disclosure of traditional knowledge requirement in patent law.[20]

As countries have differing standards of intellectual property protection, it is clear that a minimum standards framework is not the same thing as a harmonised intellectual property law. Some minimum standards are broader in scope than others, but a minimum standard allows for national autonomy over how that minimum standard is implemented. The TRIPS Agreement recognises that members may implement these minimum standards in a manner that they see fit.[21] However, a minimum standards

---

[19] See generally, Guido Westkamp, 'TRIPS Principles, Reciprocity and the Creation of Sui-generis Type Intellectual Property Rights for New Forms of Technology', (2003) 6 *Journal of World Intellectual Property Law* 827.

[20] As part of the process of the review of Article 27:3 of the TRIPS Agreement, above n. 2, there have been submissions made in the TRIPS Council to include in the TRIPS Agreement a requirement for disclosure of uses of traditional knowledge in the patent process. The EU support the general idea that there should be disclosure, but it does not support the more radical submission that disclosure should lead to a patent being invalidated. For the TRIPS Council discussion generally, see WTO, Article 27.3b, traditional knowledge, biodiversity at http://www.wto.org/english/tratop_e/TRIPs_e/art27_3b_e.htm.

[21] TRIPS Agreement, above n 2, Article 1.1 states '. . . Members shall be free to determine the appropriate method of implementing the provisions of this Agreement within their own legal system and practice'. Some TRIPS Agreement

approach means that many interpretations might be compliant with the standard. So, for example, the copyright laws of New Zealand, Argentina and the United States are not identical. Because there are many ways to implement minimum standards, this ought to mean that dispute panels and the Appellate Body recognise that the provisions of the agreement cannot be interpreted with the same degree of formalism that often accompanies domestic statutory interpretation.[22] There are rules for the interpretation of international treaties and the WTO has chosen to follow those rules.[23]

In addition to allowing members autonomy over how to implement standards, members may provide standards in excess of the TRIPS minimums.[24] Allowing higher standards was seen as important, in part, because some members already provided higher standards, but it also allows members seeking to increase standards to continue to do so. Higher standards will be enacted in national laws either as a domestic policy or as a result of bilateral or free trade agreements.[25] In pursuit of high standards,

---

provisions allow for more national autonomy over implementation than others. For example, the requirement in Article 10 to protect computer programs as literary works in copyright law leaves comparatively less scope for national autonomy than the requirement in Article 27:3(b) to protect plant variety rights as either patents or a sui generis system. See also Susy Frankel, 'Eroding National Autonomy from the TRIPS Agreement', in Meredith Kolsky Lewis and Susy Frankel (eds), *National Autonomy and International Economic Law* (Cambridge: Cambridge University Press, forthcoming).

[22] Although panel decisions have been criticised for their formulaic approach, see Graeme B. Dinwoodie and Rochelle Dreyfuss, 'TRIPS and the Dynamics of Intellectual Property Lawmaking', (2004), 36 *Case W. Res. J. Int'l* 95 ('Dynamics of Intellectual Property Lawmaking').

[23] DSU, above n. 10, Article 3.2 provides that '. . . The Members recognise that [the dispute settlement system] serves to preserve the rights and obligations of Members under the covered agreements, and to clarify the existing provisions of those agreements in accordance with the customary rules of interpretation of public international law'. Panels and the Appellate Body have recognised that the relevant customary international law is codified in Articles 31 and 32 of the Vienna Convention of the Law of Treaties, 23 May 1969, A/CONF.39/11/Add.2; 115 UNTS 331 (1980) ('Vienna Convention').

[24] TRIPS Agreement, above n. 2, Article 1:1 provides, '. . . Members may but shall not be obliged to, implement in their law more extensive protection than is required by the Agreement, provided that such protection does not contravene the provisions of this Agreement'.

[25] For a general discussion of intellectual property chapters in free trade agreements, see Susy Frankel, 'The Legitimacy and Purpose of Intellectual Property Chapters in FTAs', in Ross Buckley, Vai Io Lo and Laurence Boulle (eds), *Challenges to Multilateral Trade: The Impact of Bilateral Preferential and Regional Trade Agreements* (The Netherlands: Kluwer Law International, 2008) ('Legitimacy and Purpose of IP Chapters').

many treat TRIPS as having no limits. I have argued elsewhere that this is not a good or defensible interpretation of the TRIPS Agreement as its limits can be found in its object and purpose and in a proper interpretation of its principles.[26] The TRIPS Agreement's stated object and purpose are a balancing mechanism and include principles of innovation, development and technology transfer. Despite such legally correct arguments, the balancing principles in the TRIPS Agreement are routinely ignored by those seeking to increase intellectual property standards in order to protect their own industries and businesses. The Doha Declaration on Public Health emphasised the importance of these objectives in the interpretation of the TRIPS Agreement, so it may be hoped that panels and the Appellate Body will heed this.[27]

The article in TRIPS that allows autonomy over implementation of standards and increased standards notably also contemplates that not all increases will be TRIPS compliant.[28] An increase will not be compliant with TRIPS if it violates, for example, a non-discrimination principle. The requirement that any increased standard be compatible with the TRIPS Agreement should also be interpreted as directed at the objectives and principles of the agreement. The commonality between those articles and the non-discrimination principles is that they are designed to apply to the whole agreement.[29] In spite of the structural nature of the object and purpose of TRIPS, the agreement carries with it a presumption that increased intellectual property standards are good for trade. There is much literature contesting this notion, but the creation of TRIPS-plus intellectual chapters in FTAs, and interpretation of the TRIPS Agreement in the WTO, do not seem to contest this notion. Additionally, the TRIPS Agreement even incorporates a tool for fast-track inclusion of higher standards. It provides:[30]

> Amendments merely serving the purpose of adjusting to higher levels of protection of intellectual property rights achieved, and in force, in other multilateral

---

[26] Susy Frankel, 'WTO Application of "the Customary Rules of Interpretation of Public International Law" to Intellectual Property', (2006) 46(2), p. 365, *Virginia International Law Review* ('Application of Customary Rules').

[27] WTO 4th Ministerial Conference, 'Declaration on the TRIPS Agreement and Public Health', WT/MIN(01)/DEC/2, adopted on 14 November 2001 (Declaration on the TRIPS Agreement and Public Health), available at www.wto.irg/english/tratop_e/implem_para6_e.htm.

[28] See above n. 24.

[29] All of these provisions are found in Part I of the TRIPS Agreement, above n. 2, entitled 'General Provisions and Basic Principles'.

[30] TRIPS Agreement, above n. 2, Article 71.2.

agreements and accepted under those agreements by all Members of the WTO may be referred to the Ministerial Conference for action in accordance with paragraph 6 of Article X of the WTO Agreement on the basis of a consensus proposal from the Council for TRIPS.

Members cannot agree to lesser standards outside of the WTO because that would violate the TRIPS Agreement, although where TRIPS-plus measures are in place, Members ought not be prevented from returning to TRIPS-equivalent measures.[31] What this provision shows is, however, contextual support that despite the appearance of valuing innovation and technology, the TRIPS Agreement is fundamentally tipped towards increasing intellectual property standards and enforcing those increases whatever their effect on innovation and even trade.[32] The effect on trade ought to be considered in the interpretation of the agreements, but panels and the Appellate Body have consistently focused on whether a particular law is in compliance with a standard in isolation from whether the interpretation of the standard is consistent with the balancing goals in the agreement.[33] The GATT has been used to interpret the TRIPS non-discrimination principles, but it has not been used to discuss whether a particular aspect of the TRIPS Agreement is consistent with the free flow of goods principles contained in GATT.

2.2 *Interpretation of non-discrimination principles*

2.2.1 MFN and National Treatment

TRIPS Agreement minimum standards are coupled with the non discrimination principles of national treatment and most-favoured nation

---

[31] 'Dynamics of Intellectual Property Lawmaking', above n. 22, p. 106; the authors say that '[I]t is quite important that the TRIPS Agreement not be read to prevent member states from switching legal regimes or rolling back excessive protection to the international minimum'.

[32] Dinwoodie and Dreyfuss discuss the ratcheting-up of TRIPS as one way, even in dispute settlement, where lesser protections can be found to be non-TRIPS compliant, but greater protection will not be; see 'Dynamics of Intellectual Property Lawmaking', above n. 22, pp. 99–100. I have argued that a possible use of non-violation complaints would be that users can contest greater standards; see Susy Frankel 'Challenging TRIPS-Plus Agreements: the Potential Utility of Non-violation Complaints', *Journal of International Economic Law* (2009), 12(4), 1023–65.

[33] Panels seem to assume that such a balance has already been dealt with in setting down the standard. This approach, however, ignores the interpretative role of Articles 7 and 8. The Doha Declaration underscored that interpretative role: See above n. 27.

('MFN'). The primary effect of combining minimum standards with national treatment is to ensure that all members of the agreement can expect the application of the same minimum standards in other member countries. A minimum standards agreement would not achieve the aim of international protection without being coupled with the national treatment. Without national treatment, members would be free to apply one law to its domestic nationals and another to foreign nationals. One possibility under the TRIPS Agreement is to provide a worse standard to your own nationals than to foreign nationals.

In the GATT and GATS, the principles of MFN and national treatment have a different focus from the TRIPS Agreement non-discrimination provisions because of the coverage and nature of those agreements. In GATT, members are not permitted to apply different taxes, levies, laws or regulations to like products.[34] This has given rise to a number of disputes about the meaning and contours of like product.[35] In the GATS context, national treatment and MFN require that members give no less favourable treatment than they accord to like services and services suppliers. The TRIPS non-discrimination principles require like treatment of nationals. The focus on nationals is a reflection of the role of TRIPS in setting minimum standards for intellectual property protection as private rights at domestic law. A comparison of the agreement's core non-discrimination principles is shown in Table 1.1:[36]

In the goods and services context, the notion of like products and services is the mechanism which limits members' ability to favour a domestic industry over potential foreign competitors. Like product disputes determine whether country A's product is like country B's and, therefore, must have the same tariff or internal tax. For example, the Appellate Body concluded that Japan's local alcohol spirit, shochu, was like imported spirits.[37] In the TRIPS Agreement, the broad non-discrimination principles do not include the like products test. TRIPS national treatment and MFN do not, on their own, prevent members from giving different levels of intellectual property protection for different sorts of products. GATT and GATS function to capture the issues relevant to product or service discrimination, but as far as the protection of intellectual property protection goes,

---

34 GATT, above n. 1, Articles I and III.

35 For a general discussion of like products, see M.J. Trebilcock and Robert Howse, *The Regulation of International Trade*, 3rd edition, London: Routledge, 2005, pp. 65–80.

36 Other non-discrimination principles which are narrower in their application are found throughout the agreements.

37 *Japan – Alcohol,* above n. 5.

Table 1.1 Non-discrimination principles

WTO Agreement	Most-favoured–nation ('MFN')	National Treatment
GATT – Articles I and III	Customs duties and charges on like products	Internal taxation and regulation on like products
GATS – Articles II and XVII	Services and service suppliers	Services and service suppliers
TRIPS – Articles 3 and 4	Nationals of members	Nationals of members

the TRIPS Agreement is the primary tool. Because of the absence of any like product test in the broad non-discrimination principles of TRIPS, Article 27, which provides the minimum standards of patentable subject matter, includes a non-discrimination principle. It provides:[38]

> . . .patents shall be available and patent rights enjoyable without discrimination as to the place of invention, the field of technology and whether products are imported or locally produced.

This principle is much more tightly drafted than the GATT like products provision. It is possible that products can be in the same field of technology, but not as for GATT purposes. This is because the test for likeness involves a range of considerations, such as tariff classification, irrelevant to the notion of field of technology.[39] For example, a GATT panel held that certain Japanese dimension lumber was not like Canadian Spruce Pine Fir Dimension Lumber.[40] If patents existed, perhaps in relation to this lumber, those patents would likely be considered in the same field of technology.

The reason that this subject matter discrimination is only found in relation to patents and not other areas of intellectual property is in part because of the relative economic importance of patents, but also because the workings of copyright include subject matter tailored limits. Any copyright work is categorised into subject matter. The Berne Convention, as incorporated into TRIPS, covers what it defines as artistic and literary

---

[38] TRIPS Agreement, above n. 2, Article 27.

[39] See *The Regulation of International Trade*, above n. 35.

[40] *Japan – Tariff on Import of Spruce-Pine-Fir (SPF) Dimension Lumber*, GATT Panel Report, adopted 19 July 1989, 36 Supp. BISD 167 (1990).

works.[41] The TRIPS Agreement acknowledges and adds to this type of categorisation of copyright through the inclusion, for example, of the requirement to protect computer programs as literary works.[42] The categorisation of copyright works has the effect of eliminating subject matter discrimination. In patent law, the requirements of patentable invention are the gateway to patentability and would not, without the wording of Article 27, require non-discrimination of subject matter.

2.2.2 Interpretation of Article 27

The WTO panel in the *Canada Pharmaceuticals* dispute concluded that Article 27 also applied to exceptions to patentability made under Article 30 of TRIPS.[43] In this way, the Panel interpreted Article 27 as having a broad effect, making it applicable to all aspects of patent under TRIPS, not just Article 27. This effectively makes the Article 27 provision equivalent to the broad non-discrimination provisions.[44] Dinwoodie and Dreyfuss argue that this interpretation of Article 27 was not necessary, or in fact good, for intellectual property in trade. Their argument is that if exceptions to intellectual property are allowed to discriminate on a technology basis, they will be much more limited than exceptions that have a wider sweep in the name of technological neutrality.[45] Dinwoodie and Dreyfuss point out that discrimination is not the same thing as differential treatment. The panel stated that 'Article 27 does not prohibit bona fide exemptions to deal with problems that may exist only in certain product areas'.[46] In some circumstances, differential treatment falls way short of discrimination. 'Under a normal meaning of the term "discrimination" treating different cases differently is not discrimination.'[47]

The panel, in reaching its conclusion, did not expressly compare the GATT non-discrimination principles with the TRIPS articles. The panel stated:[48]

---

41 Berne Convention, above n. 6, Article 2, incorporated into the TRIPS Agreement, above n. 2, Article 9.

42 TRIPS Agreement, above n. 2, Article 10:1.

43 WTO Panel Report, *Canada – Patent Protection of Pharmaceutical Products ('Canada Pharmaceuticals')*, WT/DS114/R, 17 March 2000.

44 This structural effect is a point made in Graeme B. Dinwoodie and Rochelle Dreyfuss, 'Diversifying without Discrimination: Complying with the Mandate of the TRIPS Agreement', 13 *Michigan Telecommunications and Technology Law Review* 445 (2007), at 448 ('Diversifying without Discrimination').

45 'Diversifying without Discrimination', above n. 44, p. 449.

46 *Canada Pharmaceuticals*, above n. 43, para. 7.92.

47 'Diversifying without Discrimination', above n. 44, p. 450.

48 *Canada Pharmaceuticals*, above n 43, para. 7.98.

> In considering how to address these conflicting claims of discrimination, the Panel recalled that various claims of discrimination, de jure and de facto, have been the subject of legal rulings under GATT or the WTO.[49] These rulings have addressed the question whether measures were in conflict with various GATT or WTO provisions prohibiting variously defined forms of discrimination. As the Appellate Body has repeatedly made clear, each of these rulings has necessarily been based on the precise legal text in issue, so that it is not possible to treat them as applications of a general concept of discrimination.

This approach allowed the panel to construe Article 27 non-discrimination requirements more narrowly than the general GATT non-discrimination principles. From an interpretation perspective, it makes sense that the primary context for interpreting Article 27 of TRIPS is the TRIPS Agreement.[50] The more TRIPS-specific a provision is, the more panels and the Appellate Body seem to treat TRIPS as a *lex specialis*. Panels and the Appellate Body have used GATT non-discrimination principles directly, however, to interpret the TRIPS Agreement's broad national treatment and MFN principles.

2.2.3 WTO panels and TRIPS national treatment and MFN

In the *Geographical Indications*[51] dispute, the panel drew extensively on GATT jurisprudence to decide if there had been a violation of TRIPS national treatment and MFN. In the dispute, the US alleged that the EC discriminated against non-EC nationals. The discrimination was the requirement that in order for a non-EU national to register a geographical indication under EC law, there needed to be certification of equivalent geographical indication protection outside the EC. The US successfully argued that the requirement that geographical indications, from outside the EU, have to meet the requirement that the country has an equivalent system to the EC system was discriminatory. The US also submitted that the requirement contravened the TRIPS Agreement provision that allows

---

[49] Citing at footnote 436, for example, *Japan – Taxes on Alcoholic Beverages*, WT/DS8/AB/R, WT/DS10/AB/R, WT/DS11/AB/R (adopted 1 November 1996); *European Communities – Regime for the Importation, Sale and Distribution of Bananas*, WT/DS27/AB/R (adopted 17 November 1997); *EC Measures Concerning Meat and Meat Products*, WT/DS26/AB/R, WT/DS48/AB/R (adopted 15 February 1998); *United States – Import Prohibition of Certain Shrimp and Shrimp Products*, WT/DS58/AB/R (adopted 6 November 1998).

[50] However, the panel did not have full regard to the context of TRIPS, Application of Customary Rules, above n. 26.

[51] WTO Panel Report, *European Communities – Protection of Trademarks and Geographical Indications for Agricultural Products and Foodstuffs* (*EC- Geographical Indications*), WT/DS174/R, 15 March 2005.

members to implement the laws in their own way.[52] The EC said this was not discrimination against nationals under TRIPS, because all nationals had to comply with the relevant provision. However, the panel found that the provision was discriminatory because it said that the TRIPS Agreement required 'effective equality of opportunity' to have protection under the EC law. The panel, in reaching its conclusion, focused on 'actual effects of the contested provision in the marketplace'. These concepts come directly from interpretation of national treatment under GATT.[53]

In *Havana Club*,[54] the EC complained about the discriminatory effects of a US law that prevented enforcement of trademarks which had been confiscated by the Cuban government, at the time of the Castro revolution. The Appellate Body found that the US law violated national treatment and MFN because under the law, a Cuban original trademark owner was treated less favourably than a US original trademark owner. In the course of considering MFN, the Appellate Body stated:[55]

> . . . the framers of the TRIPS Agreement decided to extend the most-favoured-nation obligation to the protection of intellectual property rights under the TRIPS Agreement covered by the Agreement. As a cornerstone of the world trading system, the most-favoured-nation obligation must be accorded the same significance with respect to intellectual property rights under the TRIPS Agreement that it would have been accorded with respect to trade in goods under the GATT. It is, in a word, fundamental.

The real question with regard to MFN and TRIPS is why and in what way it is 'fundamental' in the TRIPS context. It turns out that one of the fundamental outcomes of the provision is that Free Trade Agreements ('FTAs') are not confined to the parties to the free trade agreement because the TRIPS Agreement does not have an MFN exemption for these types of agreements.

---

52 TRIPS Agreement, above n. 2, Article 1:1.

53 The United States argued that 'jurisprudence on [national treatment] Article III:4 of GATT 1994 offers useful guidance in the interpretation of Article 3:1 of the TRIPS Agreement. The broad and fundamental purpose of Article II is to avoid protectionism in the application of tax and regulatory measures. This is easily extrapolated to the TRIPS Agreement in which the national treatment obligation intend to avoid protectionism with respect to the protection of intellectual property. . .' The EC argued that there was no commonality of non-discrimination principles across all agreements. See *EC Geographical Indications*, above n. 51, para. 7.107.

54 WTO Appellate Body Report, *United States – Section 211 Omnibus Appropriations Act 1988*, WT/DS176/AB/R, 1 February 2002 ('*Havana Club*').

55 *Havana Club*, above n. 54, para. 297.

2.2.4 TRIPS HAS NO MFN EXCEPTION

A key difference between MFN in the TRIPS Agreement and MFN in both GATT and GATS is that in TRIPS there is no MFN exemption for FTAs.[56] Some commentators initially thought that there was a possibility that the MFN exemption in GATT would apply to intellectual property chapters made as an extension of the TRIPS Agreement.[57] The drafting history of the TRIPS Agreement shows that an MFN exemption was contemplated in one of the drafts, but dropped.[58] The effect of there being no MFN exemption in the TRIPS Agreement is generally thought to be that it provides a way in which intellectual property chapters in FTAs, negotiated between two or more parties, can be used to drive an increase in multilateral intellectual property standards. Such a drive occurs through a combination of mechanisms. First, countries, most notably the US, enter into several FTAs, with similar TRIPS-plus provisions, so as to have repeated standards in a number of countries. In the intellectual property context, MFN works differently from GATT. A tariff once lowered must be applied to all WTO members, unless it is subject to the MFN exemption. In the TRIPS Agreement context, a change in law as a result of an FTA applies to domestic right holders and as a result of national treatment to foreign nationals seeking rights in that jurisdiction. If other countries are to adopt that norm, they must also change their law.[59] The more countries that have a standard, the more likely it is to become a norm. Additionally, if intellectual property rights owners can achieve better protection away from home, they may pressure their government to increase intellectual property standards at home.

Given that there are not equivalent provisions permitting FTAs, under TRIPS, to those found in GATT and GATS, one might think that intellectual property chapters in FTAs are not permitted.[60] The difficulty with that interpretation is that allowing increased standards in TRIPS suggests that parties contemplated that increases would occur in an FTA forum.

---

[56] GATT, above n. 1, Article XXIV.

[57] See, for example, J.H. Reichmann, 'Universal Minimum Standards of Intellectual Property Protection under the TRIPS Component of the WTO Agreement', (1995) 29 *International Law* 345, 347.

[58] See Daniel Gervais, *The TRIPS Agreement: Drafting History and Analysis*, 2nd edition (London: Sweet & Maxwell, 2003) 10–26, where he sets out the history of the drafts and see 'Legitimacy and Purpose of IP Chapters', above n. 25, 187–8.

[59] There are some exceptions to national treatment where material reciprocity can apply; see TRIPS Agreement, above n. 1, Article 1:1.

[60] 'Legitimacy and Purpose of IP Chapters', above n. 25, 186–9.

Bilaterals, after all, have been known since pre-Berne Convention days.[61] Notably, however, the destructiveness of bilaterals was one of the reasons leading to the Berne Convention.

The provision of increased standards on an MFN basis rather than with an MFN exception as a means to achieve multilateral change has been adopted in the GATT arena. European Partnership Agreements, known as EPAs, which are trade agreements between the EU and African, Caribbean or Pacific countries, apply their provisions on an MFN basis.[62] Whether such an approach is compliant with the GATT Agreement is not clear.

Certainly, one of the principles of allowing FTAs, under GATT, is that it does not raise trade barriers[63] and 'duties and other restrictive regulations of commerce . . . are eliminated on substantially all trade'.[64] Such a concept is not directly relevant to the minimum standards structure of TRIPS. The structure does not directly ask whether increases are trade benefits. However, consistent with the goals of liberalising trade, such questions should be asked. When considered in the context of why FTAs are permitted under GATT, it is arguable that an equivalent test should be applied to intellectual property chapters made under the TRIPS Agreement.

The jurisprudence on compliance with Article XXIV of GATT is thin, but the literature vast. It seems to be generally accepted that many agreements that claim the safe haven of Article XXIV do not meet its requirements, but such agreements are tolerated.[65] This tolerance policy has spilled over into TRIPS interpretation. Intellectual property chapters in FTAs can be questioned either because they do not have the authority of

---

[61] Sam Ricketson and Jane C. Ginsburg, *International Copyright and Neighbouring Rights: The Berne Convention and Beyond* (Oxford: Oxford University Press, 2006), paras 1.29–1.30.

[62] Lorand Bartels, 'Cariforum-EU Economic Partnership Agreement Comments', available at http://www.acp-eu-trade.org/library/files/Bartels_EN_130208_EC_CARIFORUM-EU-EPA.pdf.

[63] GATT, above n. 1, Article 24:4.

[64] GATT, above n. 1, Article 24:8(b).

[65] See generally, Alberta Fabricotti, 'The Interplay between the WTO and RTAs: Is it a Question of Interrelation between Different Sources of International Law?', available at http://papers.ssrn.com/sol3/papers.cfm?abstract_id=1151386. The WTO has a review mechanism for these agreements, but it is largely ineffectual; see Report by the Consultative Board to the Director-General, 'The Future of the WTO: Addressing Institutional Change since the New Millennium' (2004) 21, available at http://wto.org.

an Article XXIV, or are not otherwise permissible, but such chapters are, like their GATT counterparts, tolerated.

3. Dispute settlement generally

3.1 Interpretation principles

As a formal matter, the TRIPS Agreement provides that disputes may be brought to the dispute settlement body in accordance with the rules of the DSU.[66] These rules include the customary law principles of interpretation of international agreements.[67]

Some of the first WTO panel and Appellate Body reports, dealing with TRIPS Agreement disputes, referred to GATT cases. There is no formal precedent system in the WTO, but many panels discuss past decisions and whether they are analogous.[68] However, as the above discussion shows, at least in relation to broad principles that are common among the agreements, panels are likely to refer to GATT decisions.[69] It is valuable to consider other ways in which GATT principles might be thought relevant to interpretation of the TRIPS Agreement. Examples where GATT principles might be used as interpretative tools include exceptions to the exclusive rights in the TRIPS Agreement and whether the prevention of parallel importing of copyright and trademarked goods is WTO consistent. Each of these is now discussed.

3.2 Parallel importing

The TRIPS Agreement does not include any overall minimum standards on the exhaustion of rights.[70] The exclusive rights to be conferred on patent

---

66 TRIPS Agreement, above n. 2, Article 64:1.

67 DSU, above n. 10, Article 3.2.

68 John Jackson has stated, 'In sum, it can be argued that there is quite a powerful precedent effect in the jurisprudence of the WTO, but that it is certainly not stare decisis, and it is not so powerful as to require panels or the Appellate Body considering new cases to follow prior cases, with the possible exception that once prior cases have been numerous regarding a particular issue and approach, and apparently accepted by all members of the WTO, then the language of the Vienna Convention about "practice under agreement," may suggest a stronger impact. But short of that situation, it appears that the "flavor" of the precedent effect in the WTO is still somewhat fluid, and possibly will remain fluid for the time being.' See John Jackson, *Sovereignty, the WTO and Changing Fundamentals of International Law*, (Cambridge: Cambridge University Press, 2006), at p. 177.

69 See above Section 2.

70 See above n. 16.

owners, under the agreement, include the import right.[71] The TRIPS Agreement does not prevent a member from having a law that permits parallel importation of copyright works and trademarked goods. The topic of parallel importation is an immense topic and cannot be done justice to in this chapter. The reason for discussing it is that parallel importing is illustrative of a clash of objectives between intellectual property and the GATT.

Intellectual property rights are used in many jurisdictions to stop importation of parallel imported products. It is important to note that parallel imports are not counterfeit products, but are genuine products made for one market that are then imported into another. Countries that prevent the parallel importation of goods usually justify this as a way of ensuring that products made for and priced according to local conditions should not be used to undercut a market where a higher price is charged for that product and sometimes for products of higher quality.[72] The main GATT objective that seems to be ignored, when parallel importing is prohibited, is liberalising the movement of goods. The assertion of an intellectual property right to prevent the importation of goods is a trade barrier, which the TRIPS Agreement allows. As one commentator has said, 'protecting the profit margin of certain producers by stopping goods at the border is precisely the sort of activity that the GATT was meant to discourage'.[73]

Intellectual property chapters in FTAs are used to prevent parallel imports of goods. Australia used to allow parallel importation of certain copyright goods, but after entering into an FTA with the US, has reversed its position on copyright products.[74] As stopping the free flow of goods in this way is not consistent with GATT, but is a feature of intellectual property law, it is difficult to see how any argument, discussed above, that intellectual property chapters in FTAs are consistent with the GATT can rationally be sustained.

---

[71] TRIPS Agreement, above n. 2, Article 28:1. Changes to the compulsory licensing regime also now allow pharmaceuticals, made under such a licence, to be imported by certain nations which have no manufacturing capacity. See TRIPS Agreement, above n. 2, Article 31 bis.

[72] See, for example, the prevention of imports of inferior quality toothpaste from Brazil to the United Kingdom, *Colgate-Palmolive Ltd and Another v. Markwell Finance Limited and Another* (1989) 106 RPC 497 (EWCA).

[73] Paul J. Heald, 'Trademarks and Geographical Indications Exploring the Contours of the TRIPS Agreement', (1996) 29 *V. and J. Transnat'l L.* 638, 658.

[74] I have argued elsewhere that this sort of change could be the subject of a non-violation complaint under the TRIPS Agreement, if non-violation complaints, which cannot be brought under TRIPS, were permitted. See 'Non-violation Disputes', above n. 32.

3.3 Exceptions to TRIPS exclusive rights

The TRIPS Agreement contains a number of flexibilities, but all of these are in the form of exceptions to exclusive rights. Patents, copyright and trademarks each have differing versions of the so-called three-step test.[75] The patent three-step test is:[76]

> Members may provide limited exceptions to the exclusive rights conferred by a patent, provided that such exceptions do not unreasonably conflict with a normal exploitation of the patent and do not unreasonably prejudice the legitimate interests of the patent owner, taking account of the legitimate interests of third parties.

These broad tests for exclusion can theoretically be adapted for any normative policy for an exception. As discussed above, the WTO panel in *Canada Pharmaceuticals* found that Article 30 was subject to the non-discrimination principles in Article 27.[77] Article 27 also contains some exceptions, which unlike the three-step tests, specify particular policies for the exceptions. These exceptions include the right to exclude from patentability inventions where such exclusions are 'necessary to protect ordre public or morality, including to protect human, animal or plant life or health'.[78] Similar wording to these exclusions is found in the

---

[75] TRIPS Agreement, above n. 2, Article 13, copyright three-step test, Article 17, Trademark three-step test and Article 30, patents three-step test.

[76] TRIPS Agreement, above n. 2, Article 30.

[77] See above Section 2.2.

[78] TRIPS Agreement, above n. 2, Article 27:2–3 provides:

2. Members may exclude from patentability inventions, the prevention within their territory of the commercial exploitation of which is necessary to protect ordre public or morality, including to protect human, animal or plant life or health or to avoid serious prejudice to the environment, provided that such exclusion is not made merely because the exploitation is prohibited by their law.
3. Members may also exclude from patentability:
   (a) diagnostic, therapeutic and surgical methods for the treatment of humans or animals;
   (b) plants and animals other than micro-organisms, and essentially biological processes for the production of plants or animals other than non-biological and microbiological processes. However, Members shall provide for the protection of plant varieties either by patents or by an effective sui generis system or by any combination thereof. The provisions of this subparagraph shall be reviewed four years after the date of entry into force of the WTO Agreement.

GATT[79] and GATS.[80] In GATT, the flexibilities function as reasons why members may be allowed to have restrictions on imports or other trade barriers that would otherwise offend the provisions of GATT. These provisions have been tested many times at the WTO and in many cases the exceptions have not been allowed because although the normative reason for the exclusion is present, such as an effect on human or animal life, the measure taken could have been less distorting. Such a conclusion is possible because of the wording of the 'chapeau', which precedes the exceptions as follows:[81]

> Subject to the requirement that such measures are not applied in a manner which would constitute a means of arbitrary or unjustifiable discrimination between countries where the same conditions prevail, or a disguised restriction on international trade, nothing in this Agreement shall be construed to prevent the adoption or enforcement by any contracting party of measures.

I have argued elsewhere that TRIPS Agreement flexibilities should not be so strictly interpreted because they do not have the same features as the GATT flexibilities.[82] In particular, TRIPS does not have the chapeau. The analogous principle of avoiding distortions of trade is found in the preamble of the TRIPS Agreement; however, from an interpretative perspective, it does not perform the same function as the GATT or indeed the GATS chapeau.[83] It is an interpretative guide to Article 27, but is not part of the article to be interpreted.

The GATT jurisprudence is, however, relevant to the way in which concepts such as 'human, animal or plant life or health' should be interpreted. These terms have a meaning that is not static and they are not defined in the TRIPS Agreement or any WTO Agreements.[84] Therefore, external sources should be used in their interpretation. This has been done in both GATT and GATS disputes and should be done in interpreting these exclusions in TRIPS.[85] The use of external sources is, however, treated as an interpretative guide and not as anything greater. The WTO does not

---

79 GATT, above n. 1, Article XX(a) and (b).

80 GATS, above n. 3, Article XIV(a) and (b).

81 GATT, above n. 1, Article XX.

82 See Application of Customary Rules, above n. 26.

83 For a discussion of the GATS chapeau, see WTO Appellate Body Report, *United States – Measures Affecting the Cross-border Supply of Gambling and Betting Services*, WT/DS285/AB/R, 7 April 2005 ('*Antigua Gambling*').

84 See Application of Customary Rules, above n. 26, 421–7.

85 For GATT examples see WTO Appellate Body Report, *United States – Import Prohibition of Certain Shrimp and Shrimp Products*, WT/DS58/AB/R, 12 October 1998 and WTO Appellate Body Report, *European Communities –*

decide disputes based on their rulings. The reasons for this are many and include the fact that the WTO has no jurisdiction to do so. The dispute settlement body has jurisdiction to interpret the WTO Agreements, not other international treaties.[86] So, for example, World Health Organization (WHO) guidance on human health might be relevant to an interpretation of that term in the TRIPS Agreement, but the WTO would not decide a dispute by ruling under WHO policies. Also, Vienna Convention interpretation rules may lead to the conclusion that an external source, that is, another international agreement, while it may be an interpretative guide, cannot be decisive unless all members of the WTO have agreed to it.[87]

4. Conclusion

GATT jurisprudence is used to interpret the TRIPS Agreement's broad non-discrimination principles of national treatment and MFN. The more TRIPS-specific a provision is, the more panels treat TRIPS as a *lex specialis*. This approach is found in the WTO panel report in *Canada Pharmaceuticals*. There are a number of areas of intellectual property that the TRIPS Agreement does not cover. One of these is parallel importing of copyright and trademarked products. This means countries can create their own laws, but in this area the GATT principles of liberalising the cross-border movement of goods should be applicable. To allow restrictions on parallel importing is to treat the movement of goods differently from GATT simply because of the involvement of intellectual property. To isolate intellectual property from GATT principles in this way does not seem justified. GATT principles many also be applicable to the interpretation of some TRIPS Agreement exceptions, particularly where those exceptions require external sources to give them a meaning in the TRIPS Agreement context. The applicability of GATT principles varies according to what is at issue. As yet, it is not clear that there is a consistent approach to the use of GATT principles in the interpretation of the TRIPS Agreement.

Measures Affecting Asbestos and Asbestos-containing Products, WT/DS135/AB/R, 12 March 2001. For a GATS example, se *Antigua Gambling*, above n. 83.

[86] DSU, above n. 10, Article 3.2 provides, '. . . The Members recognise that [the dispute settlement system of the WTO] serves to preserve the rights and obligations of the Members under the covered agreements, and to clarify existing provisions of *those agreements* . . .' (emphasis added).

[87] See Application of Customary Rules, above n. 26.

2 TRIPS-plus-plus initiatives on broad border measures: features and implications

Xuan Li

1. Introduction

Promoting TRIPS-plus-plus standards on IP enforcement has been a priority of developed countries in recent years through multilateral, regional and bilateral negotiations.[1] Traditionally, WIPO has been the major forum to negotiate intellectual property (IP). However, while facing resistance to the TRIP-plus-plus negotiations agenda under the World Trade Organization (WTO) and World Intellectual Property Organization (WIPO) from well-coordinated developing countries, developed countries launched simultaneous initiatives in other international or regional forums and in particular, shifted the battlefield to the World Customs Organization (WCO), which is relatively unknown to the international community for setting IP regulations, and through manipulating WCO, to further influence other international forums like the Universal Postal Union (UPU). Other forums include the International Medicinal Products Anti-counterfeit Taskforce (IMPACT), based at the World Health Organization (WHO), the Anti-counterfeiting Trade Agreement (ACTA); and various free trade agreements (FTAs) which bypass the WTO process in order to impose TRIPS-plus-plus standards. Under this forum-shopping strategy, the intention of developed countries is to break the deadlock through the back-door. The ongoing TRIPS-plus-plus IP enforcement initiative can be regarded as the second generation of international IP rule making, if TRIPS can be seen as the first generation. Developed countries' current strategy of promoting IP enforcement negotiations bears some similarities to that of 13 years ago when developed countries were pushing for incorporation of TRIPS into the WTO rule system, but there are also some new features. What is common in both

[1] 'TRIPS-plus' generally refers to commitments that go beyond those already included or Agreement on consolidated in the Trade-related Intellectual Property Rights (TRIPS). 'TRIPS-plus-plus' highlights the extent of the significant departure of SECURE from the existing TRIPS Agreement regarding border measures.

strategies is the tactic of forum-shopping. At that time, 'the shopping approach' was used to establish a link between WIPO and WTO. By incorporating the relatively weak WIPO treaties into the WTO, which has comparatively stronger power of enforcement, the interest groups concerned wanted to standardize, legalize and internationalize their policy objectives. The current strategy of IP promotion by developed countries is a simultaneous, multi-pronged offensive at regional, global and bilateral levels, as reflected in their attempts to cut through the weaker links and craft new IP enforcement laws and standards. Once this step is accomplished, developed countries will be able to better sell these standards in other forums, including through free trade agreements, with the purpose of eventually turning them into internationally mandatory arrangements.

Among the various initiatives promoted by the interest groups of developed countries at WCO, WHO, UPU, the G8 (Group of Eight), etc., the negotiation on the Provisional Standards Employed by Customs for Uniform Rights Enforcement (SECURE) at the WCO represented one of the most significant attempts to establish TRIPS-plus-plus initiatives on IP enforcement in recent years. It enshrines provisional enforcement rules and procedures for right-holders on one critical aspect of intellectual property rights enforcement: border measures (Li, 2008b).

The objective of this chapter is to provide an overview of recent initiatives to promote TRIPS-plus-plus standards on IP enforcement at the international level, and to draw some implications of these initiatives for international trade. It also serves the purpose of assisting developing countries in addressing the emerging global IP enforcement challenges. Following a brief introduction in Section 1, Section 2 examines the extent of the obligations under the TRIPS Agreement, highlighting the diversity of national legislation existing in this area. Section 3 elaborates on the proposed TRIPS-plus-plus initiatives in WCO, UPU and WHO. Section 4 examines the implications of broad border measures with reference to the India pharmaceutical case, with conclusions in Section 5.

2. Border measures under the TRIPS Agreement

Part III of the TRIPS Agreement establishes international obligations for WTO Members on Enforcement of Intellectual Property Rights. Part III is composed of five sections, that is, general obligations (Section 1), civil and administrative procedures and remedies (Section 2), provisional measures (Section 3), special requirements related to border measures (Section 4) and criminal procedures (Section 5). Border measures are regulated in Section 4, from Article 51 to Article 60. This section establishes the procedure and conditions under which customs authorities may, at the request of right-holders, suspend the release into circulation (seize at importation) of any suspected counterfeit trademark or pirated copyright goods. It also establishes the conditions of exemption from suspension and establishes terms of reference for customs authorities.

What are the obligations of member countries on border measures under the TRIPS Agreement? Article 51 of the TRIPS Agreement (Suspension of Release by Customs Authorities) states that 'Members shall, in conformity with the provisions set out below, adopt procedures to enable a right holder, who has valid grounds for suspecting that the importation of counterfeit trademark or pirated copyright goods may take place, to lodge an application in writing with competent authorities, administrative or judicial, for the suspension by the customs authorities of the release into free circulation of such goods'.[2] This is a very important Article which describes the key border measures in terms of procedure, definition, scope and responsibility.

In terms of procedure, Article 51 of the TRIPS Agreement only requires WTO Members to adopt a procedure for the right-holder to lodge an application for the suspension of the release of the suspected counterfeit trademark or pirated copyright goods. As clearly defined in footnote 14 to Article 51, the definition of 'counterfeit trademark goods' only refers to registered marks as 'counterfeit trademark goods', that is, 'any goods, including packaging, bearing without authorization a trademark which is identical to the trademark validly registered in respect of such goods, or which cannot be distinguished in its essential aspects from such a trademark, and which thereby infringes the rights of the owner of the trademark in question under the law of the country of importation'.[3] In terms of scope, the customs administrations can only deal with importation under the TRIPS Agreement. In terms of responsibility, according to Article 51 of the TRIPS Agreement, the customs administration's authority is expressly limited to the suspension of release into free circulation of goods suspected of bearing a counterfeit trademark or having a pirated copyright, on valid grounds (Vrins and Schneider, 2006).

Article 52 of the TRIPS Agreement contains detailed requirements regarding the application from right-holders to initiate a procedure for customs intervention. Accordingly, it is the obligation of the right-holder to provide evidence and satisfy the requirements of the customs authority in order to make a determination. To do so, two types of evidence should be provided: (a) a prima-facie infringement of an IPR under the laws of

---

[2] TRIPS Agreement.
[3] TRIPS Agreement.

the country of importation; (b) a sufficiently detailed description of the goods to enable the customs authorities to identify the goods in question.

Article 54 of the TRIPS Agreement (Notice of Suspension) defines the obligation of the customs authority to issue notice of suspension. It states that 'the importer and the applicant shall be promptly notified of the suspension of the release of goods according to Article 51'.[4] Thus, the importer is entitled to be notified of the suspension of the release of the goods under the TRIPS Agreement. Also, under the TRIPS Agreement, customs administrations have no legal authority to transmit to the right-holder information regarding detention of infringing goods.

Article 55 of the TRIPS Agreement establishes the duration of suspension for the suspected goods. It requires customs administrations to release the suspended goods within ten working days, under certain conditions, after the applicant has been served notice of the suspension.

Article 56 of the TRIPS Agreement establishes obligations for the applicant, if there is a wrongful detention of goods or through the detention of goods released pursuant to Article 55, to make 'appropriate compensation for any injury caused to them through the wrongful detention of goods'.

Article 58 of the TRIPS Agreement limits the authority of customs administrations. It establishes procedures and conditions related to ex officio action, in the absence of a legal basis for ex officio action. Ex officio measures are those taken on the initiative of the competent authorities without a request by the right-holder or other interested party. Where Members require competent authorities to act upon their own initiative and to suspend the release of goods in respect of which they have acquired prima-facie evidence that an intellectual property right is being infringed, it requires that where such measures exist in the national law of a WTO Member: (a) the importer and right-holder must be promptly notified; (b) remedial measures may be taken against public authorities and officials who did not act in good faith.[5]

Article 59 of the TRIPS Agreement establishes remedies for right-holders. Without prejudice to other rights of action open to the right-holder and subject to the right of the defendant to seek review by a judicial authority, competent authorities shall have the authority to order the destruction or disposal of infringing goods in accordance with the principles set out in Article 46.

Article 60 of the TRIPS Agreement defines exceptional circumstances where border measures are not applicable. It states that 'WTO Members

---

4 Ibid.
5 Ibid.

may exclude from the application of the above provision (border measures) small quantities of goods of a non-commercial nature contained in travellers' personal luggage or sent in small consignments'.[6] This Article takes into consideration the practical difficulty of enforcing border measures regarding small non-commercial shipments of infringed goods, in particular in travellers' private luggage. It thus excludes small quantities of goods from the obligation of applying border measures. As *de minimis* imports may impose a considerable administrative burden on customs authorities, Article 41(5) of the TRIPS Agreement becomes relevant as it provides that WTO Members are not required to divert law enforcement resources to IP enforcement.

Overall, the provisions of TRIPS define clearly the rights and obligations (including appeal and remedies) of the right-holder and importer, as well as the responsibility and authority of customs administrations in so far as border measures are concerned.

3. Features of broad border measures initiatives

Numerous TRIPS-plus-plus enforcement of IP initiatives have recently emerged, for instance, the G8 Countries' Initiative on Counterfeits; the World Customs Organization initiative on Provisional Standards Employed by Customs for Uniform Rights Enforcement (SECURE); the Universal Postal Union (UPU), the International Medical Products Anti-Counterfeiting Taskforce (IMPACT) based at the World Health Organization, WIPO's Advisory Committee on Enforcement (ACE); Interpol's initiatives on IP crime and other initiatives in the US as well as in the EU; the Anti-Counterfeiting Trade Agreement (ACTA), all aimed at TRIPS-plus-plus enforcement of IP. This section examines the characteristics of a few such initiatives and compares them with the provisions of TRIPS Agreement.

3.1 WCO

As an essential part of the forum-shopping strategy, the WCO, a relatively small international organization which is geographically distant from Geneva, the headquarters of the WIPO and WTO, has been chosen to promote SECURE, a major IP enforcement initiative from the perspective of developed countries. The WCO, with its headquarters in Brussels and 174 member customs administrations, is an international organization with a mandate to provide technical assistance to customs administrations and serves as a forum where delegates representing a wide variety

6 TRIPS Agreement.

of members can tackle customs issues on an equal footing.[7] However, in the case of SECURE, the WCO has been used to undertake norm-setting activities on IP enforcement, which is beyond its mandate.

3.1.1 SECURE at the WCO

SECURE at the WCO represents one of the most significant initiatives to establish TRIPS-plus-plus initiatives on IP enforcement. The SECURE Working Draft is a working document of the SECURE Working Group established by the WCO Enforcement Committee. It is comprised of an introduction and four sections, that is, Section I (IPR Legislative and Enforcement Regime Development), Section II (Co-operation with the Private Sector), Section III (Risk Analysis and Intelligence Sharing), and Section IV (Capacity Building for IPR Enforcement and International Co-operation). Among these, Section I of the SECURE Working Draft, 'IPR Legislative and Enforcement Regime Development', is the key component of the working draft, which contains 12 standards of IP enforcement. The expected outcome of the establishment of the SECURE Working Group at the WCO is to introduce a set of TRIPS-plus-plus standards on border measures of IP enforcement.

3.1.2 A Comparison of WCO SECURE and the TRIPS Agreement

The 12 standards under Section I of the SECURE Working Draft essentially correspond to Section 4 of Part III of the TRIPS Agreement, namely, Articles 51 to 60, dealing with Special Requirements Related to Border Measures.

The standards included in SECURE represent a significant departure from the TRIPS Agreement. The key content is to revise customs regulations with expansion of the authorities of customs administrations, and re-delineate the boundary of customs and other stakeholders. If SECURE were adopted, these TRIPS-plus-plus measures would increase the power and authority of national border and customs authorities to seize goods which are suspected of infringing intellectual property rights. For developing countries, SECURE primarily poses a five-fold threat: (1) it appears to be outside the boundary of the WCO's mandate and responsibility; (2) it could undermine the delicate balance as enshrined in the TRIPS as far as the role of customs is concerned; (3) it is contaminated by a number of TRIPS-plus-plus elements; (4) it is obviously biased in favour of the interests of right holders at the expense of other parties; (5) it is a process

---

[7] 'Our Profile', World Customs Organization, http://www.wcoomd.org/home.htm.

without transparency and participation of developing countries and observers from inter-governmental organizations and NGOs. Adoption of SECURE standards would allow developed countries to gradually legalize international TRIPS-plus-plus rules without resorting to amending the TRIPS Agreement itself.

Table 2.1 below summarizes the differences between provisions of the SECURE Working Draft and the TRIPS Agreement, and highlights the TRIPS-plus-plus elements of the former (Li, 2008a).

Therefore, the proposed SECURE standards are IP enforcement border measures that represent a significant departure from TRIPS provisions in terms of subject, scope and measures of protection, disposal methods and Member State obligations and rights. First, the proposed SECURE standards expand the subject and scope of enforcement of IPRs. Enforcement by customs administrations under the TRIPS Agreement is compulsory only with respect to importation (Article 51). However, the scope of SECURE Standard 1 is much broader than that of the TRIPS Agreement, as Standard 1 extends enforcement from importation to all types of transaction, including but not limited to export, transit, warehouses, transshipment, free zones, duty-free shops, etc. Regarding the scope of protection, it is proposed under SECURE Standard 2 that 'National legislation may extend the scope of Customs IPR legislation from trademark and copyright to other intellectual property rights'.[8] However, the procedures for border measures under TRIPS are required to be made available to 'counterfeit trademark or pirated copyright goods' only (Article 51). As clearly defined in footnote 14 to Article 51, the definition of 'counterfeit trademark goods' only refers to *registered* marks as 'counterfeit trademark goods', that is, 'any goods, including packaging, bearing without authorization a trademark which is identical to the trademark validly registered in respect of such goods, or which cannot be distinguished in its essential aspects from such a trademark, and which thereby infringes the rights of the owner of the trademark in question under the law of the country of importation'.[9]

Secondly, the proposed SECURE standards tend to favour the right-holders, thus affecting the balance between right-holders and importers under TRIPS. The balanced mechanisms under TRIPS have been bypassed under the SECURE standards, thus narrowing the flexibilities contained in TRIPS. According to Article 52 of the TRIPS Agreement, it is the obligation of the right-holders to provide evidence and satisfy the customs

---

8 SECURE, as of 25 April 2008.

9 TRIPS Agreement.

Table 2.1 Comparisons of SECURE and TRIPS provisions

SECURE	Issue	TRIPS Agreement	Comments
Standard 1	Scope	Article 51	Extends the scope from 'import' to 'export, transit, warehouses, transshipment, free zones, duty-free shops', etc.
Standard 2	Definitions	Article 51	Extends the protection from trademark and copyright to all other types of intellectual property rights.
Standard 3	Procedures	Article 51	Extends the procedure from 'suspension of the release of goods' to other types of procedures.
Standard 4	Application and right of Information	Articles 52, 57	Unclear definition of 'costs to right-holders' and no justification why the costs to right-holders should be reduced. Removes the obligations of right-holders to provide adequate evidence to satisfy the competent authorities that there is prima facie an infringement to initiate the procedure.
Standard 5	Central Office	Article 41	A single contact point governing applications should be designated by the customs authorities which imposed an additional burden. Under Article 41(5) of the TRIPS Agreement, however, WTO Members are not obliged with respect to the distribution of limited resources as between enforcement of IPR and the enforcement of law in general.
Standard 6	*De minimis* import	Article 60	Establishes a principle that the quantities of exempted goods should be 'as low as possible'.

Table 2.1 (continued)

SECURE	Issue	TRIPS Agreement	Comments
Standard 7	Ex officio	Article 58	• Expands the right of customs authorities to take action upon own initiatives, but removes the obligations from remedial measures when they did not act in good faith, • Specifies the right of right-holders to make a request, but the importer's minimum right of being notified promptly and properly is decreased.
Standard 8	Application	Articles 52, 58	Transfers the burden to provide evidence from the right-holders to customs administration. • Under TRIPS, it is the obligation of the right-holders to provide evidence and satisfy the customs authority making the determination. • To satisfy, two evidences should be provided: (a) a prima-facie infringement of an IPR under the laws of the country of importation; (b) a sufficiently detailed description of the goods to enable the customs authorities to identity the goods in question.
Standard 9	Notification	Article 54	• Under TRIPS, the importer and the applicant shall be promptly notified of the suspension of the release of goods. • Under SECURE, no safeguard is available for importers regarding the right of notification of suspension and detention.

Standard 10	Remedies	Article 59	• Under TRIPS, (a) it is the responsibility of the judicial body, rather than the customs administration to dispose of or destroy the infringed goods; (b) it rests upon the decision of the competent body to decide upon either the destruction or disposal of infringing goods; (c) it is established the procedure that any order to destroy or dispose of the goods is subject to a right of review by the importer or other defendant and without prejudice to the right-holder's rights of action. • Under Standard 10, it (a) expands the authority of the customs administration, (b) it regulates that all infringing goods shall be destroyed.
Standard 11	Disposal	Article 51	Under SECURE, (a) The customs administration has the authority to detail, move, or seize IPR infringing goods; (b) while specifying that the burden of fee should not be unreasonable on right-holders, there is no security for other stakeholders.
Standard 12	Criminal procedure	Article 61	• Under TRIPS, Members shall provide for criminal procedures and penalties for . . . trademark counterfeiting and copyright piracy on a commercial scale. • Under SECURE, the customs administration has the legal authority to impose deterrent penalties against entities knowingly involved in the importation/exportation of goods under customs control which violate *any* IPR laws.

authority in their assessment of whether a product is a counterfeit. The aim of the TRIPS Agreement is to ensure that customs authorities would not impede legitimate trade and prevent right-holders from taking undue advantage of the border seizures and detentions to delay legitimate trade. As stated above, to satisfy Article 52, two forms of evidence should be provided: (a) a prima-facie infringement of an IPR under the laws of the country of importation; (b) a sufficiently detailed description of the goods to enable customs authorities to identify the goods in question. However, when the SECURE Standards 4 and 8 are read together, they point to an intention to shift the burden of proof from right-holders to customs administrations by requesting customs administrations to provide samples of suspicious goods to right-holders, and for right-holders to determine the counterfeit nature of those samples.[10]

Thirdly, the proposed SECURE standards may disrupt normal trade of non-infringing goods by re-delineating the responsibilities of determination of IP infringement among various authorities. Under TRIPS, it is the responsibility of a judicial body, rather than the customs administrations, to dispose of or destroy the infringing goods. It falls to the competent body to decide upon either the destruction or disposal of infringing goods, as stated in Article 46 that 'the judicial authorities shall have the authority to order that goods that they have found to be infringing be, without compensation of any sort, disposed of outside the channels of commerce. . . or, destroyed'. The established procedure is that any order to destroy or dispose of the goods is subject to a right of review by the importer or other defendant and without prejudice to the right-holder's rights of action (Biadgleng and Munoz, 2008). However, under Standard 10, while expanding the authority of the customs administrations, it also regulates that all infringing goods should be destroyed. Therefore, the proposed border measures for the enforcement of IPRs embedded in the SECURE standards may significantly disrupt legitimate trade of non-infringing goods. Notably, SECURE provides no mechanism for appeal and review, which undermines the fairness of a system.

---

[10] Standard 4 proposes that 'with respect to requests from rights holders for Customs intervention, Customs Administrations should develop standardized application forms requesting information consisting of basic, standard data at a cost not exceeding the costs of the processing of the application. . . . The initial period should be extended by simple notification, including evidence of the continuing right and prima facie evidence of infringement.' Standard 8 proposes that 'Customs Administrations should adopt procedures enabling them to provide to rights holders free of charge samples of suspicious goods to determine the counterfeit nature of those samples . . .'. SECURE, as of 25 April 2008.

3.2 UPU

With the forum-shopping strategy, it is not surprising to see that a similar attempt by developed countries is under way to promote a TRIPS-plus-plus agenda on international border enforcement through another route. UPU is a specialized agency of the United Nations with 191 Member States, with its headquarters in Berne, Switzerland. As the primary forum for cooperation between postal sectors, UPU sets the rules for international mail exchanges and makes recommendations to stimulate growth in mail volumes and to improve the quality of service. Postal services may be regarded as part of the custom authorities because of their important role in international trade. In this context, initiatives involving postal services are also part of developed countries' TRIPS-plus-plus agenda.

3.2.1 Resolution 40 and its negotiation

Resolution 40, entitled 'Counterfeit and Pirated Items Sent through the Post', was presented to the 24th Congress of the Universal Postal Union (UPU), held in Geneva, from 23 July to 12 August 2008.

The preamble to draft Resolution 40 stipulated that:

- 'the postal channel is used, together with other distribution channels, for the sending of counterfeit and pirated items';
- 'that the POC Committee 3 Customs Support Project Group has carried out a study on UPU customs and security-related issues concerning intellectual property matters';
- 'that the results of the study revealed that postal administration have no legal competence in determining whether or not an item is a counterfeit or whether a customs declaration has been falsely completed';
- 'that the Customs and experts on intellectual property rights are primarily responsible for determining whether an item is counterfeit';
- 'that the legislation of member countries on how to deal with counterfeit and pirated items varies from country to country'; and finally
- 'that the above problems cause operational difficulties and legal problems for the countries concerned'.

Draft Resolution 40 stated in its operative paragraphs:

> Urges UPU member countries in the context of national legislation to encourage their postal administrations to:
>
> - take all reasonable and practical measures to support Customs in their role of identifying counterfeit and pirated items in the postal network;

- cooperate with the relevant national and international authorities to the maximum possible extent in awareness-raising initiatives aimed at preventing the illegal circulation of counterfeit goods, particularly through postal services.

Resolution 40 was proposed by France, as part of the 'Proposal of a General Nature' submitted by Postal Operations Council (POC). Previously, it was presented by the WCO-UPU (Universal Postal Union) Contact Committee and the POC 3 Customs Support Project Group to the POC for examination in January 2008.

WCO appeared to be primarily responsible for the birth of Resolution 40. Resolution 40, unlike many other such proposals, was presented by the World Customs Organization (WCO)-UPU Contact Committee and the Postal Operational Council (POC) 3 Customs Support Project Group to the POC for examination in January 2008. It can be further traced back to a Memorandum of Understanding, signed by the UPU and the WCO in July 2007. Noting that the SECURE Working Group was established during the same period at WCO, there is clearly a coherent strategy by developed countries to have the same agenda, promoted simultaneously in various international and regional forums. During the 24th Congress of UPU, the draft Resolution 40 was first adopted on 1 August 2008, but an appeal by developing countries was adopted subsequently on 8 August 2008. The appeal was co-sponsored by Egypt, India, Jordan, Libya, Malaysia, Pakistan, Saudi Arabia, South Africa, Syria and Turkey.

3.2.2 A comparison of UPU Resolution 40 and the TRIPS Agreement

There were two versions of Resolution 40. The original draft Resolution 40 of UPU implied a shift of responsibility from the judiciary to customs over the determination of IP infringement and expansion of the terms of reference of postal authorities.

Article 46 of the TRIPS Agreement ('Other Remedies') states:

> In order to create an effective deterrent to infringement, the judicial authorities shall have the authority to order that goods that they have found to be infringing be, without compensation of any sort, disposed of outside the channels of commerce in such a manner as to avoid any harm caused to the right holder, or, unless this would be contrary to existing constitutional requirements, destroyed.

According to TRIPS, it is 'the judicial authorities to have the authority to order that goods that they have found to be infringing be, without compensation of any sort, disposed of outside the channels of commerce . . .

or, destroyed'. However, given the fact that customs administrations have neither the mandate nor legal competence to determine whether an item is counterfeit, the shift of responsibility would imply a new trade barrier in the global economy. If the original draft Resolution 40 was adopted without amendment, it would legitimize the role of the customs administration in the determination of IP infringement.

Considering the original draft indicating that 'the Customs and experts on intellectual property rights are primarily responsible for determining whether an item is counterfeit', amendments were proposed and adopted to the preamble of the Resolution as follows:

> PP 1 (bis) – 'Without prejudice to the ongoing IP related work in other competent international organizations'.
> PP 4 (alt) – 'Understanding that determination of counterfeit items is the responsibility of relevant national authorities, in accordance with national legislation'.

The adoption of the appeal implies that the deviation from TRIPS Agreement on the role of customs in determination of counterfeit has been diminished.

3.3 WHO

The World Health Organization (WHO) has been targeted as another multilateral platform of the TRIPS-plus-plus IP enforcement agenda promoted by developed countries and major multinational pharmaceutical companies. WHO is a specialized agency of the United Nations (UN) that acts as a coordinating authority on international public health.

3.3.1 WHO IMPACT AND ITS NEGOTIATION

A WHO Secretariat report and a draft resolution entitled 'counterfeit medical products' (EB 124/14) prepared for the WHO Executive Board meeting in January 2009 proposes resolving health problems through mechanisms related to IP enforcement. The draft resolution and report seek a strong mandate on 'counterfeit' and to endorse the activities of a multi-stakeholder initiative called IMPACT. IMPACT is a process initiated by multinationals and developed countries and has taken shelter at the WHO without endorsement of WHO member states. IMPACT developed a one-size-fits-all model – Principles and Elements of National Legislation against Counterfeit Medical Products. The IMPACT Principles advance an IP enforcement agenda designed to enforce stringent standards of IP enforcement against IP-infringing medical products through public health standards.

The WHO Secretariat's report and draft resolution use the terminology of 'counterfeit' and label this term as a central health problem. It refers to the definition of 'counterfeit' proposed in the context of IMPACT:

> The term counterfeit medical product describes a product with a false representation (a) of its identity (b) and/or source (c). This applies to the product, its container or other packaging or labelling information. Counterfeiting can apply to both branded and generic products. Counterfeits may include products with correct ingredients/components (d), with wrong ingredients/components, without active ingredients, with incorrect amounts of active ingredients, or with fake packaging.

Violations or disputes concerning patents must not be confused with counterfeiting of medical products. Medical products (whether generic or branded) that are not authorized for marketing in a given country but authorized elsewhere are not considered counterfeit. Substandard batches of, or quality defects or non-compliance with Good Manufacturing Practices/Good Distribution Practices (GMP/GDP) in legitimate medical products must not be confused with counterfeiting.

The notes referred to above as (a), (b), (c) and (d) of the definition are as follows:

(a) Counterfeiting is done fraudulently and deliberately. The criminal intent and/or careless behaviour shall be considered during the legal procedures for the purposes of sanctions imposed.
(b) This includes any misleading statement with respect to name, composition, strength, or other elements.
(c) This includes any misleading statement with respect to manufacturer, country of manufacturing, country of origin, marketing authorization holder or steps of distribution.
(d) This refers to all components of a medical product.

Thus, the WHO Secretariat report uses the term 'counterfeit' in a confusing manner. The connotations of the word 'counterfeit' used in the WHO Secretariat report may be misleading in the context of public health. Further, it is stated in paragraph 5 of the Secretariat's report that 'often no distinction is made between patent violations, patent or trademark disputes, copyright violations and actual counterfeiting'. Paragraph 12 of the Secretariat report states that the intellectual property rights approach identifies the right-holder as the main victim of counterfeiters and as the main trigger of enforcement and prosecution while, in the case of medical products, the real victim of counterfeiting is the patient'. Consequently, the EB document 124/14 could be used to advance a flawed

IP enforcement agenda through public health. It reflects a concerted strategy by developed countries and major pharmaceutical companies to push for a TRIPS-plus-plus IP enforcement agenda in multinational negotiation forums.

3.3.2 A COMPARISON OF THE PROPOSED DEFINITION OF COUNTERFEIT MEDICAL PRODUCT AND TRIPS

The IPR-related issue in the Draft Resolution EB124/14 is the proposed definition of counterfeit medical product. There are legitimate health concerns pertaining to quality, safety and efficacy of medicines as there are problems concerning products with wrong information on the label with regard to the content, date of manufacture, place of manufacture, date of expiry (known as false labelling), products which, contrary to the label, contain no active ingredient or a wrong active ingredient or an insufficient amount of an active ingredient (known as spurious drugs); and low-quality drugs caused by poor manufacturing practices, poor transportation techniques or poor storage facilities (known as substandard drugs).[11] However, some of these legitimate health concerns have been subsumed under the term 'counterfeit', a term used in the context of IP. The issue is that it is likely to be oriented towards protecting and enforcing the interests of the IP right holder to an extent that may damage access to medicines.

'Counterfeit' is a term used in the WTO TRIPS Agreement in connection with intellectual property rights, particularly trademark infringements. Compared with the TRIPS Agreement, the proposed IMPACT definition of counterfeit medical products is controversial particularly because it is an attempt to conflate issues of IP and public health. It should be noted that IP violations are not problems of quality per se and not an issue for WHO which is tasked with a mandate on public health. This definition, which is presented in the Secretariat's report, applies to *all medical products* and not just medicines. While it explains that counterfeiting is done fraudulently and deliberately, it raises the presumption that any act of false representation as to the identity or source of the medical product is necessarily done fraudulently and deliberately. Instead of bringing in the requirement of deliberate and fraudulent intent within the main definition, this explanation shifts the burden of proving the lack of fraudulent intent onto the defendant, rather than requiring the prosecution to

---

[11] Sangeeta Shashikant, 'WHO: Approach to "Counterfeit" Drugs may Affect Access to Medicines', *SUNS*, 15 January 2009.

establish fraudulent intent. Thus, it lowers the standard of proof required to establish counterfeiting.[12]

Moreover, fraudulent intent is made relevant only for determining sanctions and not for establishing culpability. While it attempts to exclude patent disputes and violations from the definition, the explanation does not exclude other IP issues, particularly trademark violations. Further, the IMPACT principles also lay down responsibilities for governments and other parties which are designed to enforce measures such as criminal sanctions against broadly defined acts of counterfeiting. It also requires governments to seize such broadly defined counterfeit medical products while in transit through their ports.[13]

3.4 Feature and strategy of WCO, UPU and WHO IP initiatives

Overall, these TRIPS-plus-plus IP enforcement initiatives at the WCO, UPU and WHO aim at designing an extensive legal framework to ensure that customs authorities and right-holders have broader rights and means for strong IPR enforcement. There are three distinguished features to be noted:

First, these initiatives tend to expand the definition of IP under border measures. On the one hand, these ongoing initiatives, as in the case of WCO SECURE, substantially enlarge the limited obligations of IP enforcement under the TRIPS from copyright and trademark to all types of IPRs, particularly patent infringement. On the other hand, these initiatives, as in the case of the WHO IMPACT, mislead the public and confuse the issue of low quality medicines with infringement of pharmaceutical patents and other IP rights.

Secondly, these initiatives attempt to expand the scope of protection and enforcement of IPR. These initiatives also attempt to extend the scope of seizure from import required by TRIPS, to export, transshipment of goods suspected of infringing IP and others, as proposed at WCO SECURE.

Thirdly, these initiatives expand the authority of customs administrations, but reduce their obligations. For instance, it is proposed to give authority to customs administrations to determine infringement and take action against suspected infringers even in the absence of complaint by right-holders; grant extensive powers to customs authorities to seize documentary evidence relating to the suspected infringement and the suspected goods themselves and for the granting of preliminary injunctions; give

12 South Centre Summary Note of Analysis on the IMPACT Taskforce on Counterfeit Medicines. 14 January 2009.

13 Ibid.

rights to customs administrations to destroy suspected IPR-infringing goods and seize equipment and materials used to make IPR-infringing goods, without going through proper judicial procedure; and remove the obligation of issuing notice by customs authorities as required by TRIPS (SECURE, UPU).

These various initiatives at WCO, UPU, WHO and other international forums are not isolated, as they all form part of an overall TRIPS-plus-plus strategy on the part of developed countries. The origins of these TRIPS-plus-plus initiatives are in the July 2005 declaration of the G8, as summit leaders, urging collective and concerted international action to combat counterfeiting and piracy, empowered the WCO through a political boost to substantially increase their mandate to develop IP enforcement legislation. As shown in Table 2.2, the WCO's proposal (SECURE) contains

Table 2.2 Comparison of TRIPS-plus-plus proposals on IP enforcement at WCO, UPU and WHO

	WCO's Proposal (SECURE)	UPU's Proposal (Resolution 40)	WHO's Proposal (EB 124/14 of Secretariat report)
Definition of protection	(a) Extend the definition from copyright and trademark to all IPRs, i.e., patent	Extend the protection from copyright and trademark to all IPRs, i.e., patent	Confuse IP and public health by proposing new definition of 'counterfeit medical product'
Scope of protection and enforcement	(a) Extend the scope of protection from exportation to importation, in-transit, etc.		
Authority of customs administration	(a) Expand the authority's right to determine the IP infringement (b) Narrow down the authority's responsibility	Extend the authorities of customs administrations to determine IP infringement	

extensive border measures involving the definition and scope of protection, right and obligations of right-holders and authority of customs administrations. Echoing the WCO's proposal, UPU's proposal (Resolution 40 of UPC) focuses on the expansion of customs administrations' authority to determine infringement. As a specialized agency in international health matters, the WHO proposal (EB 124/14 of Secretariat report) involves expanding the definition and scope of protection by introducing a newly defined 'counterfeit medical product'. The analysis of the implications of these broad border measures is provided in the next section.

4. Implications of broad border measures

4.1 Implications of a broad definition of IP

Expanding the definition of counterfeit and piracy to include all forms of IPR infringement may have significant implications. Notably, a broad definition, which includes patent and other forms of IPR, would form a basis for taking border measures over patent infringement. In the field of public health, for instance, a broad definition of 'counterfeit medical product' raises a few concerns. The mixture of IP in the definition will result in shifting the focus from quality, safety and efficacy to IP infringement. Such a mixture, together with broad border measures by customs administrations, will result in seizures at the border that have more to do with IP violations and little relevance to quality, safety and efficacy. The second concern is that the scope of the definition appears to be beyond the mandate of WHO, with 'medical products' covering a broad range of items, that is, drugs, vaccines, diagnostic kits, medical devices (for instance, surgical devices, scanners, x-ray machines), as well as the raw material used for production. This is because World Health Assembly (WHA) resolutions 41.16, 47.13 and 52.19 only refer to medicines, drugs and pharmaceutical preparations, without providing a mandate to deal with 'medical products'. The expansion of these definitions would form the basis of expanding the powers of customs administrations, which would have discretion to seize goods suspected of being in violation of IPRs, for example, patent-infringing products.

Evidence of this can be found in the emerging case of shipments of Indian generic drug destined for Venezuela being seized at Dutch ports on charges of counterfeiting and patent infringement in December 2008. While the Indian Pharmaceuticals Export Promotion Council (Pharmexcil), an agency set up by India's commerce ministry, considered the seized drugs to be genuine and legal, EU authorities upheld the seizures and claimed the drugs were in violation of intellectual property rights and were hence counterfeit.[14] It should be noted that the seized drugs had nothing to do with trademark issues as the exports were unbranded Active Pharmaceutical Ingredients (APIs) or counterfeiting as defined under TRIPS. The reason why this consignment was seized at the border under the claim of patent infringement is because of the introduction of TRIPS-plus-plus border measures at EU borders, particularly the expansive and unclear definition of IP, that is, the inclusion of patent in the definition of IP enforcement, and problematic definitions of counterfeit drugs by the WHO and IMPACT lead to misinterpretation of counterfeit drug consignments from India. The seizure of the Indian shipment is one concrete case that shows how a broad definition of IP violation and a term such as 'counterfeit' when used to address health problems, can result in national legislation aimed at protecting the interests of IP holders, with potentially damaging effects on access to medicines. While the term, counterfeit medical product, was used to ensure good quality, safe and effective medicines, it has become a barrier, blocking access to and availability of generic medicines in developing countries.

4.2 Implications of expanded scope of protection and enforcement

Expanding the scope of protection and enforcement from import to export, in-transit, and others, would create substantial risks for legitimate trade. Such an impact on developing countries could be at least twofold: (i) within their territory, there will be increased obligations on exports for their customs administrations, which would generate additional costs of enforcement; (ii) externally, developing countries' enterprises are likely to face greater uncertainties resulting from potential trade barriers during transit.

On the first issue, an additional burden is imposed on customs administrations to spend more public resources to enforce IP as a private right, which is the opposite of the basic principle of enforcement. If these broad border measures are implemented, these may lead to some internal restructuring and shifts of focus and priorities in a given customs administration. At present, many customs authorities in developing countries are facing the challenge of adapting to the changes in their roles in an increasingly globalized world, while coping with the difficulties of limited availability of human, financial and material resources. In terms of capacity building, developing countries in general, and least developed countries in particular, need sufficient time and resources to prepare and update the

[14] Lison Joseph, 'Shipments Seizure: India's Drug Makers may Avoid EU Route', *The Wall Street Journal*, Livemint.com, 11 Dec 2008. http://www.eu-digest.com/2008/12/livemintcom-shipments-seizure-of.html.

dynamic content of training for their competent functionaries, including customs officials, in accordance with the relevant provisions of the TRIPS Agreement. It should be noted that developing countries have no legal obligations to extend border measures beyond the requirements of the TRIPS Agreement on a mandatory basis, but may choose to do so if they are able and willing.

On the second issue, if broad border measures like expanding scope of protection to shipment in-transit are implemented, customs would be accorded higher than appropriate powers in international trade. In the case of customs, with such new powers, developed countries would be able to put in place new border barriers to restrict imports from developing countries during transit. As such, it would become hard for importers/exporters to predict whether their shipment would be seized as a result of suspected infringement during transit through a third country. Consequently, importers/exporters would have to bear additional risk with associated costs. Normally, the allegation of infringement should be raised by right-holders with appropriate evidence and proof to judicial authorities that have jurisdiction over IP enforcement in a given country. Due to the fact that IP may have a geographically distinct nature, if a shipment in-transit is put under IP enforcement, it would mean a major departure from general principle of IP enforcement and disrupt normal international trade. With such practices, right-holders would also be tempted to engage in lobbying activities in third countries, which would negatively affect normal international trade. There have been a few cases where seizures in-transit have affected the international trade order. Indian generic drugs destined for Venezuela being seized in-transit at a Dutch port in 2008 is an example. Apart from this, according to the Pharmaceuticals Export Promotion Council (Pharmexcil), Chandigarh-based Ind-Swift Laboratories Ltd and several other Mumbai-based bulk drug makers have had their shipments seized at EU ports, including in Germany, France, the UK and the Netherlands in 2008. The 'in-transit' seizures of Indian consignments of Pharmexcil member companies in the EU raise concerns about the current trend towards the proliferation of more expansive border measures globally.

4.3 Implications of expanding the authority of customs administrations

The implications of the proposed expansion of customs administrations' authority to determine IP infringement, or seize products on right-holders' complaints, or even the duty to act ex officio, so as to suspend the release of goods suspected to be infringing, even in the absence of any request by right-holders, could be significant. Notably, the question of who can determine patent infringement would have a most significant impact.

Authorizing customs to determine IP infringement may result in unpredictability and constitute a barrier to legitimate trade. Why? Patent infringement determination is a highly sophisticated process which has been dealt with by judicial bodies according to the jurisdictions of most countries. A patent contains several parts – a specification, drawings, and claims. No matter how much a questioned machine, manufacture, composition of matter or process may look like the specification and drawings of a patent, it is only the claims of the patent which can be infringed (Walter J. Blenko, 1990). Determination of infringement requires a construction of the meaning of the claim language and then application of the claims so construed to the accused product or process. The determination of patent infringement is a two-step process: (1) derivation of the meaning of the claims 'by a study of all relevant patent documents . . .' and interpreting the language of the claims, and (2) a reading of the claims on the accused product or process, which is whether the claimed invention is being made, used, or sold by the alleged infringer. Whether an alleged equivalent to an element of a patent claim must have been in existence and known in the relevant art as an equivalent is a long-standing problem with the Doctrine of Equivalents (Holzmann, 1995). The Doctrine of Equivalents considers the literal meaning of the claims and several other factors including the scope and content of the prior art and the prosecution history. Under the Doctrine of Equivalents, an accused device that is not literally described by the claims of a patent may still be found to infringe if the accused device performs substantially the same function, in substantially the same way, to achieve substantially the same result, as the claimed invention. Such a highly technical process is beyond the authority and competence of customs administrations.

Other measures allow customs administrations to seize products at the border on the complaint by an IP right-holder. The process for complaint is simpler in that the owner of an intellectual property right that has valid grounds for suspecting that the importation of counterfeit goods may take place, can make an application for seizure of the product to the relevant authority. The IP holder has to provide some evidence of an IP right subsisting, and the relevant authority has to consider and deal with the application within a certain period of time to be satisfied that there are reasonable grounds that the applicant is prima facie the owner of an IP right. However, with relaxed regulation, multinational pharmaceutical companies could raise complaints about intellectual property rights infringement with customs authorities, where such complaints are not necessarily based on valid evidence and court decision, effectively in order to stop the suspected products at the border. If customs were to be accorded such powers and to exercise them, where such powers are higher than the appropriate powers in international trade, developed countries would be able to put in place new border barriers to restrict imports from developing countries. Moreover, with more powers accorded to IP holders, exports from developing countries could easily be alleged to be infringing patents, and hence blocked or even destroyed by customs, as in the recent seizure of importation of GMO soybean meal from Argentina (Correa, 2006; 2009). Since there is no dispute resolution mechanism or channel for appeal in place, exports from developing countries are more likely to be treated unfairly. Consequently, the process of determining IP infringement at the border becomes highly unpredictable and may not be 'fair and equitable', as required by Article 41(3) of TRIPS. As stated above, evidence of this emerged in the recent case of shipments of drug products of Indian companies in-transit which were seized at Dutch ports.

5. Conclusion

This chapter provides an overview of recent initiatives to promote TRIPS-plus-plus standards on IP enforcement in the international arena, including WCO, UPU and WHO. These initiatives are not isolated; they form part of an overall TRIPS-plus-plus IP enforcement strategy by developed countries. The aim of these initiatives is to design an extensive legal framework to ensure that customs authorities and right-holders have broader rights and means for strong IPR enforcement. By comparing the border measures under new initiatives and TRIPS, three distinct features are found: first, these initiatives aim to expand the definition of IP, notably patent infringement. Secondly, these initiatives attempt to expand the scope of protection and enforcement of IPR, particularly exports and in-transit. Thirdly, these initiatives tend to expand the authority of the customs administration; in particular, they grant authority to customs administrations to determine infringement.

In conclusion, broad border measures beyond TRIPS would constitute a new type of barrier to legitimate trade by expanding the definition and scope of IP enforcement, as well as shifting the state's responsibility for the determination of IP infringement from the judiciary to an administrative body like customs. If adopted for implementation globally, such measures would be detrimental to the normal trade and economic growth of developing countries, as is evident in the recent seizure of a drug consignment from India to Latin America in-transit in an EU port. However, it should be highlighted that broad border measures that put an undue burden on trade can be challenged for their abuse at the WTO.

References

Biadgleng, Ermias and Munoz, Viviana (2008), 'The Changing Structure and Governance of Intellectual Property Enforcement', Research Papers No. 15, South Centre, Geneva.

Blenko, Jr., Walter J. (1990), 'When Does Patent Infringement Become Unfair Competition?', The Minerals, Metals and Materials Society, 42(10), p. 55.

Correa, Carlos (2006), 'La disputa sobre soja transgénica. Monsanto vs. Argentina', in *Le Monde Diplomatique/El Dipló*.

Correa, Carlos (2009), 'Enforcing Border Measures: Importation of GMO Soybean Meal from Argentina', in Xuan Li and Carlos Correa (eds), *Intellectual Property Enforcement: International Perspectives*, Cheltenham, UK and Northampton, MA, US: Edward Elgar.

Holzmann, Richard T. (1995), *Infringement of the United States Patent Right: A Guide for Executives and Attorneys*, Westport, CT: Quorum Books, p. 84.

Li, Xuan (2008a), 'SECURE: A Critical Analysis and Call for Action', *South Bulletin* (15), 16 May.

Li, Xuan (2008b), 'WCO SECURE: Lessons Learnt from the Abortion of the TRIPS-plus-plus IP Enforcement Initiative', Research Papers No. 19, South Centre, Geneva.

Vrins, Olivier and Schneider, Marius (2006), *Enforcement of Intellectual Property Rights through Border Measures, Law and Practice in the EU*, Oxford: Oxford University Press.

3 Lessons from the United States in regard to the recent, more flexible application of injunctive relief

*Joshua D. Sarnoff**

Introduction

Although the existence of a right normally implies the existence of a remedy for its violation, substantial judicial discretion may exist in determining what particular remedy to apply. Such discretion provides flexibility to accomplish policy goals, and thus may be considered one of many important 'policy levers' that may be applied to accomplish legislative purposes and enhance social welfare, without creating excessive specificity or differentiation in the legislation itself.[1] Retail differentiation of remedies by judges in particular cases may be less risky for innovation policies, less costly to administer, more sensitive to contextual information, or more politically feasible than wholesale differentiation of rights and remedies at the legislative level.[2] Such legislative specificity, moreover, would encourage rent-seeking. Few (except perhaps lawyers) would want intellectual property legislation to look like the tax code or environmental regulations.

In both common law and civil law jurisdictions, some form of equity jurisprudence invariably exists as an alternative to or correction for a more rigid, codified, and universal system of enforcing legal rules, whether or not this alternative system of justice is applied by separate municipal courts.[3] Nevertheless, separate courts of equity have a long

* The author thanks Michael Carroll, Peter Jaszi, and David Ryan for helpful insights and Ida Wahlquist-Ortiz for research assistance.

1 *See* Michael W. Carroll, 'Patent Injunctions and the Problem of Uniformity Cost', *Mich. Telecomm. & Tech. L. Rev.* 13 (2007): 422–26. *See generally* Dan L. Burk & Mark A. Lemley, 'Policy Levers in Patent Law,' *Va. L. Rev.* 19 (2003): 1575.

2 *See* Michael W. Carroll, 'One for All: The Problem of Uniformity Cost in Intellectual Property Law', *Am. U. L. Rev.* 55 (2006): 848.

3 *See, e.g.*, Joseph Story, *Commentaries on Equity Jurisprudence as Administered in England and America* 1 (1870): § 3, at 3–4 (Isaac F. Redfield ed. 10th ed. Little Brown); *id.*, §§ 7–9, at 6–10; *id.*, §§ 25–35, at 19–26.

pedigree, tracing back at least to Roman law.[4] The basic nature of equity jurisprudence is for courts to have 'jurisdiction in cases of rights, recognized and protected by the municipal jurisprudence, where a plain, adequate, [or] complete remedy cannot be had in the courts of common law.'[5] Equitable jurisdiction and remedies thus are sometimes concurrent with, exclusive of, or auxiliary to the remedies available at law, and provide the flexibility to render complete justice among the parties.[6] Equity jurisprudence is distinguished by its flexible application to factual context and by the policy discretion vested in the judiciary to achieve substantive justice and more complete relief.[7] Foremost among the remedies authorized by equity is the prospective injunction, which is directed to a party so as to prevent a wrong, when courts at law can only redress the wrong after it occurs.[8]

1. Recent limits on judicial discretion to deny injunctions to stop infringing activity

Although substantial judicial discretion may exist to determine what particular remedy to apply, for many decades judges in the United States have with ever-increasing rigidity applied one specific and extremely powerful equitable remedy for cases of patent infringement – injunctive relief in the inflexible form of an order to cease any continued infringing activity.

In contrast, judicial flexibility may accomplish various policy goals and legislative purposes, without requiring excessive specificity or differentiation in legislation itself. Differentiation of remedies by judges in particular cases may be less risky for innovation policies, less costly to administer, more sensitive to contextual information or more politically feasible than at the legislative level. Before the creation of the US Court of Appeals for the Federal Circuit (Federal Circuit) – which has nearly exclusive jurisdiction over patent appeals – federal Circuit Courts of Appeals frequently granted injunctive relief once a patent was found (or found likely) to be valid and infringed.[9] At least by 1988, the Federal Circuit had stated that

---

4 *See id.*, §§ 4–6, at 4–6; *id.*, §§ 36–37, at 26–27.

5 *Id.*, § 33, at 24.

6 *See id.*

7 *See, e.g., id.*, § 28, at 20–21 ('one of the most striking and distinctive features of courts of equity is, that they can adapt their decrees to all the varieties of circumstances, which may arise, and adjust them to all the peculiar rights of all the parties in interest'); Hecht Co. v. Bowles, 321 U.S. 321, 329 (1944).

8 Story, *Commentaries on Equity, supra,* 1: § 30, at 21–22.

9 *See* Carroll, 'Patent Injunctions', *supra* note 1, at 422–26. Carroll, 'One for All', *supra* note 2, at 848.

a permanent injunction 'should issue once infringement has been established unless there is a sufficient reason for denying it'.[10] This presumption in favor of injunctive relief had expanded by 2005 to limit the reasons for denying injunctions to the point that the Federal Circuit could state a 'general rule that courts will issue permanent injunctions against patent infringement absent exceptional circumstances'.[11] In regard to preliminary injunctions, which are an 'extraordinary remedy',[12] the Federal Circuit had developed a strong presumption of irreparable harm upon a sufficient showing that a patent was valid and was infringed, which applied without regard to differences among patent holders who licensed their inventions and those who made and sold their inventions in the market.[13]

Similar presumptions in favor of prospective injunctive relief to stop infringing conduct have also been applied for a longer time in trademark and copyright cases within all of the federal circuits. In trademark cases, the difficulties of quantifying harm to market share, goodwill or reputation and the public interest in avoiding consumer confusion typically resulted in granting permanent injunctions, and courts provided a presumption of irreparable harm for preliminary injunctions when there was a sufficient showing of likely success on the merits.[14] Similarly, in copyright cases courts have traditionally granted permanent injunctions once copyright infringement was proven, and have presumed irreparable harm upon a sufficient showing of a likelihood of success. Such injunctions and presumptions reflected concerns over the forced sharing of the creative works of authors, although courts also sometimes refused to order infringement to stop when to do so would impose harms that were disproportionate to the infringement or based on the public's interest in free expression or in access to the infringing work.[15]

---

[10] *W.L. Gore & Assocs., Inc. v. Garlock, Inc.*, 842 F.2d 1275, 1281 (Fed. Cir. 1988). *See, e.g., Chisum on Patents* 7–20 (2008): § 20.04[1][e] (Matthew Bender & Co. on-line edition).

[11] *MercExchange, LLC v. eBay, Inc.*, 401 F.3d 1323, 1339 (Fed. Cir. 2005), rev'd in part, 547 US 388 (2006).

[12] *Roper Corp. v. Litton Sys., Inc.*, 757 F.2d 1266, 1273 (Fed. Cir. 1985).

[13] *See, e.g., id.* at 1271–3.

[14] *See, e.g., Opticians Ass'n of Am. v. Indep. Opticians of Am.*, 920 F.2d 187, 196 (3d Cir. 1990); *Talley-Ho, Inc. v. Coast Cmty. Coll. Dist.*, 889 F.2d 1018, 1029 (11th Cir. 1989); *Int'l Kennel Club, Inc. v. Mighty Star, Inc.*, 846 F.2d 1079, 1092 (7th Cir. 1988); *Omega Importing Corp. v. Petri-Kine Camera Co.*, 451 F.2d 1190, 1195 (2d Cir. 1971). *See generally Gilson on Trademarks* 3–14 (2008): § 14.02[3][b][ii] (Matthew Bender & Co. 2008 on-line edition).

[15] *See, e.g., Taylor Corp. v. Four Seasons Greetings, LLC*, 403 F.3d 958, 967 (8th Cir. 2005); *Silverstein v. Penguin Putnam, Inc.*, 368 F.3d 77, 84–5 (2d Cir.

Because intellectual property infringement normally does not require culpable intent, infringers often may have made substantial but reasonable investments in creativity, manufacturing, marketing, and other activities. By 1986, however, the Federal Circuit had stated that the potential to put the infringer out of business was not a sufficient reason to deny a prospective injunction to cease infringement, even though patent injunctions are authorized by law only 'in accordance with the principles of equity'.[16] Equitable principles traditionally required consideration of (among other factors) the balance of hardships to the parties, but the Federal Circuit's rigid approach precluded the flexible and contextual weighing of the equities.[17] As the Federal Circuit put it, '[o]ne who elects to build a business on a product found to infringe cannot be heard to complain if an injunction against continuing infringement destroys the business so elected'.[18] Thus, particularly when the infringement related only to a component of a larger product, the potential for injunctive relief and the presumption of irreparable harm from proof of likely infringement over the last two decades has posed a significant 'holdup problem' that may have resulted in extortionate settlements and unreasonable licensing demands and fees.[19]

In earlier times, decisions about whether to grant such injunctive relief were left to the sound discretion of trial courts, which applied equitable principles in their traditional, flexible, and context-specific manner. For example before the 20th century, patent injunctions were refused where: they would cause disproportionate harm to defendants relative to the benefits to plaintiffs or would prevent the use of an essential process or device;[20] they would be harmful to the convenience as well as the safety of the public;[21] the defendant acted in a good faith belief in the

---

2004); *Johnson Controls, Inc. v. Phoenix Control Sys., Inc.*, 886 F.2d 1173, 1174 (9th Cir. 1989); *Abend v. MCA, Inc.*, 863 F.2d 1465, 1478–80 (9th Cir. 1988); *Pac. & S. Co. v. Duncan*, 744 F.2d 1490, 1499 (11th Cir. 1984). *See generally Nimmer on Copyright* 4–14 (2008): § 14.06[A]&[B] (Matthew Bender & Co. 2008 on-line edition).

16 35 USC § 283. *See generally* Joseph Story, *Commentaries on Equity Jurisprudence as Administrated in England and America* (Isaac F. Redfield, ed., 10th edition; Boston: Little, Brown; 1870).

17 *See eBay, Inc. v. MercExchange, LLC*, 547 US 388, 391 (2006).

18 *Windsurfing Int'l, Inc. v. AMF, Inc.*, 782 F.2d 995, 1003 n.12 (1986).

19 *See* Mark A. Lemley & Carl Shapiro, 'Patent Holdup and Royalty Stacking', *Tex. L. Rev.* 85 (2007): 1992–3.

20 *See* William C. Robinson, *The Law of Patents for Useful Inventions* 3 (1890): § 1200, at 619 & n. 3 (Boston, Little, Brown).

21 *See id.* § 1200, at 620 & n.4.

inapplicability of or in ignorance of the patent when making substantial business investments,[22] or the patent holder had an established fee for licensing the invention (and the defendant was solvent).[23]

At the beginning of the 20th century, the Supreme Court in *Continental Paper Bag Co v. Eastern Paper Bag Co.* had stated that exclusion is 'the very essence of the right conferred by the patent', and 'that the right can only retain its attribute of exclusiveness by a prevention of its violation', holding that equity jurisdiction exists to grant injunctive relief even when the patent holder did not itself use or license the patented invention.[24] Given this language, some have argued that appellate courts have been justified in routinely granting injunctive relief, finding a presumption of irreparable harm and inadequacy of damages for infringements of valid patents.[25] Nevertheless, the Court in *Continental Paper Bag* had reiterated general equitable principles in reaching its conclusion, specifically the concern that damages at law might not remedy continuing harms, and expressly refused to decide whether 'the situation of the parties in view of the public interest' might justify withholding an injunction.[26] Further, the view expressed in *Continental Paper Bag* – and a later Supreme Court case affirming *Continental Paper Bag*'s holding in the context of a refusal to grant a patent allegedly intended for non-use or misuse to protect the value of a broader invention[27] – addresses only whether the patent holder must work or license the patented invention in order to assert the patent right and not what the remedy should be for any specific violation of that right. In the 1952 Act, Congress reaffirmed the right to relief and simultaneously retained judicial discretion over the remedy.[28]

As with the patent experience, during the 20th century courts also became less willing to refuse copyright injunctions than in an earlier era when no presumption of such relief existed, no 'overheated rhetoric about copyright being a sanctified form of property' was employed, courts 'revealed a balanced, and in some cases skeptical attitude toward the need for such relief', and copyright holders were required as a condition

---

22 *See id.* § 1197, at 611 & n.1.

23 *See id.* § 1088, at 400 & n.2.

24 *Continental Paper Bag Co. v. Eastern Paper Bag Co.*, 210 US 405, 429–30 (1908).

25 *See, e.g.,* David F. Ryan, 'Patent Jurisprudence after *Quanta* and *eBay*: Is the Supreme Court Moving the Patent Clause to Article III?', at 3–18 (unpublished draft 28/07/2008).

26 *Id.* at 430.

27 *See Specialized Equipment Co. v. Coe,* 324 US 370, 375–80 (1945).

28 *See* 35 §§ 271(d)(4), 283. *Cf.* Ryan, *supra,* at 88.

for injunctions to reimburse innocent infringers who lacked notice before making investments that would be destroyed.[29]

2. The *eBay* decision and restored judicial flexibility to deny injunctions

In 2006, in *eBay, Inc. v. MercExchange, LLC,*[30] the US Supreme Court explicitly rejected the Federal Circuit's 'general rule' that after finding infringement of a valid patent, a permanent injunction to cease infringement should issue. The Supreme Court made clear that the right to exclude does not necessarily imply the powerful exclusionary remedy of such an injunction.

> According to the Court of Appeals, this statutory right to exclude alone justifies its general rule in favor of permanent injunctive relief . . . But *the creation of a right is distinct from the provision of remedies for violations of that right.* Indeed, the Patent Act itself indicates that patents shall have the attributes of personal property '[s]ubject to the provisions of this title' . . . including, presumably, the provision that injunctive relief 'may' issue only 'in accordance with the principles of equity'. . .[31]

The importance of the highlighted statement cannot be overstated. It denies any necessary legal entitlement to an injunction, and reflects a fundamentally different understanding than that expressed by the Federal Circuit regarding nature of exclusive patent rights and of equitable limitations on enforcing that right.

In contrast, the Federal Circuit has repeatedly stated its view that an exclusionary right implies the need for an exclusionary remedy, because a patent grants 'the right to invoke the state's power in order to exclude others from utilizing the patentee's discovery without his consent', and without this power, 'the right to exclude granted by the patent would be diminished, and the express purpose of the Constitution and Congress, to promote the progress of the useful arts, would be seriously undermined'.[32] Although the Federal Circuit's language reflects a view of the importance of exclusivity granted by the patent right similar to that expressed in *Continental Paper Bag,* the Supreme Court in *eBay* had requested briefing

---

[29] William F. Patry, *Patry on Copyright* 6 (2008): § 22.3 (Thomson Reuters/West, on-line edition). *See id.* § 22.4 (citing Copyright Act of 1909, § 21).

[30] 547 US 388 (2006).

[31] *Id.* at 392 (emphasis added) (quoting 35 USC § 283).

[32] *Smith Int'l, Inc. v. Hughes Tool Co.*, 718 F.2d 1573, 1577–8 (Fed. Cir. 1983). *See* Paul M. Schoenhard, 'Who Took My IP? – Defending the Availability of Injunctive Relief for Patent Owners', *Tex. Intell. Prop. L.J.* 16 (2008): 196 ('Logically, a right to exclude mandates exclusion.').

on whether to reconsider its prior precedents and referenced *Continental Paper Bag* only to reject any categorical rule precluding injunctive relief.[33] Further, the Supreme Court implicitly reiterated that the burden is on the patent holder to prove each of the traditional equitable factors, when noting that even non-working entities 'may be able to satisfy the traditional four-factor test'.[34]

The Supreme Court's reaffirmation of the right–remedy distinction in *eBay* also implicitly overruled a line of Federal Circuit cases dating back at least to 1987 regarding preliminary injunctive relief. The Federal Circuit had held in that context that irreparable harm should be 'presumed when a clear showing has been made of patent validity and infringement', because the patent's term will continue to run during any litigation and because the '*nature of the patent grant* . . . weighs against holding that monetary damages will always suffice to make the patentee whole, for *the principle value of a patent is its statutory right to exclude*'.[35] As the Supreme Court noted in *eBay*, however, the exclusive right does not as a matter of law mandate an exclusionary remedy; this is true whether or not a diminution in the value of that right to the patent holder might result. It is only the flexible judicial decision to afford substantive justice in equity (considering the effects on a patent's value of any infringement of the exclusive right) that supplies the basis for an injunctive remedy.

Nevertheless, as discussed below, some courts have refused to abandon this presumption of irreparable harm, seeking instead to limit the effects of *eBay* to the permanent injunction context. Such courts either have refused to resolve the presumption of irreparable harm question or have held that the Supreme Court at most overruled only a presumption that injunctive relief must be granted following proof of patent validity and infringement. That consequence of the Supreme Court's *eBay* decision is crystal clear. The Court had analogized its decision in patent cases to that in earlier copyright cases, where it had refused to 'replace traditional equitable considerations with a rule than an injunction automatically follows a determination that a copyright has been infringed'.[36]

---

33 *See eBay,* 547 US at 393.

34 *Id.*

35 *H.H. Robertson Co. v. United Steel Deck, Inc.*, 820 F.2d 384, 390 (1987) (emphasis added) (citing *Smith Int'l, Inc.*, 715 F.2d at 1581, and *Connell v. Sears Roebuck & Co.*, 722 F.2d 1542, 1548 (Fed. Cir. 1983)). *See Chisum on Patents, supra,* 7–20, § 20.04[1][e][i].

36 *Id.* at 392–3 (citing *New York Times Co. v. Tasini*, 533 US 483, 505 (2001), *Campbell v. Acuff-Rose Music, Inc.*, 510 US 569, 578 n.10 (1994), and *Dun v. Lumbermen's Credit Ass'n*, 209 US 20, 23–4 (1908)).

The Supreme Court also reiterated that injunctive relief in regard to patent infringement is subject to the traditional four-factor test established by courts in equity, which places the burden on the plaintiff to prove:

> (1) that it has suffered an irreparable injury; (2) that remedies available at law, such as monetary damages, are inadequate to compensate for that injury; (3) that, considering the balance of hardships between the plaintiff and defendant, a remedy in equity is warranted; and (4) that the public interest would not be disserved by a permanent injunction.[37]

In remanding the case for proper evaluation under the traditional test, the Court rejected both: (1) the 'broad classifications' of the District Court that the patent holder's willingness to license and failure to practice the patent necessarily precludes injunctive relief; and (2) the Federal Circuit's 'categorical grant' of relief except in 'the "unusual" case, under "exceptional circumstances" and "in rare instances . . . to protect the public interest"'.[38]

Thus, the Supreme Court also made clear that these equitable principles should be applied in their traditional, context-specific manner and that the 'public interest' factor should encompass and should properly weigh all relevant public interests and was not constrained by the small list of exceptions previously recognized by the Federal Circuit. Those exceptions were limited to when the '"patentee's failure to practice the invention frustrates an important public need for the invention," such as the need to use an invention to protect public health'.[39]

Since the 2006 *eBay* decision, a body of case law has been developing regarding the conditions under which preliminary and permanent injunctions should and should not issue in patent, trademark, copyright, and other intellectual property law cases. In an increasing number of cases, which inform the discussion below, preliminary or permanent injunctive relief is being denied (although permanent injunctions continue to be routinely granted in cases of direct competition[40]). Following

---

37 *eBay,* 548 US at 391. *But see* Thomas F. Cotter, 'Patent Holdup, Patent Remedies, and Antitrust Responses', 34, *J. Corp. Le* 1151, 1174 & n. 116 (2009), (disputing that the four-factor test was traditional for permanent injunction decisions).

38 *Id.* at 393–4 (citations omitted).

39 *MercExchange, LLC,* 401 F.3d at 1338 (quoting *Rite-Hite Corp. v. Kelley Co.*, 56 F.3d 1538, 1547 (Fed. Cir. 1995) (en banc)). *See, e.g., Hybritech, Inc. v. Abbott Labs*, 4 USPQ 2d 1001, 1015 (C.D. Cal., 1987) (excepting infringing medical test kits for cancer and hepatitis from permanent injunction, to avoid requiring switching to unavailable or less effective technologies).

40 *See, e.g.,* Douglas Ellis John Jarosz, Michael Chapman & L. Scott Oliver,

judgments of validity and infringement, prospective compensation is sometimes being awarded in the form of an equitable 'ongoing royalty' injunction,[41] which some argue (wrongly, as explained below) is a compulsory license[42] even if limited to the defendant in the dispute.[43] These decisions to deny injunctions to stop infringement reflect the roots of injunctive relief in equity, demonstrating its flexibility and its sensitivity to the factual context and the positions of the parties in achieving substantive justice. Moreover, the developing case law reflects renewed recognition of the fact that equitable remedies were not to be supplied where damage remedies at common law were adequate to compensate the plaintiff.[44] The increased flexibility to deny injunctive relief restored to trial court judges by the *eBay* decision, moreover, may encourage judges to uphold the validity of intellectual property rights and to find liability more often in difficult cases, where they would otherwise have been reluctant to impose the high costs of injunctive relief on defendants or on society, thereby bringing 'into alignment the issues of liability and remedy'.[45]

The body of case law that is being developed in the United States through the discretionary judgments of trial judges may be highly instructive to other developed and to developing countries in assessing whether, when, and how to grant prospective injunctive relief. This is true even if judges and legislators in those countries choose to exercise their policy discretion differently than judges in the United States. To the extent that social conditions or policy preferences differ from those in the United States, moreover, legislators in those countries may choose to further limit or to further specify the conditions under which injunctive relief should be granted. Similarly, legislators may choose to codify different factors for judges to consider, different weights to be accorded, or different degrees of delegated policy discretion.

Footnote 40 (*cont.*)
'The Economic Implications (and Uncertainties) of Obtaining Permanent Injunctive Relief after eBay v. MercExchange', *Fed. Cir. B.J.* 17 (2008): 442–3.

41 *Paice LLC v. Toyota Motor Corp.*, 504 F.3d 1293, 1313 & n.13 (Fed. Cir. 2007).

42 *See id.* at 1316–17 (Rader, J., concurring).

43 *See id.* at 1314–16.

44 *See Root v. Lake Shore & M.S. Ry. Co.*, 105 US 189, 206–16 (1881); Robinson, *Law of Patents, supra,* 3: § 1084, at 394–5; *id.*, § 1086, at 396–7.

45 Richard Dannay, 'Copyright Injunctions and Fair Use: Enter *eBay* – Four-Factor Fatigue or Four-Factor Freedom?', *J. Copyright Soc'y of the U.S.A.* 55 (2008): 459.

3. Domestic policy flexibility for injunctive relief under the TRIPS Agreement

US legislation regarding intellectual property rights has always authorized the flexibility reflected in the recent injunctive relief case law. The US Congress has supplied an express, discretionary authorization for federal courts to grant injunctive relief in patent and copyright cases since 1819, although federal courts granted injunctive remedies even earlier in diversity jurisdiction cases.[46] Specifically, the 1819 Act provided that federal courts 'should have authority to grant injunctions, *according to the course and principles of courts of equity*'.[47] As currently phrased, federal courts '*may* grant injunctions in accordance with the principles of equity to prevent the violation of any right secured by the patent, *on such terms as the court deems reasonable*'.[48] Similar discretionary language and references to equity exist in regard to providing injunctive authority to redress violations of other intellectual property rights.[49]

The discretionary authority vested in trial courts by the US Congress is further reinforced by deferential appellate review standards for grants and denials of preliminary and permanent patent injunctions. Such judgments are subject to reversal or modification only for an 'abuse of discretion', that is, 'a clear error of judgment in weighing the relevant factors, or based a decision upon a clearly erroneous factual finding or an erroneous legal standard'.[50] Similar discretionary deferential review standards apply in regard to other intellectual property rights.[51]

Such domestic policy flexibility in determining whether, when, and how to award injunctive relief for infringements of intellectual property

---

46 *See* Robinson, *Law of Patents, supra,* 3: §§ 1082–3, at 891–3.

47 Patent Act of 1819, ch. 19, 3 Stat. 481–2 (Feb. 15, 1819) (emphasis added).

48 35 USC § 283 (emphasis added).

49 *See, e.g.,* 17 USC § 502(a) ('may . . . grant temporary and final injunctions on such terms as it may deem reasonable' for copyright infringement), 15 USC § 1116(a) ('shall have power to grant injunctions, according to the principles of equity and upon such terms as the court may deem reasonable' for registered and unregistered trademark infringement and unfair trade practices). *See also* 15 USC § 1116(a), § 1125(c) (trademark dilution).

50 *Tate Access Floors, Inc. v. Interface Architectural Resources, Inc.*, 297 F.3d 1357, 1364 (Fed. Cir. 2002) (preliminary injunctions). *See Int'l Rectifier Corp. v. Samsung Elecs. Co.*, 361 F.3d 1355, 1359 (Fed. Cir. 2004) (same for permanent injunctions).

51 *See, e.g., Perfect 10, Inc. v. Amazon.com, Inc.*, 487 F.3d 701, 713 (9th Cir. 2007) (copyright preliminary injunctions); *Boston Duck Tours, LP v. Super Duck Tours, LLC*, 531 F.3d 1, 11 (1st Cir. 2008) (trademark preliminary injunctions); *Christopher Phelps & Assocs., LLC v. Galloway*, 492 F.3d 532, 543–7 (4th Cir. 2007) (copyright permanent injunctions); *Angel Flight of Georgia, Inc. v. Angel Flight America, Inc.*, 522 F.3d 1200, 1208 (11th Cir. 2008) (trademark permanent injunctions).

rights was expressly authorized by the TRIPS Agreement.[52] Article 44.1 of the TRIPS Agreement requires only that 'judicial authorities *shall have the authority* to order a party to desist from an infringement, *inter alia* to prevent the entry into the channels of commerce . . . immediately after customs clearance of such goods'.[53] Article 44.1 also recognizes that Members are not required to provide such injunctive relief authority in regard to protected subject matter (typically products that infringe patents, copyrights, or trademarks) against parties that lack 'reasonable grounds to know' of infringement.[54] Similarly, Article 45.1 of TRIPS requires that the judicial authorities 'shall have the authority to order' payment of damages 'adequate to compensate for the injury the right holder has suffered' from infringers with 'reasonable grounds to know' of the infringement.[55] And Article 50.1 requires that the judicial authorities 'shall have the authority to order prompt and effective provisional measures . . . to prevent an infringement . . . from occurring', preserving domestic discretion in regard to whether, when, and how to grant preliminary injunctive relief.[56]

Article 44.2 of TRIPS provides additional policy flexibility. Members are not required to provide injunctive relief authority but rather may limit judicial remedies to the 'payment of remuneration' in accordance with Article 31(h)[57] – which requires payment of 'adequate remuneration'[58] – in the special circumstances of governmental use or compulsory licensing, so long as they comply with other TRIPS provisions applicable to governmental use or compulsory licensing.[59] Article 44.2 specifically refers to the ability to limit remedies 'against such use',[60] which necessarily refers only to these special circumstances. Finally, Article 44.2 provides that where injunctive relief would be inconsistent with national law, Members may provide for a declaratory judgment and 'adequate compensation'.[61] For this reason, resort to Article 13, Article 30, or any other limited authorizations[62] to adopt domestic exceptions to exclusive rights are wholly unnecessary to justify even categorical legislative exclusions of injunctive relief.

---

52 Agreement on Trade-Related Aspects of Intellectual Property Rights (TRIPS Agreement), Apr. 15, 1994, 33 ILM 81.

53 *Id.* Art. 44.1 (first emphasis added).

54 *Id.*

55 *Id.* Art. 45.1.

56 *Id.* Art. 50.1.

57 *Id.* Art. 44.2.

58 *Id.* Art. 31(h).

59 *Id.* Art. 44.2.

60 *Id.*

61 *Id.*

62 *See, e.g., id.* Arts. 13, 30.

Because Article 44.2 provides additional flexibility rather than imposes additional restrictions on the required injunctive relief authority under Article 44.1, Article 44.2 *has no application whatsoever* to judicial decisions to provide ongoing royalty injunctions (or other conditional injunctions that do not stop continuing infringement) in particular cases. Such injunctions are simply a particular equitable remedy exercised as part of the broader injunctive relief authority required by Article 44.1. The reference to compulsory licensing in Article 44.2, moreover, is the object (rather than the consequence) of the additional authorization for Members to dispense with injunctive relief authority in specified circumstances. Nor would Article 44.2 apply to damage awards that include a market entry fee or other prospective compensation, thereby authorizing prospective infringing conduct; rather, the only limitation for such a damage award is that it be 'adequate to compensate for the injury the right holder has suffered' under Article 45.[63]

It is critically important not to confuse such ongoing royalty injunctions, damage awards authorizing future conduct, or refusals to grant preliminary injunctive relief with compulsory licenses granted by the government.[64] (For this reason, the Paris Convention's authorization for and limits on the grants of compulsory licenses also are inapplicable.[65]) Ongoing royalty injunctions (or other injunctions that do not order infringement to stop) and damage awards incorporating payment for prospective infringing conduct have long been a part of the judicial arsenal of equitable and legal remedies.[66] Given such long-standing practises,

---

[63] *Id.* Art 45.1. *See id.* Art. 31(a)–(l).

[64] *See, e.g.,* Harold C. Wegner, 'Post-*eBay* Compulsory Licenses: TRIPS Standards', paper prepared for the 41st World Congress of the Association Internationale pour la Protection de la Propriété Industrielle (Sept. 9, 2008): 1 (referring to an '"ongoing royalty license"' as a compulsory license); *id.* at 2–18 (suggesting that such remedies are subject to TRIPS Art. 31 and may violate treaty requirements). *Cf. Innogenetics, N.V. v. Abbott Labs.*, 512 F.3d 1363, 1381 (Fed. Cir. 2008) (referring to a judgment imposing a 'running royalty' damage award as a compulsory license); *Finisar Corp. v. The DirecTV Group, Inc.*, 2006 WL 2037617 (E.D. Tex. July 7, 2006) (final judgment denying injunctive relief, granting a 'compulsory license' and ordering payment of an 'ongoing royalty'), vacated, 523 F.3d 1323 (Fed. Cir. 2008).

[65] Paris Convention for the Protection of Industrial Property, Mar. 20, 1883, revised July 14, 1967, 21 UST 1583, 828 UNTS 305, Art. 5.A(2) & (4) ('Paris Convention').

[66] *See, e.g., Shatterproof Glass Corp. v. Libbey-Owens Ford Co.*, 758 F.2d 613, 628 (Fed. Cir. 1985); *Foster v. Am. Mach. & Foundry Co.*, 492 F.2d 1317, 1324 (2d Cir. 1974); *Royal-McBee Corp. v. Smith Corona Marchant, Inc.*, 295 F.2d 1, 6 (2d Cir. 1961).

it seems highly unlikely that the negotiating parties would (without any discussion) have subjected the continued use of such remedies (or denials of preliminary injunctions having a similar, albeit temporary, effects) to the highly controversial administrative procedures and substantive restrictions employed for compulsory licenses in Article 31.[67] Articles 44, 45, and 50 all use the standard, discretionary language employed for the powers that Members must supply to their judicial branches – 'shall have authority to' – and do not require any specific actions by the judiciary in particular cases.

Further, the negotiating history of the TRIPS Agreement reflects significant concerns to preserve differences among national legal systems in regard to enforcement authorities. These concerns resulted not only in a provision assuring that Members were not required to enforce intellectual property laws differently from other laws, but more importantly on the limitation in Article 44.1 on the requirement for Members to supply injunctive relief authority in cases of innocent infringement.[68] It is only in this context of *limiting* Members' judicial obligations that any reference is made to compulsory licenses, and it seems highly unlikely that the drafting parties would have imposed *additional* obligations for judges to comply with Article 31 when doing so. Any argument of nullification or impairment of benefits from judicial decisions not to order parties to cease infringement in particular cases would similarly be very difficult to sustain, absent 'a systematic refusal (which would be difficult to demonstrate)'.[69]

In summary, TRIPS Members retain substantial discretion to determine their legislative policies and to delegate policy discretion to their judges to decide whether, when, and how to grant preliminary and permanent injunctive relief. Thus, we should expect significant differences of national treatment in this regard.

---

[67] *See, e.g.,* Mohammed Omar Gad, *TRIPS Dispute Settlement and Developing Country Interests,* in *Intellectual Property and International Trade: The Trips Agreement* (2008): 355–63 (2d ed., Carlos M. Correa & Abdulqawi A. Yusuf, eds., Alphenaan der Rijn, The Netherlands: Wolters Kluwer) (discussing WTO dispute settlement understanding panels and appellate body approaches regarding general principles of interpretation and deference to national law under the TRIPS Agreement).

[68] *See* Daniel Gervais, *The TRIPS Agreement: Drafting History and Analysis* (2nd edition, Sweet & Maxwell, London; 2003): 289, 296, 299 (discussing TRIPS Arts. 41.5, 44.1, 44.2, and 45.1).

[69] *Id.* at 293 (discussing the 'shall have the authority' language in Art. 43.1).

4. The developing equitable jurisprudence of injunctive remedies after *eBay*

An exhaustive survey of recent decisions regarding injunctive relief and of each factor of the four-factor test in each of the different fields of intellectual property law is beyond the scope of the present discussion, and in any event would soon become outdated. Rather, this section seeks to identify some critical issues by reference to the developing equitable jurisprudence, focusing principally (but not exclusively) on the patent cases. These issues are to some extent interrelated, and raise important choices for policy-makers on fundamental questions regarding the nature of intellectual property rights and their functions in society. The issues are: (1) the adequacy of damage remedies and irreparable harm in regard to rights holders who make and sell products or services (practicing entities), as well as for those who only license their rights (non-practicing entities); (2) judicial supervision and holdout concerns in regard to determining compensation and prospective remedies; (3) the potential for injunctive relief to deter socially beneficial challenges to the validity of intellectual property rights; and (4) the balancing of various public interests in permitting or prohibiting continuing infringement. In particular, judges in the United States (and by extension judges and legislators in other countries) must make policy choices regarding: (1) the types of harms that should be compensable, and whether to protect intellectual property owners' subjective valuations of the worth of their rights; (2) the degree of remedial precision required for fairness (that is, whether rough judgments should be considered adequate compensation), whether courts should be actively involved in supervising the parties' obligations, and whether in doing so courts can avoid sending signals that may exacerbate holdout behaviors; (3) the degree to which decisions to grant injunctions, and the timing of preliminary injunction decisions, may deter potentially successful, socially beneficial validity challenges; and (4) the kinds and weights of public interests to recognize, and in particular whether and when to exert judicial control over market prices and anticompetitive behaviors. Again, different jurisdictions may and do adopt very different policies.

4.1 Assessing adequacy of damages and the potential for irreparable harm

4.1.1 Practicing entities

Patent law provides practicing patent holders with the ability to recover not only for lost sales, but also for the erosion of prices affecting the profits made on sales that are nevertheless completed by the patent holder.[70] Thus, it is principally the practical problem of determining lost sales and price erosion[71] – and other effects on market share or future activities resulting from infringing competition (such as lost goodwill, lost licensing and cross-licensing opportunities)[72] – that might render a prospective damage award inadequate. To the extent that a retrospective damage award includes a rights-holder requested prospective, paid-up license or market-entry fee, then there is no inadequacy to the award, no potential for irreparable harm, and no basis for prospective injunctive relief.[73]

The adequacy of a prospective damage award and the corresponding potential for irreparable harm also reflects policy judgments regarding the kinds of harms that should or should not be compensable. Damages should be considered inadequate to remedy more remote consequences (for example, loss of cross-licensing abilities) only when those harms are legally or equitably cognizable and rise above a level where their exclusion from the damage remedy renders it not 'adequate to compensate for the infringement'.[74] As with proximate causation in tort cases, not all but-for harms are legally compensable, but rather only those 'fairly attributable to the defendant'.[75] The issue of what damages are legally cognizable, proximate, and sufficient to warrant recovery most commonly arises in regard to whether lost profits should include the value of either: (1) unpatented components sold with the patented invention (under the 'entire market value' rule, where the value of the patented invention is the source of demand for the entire product); or (2) product sales not directly incorporating the patented invention but competing with the infringing product (so-called 'diverted' or 'convoyed' sales).[76] Further, in order to assert that damages are inadequate, the plaintiff itself must be the party suffering the relevant harms (for example, non-practicing entities cannot assert the inadequacy of damages on behalf of their exclusive licensees).[77] These

---

[70] *See, e.g.*, 35 USC § 284; *Crystal Semiconductor Corp. v. Tritech Microelectronics Int'l, Inc.*, 246 F.3d 1336, 1357 (Fed. Cir. 2001).

[71] *See, e.g., Canon, Inc. v. GCC Int'l Ltd.*, 263 Fed. Appx. 57, 62 (Fed. Cir. 2008); *Sanofi-Synthelabo v. Apotex, Inc.*, 470 F.3d 1368, 1381–3 (Fed. Cir. 2006).

[72] *See, e.g., Sanofi-Synthelabo,* 470 F.3d at 1383; Carroll, 'Patent Injunctions', *supra,* at 433.

[73] *See, e.g., Innogenetics, N.V. v. Abbott Labs.*, 512 F.3d 1363, 1379–81 (Fed. Cir. 2008); *Rite-Hite Corp.*, 56 F.3d at 1574 & n.21 (Nies, J., dissenting).

[74] 35 USC § 284.

[75] *Anza v. Ideal Steel Supply Corp.*, 547 US 451, 466 (2006).

[76] *Compare, e.g., Rite-Hite Corp.*, 56 F.3d at 1546–51, *with id.,* 56 F.3d at 1556–74 (Nies, J., dissenting).

[77] *See Voda v. Cordis Corp.*, 2008 WL 3822801, at *15 (Fed. Cir. Aug. 18, 2008).

rules are controversial precisely because they incorporate basic notions of fairness, which differ not only domestically but internationally.

4.1.2 Non-practicing entities

In contrast to practicing entities who may recover lost profits from infringing competitors, non-practicing entities (both those that have licensing programs and those that do not) are entitled to damages that 'in no event [are] less than a reasonable royalty for the use made of the invention'.[78] The question thus arises as to whether such entities are entitled to any damages beyond a reasonable royalty, including royalties that by definition are in excess of what is objectively reasonable. For non-practicing entities that have established licensing programs, the answer is typically no.[79] Damage awards in such cases can be based on straightforward prospective royalty calculations that will be considered fully adequate to compensate for any harm to the patent holder. This is true even though the patent holder *could have* chosen to hold out for a higher voluntary licensing fee (ex ante or in settlement) in regard to the particular infringer.

Where there is not an established program of licensing, courts have recognized that non-practicing entities may suffer irreparable harm to goodwill, reputation, potential licensing prospects, or other opportunities that are difficult to measure.[80] Nevertheless, the majority of courts since *eBay* have denied permanent injunctions to stop infringing activities for non-practicing patent holders, given that the infringers do not directly compete with them, and thus reasonable royalty damages are considered to be fair and adequate compensation for such entities even if some remote harms to their interests result.[81] Similarly, although courts 'are understandably reluctant to "set" prices or rates or interfere with the freedom of copyright owners to establish their own fees', they nevertheless evaluate the adequacy of damages and market harm by carefully scrutinizing proposed licensing fees 'in the context of prevailing rates in the industry and

---

[78] 35 USC § 284.

[79] *Cf.* Carroll, 'Patent Injunctions', *supra* note 1, at 434–5 (distinguishing 'productive licensing' patent holders from other non-practicing entities that either do not license or do not have established rates, based on the uncertain effects on licensing market behaviors).

[80] *See, e.g., Commonwealth Scientific and Indust. Res. Org. (CSIRO) v. Buffalo Tech. Inc.*, 492 F. Supp. 2d 600, 604–06 (E.D. Tex. 2007).

[81] *See, e.g.,* Gauri Prakash-Canjels & Kristen Hamilton, 'Implication of EBay for Noncompetes, Other Entities', *Law 360* (Sept. 2, 2008, on-line edition); Eric Keller, 'Time-varying Compulsory License: Facilitating License Negotiation for Efficient Post-verdict Patent Infringement', *Tex. Intell. Prop. L.J.* 16 (2008): 434.

the licensing history and fees of copyright owners and users'.[82] Judges thus routinely engage in market regulation, as discussed further below.

So long as a court can fairly determine a prospective 'reasonable royalty' – which they are required to do for retrospective damage award calculations based on past history and objective market norms, using a complicated multi-factor test[83] – an injunction to cease infringement necessarily must protect either *more than objectively reasonable* compensation for the value of the invention or the *subjective* value to the patent holder of refusing to license the invention at all. Refusal to license an invention may be a right conveyed to the patent holder, subject over time to any working requirements, compulsory licensing, or government use imposed by national law.[84] But jurisdictions are not required to provide equitable remedies to protect against harms to objectively excessive valuations or to the subjective value of suppressing exclusive rights, particularly when those valuations are balanced against harms to infringers or to public interests of which equitable injunctive relief also requires consideration. TRIPS Article 44 clearly does not require that result. TRIPS Article 45 similarly requires judges only to have authority to order the recovery of damages 'adequate to compensate for the injury the right holder has suffered',[85] leaving to national law decisions about what injuries are cognizable and what compensation is adequate. Any concerns that the judicial refusal to prohibit infringement compels the patent holder to license its invention against its will, moreover, are likely to be much less strong in the patent context than similar concerns in copyright and trademark contexts, where creative expressions and public confusion are at issue. This is particularly true in countries other than the US that have a strong tradition of protecting moral rights.[86]

Thus, for non-practicing entities, whether damages are adequate and whether irreparable harm will occur absent an injunction thus will depend principally on fundamental policy choice regarding the fairness of rejecting compensation for rights holders who refuse to license unless

---

82 Dannay, *supra,* at 458.

83 *See Georgia-Pacific Corp. v. U.S. Plywood Corp.*, 318 F. Supp. 1116 (SDNY 1970).

84 *See, e.g.,* Paris Convention, *supra,* Art. 5.A; TRIPS Agreement, *supra,* Art. 31; 42 USC § 28 USC § 1498(a).

85 TRIPS Agreement, Art. 45.1.

86 *See, e.g.,* Marina Santilli, 'United States Moral Rights Developments in European Perspective', *Marquette Intell. Prop. L. Rev.* 1 (1997): 89; Russell J. DaSilva, 'Droit Moral and Amoral Copyright: A Comparison of Artists' Rights in France and the United States', *Bull. Copyright Soc'y* 28 (1980): 1.

they receive a subjectively desired and voluntarily accepted level of compensation. Such decisions reflect a larger policy debate, commonly referred to as the choice between property rules (leaving valuations to private, market-based determinations) and liability rules (authorizing governmental determinations of prices).[87] Again, countries have substantial policy discretion to make different choices in different contexts, in general as well as in regard to intellectual property rights. But even the rhetoric may matter here, as it may determine whether to view patents, copyrights, and trademarks as private property rights subject to constitutional protections or as governmental privileges subject to governmental adjustment and regulation.[88]

4.2 Precision in determining remedies, supervision of relief, and concerns over holdout behaviors

Some patent cases after *eBay* continue to state that irreparable harm *necessarily* follows from the fact of infringement by direct competition and the consequent diminution of value of the exclusive right.[89] Other cases reject the existence of a presumption of irreparable harm from proof of validity and infringement.[90] In these cases, the courts have focused on the potential for price erosion and consequent effects on sales, market share, licensing opportunities, and goodwill to demonstrate irreparable harm.[91] The trademark cases have long recognized the difficulty of assessing the effects of infringing conduct on market behaviors resulting from reductions in goodwill and reputation, and courts in cases decided since *eBay*

---

87 *See generally* Stewart E. Sterk, 'Property Rules, Liability Rules, and Uncertainty about Property Rights', *Mich. L. Rev.* 106 (2008): 1285.

88 *See, e.g.,* Davida H. Isaacs, 'Not All Property is Created Equal: Why Modern Courts Resist Applying the Takings Clause to Patents, and Why they are Right to Do So', *Geo. Mason L. Rev.* 15 (2007): 23–5, 40–41; Peter Drahos, *A Philosophy of Intellectual Property* (Ashgate, Dartmouth; 1996): 32–3.

89 *See, e.g., Visto Corp. v. Seven Networks, Inc.*, 2006 US Dist. Lexis 91453, at *12 (E.D. Tex. Dec. 19, 2006); *Muniauction, Inc. v. Thomson Corp.*, 502 F. Supp. 2d 477, 482 (W.D. Pa. 2007). *See also, e.g., Perdue Pharma L.P. v. Boehringer Ingelheim GmbH*, 237 F.3d 1359, 1363 (Fed. Cir. 2001) (rebuttable presumption of irreparable harm from likelihood of success in preliminary relief context). *See generally* Aron Stiefel, 'Two Years Since *eBay*: The Impact on Permanent Injunctive Relief in Patent Cases', *Pat., Trademark & Copyright J.* 76 no. 1867 (2008): 62 (BNA).

90 *See, e.g., MercExchange, L.L.C. v. eBay, Inc.*, 500 F. Supp. 2d 556, 568 (E.D. Va. 2007); *z4 Technologies, Inc. v. Microsoft Corp.*, 434 F. Supp. 2d 437, 440 (E.D. Tex. 2006).

91 *See, e.g., Sanofi-Synthelabo,* 470 F.3d at 1382; *Abbott Labs. v. Sandoz, Inc.*, 500 F. Supp. 2d 807, 843 (N.D. Ill. 2007).

continue to make the same point.[92] Similarly, copyright cases since *eBay* continue to recognize irreparable harm either from the mere fact of continued infringement[93]or from specific facts that typically exist in regard to copyright infringement, such as the reduced incentives and value for further works of the same author or of potentially competing works.[94]

The cases have not provided any meaningful analysis of a threshold for determining inadequacy of damages in regard to these hard-to-measure effects or of the degree of diminished value to the exclusive right that is sufficient to render a damage remedy inadequate and the harm irreparable. 'Normal business losses' associated with direct competition are not necessarily incalculable, and economists and accountants regularly calculate such damages.[95] Thus, a key question arises as to the degree of 'reasonable precision' required in determining whether a damage award would be adequate to compensate the right holder, the absence of which requires resort to equitable remedies.[96] Stated differently, the question is whether the somewhat rougher justice of legal remedies is considered sufficient to assure fair treatment.[97]

The increased precision involved in providing equitable remedies to assure fairer treatment than that available at law, however, comes at the cost of greater judicial involvement and greater expenditure of governmental resources. Prospective injunctions require monitoring. Injunctions ordering prospective compensation may require more monitoring (to address potential changes in market conditions relating to the relevant technologies[98]) than injunctions that simply prohibit continuing infringement (although they may trigger contempt proceedings or subsequent requests for modification or dissolution).

However, the very premise of equitable injunctive relief is to *minimize*

---

[92] *See, e.g., JA Apparel Corp. v. Abboud*, 2008 WL 2329533, at *22 (SDNY June 5, 2008).

[93] *See, e.g., Propet USA, Inc. v. Shugart*, 2007 WL 4376204, at *2 (W.D. Wash. Dec. 13, 2007).

[94] *See, e.g., Warner Bros. Ent. Inc. v. RDR Books*, No. 07 Civ. 9667 (RPP) Opinion and Order (Sept. 8, 2008) at *63–*65.

[95] Ellis et al., 'Economic Implications', *supra* note 32, at 446.

[96] *Power-One, Inc. v. Artesyn Techs., Inc.*, 2008 US Dist. Lexis 30338, at *5 (E.D. Tex. Apr. 11, 2008).

[97] *See, e.g., Visto Corp.*, 2006 US Dist. Lexis 91453, at *13; *Brooktrout, Inc. v. Eicon Networks Corp.*, 2007 US Dist. Lexis 43107, at *4–*5 (E.D. Tex. Jun. 14, 2007); Carroll, 'Patent Injunctions', *supra* note 1, at 422 & n.47.

[98] *See, e.g., CSIRO*, 492 F. Supp. 2d at 606; *The Mortg. Mkt. Guide, LLC v. Freedman Report, LLC*, 2008 US Dist. Lexis 56871, at *131–*132 (DNJ July 28, 2008).

the burdens on courts and the unfairness to property owners of repetitive judicial damage actions at law.[99] Injunctions that prohibit continued infringement thus may induce the parties to enter settlement agreements or consent decrees that authorize the conduct, thereby restoring to the parties themselves the obligation to monitor compliance and to assess changes in market conditions. But even then, such settlements or consent decrees may simply defer conflicts to the future, requiring judicial resources to resolve continuing disputes in contempt proceedings or to address future infringements that are not authorized by the earlier voluntary resolution or addressed by the earlier injunction.

The question of whether to grant injunctive relief thus may ultimately depend less on what is best for the particular parties to the dispute than on decisions about the best uses of scarce judicial resources. Such decisions are likely to be better made on a retail basis by judges in particular cases than on a wholesale basis by legislative directives. Determining whether to grant and the form of prospective injunctive relief requires careful consideration and calibration to the conditions.

Intellectual property injunctions, however, are not necessarily harder to supervise than other types of injunctions. In many contexts, courts must supervise compliance in ways that pose much greater judicial burdens, for example, when addressing such controversial and recalcitrant issues as school desegregation and prison conditions.[100] Courts thus have not hesitated to impose or uphold ongoing royalty injunctions when they have thought it appropriate, even when they have recognized that it would be preferable to have the parties voluntarily reach agreement over the financial terms.[101] Accordingly, there may be substantial wisdom to the preservation of the traditional flexibility of equitable remedial discretion in determining the need for and the form of injunctive remedies.

Nevertheless, the mere potential for judicial involvement to prohibit continued infringement raises concerns about potential direct costs and sequential innovation effects on infringers and on the public (to whom

---

[99] *See, e.g., Continental Paper Bag Co.,* 210 U.S. at 430; Brief for General Elec. Co., 3M Co., The Proctor & Gamble Co., E.I. DuPont De Nemours and Co., and Johnson & Johnson as Amici Curaie Suggesting Affirmance, *eBay, Inc. v. MercExchange LLC,* 547 US 388 (2006), at 14 (citing Story, *Commentaries,* 2 (Bigelow ed., 13th ed. 1886, *supra* note 8 for a different edition) at 236 (Fred B. Rothman & Co Littleton, Colo.; 1988), and *Archer v. Greenville Sand & Gravel Co.,* 233 US 60, 63–6 (1911)).

[100] *See, e.g., Swann v. Charlotte-Mecklenburg Bd. of Ed.,* 402 US 1, 22–32 (1971).

[101] *See, e.g., Paice,* 504 F.3d 1314–15; *id.* at 1316–17 (Rader, J., concurring).

competitors pass on the costs and harms). Infringers may have to pay higher settlements or higher licensing fees than they would otherwise voluntarily negotiate in the absence of the threat of injunctive relief. These holdup-cost concerns are particularly great in regard to patents held by non-practicing entities, including universities.[102] Non-practicing entities may not need to cross-license their intellectual property rights, and are unlikely to be defendants (or, if state entities, may not have to pay damages due to sovereign immunity[103]). Thus, universities and other non-practicing entities may exercise significantly less restraint in seeking to maximize litigation and licensing revenues. The lack of restraint, coupled with the potential for injunctive relief, may threaten payments far exceeding any objectively reasonable royalty. Similar holdout concerns also apply to patents for inventions that are only components of larger products, as the attendant costs to the infringer of an injunction are correspondingly greater,[104] and to patents of dubious validity or uncertain scope, given the questionable value of the patent and the attendant difficulties of avoiding its application.[105]

The decisions that courts make in granting or denying injunctions, and in deciding on their form, send important signals to rights holders and potential infringers that either may encourage holdout behaviors or that may inadequately deter infringement. The existence of strong expectations in regard to such injunctions may predetermine these behaviors. In contrast, the greater uncertainty resulting from increased judicial flexibility and sensitivity to factual context may limit transmission of signals that would encourage either set of behaviors. Again, the flexibility provided by equity jurisprudence and discretionary review standards may be the best solution to avoid sending the wrong signals.

These holdout and signaling concerns, moreover, apply to decisions to grant adequate compensation in damage awards, given the potential to recover under the 'entire market value' rule, lost profits based on the larger products sold by the patent holder or royalties based on the larger products sold by the infringer.[106] A vigorous debate thus is currently

---

102 *See, e.g.,* Mark A. Lemley, 'Are Universities Patent Trolls?', *Fordham Intell. Prop. Media & Ent. L.J.* 18 (2008): 611–19. *See generally* Lemley & Shapiro, 'Patent Holdup', *supra.*

103 *See, e.g., Biomedical Pat. Mgmt. Corp. v. State of Cal.*, 505 F.3d 1328 (Fed. Cir. 2007), petition for cert. pending.

104 *See eBay,* 547 US at 396–7 (Kennedy, J., concurring); *z4 Technologies, Inc.,* 434 F. Supp. 2d at 440–41.

105 *See* Carroll, 'Patent Injunctions', *supra* note 1, at 436–9.

106 *See, e.g.,Rite-Hite Corp.,* 56 F.3d at 1549 (citing *State Indus. Inc. v. Mor-*

raging in regard to whether to amend US patent law to further limit royalty damages to the apportioned value of the inventive contribution of the patent to the infringing product.[107] So long as the entire market value rule authorizes recoveries that may extend beyond the objective contribution of the patented invention to the value of the products at issue, greater judicial flexibility to determine adequate compensation may be justified not only as providing fairer compensation but also to avoid having judges send the wrong signals.

4.3 Concerns about deterring legitimate challenges to validity

Because injunctions that stop infringing activity may result in substantial lost investments for innocent infringers and may increase the litigating power of patent holders to obtain greater than objectively reasonable compensation, they may excessively deter socially valuable infringing conduct. Of perhaps greater concern, such injunctions may deter legally permissible conduct that does not infringe any valid intellectual property right. The potential to grant permanent injunctive relief potentially discourages challenges to intellectual property rights that are not valid (or challenges to overbroad assertions of valid rights). Strong public policy interests exist in assuring vigorous challenges to invalid intellectual property rights, so as to free the public from the burdens that such rights impose.

At least since 1969, the US Supreme Court has affirmatively encouraged litigation challenges to the validity of granted patents, prohibiting contractual licensing provisions that would foreclose or deter such challenges by parties with the greatest incentives to litigate.[108] Nevertheless, it is widely recognized that inadequate incentives exist for bringing validity challenges or for maintaining validity defenses, in light of the costs and

---

Flo Indus., Inc., 883 F.2d 1573, 1577 (Fed. Cir. 1989), *Velo-Bind, Inc. v. Minnesota Mining & Mfg. Co.*, 647 F.2d 965 (9th Cir. 1981), and various cases applying the entire market value rule to lost profit and reasonable royalty damage awards).

107 *See, e.g,* S.1145, 110th Cong., 2d Sess. § 4 (2008) (as reported by Committee on Judiciary); *Georgia-Pacific* 1120 (factor 13, discussing the 'portion of the realized profit that should be credited to the invention as distinguished from non-patented elements'). *See generally* Eric E. Bensen & Danielle M. White, 'Using Apportionment to Rein in the Georgia Pacific Factors', *Colum. Sci. & Tech. L. Rev.* 9 (2008): 1.

108 *See Lear v. Adkins*, 395 US 653, 670–72 (1969). *Cf. Medimmune, Inc. v. Genetech, Inc.*, 127 S.Ct. 764, 769–77 (2007) (holding that licensees need not breach their agreements in order to have standing to file declaratory actions challenging patent validity). *See generally* Joshua D. Sarnoff, '*Bilcare, KSR,* Presumptions of Validity, Preliminary Relief, and Obviousness in Patent Law', *Cardozo Arts & Ent. L.J.* 25 (2008): 1044–50.

risks of litigation compared to license fees or settlements that may be demanded by the patent holder.[109] Collective action problems also exist in regard to such challenges, resulting in part from the legal rule that patent holders cannot assert validity in future litigation once their patent has been declared invalid.[110]

Concerns about deterring potentially successful challenges to the validity of granted intellectual property rights are particularly strong in regard to grants of preliminary injunctive relief. (Determining the likelihood of success on the merits when seeking preliminary relief may differ from the standards of proof at trial, as some cases require the party opposing such relief to show only a 'substantial question' concerning validity, enforceability or infringement that the party seeking such relief cannot show to 'lack[] substantial merit'[111]). Such relief may induce parties to settle prematurely rather than to litigate validity issues to their conclusion. Although such settlements may be subject to antitrust scrutiny for collusive behavior, as with recent reverse-payments settlements in pharmaceutical patent litigation, such scrutiny in the United States is highly deferential.[112]

Judges thus may need to consider more carefully the effects that preliminary injunction decisions may have on prematurely terminating what would otherwise be successful validity challenges. To do so, however, may conflict with other important public policies, such as encouraging settlements of complex disputes to avoid expending judicial resources.[113] Further, it may require not only careful balancing of the relative hardships to the parties (as already required by equitable principles), but also careful assessment of whether these hardships will lead to premature settlements.

---

[109] *See, e.g.,* Joseph Farrell & Robert P. Merges, 'Incentives to Challenge and Defend Patents: Why Litigation Won't Reliably Fix Patent Office Errors and Why Administrative Patent Review Might Help', *Berkeley Tech. L.J.* 19 (2004): 948–60; Matthew Sag & Kurt Rohde, 'Patent Reform and Differential Impact', *Minn. J.L. Sci. & Tech.* 8 (2007): 22–3.

[110] *See Blonder-Tongue Labs., Inc. v. Univ. of Ill. Found.*, 402 US 313, 317–49 (1971).

[111] *Genentech, Inc. v. Novo Nordisk A/S*, 108 F.3d 1361, 1364 (Fed. Cir. 1997). *But see Abbott Labs. v. Sandoz, Inc.*, 544, F.3rd, 1341, 1363-71 (Fed. Cir., 2008) (suggesting a substantial question of validity may be insufficient to negative likelihood of success on the merits under the applicable burden of proof).

[112] *See, e.g., In re Ciprofloxacin Hydrochloride Antitrust Litig.*, 2008 WL 4570669, at *6–*10 (Fed. Cir. Oct. 15, 2008); *In re Tamoxifen Citrate Antitrust Litig.*, 466 F.3d 187, 205 (2d Cir. 2006). *See generally* Christopher M. Holman, 'Do Reverse Payments Settlements Violate the Antitrust Laws?', *Santa Clara Comp. & High Tech. L.J.* 23 (2007): 490.

[113] *See, e.g., Gambale v. Deutsche Bank AG*, 377 F.3d 133, 143 (2d Cir. 2004); Holman, 'Reverse Payments', *supra,* at 549–50.

More routinely denying the extraordinary relief of preliminary injunctions to encourage validity challenges also will diminish somewhat (albeit temporarily) the value of granted intellectual property rights ultimately held valid (which is already considered under equitable balancing principles), and thus will diminish somewhat the incentives provided for investment, invention, disclosure, or distribution.[114]

Although the cases since *eBay* have not directly addressed this issue, they have implicitly done so when evaluating the relationship (if any) that exists between proof of success on the merits and other preliminary injunction factors, particularly irreparable harm. Some cases have called into question the presumption of irreparable harm for proof of likely patent infringement,[115] as well as for proof of likely trademark infringement or false advertising.[116] Others have limited the presumption of irreparable harm to cases where a clear showing of likely success on the merits has been made, and have refused to find irreparable harm based on the possibility of lost revenues and price erosion, lost market share, lost research opportunities, inability to service debts and lost employees where the defendants were solvent.[117] As one court noted, it 'would convert the "extraordinary" relief of a preliminary injunction into a standard remedy'.[118] Nevertheless, other cases (including those decided by the Federal Circuit) have consciously avoided resolving whether a presumption of irreparable harm should exist resulting from a strong showing of validity and infringement.[119] In the copyright context, some cases continue to hold that a presumption of irreparable harm should exist upon a prima facie showing of copyright infringement,[120] and other cases question the

---

[114] *See* Sarnoff, '*Bilcare, KSR*', *supra,* at 1000.

[115] *See, e.g., Tiber Labs. LLC v. Hawthorn Pharms. Inc.*, 527 F. Supp. 2d 1373, 1380 (N.D. Ga. 2007); *z4 Technologies, Inc.*, 434 F. Supp. 2d at 440. *See generally* Stiefel, 'Two Years Since *eBay*', *supra,* at 62.

[116] *See, e.g., N. Am. Med. Corp. v. Axiom Worldwide, Inc.*, 522 F.3d 1211, 1226–9 (11th Cir. 2008).

[117] *See, e.g., Altana Pharm. AG v. Teva Pharms. USA, Inc.*, 532 F. Supp. 2d 666, 681–4 (DNJ 2007) (citing *Nutrition 21 v. United States*, 930 F.2d 867, 871 (Fed. Cir. 1991)).

[118] *Id.* at 683 (DNJ 2007) (quoting *Eli Lilly & Co. v. Am. Cyanamid Co.*, 82 F.3d 1568, 1578 (Fed. Cir. 1996), and *Illinois Tool Works, Inc. v. Grip-Pak, Inc.*, 906 F.2d 679, 683 (Fed. Cir. 1990)).

[119] *See, e.g., Everett Labs., Inc. v. Breckenridgue Pharm., Inc.*, 2008 WL 4053447, at *8–*9 (DNJ Aug. 26, 2008) (*citing, inter alia, Amado v. Microsoft Corp.*, 517 F.3d 1353, 1359 (Fed. Cir. 2008)).

[120] *See, e.g., Lennon v. Premise Media Corp.*, 556 F. Supp. 2d 310, 319 & n.1 (SDNY June 2, 2008).

presumption but find irreparable harm on the facts anyway without significant analysis.[121]

Of more explicit relevance, some courts have adopted a presumption that absent a showing of likely success on the merits, the public interest factor weighs strongly in favor of denying a preliminary injunction.[122] Clearly, this presumption is more favorable to the policy of not discouraging validity challenges. But it could also be more nuanced, distinguishing more clearly likelihood of success in regard to validity and infringement. Courts also could be more conscious about the timing of their preliminary injunction rulings, deciding explicitly whether to defer decisions on preliminary injunctive relief that might cause litigation to terminate before evidence of invalidity can be fully developed and evaluated.

4.4 Competing conceptions of the public interest and of judicial control over market prices and behaviors

Courts since *eBay* differ significantly in their views regarding whether public interests other than those relating to health and safety (and sometimes even those) are sufficient to warrant denying injunctive relief. Recall that the Supreme Court in *eBay* expressly rejected the Federal Circuit's constricted view (as unusual, exceptional, or rare) of the public interest grounds for denying injunctions. Nevertheless, some courts have repeated the earlier view that exceptions to injunctive relief on public interest grounds are 'rare and limited',[123] and that the diminution in value of the exclusive right by permitting continued infringement (and consequent diminution in ex ante incentives provided by the right) will necessarily outweigh any other public interest concerns. Thus, one court granted a permanent injunction by according (without reference to the particular facts of the case) superior weight to the public interest of encouraging investments in research and development over the public interest in obtaining lower prices and increased access to products.[124] Another court did the same, explaining that without an injunction, the exclusive right 'would have only a fraction of the value it was intended to have, and would no longer be as great an incentive to engage in the toils of scientific and technological research'.[125] Yet another court suggested

---

[121] *See, e.g., Warner Bros. Ent. Inc., supra,* at *63–*65.

[122] *See, e.g., Abbott Labs. v. Andrx Pharms., Inc.*, 452 F.3d 1331, 1384 (Fed. Cir. 2006).

[123] *CSIRO,* 492 F. Supp. 2d at 607.

[124] *See, e.g., id.*

[125] *Telequip Corp. v. The Change Exchange*, 2006 WL 2385425, at *2 (NDNY

categorically that any diminution in the value of a patent would favor the patent holder when balanced against any harm incurred by an infringer, and that the public interest in 'protecting patent rights, which encourage the development of useful inventions' categorically outweighs the public interest in 'low cost generic alternatives to branded drugs' resulting from earlier market entry.[126] Yet other courts may have focused on the particular language of the four-factor equitable balancing test articulated in *eBay* (that 'the public interest would not be disserved') to require the defendant to show that the public interest would be disserved by granting an injunction, even though *eBay* makes clear that the plaintiff bears the burden of proof.[127] In the context of preliminary relief, moreover, one court suggested that the public interest factor should be governed by the likelihood of success, because of the public interest to enforce patents or copyrights.[128]

Significantly, many of these cases rely on pre-*eBay* Federal Circuit dicta suggesting that continuing an infringement can never be found to be of paramount public interest. For example, '"selling a lower-priced product does not justify infringing a patent" . . . or "excuse infringement of a valid pharmaceutical patent"'.[129] Similar categorical language can be found in some copyright cases. For example, since 'Congress has elected to grant certain exclusive rights to the owner of a copyright in a protected work, it is virtually axiomatic that the public interest can only be served by upholding copyright protections and, correspondingly, preventing the misappropriation of the skills, creative energies, and resources which are invested in the protected work'.[130] But even without such generalized language, in many copyright cases the policy balance of production incentives is categorically determined (without reference to the particular facts) to

---

Aug. 15, 2006) (quoting *Honeywell Int'l, Inc. v. Universal Avionics Sys. Corp.*, 397 F. Supp. 2d 537, 547 (D. Del. 2005)).

[126] *Everett,* 2008 WL 4053447, at *11.

[127] *See, e.g., Brooktrout, Inc., supra,* 2007 US Dist. Lexis 43107, at *5; *O2 Micro Int'l Ltd. v. Beyond Innovation Tech. Co.*, 2007 US Dist. Lexis 25948, at *9 (ED Tex. Mar. 21, 2007). *Cf. eBay,* 547 US at 391.

[128] *See, e.g., Sun Optics, Inc. v. FGX Int'l, Inc.*, 2007 US Dist. Lexis 56351, at *3 (Aug. 2, 2007); National League of Junior Cotillions v. Porter, 2007 U.S. Dist. Lexis 58117, at *34 (WDNC Aug. 9, 2007).

[129] *Id.* (quoting *Pfizer, Inc. v. Teva Pharms, USA, Inc.*, 429 F.3d 1364, 1382 (Fed. Cir. 2005)).

[130] *Advance Magazine Pubs. v. Leach*, 466 F. Supp. 2d 628, 638 (D. Md. 2006) (quoting *Apple Computer, Inc. v. Franklin Computer Corp.*, 714 F.2d 1240, 1254–5 (3rd Cir. 1983)). *See also UMG Recordings, Inc. v. Blake*, 2007 US Dist. Lexis 46414, at *8 (EDNC June 26, 2007).

outweigh access concerns. For example, '[t]he public interest in receiving copyrighted content for free is outweighed by the need to incentivize the creation of original works'.[131]

Nevertheless, some courts have made the opposite error of categorically ignoring the public interest in the greater incentives provided by the increased value of patents when injunctions to cease infringement are granted. For example, in a case that refused to enjoin a product incorporating the patented invention as a small component, the court focused on the somewhat speculative negative effects that would result from an injunction and stated that it was 'unaware of any negative effects that might befall the public in the absence of an injunction'.[132]

These categorical views of the public interests and their relative weights are untenable in light of *eBay,* which required elaboration and careful consideration of the competing harms. As one court put it when denying an injunction, 'although it is true that the protection of patent rights generally fosters innovation, that, in itself, is insufficient to justify permanent injunctive relief. As the Supreme Court has cautioned us, we must consider the facts of each patent case on its own merits, and not grant permanent injunctive relief based on broad principles, and generalities, of patent law.'[133] However, it is difficult to determine how the courts are actually weighing the competing interests, as they may identify the competing interests and state their balancing outcome without detailing their reasoning.[134]

Thus, more nuanced attention by judges to the factual context and the different public interests, and more explicit development and articulation of the competing policy judgments, is clearly warranted. In particular, determining the public interest in regard to injunctive relief requires explicit balancing of the short-term interest in reduced prices, increased access, and cumulative innovation that denying injunctions may provide against the long-term interest in promoting investment, creativity, disclosure, and distribution that enforcing the exclusive right may provide.[135] Yet, such policy-based judgments are often intentionally eschewed by

---

[131] *Metro-Goldwyn-Meyer Studios, Inc. v. Grokster, Ltd.*, 518 F. Supp. 2d 1197, 1222 (CD Cal. 2007). *See also Disney Enters. Inc. v. Delane*, 446 F. Supp. 2d 402, 408 (D. Md. 2006).

[132] *z4 Technologies, Inc.,* 434 F. Supp. 2d at 444.

[133] *Respironics, Inc. v. Invacare, Corp.*, 2008 US Dist. Lexis 1174, at *17 (WD Pa. Jan. 8, 2008).

[134] *See, e.g., Sanofi-Synthelabo v. Apotex, Inc.*, 492 F. Supp. 2d 353, 397 (SDNY 2007).

[135] *See, e.g.,* Carroll, 'Patent Injunctions', *supra* note 1, at 440–41.

judges as best left to legislators,[136] even though the legislature in the case of injunctions has delegated the policy-making decisions to the courts in equity.

The concerns typically expressed in opposing compulsory licensing regimes regarding the fairness and social efficiency of involuntary compensation are highly relevant to the choice to grant injunctions to stop infringement and/or to impose ongoing royalties. These concerns include: (1) depriving rights holders of liberty and compelling actions they would otherwise refuse; (2) failing to include valuable terms that would be included in voluntary licenses or to adjust for changes to market conditions and the value of the rights over time;[137] (3) converting courts into regulatory bodies that set prices, licensing terms, and other industry requirements;[138] (4) interfering with markets in ways that are not economically efficient and that reduce dynamic product competition;[139] and (5) diminishing incentives for investment, invention, disclosure, and dissemination.[140] Similar concerns have already been expressed in the academic literature in regard to refusing to enjoin continuing infringement, including: (1) unfairly depriving inventors of the worth of their contributions (including when it is incorporated into complex products); (2) increased resort to trade secrecy (and consequent reductions in public disclosure); (3) reduction of capital investments and of consequent market competition (particularly for individuals and small enterprises); and (4) discouragement of the transition from university-based research to commercial products.[141] But the competing values of access and of assuring only objectively reasonable compensation and market behaviors by rights holders have not been thoroughly explored. These issues are ripe for additional scholarly analysis. As part of such analysis and of the developing jurisprudence on

---

[136] *Cf. Festo Corp. v. Shoketsu Kinzoku Kogyo Kabushiki Co.*, 535 US 722, 732 (2002) (referring policy objections to the doctrine of equivalents to Congress); *Novartis Pharms Corp. v. Teva Pharms. USA, Inc.*, 2007 US Dist. Lexis 65792, at *43 (Sept. 6, 2007) (recognizing valid public interest arguments of both parties but denying a preliminary injunction 'based on the other parts of the analysis').

[137] *See, e.g., CSIRO*, 492 F. Supp. 2d at 606.

[138] *See, e.g.,* Carol M. Nielsen & Michael R. Samardzija, 'Compulsory Patent Licensing: Is it a Viable Solution in the United States?', *Mich. Telecomm. & Tech. L. Rev.* 13 (2007): 535.

[139] *See, e.g.,* Leroy Whitaker, 'Compulsory Licensing – Another Nail in the Coffin', *Am. Pat. L. Ass'n Q.J.* 2 (1974): 165–8.

[140] *See id.* at 161.

[141] *See, e.g.,* Andrew Beckerman-Rodau, 'The Supreme Court Engages in Judicial Activism in Interpreting the Patent Law in *eBay, Inc. v. MercExchange, L.L.C.*', *Tulane J. of Tech. & Intell. Prop.* 10 (2007): 194–202.

preliminary and permanent injunctions, and notwithstanding the traditional hostility in the United States to the issue,[142] it may be appropriate to look to earlier precedents granting compulsory licenses (typically by the judiciary to remedy patent misuse and antitrust violations, but also by the Federal Trade Commission).[143] The compulsory licensing precedents may be particularly relevant to determinations of whether, when, and on what conditions to grant ongoing royalty awards. Similarly, courts could look for guidance for ongoing royalties to the developing body of decisions of the Copyright Royalty Board in establishing royalty rates for statutory copyright licenses.[144]

Perhaps more importantly, the concerns expressed against compulsory licensing reflect a philosophic view that intellectual property rights, as exclusive market rights, should convey power to be free not only from competition but also from price regulation[145] and from antitrust (competition law) scrutiny and misuse doctrines when selling products within the scope of the granted rights.[146] As noted above, courts tend to believe that the public's long-term interest in promoting innovation necessarily trumps its short-term interest in obtaining low-cost access to protected goods, and thus price regulation and competition concerns should not be applied to limit intellectual property rights during their term. Similarly, a recent Federal Circuit decision has held that the grant of a patent conveys broad immunity from state price regulation of patented products, at least for pharmaceuticals and other medical inventions subject to patent term

---

142 *See, e.g.,* Jay Dratler, *Licensing of Intellectual Property* (Law Journal Press, New York; 2001): § 3.03[2].

143 *See, e.g.,* Jerome H. Reichman & Catherine Hasenzahl, 'Non-voluntary Licensing of Patented Inventions: Historical Perspective, Legal Framework under TRIPS, and an Overview of the Practice in Canada and the United States of America', UNCTAD-ICTSD Project on IPRs and Sustainable Development Series Issue Paper 5 (June 2003): 21–2.

144 *See* 17 USC § 114. *See generally* Mark D. Robertson, 'Sparing Internet Radio from the Real Threat of the Hypothetical Marketplace', *Vand. J. Ent. & Tech. L.* 10 (2008): 543.

145 *See, e.g.,* Richard A. Epstein, 'Introduction to the Italian Edition of Overdose', *Cumb. L. Rev.* 38 (2008): 227.

146 *See, e.g., Professional Real Estate Investors, Inc. v. Columbia Pictures Indus., Inc.*, 508 US 49, 56–60 (1993); *Monsanto v. McFarling*, 363 F.3d 1336, 1341 (Fed. Cir. 2004); *Virginia Panel Corp. v. Mac Panel Co.*, 133 F.3d 860, 868–74 (Fed. Cir. 1997); *Mallinkrodt, Inc. v. Medipart, Inc.*, 976 F.2d 700, 703–09 (Fed. Cir. 1992). *Cf. Ill. Tool Works Inc. v. Indep. Ink, Inc.*, 547 US 28, 42–3 (2006); *United States v. Masonite Corp.*, 316 US 265, 277 (1942). *See generally* Nicholas Economides & William N. Herbert, 'Patents and Antitrust: Application to Adjacent Markets', *J. Telecomm. & High Tech. L.* 6 (2008): 460–68.

extensions, because of the careful balance of incentives established by the national legislature to permit such patent holders to charge what the market will bear so as to create incentives for investment, invention, regulatory approval, and ultimate marketing.[147] There are reasons to believe that these cases are wrongly decided and overbroad,[148] given that federal price and product regulation may co-exist with intellectual property rights[149] and given the long-standing recognition that patents grant only a right to exclude and not any affirmative rights (including 'rights to a return on investments in creating patented inventions') or any authorization for market conduct or other immunity from market regulation for patented products.[150] As the Supreme Court held many years ago, '[t]he franchise which the patent grants *consists altogether in the right to exclude* every one from making, using, or vending the thing patented without the permission of the patentee. *This is all that he obtains by the patent.*'[151]

Here, in particular, differences of philosophical approach exist between the US experience and that of other developed and developing countries. Other jurisdictions view intellectual property rights grants and their relation to market regulation differently, adopting disparate approaches to price regulation of goods and services embodying exclusive rights[152] and

---

147 *See Biotechnology Indus, Org. v. Dist. of Columbia,* 496 F.3d 1362, 1371–4 (Fed. Cir. 2007) (citing the Drug Price Competition and Patent Term Restoration Act of 1984 (the 'Hatch-Waxman Act'), Pub. L. No. 98-417, 98 Stat. 1585 (codified as amended at 35 USC §156)), pet. for reh'g denied, 505 F.3d 1344 (Fed. Cir. 2007).

148 The decision did not properly apply the standard for federal conflicts preemption of state laws. *See* Joshua D. Sarnoff, 'Bio v. DC and the New Need to Eliminate Federal Patent Law Preemption of State and Local Price and Product Regulation', *2007 Patently-O Pat. L.J.* 31–2.

149 *See id.* at 32–3.

150 *Id.* at 33. *See id.* at 34.

151 *Bloomer v. McQuewan*, 55 US 539, 549 (1852) (second emphasis added).

152 *See, e.g.*, John Abraham, 'The Political Economy of Medicines Regulation in Britain', 221, 236, in *The Regulation of Science and Technology* (Helen Lawton-Smith, ed., Palgrave, New York; 2002) (discussing price regulation of pharmaceuticals in the UK); John A. Vernon, Joseph H. Golec & W. Keener Hughen, 'The Economics of Pharmaceutical Price Regulation and Importation: Refocusing the Debate', *Am. J. L. & Med.* 32 (2006): 182 (noting that lower drug prices result from price regulation and lower incomes in countries such as Canada); John M. Wechkin, 'Drug Price Regulation and Compulsory Licensing for Pharmaceutical Patents: The New Zealand Connection', *Pac. Rim L. & Pol. J.* 5 (1995): 247–50 (discussing drug price regulation in New Zealand); T.A. Faunce, 'Reference Pricing for Pharmaceuticals: Is the Australia-United States Free Trade Agreement Affecting Australia's Pharmaceutical Benefits Scheme?', *Medical Journal of Australia* 187 (2007): 1–3 (discussing price reimbursement regulation in Australia).

to determining whether and when intellectual property rights convey antitrust immunity.[153] The TRIPS Agreement does not address price regulation of patented products, except potentially as a non-violation complaint,[154] and at most imposes minimal restrictions on domestic competition policies that regulate intellectual property rights.[155] Accordingly, countries may choose to permit greater judicial policy-making discretion to regulate market conduct than is thought to exist in the United States, or alternatively may further specify by legislation when the violation of an exclusive intellectual property right either should not entail an injunctive remedy or should entail only a remedy that regulates price and private market conduct through prospective conditions (that may include ongoing royalties).

Conclusion

Although the developing US experience with injunctive relief after *eBay* is highly instructive, other developed and developing countries may choose different approaches in light of the TRIPS Agreement's flexibilities, and thus may and do make different choices regarding each of the many issues involved. Further, countries may point to the increasing flexibility in the developing equitable jurisprudence in the United States to respond to recent pressures being applied in the context of trade negotiations to restrict such flexibility and policy discretion in regard to injunctive relief.

In the context of efforts to negotiate an Anti-counterfeiting Trade Agreement (ACTA), a proposal circulated that would have required countries to adopt border 'measures to ensure that goods are not released into channels of commerce . . . in cases where goods have been determined by the competent authorities to be infringing IPR'.[156] Such measures would therefore significantly restrict the equitable discretion to determine to refuse to grant permanent injunctions or to grant injunctions on specific terms that would authorize continued infringement. Similarly, trade pres-

---

153 *See, e.g.,* Rita Coco, 'Antitrust Liability for Refusal to License Intellectual Property: A Comparative Analysis and the International Setting', *Marq. Intell. Prop. L. Rev.* 12 (2008): 10–24.

154 *See, e.g.,* Frederick M. Abbott, 'TRIPS in Seattle: The Not-so-surprising Failure and the Future of the TRIPS Agenda', *Berkeley J. Int'l L.* 18 (2000): 172.

155 *See, e.g.,* Haris Apostolopoulos, 'Anti-competitive Abuse of IP Rights and Compulsory Licensing through the International Dimension of the TRIPS Agreement and the Stockholm Proposal for its Amendment', *Richmond J. Global L. & Bus.* 6 (2007): 267–8, 273.

156 Discussion Paper on a Possible Anti-counterfeiting Trade Agreement (leaked draft 2008): 3, available at http://ipjustice.org/wp/wp-content/uploads/ACTA-discussion-paper-1.pdf.

sures are being exerted when injunctive relief is not ordered in particular cases, even though such decisions may properly reflect the facts of specific cases, judicial discretion, and domestic policy choices. For example, in the context of a report identifying perceived unfair trade practices, the United States stated that 'Argentina amended its patent law in December 2003, as required by a May 2002 agreement between Argentina and the United States. The intention of the amendment was to provide protections for process patents and to ensure that preliminary injunctions were available in intellectual property court proceedings. However, the injunctive relief process has thus far been too slow to be an effective deterrent to patent [infringement].'[157]

Whether or not the failure to grant preliminary injunctions adequately deters infringement in the view of any specific country, all countries retain substantial discretion to determine their policies for assessing the adequacy of damages and deciding whether to grant injunctive relief, and to apply those policies flexibly in specific cases. Such retained discretion and flexible application are particularly important for developing countries, given recognition of 'differential and more favourable treatment' under Articles 7 and 8 of the TRIPS Agreement[158] and of the universal premise that the increased flexibility of equity jurisprudence improves the quality of substantive justice.

157 2008 National Trade Estimate Report on Foreign Trade Barriers (2008): 24, available at http://www.ustr.gov/assets/Document_Library/Reports_Publications/2008/2008_NTE_Report/asset_upload_file365_14652.pdf.

158 Jerome H. Reichman, 'Universal Minimum Standards of Intellectual Property Protection under the TRIPS Component of the WTO Agreement', in *Intellectual Property and International Trade, supra,* at 80 (discussing TRIPS Agreement, *supra,* Arts 7, 8).

4 Accession to the WTO, intellectual property rights and domestic institutions

Ermias Tekeste Biadgleng

In 2007 Russia notified the World Trade Organization (WTO) of the enactment of its national law 'On the Procedure for Consideration of Appeals by Citizens of the Russian Federation' (WT/ACC/RUS/55, 14 August 2007). Russia informed the WTO that the law established the procedure for dealing with appeals and complaints by Russian and foreign persons to state authorities concerning the realization or violation of their rights and legal interests, violations of laws or other normative legislative acts or decision, action (or inaction) of the state agencies. Russia also declared that the law met the requirements of Article X of the General Agreement on Tariffs and Trade (GATT) 1994. In addition to the GATT, Article 41 of the Agreement on Trade-related Intellectual Property Rights (TRIPS) and Article VI of the General Agreement on Trade in Services (GATS) contain the obligation to provide for prompt judicial review of administrative decisions. Russia was led to the adoption of more rigorous standard for judicial review of administrative actions than provided under the GATT, GATS and TRIPS primarily due to the procedures for accession to the WTO.

The European Union is the only other international entity that seeks domestic reform through its accession procedure to establishing stable and strong domestic institutions capable of advancing the rule of law and human rights. No international organization other than the WTO has the ability to penetrate deep into the domestic procedural rules on administration of justice, transparency in government policy-making and induce institutional, legal and economic reform in a country. The WTO can do so not merely because of its rules as generally assumed but due to the unyielding power that members of the WTO maintain in deciding the accession of any country to the multilateral trading system.

The WTO was established at the end of the 1986–94 Uruguay Round of Multilateral Trade Negotiations concluded in Marrakesh in April 1994. The results of the negotiations include the Agreement Establishing the WTO (containing annexes, namely, the Multilateral Agreement on Trade in Goods, GATS, and the TRIPS Agreement), the Understanding on Rules and Procedures Governing the Settlement of Disputes, the Trade

Policy Review Mechanism, Plurilateral Trade Agreements and various decisions, understandings and declarations. The schedules of commitments by individual WTO members allowing specific foreign products or service-providers access to their markets also form part of the Uruguay Round agreements. All of these legal instruments are attached to the Final Act Embodying the Results of the Uruguay Round of Multilateral Trade Negotiations signed in Marrakesh in 1994 (Final Act, 1). The Final Act and Article XIV of the Agreement Establishing the WTO opened the agreement for acceptance as a whole, by signature or otherwise, by all contracting parties to the GATT 1947, and the European Communities, which are eligible to become *original members* of the WTO.

The participants at the Uruguay Round of Multilateral Trade Negotiations declared that the establishment of the WTO ushers in a new era of global economic cooperation, reflecting the widespread desire to operate in a fairer and more open multilateral trading system for the benefit and welfare of their peoples (Marrakesh Declaration of 15 April 1994, 2). They opened the possibility of membership to the WTO to all countries that were not members of the GATT or were not participating in the Uruguay Round of Multilateral Trade Negotiations. According to Articles XI and XV of the Agreement Establishing the WTO, Paragraph 3 of the Final Act and the Decision on the Acceptance of and Accession to the Agreement Establishing the WTO, there were three ways of being a member of the WTO:

1. members of the GATT that ratified the Agreement Establishing the WTO before 1 January 1995 or 1 January 1997 constituted original members of the WTO;
2. countries that acceded to GATT 1947 at an advanced stage of negotiation could be members after verification of their schedule of commitments;
3. countries that were acceding to GATT 1947 but had not completed negotiation on their respective schedule of commitments for goods and had yet to negotiate a schedule of commitment for service and countries that apply for membership after 1995 could be members upon the establishment of working parties to examine their application.

According to Article XI of the Agreement Establishing the WTO, the original members of the WTO are:

> The contracting parties to GATT 1947 as of the date of entry into force of this Agreement, and the European Communities, which accept this Agreement and

> the Multilateral Trade Agreements and for which Schedules of Concessions and Commitments are annexed to GATT 1994 and for which Schedules of Specific Commitments are annexed to GATS . . .

When the WTO became effective on 1 January 1995, there were 76 original WTO members (WTO, Press release, PRESS/3, 31 January 1995). Another 50 countries ratified and finalized their schedule of commitment within the period established by Article XV of the Agreement Establishing the WTO, the last being Congo in March 1997. Seven countries, namely, Angola, Burundi, Mali, Qatar, Saint Kitts and Nevis, Grenada, the United Arab Emirates and Papua New Guinea had straightforward accession to the WTO upon verification of their respective schedule of concessions and commitments to GATT 1994 and GATS (Decision on the Establishment of the Preparatory Committee for the World Trade Organization, Article 8(b) and PC/W/32). These lead to 131 original members of the WTO.

Upon the completion of the original membership of the WTO, a new process of accession to the WTO started in accordance with Article XII of the Agreement Establishing the WTO. These accessions are different from membership through ratification of the results of Uruguay Round of Multilateral Trade Negotiations by original members or verification of a schedule of commitments. The accession negotiations expanded in scope and started to revise trade policies beyond tariffs and market access to services. By the end of 2008, 25 countries had acceded to the WTO under this procedure. Accession to the WTO requires the acceding countries to confirm, at a minimum to the provisions of the WTO agreements, or beyond that to meet the trade interests of the WTO member states.[1] Countries have to revise their whole set of domestic laws, regulations and practices in order to be able to accede to the WTO, in addition to offering concessions and commitments on access to market of the goods and services of WTO member states.

This chapter will review how IP right issues are addressed under the accession negotiations to the WTO and the implications for domestic institutional reform. It also addresses the legal aspect of commitments of acceding countries under the WTO rules. The first section sets out to examine the nature of accession procedures and the status of current accession negotiations. The second section provides a thorough analysis of the nature of the commitments of acceding countries on IP rights. Here, the analysis will show how far the commitments of the acceding countries

---

[1] Autonomous custom territories are eligible to become members of the WTO. This chapter refers to countries for ease of reference.

conform to or exceed the minimum standard established under the TRIPS Agreement. The third section discusses institutional matters, in particular transparency in legislative practices, the role of the judiciary and legislative reforms as a result of accession negotiations. The final section concludes.

1. WTO accession procedures and recent developments

The accession negotiation starts with an application from the acceding country requesting admission to the WTO. The working party that will consider the application of the acceding country is established by the General Council of the WTO. The generic terms of reference of the working parties state that:

> . . . to examine the application of the Government of [name of applicant] to accede to the World Trade Organization under Article XII and to submit to the General Council/Ministerial Conference recommendations which may include a draft Protocol of Accession. (Handbook on Accession to the WTO, 4.2)

These working parties are open to all WTO members who take an interest in any particular acceding country. There are 25 countries that have completed accession negotiations and have been full members of the WTO since 1996. Out of the 25 countries, 13 are transition economies, three are developing countries and two are least-developed countries (LDCs). Jordan, Chinese Taipei and Saudi Arabia are both developing country and emerging markets.[2] China and Viet Nam qualify as developing countries, transition economies and emerging markets. Another country, Tonga, completed its accession with recognition of its economy as a small island economy. The terms 'developed country', 'transition economy', 'developing country', 'least developed country' and 'small vulnerable/ island economies' are classifications recognized under the WTO that lead to differentiation in certain obligations. There are no clear definitions of which countries can be classified as 'developed' or 'developing' countries in the WTO. Every WTO member can declare itself to be a developed or developing country in participation, negotiation and implementation of the WTO agreements. There has been no dispute as to status of a country in the WTO. Some of the 'developing countries' can be further considered

---

[2] 'Emerging markets' include Saudi Arabia, which appears in the list of markets given in the weekly report of economic and finance indicators for the *Economist*, in addition to those classified under the MSCI Index Country Membership. See, for example, the print edition of *the Economist*, 30 December 2008.

to be 'emerging markets'. This, however, does not have any relevance for determining the level of obligations under WTO Agreements or expected commitment in trade negotiation and accession procedures.

LDCs are defined by reference to the United Nations list of LDCs (Agreement Establishing the WTO, Article XI). Transition economies are defined as those that are transferring from a central command economy to a market economy (TRIPS Agreement, Article 65).

Out of the remaining 29 countries with pending accession negotiations, only one (Andorra) can be considered as a developed country, eight are transition economies, one other country, Russia, is both a transition economy and an emerging market, another six countries can be considered as developing countries, and the remaining 12 appear on the United Nations list of LDCs.

Vanuatu completed its accession negotiations in 2001, but it has not taken the final steps to become a member of the WTO. Negotiations for accession of the 28 countries continue to be pending in the respective working parties. The accession of the Bahamas, which has not submitted its memorandum of foreign trading regime since the establishment of the working party in 2001 and the Seychelles, whose draft working party reports was circulated in 1997, remain frozen.

The pending accession negotiations are taking place along two tracks: negotiation within the working party established to consider the application for accession and bilateral negotiations covering tariff rates and specific market access commitments for services, and related rules in goods and services. Once the working party completes its consideration of the applicant's trade regime, it finalizes the terms of accession, including the outcomes of the parallel bilateral market access negotiations. This leads to the preparation of the final packages for accession, consisting of the report of the working party, protocol and schedule of commitments for goods and services.

The results of the negotiations in the respective working parties and bilateral negotiations are extended to all members of the WTO, based on principles of national treatment and most-favoured nation treatment. The final package is passed to the WTO General Council or the Ministerial Conference for approval. Once approved, the accession package is subject to domestic ratification process where applicable (Handbook on Accession to the WTO, 4.2).

Upon completion of the pending accession negotiations, the WTO is set to be one of the most universal international organizations managing the negotiation, implementation and dispute administration of a range of trade issues, especially cross-border trade in industrial goods and services, domestic support to agricultural, manufacturing and service industry as

Table 4.1 Accession to WTO

Countries that completed accession			Countries negotiating accession		
Acceding country	Year of accession	*Ease of doing business rank	Acceding country	Working party established on accession	*Ease of doing business rank
Transition economy			Developed Country		
1. Bulgaria	1996	45	1. Andorra	October, 1997	–
2. Mongolia	1997	58	Transition economy		
3. Kyrgyz	1998	68	2. Kazakhstan	February, 1996	70
4. Latvia	1999	29	3. Belarus	October, 1993	85
5. Estonia	1999	22	4. Montenegro	February, 2005	90
6. Georgia	2000	15	5. Serbia	February, 2005	94
7. Albania	2000	36	6. Azerbaijan	July, 1997	33
8. Croatia	2000	106	7. Bosnia and Herzegovina	July, 1999	119
9. Lithuania	2001	28	8. Uzbekistan	December, 1994	138
10. Moldova	2001	103	9. Tajikistan	July, 2001	159
11. Armenia	2003	44	Transition economy/emerging market		
12. Macedonia	2003	71	10. Russian Federation	June, 1993	120
13. Ukraine	2008	145	Developing country		
Transition economy/ developing country /emerging market			11. Bahamas	July, 2001	55
14. China	2001	83	12. Lebanon	April, 1999	99
15. Viet Nam	2007	92	13. Iran	May, 2005	142
Developing country /emerging market			14. Iraq	December, 2004	152
16. Jordan	2000	101	15. Libya	July, 2004	–
17. Chinese Taipei	2002		16. Algeria	June, 1987	132

Table 4.1 (continued)

Countries that completed accession			Countries negotiating accession		
Acceding country	Year of accession	*Ease of doing business rank	Acceding country	Working party established on accession	*Ease of doing business rank
18. Saudi Arabia	2005	16	Least developed country		
Developing country			17. Vanuatu	July, 1995	60
19. Ecuador	1996	136	18. Samoa	July, 1998	64
20. Panama	1997	81	19. Yemen	July 2000	98
21. Oman	2000	57	20. Seychelles	July, 1995	104
Least developed/small island countries			21. Ethiopia	February, 2003	116
22. Nepal	2004	121	22. Bhutan	October, 1999	124
23. Cambodia	2004	135	23. Sudan	October, 1994	147
24. Tonga	2007	43	24. the Comoros	October, 2007	155
25. Cape Verde	2008	143	25. Liberia	December, 2007	157
			26. Afghanistan	December, 2004	162
			27. Lao PDR	February, 1998	165
			28. Equatorial Guinea	February, 2008	167
			29. Sao Tomé and Principe	May, 2005	176

Note: *World Bank Ease of doing business, 2008.

well as domestic regulations. East Timor and a number of micro-states in Europe and the Pacific (Monaco, San Marino, Nauru, Tuvalu, Palau, Kiribati, Micronesia, and the Marshall Islands) have yet to show any interest in acceding to the WTO. The Palestinian Authority, Somalia and the Western Saharawi Republic do not have an established government that allows them to pursue accession to the WTO. Turkmenistan, Eritrea and North Korea have policies that do not favour proactively seeking membership in the WTO. The Holy See is the only country allowed to maintain observer status in the WTO indefinitely without seeking membership.

2. Overview and nature of commitments of acceding countries on intellectual property rights

Analysis of the commitments of acceding countries can be based on the accession instruments of 25 countries that completed their accession by the end of 2008. The accession instruments for each acceding country consist of the following documents:

1. Decision of the General Council of the WTO allowing the country to accede to the WTO Agreement on the terms and conditions set out under the protocol on accession which is annexed to the Decision;
2. The protocol on accession which is annexed to the Decision of the General Council;
3. Working party reports that consist of commitments of the acceding countries;
4. Schedule of Concessions and Commitments under the GATT 1994;
5. Schedule of Specific Commitments under the GATS.

The schedules of commitments and concessions under the GATT and GATS do not relate to the TRIPS Agreement and hence are not relevant for the analysis of commitments on IP rights. The decisions of the General Council of the WTO and the protocols on accession apply to all issues under accession procedure and to the final terms and conditions of accession. Both the Decision of the General Council of the WTO allowing the country to accede to the WTO Agreement and the protocol on accession affirm the commitments made by the acceding country as contained in each Working Party Report. Analysis of the commitments of acceded countries would then be primarily based on the Working Party Reports. The Working Party Report contains detailed explanations, offers and commitments of the acceding countries on every trade issue covered by the WTO agreements and beyond. The reports have a section on TRIPS that contain a series of paragraphs on IP rights issues, some of which are commitments by the acceding countries. (Please see the bibliography for the list of reports that are the subject of the analysis in this chapter.[3])

The Working Party Report documents are compiled after a series of negotiations between WTO members that have an interest in the acceding countries trade regime and the acceding countries. All WTO members can negotiate on the membership of any country in the WTO. However, not all member states take an interest in the trading regime of all countries that have applied for membership to the WTO. Major trading economies, such as the United States, European Commission and other European countries, China, India, and Brazil, usually form part of the working parties established to consider applications for membership of the WTO. Countries neighbouring the acceding countries and other WTO members that have competing trade sectors or have an interest in the export of their products and services also usually form part of the working parties.

One can take Saudi Arabia, as an example, to explain how the members of the working parties consider the application of countries for accession to the WTO. The application of Saudi Arabia for membership to the GATT was circulated to WTO members (WTO, Accession of Saudi Arabia, WT/ACC/SAU/1, 21 December 1995, p. 2) in light of the new rules and institutional structure that came with the establishment of the WTO in 1994. The invitation for membership of the Working Party on Accession of Saudi Arabia was circulated by February 1995 (WTO, Accession of Saudi Arabia, WT/ACC/SAU/2, 19 February 1996). By May 1996, the membership included Australia, Canada, Czechoslovakia (later, the Czech Republic and Slovakia Republic), the European Communities and member states, New Zealand, Norway, Poland, Switzerland, Turkey, United States, Argentina, Bangladesh, Brazil, Chile, Colombia, India, Indonesia, Israel, Japan, Korea, Egypt, Kuwait, Malaysia, Mexico, Pakistan, Sri Lanka, Thailand, Tunisia, Venezuela (see WTO, Accession of Saudi Arabia, WT/ACC/SAU/2/Rev.1, 13 May 1996). Later this was revised, increasing the membership to 57 countries, including Bahrain, Senegal, Uruguay, Costa Rica, Morocco, Qatar, Romania, United Arab Emirates, Hungary, South Africa, Cuba, Dominican Republic, Ecuador, El Salvador, Honduras, Iceland, Mauritania, Nicaragua, Nigeria, Paraguay, Philippines, Singapore, and a number of countries that acceded to the WTO between 1996 and 2005, namely, Bulgaria, the Kyrgyz Republic,

[3] There are differences between the adoption of the Working Party Reports and the accession dates. The Working Party Reports hereinafter will be referred to on the basis of their respective document numbers. All of the reports were concluded at Geneva, and are available at http://www.wto.org/english/thewto_e/acc_e/completeacc_e.htm, last visited on 18 December 2008.

Latvia, Armenia, China, Chinese Taipei, and Jordan (WTO, Accession of Saudi Arabia, WT/ACC/SAU/2/Rev.23, 25 October 2005). It is clear that the dynamics of this group of countries reflects those WTO members that are interested in the market of Saudi Arabia for export and investment, neighbouring countries that share border and regional trade, oil exporters and importers, countries that export skilled and non-skilled workers and Israel, which has broad economic and other interests.

The membership of the working parties influences the nature of commitments undertaken on IP rights and other WTO rules. The working party reports do not specifically mention which countries demanded a specific commitment by the acceding countries on IP rights issues. Besides, the interest of the members of the working parties may not always be to demand a specific commitment or adherence to certain IP standards. Brazil supported acceding countries that are LDCs in taking lesser commitments in IP rights:

> At the meeting of the Working Party held on 15 August 2003, with reference to paragraph 134 of the Draft Working Party Report circulated in document WT/ACC/SPEC/NPL/5/Rev.2, the representative of Brazil stated that this paragraph in no way affected the right of Nepal, or for that matter any developing country and LDC, with respect to the provisions of the Doha Declaration on the TRIPS Agreement and Public Health (WT/MIN(01)/DEC/2). The representatives of India and Malaysia associated their delegations with this statement (WT/ACC/NPL/17, 28 August 2003).

The section of the reports of the working parties on 'Trade-related Aspects of Intellectual Property' contains detailed information on existing levels of IP rights protection as well as the further terms on offer for the acceding countries. All the information contained in the reports is part of the terms of accession. There are paragraphs of the Working Party reports that conclude with a sentence that the 'Working Party took note of this commitment' or the 'Working Party took note of these commitments'. These paragraphs are restated in the conclusion of the respective working parties, which is, in turn, cross-referenced under the protocol of accession as part of the Decision of the General Council of the WTO allowing the country to accede to the WTO Agreement. Under each working party report, there are additional paragraphs that state the commitment of the parties with respect to transparency and requirements for notification of laws applicable to all WTO Agreements, including the TRIPS Agreement. Furthermore, there are various paragraphs containing declarations or information by the acceding countries on IP property protection that do not impose any commitment.

The paragraphs of commitments of acceding countries identified in the working party reports can be classified into three categories that respectively concern:

1. the full implementation of the TRIPS agreement by the date of accession or with a specific period of transition;
2. less than full implementation, largely by LDCs and small developing country (Tonga);
3. full implementation, with interpretation of the provisions of the TRIPS Agreement favoured by the members of the respective working parties and, at times, going beyond what is required for the full implementation of the TRIPS Agreement.

2.1 Commitments for full implementation of the TRIPS Agreement

All 25 countries have committed to the full implementation of the TRIPS Agreement. The nature of the commitment for full implementation of the TRIPS Agreement is slightly different for acceding countries, depending on the status of IP rights protection under domestic laws, the level of development and year of accession. Saudi Arabia was congratulated by some members of the working party established to consider its accession on its generally high level of protection of IP rights. As a result of the higher protection of IP rights in Saudi Arabia, the only commitment entered by Saudi Arabia at the conclusion of the accession negotiation was to fully apply the provisions of the TRIPS Agreement from the date of accession to the WTO without recourse to any transition period (WT/ACC/SAU/61, 246 and 272). This suggests that working parties considering the application for accession to the WTO do not require commitments other than the full importation of the TRIPS Agreement from acceding countries that already provide protection of IP rights consistent with or more extensive than required by the TRIPS Agreement. For fourteen of the countries that acceded the full implementation of the TRIPS Agreement by the date of accession was the only commitment they made in acceding to the WTO. These countries were Bulgaria, Mongolia, Panama, the Kyrgyz Republic, Latvia, Estonia, Jordan, Georgia, Albania, Oman, Croatia, Lithuania, Moldova, and Saudi Arabia.

2.1.1 Transition period

The main issue for full implementation of the TRIPS Agreement by the date of accession is whether the acceding country may apply a transition period for implementation of its obligation, as provided for all WTO member states under Article 65 of the TRIPS Agreement. The transition period for full implementation of the TRIPS Agreement by WTO member developing countries and transition economies was for five years until

1 January 2000. Developing countries that did not provide pharmaceutical product patents by 1 January 2000 were further granted an additional five-year transition period that expired on 1 January 2005 for the availability and protection of the pharmaceutical product patent.

All of the transition economies that acceded before 1 January 2000 committed to fully implementing the TRIPS Agreement by the date of their accession without any recourse to a transition period. In most cases, the paragraph of commitment read as:

> . . . Government would apply fully the provisions of the Agreement on Trade-related Aspects of Intellectual Property Rights (TRIPS) by the date of its accession to the WTO without recourse to a transitional period. The Working Party took note of this commitment (Bulgaria, WT/ACC/BGR/5, 85, Latvia, WT/ACC/LVA/32, 116, Kyrgyz Republic, WT/ACC/KGZ/26, 164, and Estonia WT/ACC/EST/28, 126, Mongolia, WT/ACC/MNG/9, 54).

The transition period for transition economies was available only where countries experienced special problems in the preparation and implementation of IP rights laws. Since the accession process involved extensive negotiation on IP rights and the review and amendment of domestic IP legislations, it could be argued that the transition economies had overcome the special difficulty in implementing IP laws. In contrast to the transition economies, a transition period was available for developing countries and LDCs, considering their economic development. They could delay implementation without giving any particular reason to the extent provided under Article 65 of the TRIPS Agreement. Of the two developing countries that were able to accede to the WTO before 1 January 2000, only Ecuador was permitted to delay the full implementation of the TRIPS Agreement. The commitment of Ecuador states that:

> The representative of Ecuador confirmed that the date of application of the provisions of the Agreement on Trade-Related Aspects of Intellectual Property Rights for Ecuador will be no later than 31 July 1996. The Working Party took note of this commitment (WT/L/77, 78).

Since Ecuador acceded to the WTO on 21 January 1996, the period available for full implementation of the TRIPS Agreement by Ecuador was less than six months.

Chinese Taipei, Jordan, Oman, Panama, and Saudi Arabia, which acceded before 1 January 2005, committed to full application of the provisions of the TRIPS Agreement by the date of accession, without recourse to any transition period. This commitment basically excludes the additional transition period available for developing countries under Article 65.4, allowing a period to make available patent protection for pharmaceutical products. The transition period for the introduction of pharmaceutical patent protection was important for countries such as Jordan that had no such patents before accession to the WTO. If Jordan had already been a WTO member, it would have availed itself of the transition period for the introduction and enforcement of pharmaceutical patents. However, during the accession negotiation, Jordan had to amend its laws to introduce patent protection for pharmaceuticals well ahead of other WTO member developing countries. In the Report of the Working Party, Jordan indicated that:

> Moreover, the Patents Law No. 8 of 1986 [of Jordan] limited the patentability of chemical products, and would be amended to extend patent protection to pharmaceuticals and agricultural chemical products. He added that the new Patent Law provided protection to patents in respect of pharmaceutical products, but entrusted Cabinet with the authority to implement these provisions. Article 36/E/2 stated that 'The provisions of paragraphs (C) and (D) of this Article shall come into force one month after the issuance of a decision to the effect by Cabinet during a period which does not exceed three years from the date of Jordan's accession to the World Trade Organization' (WT/ACC/JOR/33, 211).

China acceded to the WTO in 2001. If China was considered as a 'developing country', it could benefit from the transition period for introduction and enforcement of pharmaceutical patent. The commitment of China states that 'upon accession China would fully apply the provisions of the TRIPS Agreement'. The commitment does not waive recourse to any transition period. However, China informed the Working Party in consideration of its accession, that

> The representative of China stated that so far as the range of patent protection and protection for new plant varieties were concerned, China had already met the requirements of Article 27 of the TRIPS Agreement. When amending the Patent Law in 1992, China modified Article 25 therein with reference to the relevant stipulations in the draft of the TRIPS Agreement and expanded the coverage of patent protection to food, beverages, flavourings, pharmaceuticals and materials obtained by chemical methods. The scope of patent exclusions would be limited to 'scientific discoveries, rules and methods of intellectual activities, diagnostic and therapeutic methods for the treatment of diseases, animals and plant varieties, as well as materials obtained by the change of nucleus' (WT/ACC/CHN/49, 269).

Since the transition period for the introduction and enforcement of pharmaceutical patents was available only for developing countries that did not provide such patents on the date of application of the TRIPS Agreement, Chinese Taipei, Jordan, Oman, Panama, and Saudi Arabia could not change their patent laws after accession to the WTO to benefit from the transition period. In sum, it is clear that countries that acceded before 1 January 2001 were required to implement the TRIPS Agreement fully and ahead of WTO member transition economies and developing countries.

2.1.2 The full implementation of the TRIPS agreement

Beyond the issue of transition period, working parties considering the application for accession by Armenia, China, Chinese Taipei, the Former Yugoslav Republic of Macedonia (FYRM), Viet Nam, and Ukraine took note of the commitments of the countries on various specific IP rights issues. Some of the commitments can be considered as drawing attention to specific domestic law that is inconsistent with the provisions of the TRIPS Agreement. Since the countries had already made commitment to fully implement the TRIPS Agreement by the date of accession, a more specific commitment to bring domestic legislations into conformity with the TRIPS Agreement would only be complementary and in some cases simply redundant. Other commitments can be considered as going beyond the full implementation of the TRIPS Agreement or addressing an interpretation and method of implementation of the provisions of the TRIPS Agreement. In this section, we consider only the commitments that complement the commitment for full implementation of the TRIPS Agreement by the date of accession.

Chinese Taipei committed to fully implementing the provisions of the TRIPS Agreement by the date of its accession, without recourse to any transitional period. The final paragraph regarding full implementation of the TRIPS Agreement by the date of accession adds further specific intellectual property issues; namely, that Chinese Taipei ensure by the date of accession:

> (a) full protection of geographical indications (including against trademarks which contain or consist of such an indication), as well as of well-known marks (including the enhanced protection pursuant to Article 16.2 and 3 of the TRIPS Agreement);
> (b) the establishment of a registration system for trademarks which incorporates all conditions as set out in the TRIPS Agreement;
> (c) the amendment of Chinese Taipei Copyright Law to comply with Article 14(1) of the TRIPS Agreement;
> (d) the extension to all WTO members of advantages currently given on the basis of reciprocity, the elimination of any reciprocity requirements; and in particular,
> (e) effective enforcement (including implementation of the special requirements related to border measures) (WT/ACC/TPKM/18, 1 January 2002, 209).

Chinese Taipei also committed to amending its copyright law to protect computer programs as literary works and to extend the term of protection to life plus 50 years or 50 years from the date of publication (WT/ACC/TPKM/18, 187) and on the need for effective enforcement of its IP laws as part of its obligation under the TRIPS Agreement (WT/ACC/TPKM/18, 207). All these commitments are only complementary to the full implementation of the TRIPS Agreement.

China also committed to full implementation of the TRIPS Agreement by the date of accession and to a number of other specific IP rights issues. China confirmed that it would modify the relevant laws, regulations and other measures so as to ensure national and MFN treatment to foreign right-holders regarding all IP rights across the board in compliance with the TRIPS Agreement. This commitment would include adjustments of the clearance requirement by the National Copyright Administration for copyright enforcement action by local copyright bureaux involving foreign right-holders to ensure national treatment (WT/ACC/CHN/49, 256). Some of the commitments of China start with the recognition or agreement of China on the failure of or the need to amend domestic legislation to fully comply with the TRIPS Agreement. For example, with respect to compulsory licence, the Working Party on the Accession of China took note of the commitment of China that:

> the representative of China *agreed that still not all the requirements of Article 31 of the TRIPS Agreement had been incorporated into Chinese law,* and that the Implementing Rules of the Patent Law would therefore be modified so as to ensure that: (1) use without authorization of the right-holder would only be permitted if, prior to such use, the proposed user had made efforts to obtain authorization from the right-holder on reasonable commercial terms and conditions, on the understanding that this requirement could be waived in the case of a national emergency or other circumstances of extreme urgency or in cases of public non-commercial use and subject to the other provisions of subparagraph (b) of Article 31; (2) the right-holder would be paid adequate remuneration in the circumstances of each case, taking into account the economic value of the authorization (Article 31(h)); (3) any such use would be authorized predominantly for the supply of the domestic market (Article 31(f)); and (4) in the case of semi-conductor technology, the scope and duration of such use would only be for public non-commercial use or to remedy a practice determined after judicial or administrative process to be anti-competitive (Article 31(c)). The Working Party took note of these commitments (WT/ACC/CHN/49, 275, emphasis added).

China also agreed to fully comply with the relevant articles in the TRIPS Agreement on geographic indications (WT/ACC/CHN/49, 265); the requirements of Article 40 of the TRIPS Agreement, in particular with respect to consultation with WTO members over anti-competitive practices in contractual licence of IP rights (WT/ACC/CHN/49, 286); to modify the existing trademark right confirmation system and offer interested parties the opportunity for judicial review concerning the confirmation of trademark rights and to improve the system for providing damages for trademark infringement (WT/ACC/CHN/49, 263); to effectively implement Articles 42 and 43 of the TRIPS Agreement under the judicial rules of civil procedures (WT/ACC/CHN/49, 291) and ensure compliance with Articles 45 and 46 of the TRIPS Agreement (WT/ACC/CHN/49, 292). These commitments simply refer to or restate the requirements of the TRIPS Agreement for full compliance by China. In other instances, the exact text of the provisions of the TRIPS Agreement is quoted. China would amend the Implementing Rules of Article 5 of China's Patent Law that stipulated that inventions that violate the laws of China or social morality or prejudice public interest would not be entitled to patent right in order to ensure that this provision would be implemented in full compliance with Article 27.2 of the TRIPS Agreement. In making such a commitment, China stated that in practice, during the review of patent applications, the interpretation of 'violating laws of China' had been restricted to 'if laws of China prohibit the sale of a certain patented product, or prohibit the sale of products manufactured by a patented method, the granting of patent right cannot be denied to this product invention or this invention of product manufacturing method by relying on Article 5 of the Patent Law' (WT/ACC/CHN/49, 270). China, in stating its commitment on provisional measures, quoted Article 50.3 of the TRIPS Agreement indicating that:

> . . . 'reasonable evidence' in Article 61 of the Patent Law [of China] would be, through implementing rules, clarified to mean 'any reasonably available evidence in order to satisfy with sufficient degree of certainty that the applicant is the right-holder and that the applicant's right is being infringed or that such infringement is imminent, and to order the applicant to provide a security or equivalent assurance sufficient to protect the defendant and to prevent abuse' (WT/ACC/CHN/49, 296).

The direct reference, restatement on quotation of a specific provision of the TRIPS Agreement is usually in reply to the request of the members of the working party considering the application for accession to the WTO. In the case of China, it committed to providing holders of IP rights with procedures related to border measures that complied fully with the relevant provisions of the TRIPS Agreement (Articles 51 to 60). This commitment was in reply to the more detailed demand by the members of the Working Party on Accession of China that stated:

> Some members of the Working Party expressed concerns as to the compatibility of existing border measures with obligations under Articles 51 to 60 of

> the TRIPS Agreement; particularly the provisions on suspension of release into free circulation by customs authorities (Article 51), rules on evidence for initiating this procedure (Article 52), requirements on the security needed to protect the defendant (Article 53), rules on notice of the suspension (Article 54) and its duration (Article 55), rules on indemnification of the importer in case of wrongful detention (Article 56) and opportunity for the right-holder to have the goods detained inspected (Article 57). Moreover some expressed their concern as to compatibility of rules on actions ex-officio by competent authorities and the conditions attached (Article 58), as well as to the remedies provided against infringing goods (Article 59) and the quantities subject to the *de minimis* rules (Article 60) (WT/ACC/CHN/49, 301).

Several commitments refer to the amendment, revision or submission for adoption of domestic legislation that is to be approved and implemented prior to or on the date of accession. This concerns commitments the working parties took note of in the case of Armenia (WT/ACC/ARM/23, 193), China (WT/ACC/CHN/49, 252 and 259), FYROM (WT/ACC/807/27, 211) and Chinese Taipei (WT/ACC/TPKM/18, 198). Since the commitments were focused on the adoption or implementation or approval of domestic law, they did not necessarily translate into a commitment to all substantive contents contained in the domestic legislations concerned. FYROM, on the other hand, committed itself to including comments from WTO members on its draft IP law in the final version of the legislation ((WT/ACC/807/27, 211). Armenia committed to amending its Criminal Code in order to implement Articles 10bis, 10ter of the Paris Convention and Articles 46, 47, 50, 61 of the TRIPS Agreement (WT/ACC/ARM/23, 166). Since this commitment does not reflect a certain interpretive approach to the provisions of the TRIPS Agreement and Paris Convention, its implementation by Armenia would not demand going beyond what is expected under the TRIPS Agreement.

Finally, China stated that its 'legislative and law enforcement bodies had also realized that the existing trademark law fell somewhat short of fulfilling the requirements of the TRIPS Agreement and the Paris Convention in a few aspects and were therefore preparing to amend the existing trademark law to fully meet the requirements of the TRIPS Agreement' (WT/ACC/CHN/49, 263). The amendments would include the registration of three-dimensional symbols. Article 15(1) of the TRIPS Agreement defines eligible subject matter for trademark protection as 'any sign or combination of signs . . .' with the option for member states to require that signs be visually perceptible as a condition for registration – basically to exclude sounds, smell, and texture etc. The definition is supported by a non-exhaustive list of signs which are eligible for registration, namely words, including personal names, letters, numerals, figurative elements and combinations of colours, as well as any combination of such signs. During the negotiations, the United States had proposed that three-dimensional marks be explicitly included in the list (Suggestion by the United States for Achieving the Negotiating Objective dated 19 October 1987, MTN.GNG/NG11/W/14, 20 November 1987, at Annex). The Europeans proposed to mention the 'shape of goods or of their packaging' (The European Communities' 1988 submission of Guidelines and Objectives Proposed by the European Community for the Negotiations on Trade Related Aspects of Substantive Standards of Intellectual Property Rights, MTN.GNG/NG11/W/26, 7 July 1988). Developing countries, however, favoured the determination by domestic law of the subject (submission of Argentina, Brazil, Chile, China, Colombia, Cuba, Egypt, India, Nigeria, Peru, Tanzania and Uruguay, MTN.GNG/NG11/W/71, 14 May 1990). However, a trademark as 'any sign' under Article 15.1 would arguably include shapes, such as three-dimensional marks. The commitment of China to introduce three-dimensional trademarks reflects the interest of some members in advancing a specific interpretation of the TRIPS Agreement. Similar approaches are noticeable in the commitments of China, and Viet Nam on criminal responsibility against certain types of IP rights infringement, as required by Article 61 of the TRIPS Agreement.

2.1.3 Full implementation of the provisions of the TRIPS Agreement as understood by the members of the working party on enforcement

The provisions of the TRIPS Agreement are subject to various interpretations. The negotiating history of the Agreement, a number of disputes before the panels and appellate Body of the WTO Dispute Settlement Body, the Ministerial Declaration on the TRIPS Agreement and Public Health (WT/MIN(01)/DEC/2, 20 November 2001) and on-going negotiations under the so-called Doha Round of trade negotiation (WT/MIN(01)/DEC/1, 14 November 2001) attest to the controversies over the possible interpretation of some of the provisions of the TRIPS Agreement. The accession procedure provides a chance for the WTO members to advance certain approaches to the implementation and interpretation of the provisions of the Agreement. This section considers the commitments of acceding countries that require changes in domestic legislation in order to take account of the substantive requirements of the TRIPS Agreement. Those commitments that are beyond what is required by the TRIPS Agreement are discussed in the subsequent section.

The availability of effective criminal procedures for enforcement of IP rights has attracted the attention of the working parties on Armenia, China and Viet Nam. Article 61 of the TRIPS Agreement specifically

BOX 4.1 ARTICLE 61 OF THE TRIPS AGREEMENT

Members shall provide for criminal procedures and penalties to be applied at least in cases of wilful trademark counterfeiting or copyright piracy on a commercial scale. Remedies available shall include imprisonment and/or monetary fines sufficient to provide a deterrent, consistently with the level of penalties applied for crimes of a corresponding gravity. In appropriate cases, remedies available shall also include the seizure, forfeiture and destruction of the infringing goods and of any materials and implements the predominant use of which has been in the commission of the offence. Members may provide for criminal procedures and penalties to be applied in other cases of infringement of intellectual property rights, in particular where they are committed wilfully and on a commercial scale.

indicates the cases of infringement of IP rights that should be subject to criminal procedures and penalties and the option for member states to subject other cases of infringement to criminal procedures and penalties. It also indicates the kinds of remedies that should be available in all cases or in specific cases (see Box 4.1).

In the case of China, the paragraph of commitments on effective criminal procedure states that:

> Some members of the Working Party expressed concerns that criminal procedures could not be used effectively to address piracy and counterfeiting. In particular, the monetary thresholds for bringing a criminal action, as currently applied, were very high and seldom met. Those thresholds should be lowered so as to permit effective action that would deter future piracy and counterfeiting. In response, the representative of China stated that China's administrative authority would recommend that the judicial authority make necessary adjustments to lower the thresholds so as to address these concerns (WT/ACC/CHN/49, 304).

In addition, China has committed that in 'appropriate cases, including those involving repeat offenders and willful piracy and counterfeiting [that were subject to administrative procedures and remedies], would be referred to relevant authorities for prosecution under the criminal law provisions' (WT/ACC/CHN/49, 299). In the case of Viet Nam, the paragraph of commitment on effective criminal procedures states that:

> A Member noted that Article 131 of the Criminal Code did not appear to provide criminal liability for all commercial scale copyright piracy. The Member also noted that Viet Nam's laws did not provide criminal liability for all activities involving commercial scale trademark counterfeiting nor did they provide the authority to their competent authorities, in criminal cases, to seize and destroy infringing goods and material and implements the predominant use of which had been in the commission of the offence. The representative of Viet Nam explained that a circular was currently being drafted to clarify that all commercial scale trademark counterfeiting and copyright piracy was subject to criminal prosecution and that competent authorities had seizure and destruction authority in criminal cases (WT/ACC/VNM/48, 11 January 2007, 465).

These commitments appear as efforts by some members of the working parties to push a certain type of interpretation providing for criminal liability to all *commercial-scale* piracy and counterfeiting. The threshold for criminal responsibility in China has led to a WTO dispute with the United States. The United States quoted the commitment made by China at the working party. It stated that during the accession negotiations members of the working party were unable to secure a firm commitment from China to solve the problem of Chinese law failing to provide criminal liability for all cases of commercial-scale counterfeiting and piracy. The United States considered that China had acknowledged the concerns that had been expressed regarding the impediments to the application of criminal procedures to counterfeiting and piracy created by the Chinese thresholds for criminal liability, but 'China only committed to recommending to its judicial authorities that these criminal thresholds be adjusted to address the concerns' (WT/DS362, 27–30). The commitment by Viet Nam was also limited to preparation of a circular clarifying that all commercial-scale trademark counterfeiting and copyright piracy was subject to criminal prosecution and that the competent authorities had seizure and destruction authority in criminal cases. These commitments do not have a clear substantive content that would allow an assessment if Viet Nam and China were required to adopt standards beyond what is required by the TRIPS Agreement.

The interpretation of 'commercial scale' was the main grounds for the United States challenging the implementation of its TRIPS obligations by China. The negotiating history of Article 61 does not reveal much detail on the negotiating parties' understanding of these terms ((MTN.GNG/NGll/W/5/Add.6). A document by the WIPO Committee of Experts on Measures against Counterfeiting and Piracy included an explanation of 'commercial scale'. It stated that:

> 'Commercial scale' is a notion which will have to be applied taking into consideration the circumstances accompanying the manufacture. The quantity of the

> goods manufactured, the way in which they were, is or are intended to be used and the will to make profit are among the factors that the courts will have to take into consideration (C&P/CE/2, 1988 and C&P/CE/4, April 1988).

In its complaint against China, the United States construed the term 'commercial scale' based on the ordinary meaning of 'scale' and 'commercial'. It argued that 'WTO Members must criminalize acts that reach a certain extent or magnitude; in other words, that WTO Members must do so even where there is no evidence that the infringer has a commercial motive or purpose. In addition the term draws a link to the commercial marketplace – where those "interested in a financial return" or engaged in "a matter of business" operate, and where business-minded IP rights infringers take the fruits of their counterfeiting or piracy. Thus, according to the United States the concept of "commercial scale" extends both to those who engage in commercial activities in order to make a "financial return" in the marketplace, and who are, by definition, therefore operating on a commercial scale, as well as to those whose actions, regardless of motive or purpose, are of a sufficient extent or magnitude to qualify as "commercial scale" in the relevant market' (WT/DS362, 109 and 110). The panel in *China – Certain Measures affecting the Protection and Enforcement of Intellectual Property Rights,* concluded that:

> a 'commercial scale' is the magnitude or extent of typical or usual commercial activity. . . . counterfeiting or piracy 'on a commercial scale' refers to counterfeiting or piracy carried on at the magnitude or extent of typical or usual commercial activity with respect to a given product in a given market. The magnitude or extent of typical or usual commercial activity with respect to a given product in a given market forms a benchmark by which to assess the obligation in the first sentence of Article 61. It follows that what constitutes a commercial scale for counterfeiting or piracy of a particular product in a particular market will depend on the magnitude or extent that is typical or usual with respect to such a product in such a market, which may be small or large. The magnitude or extent of typical or usual commercial activity relates, in the longer term, to profitability (WT/DS362/R, para. 7.577).

Finally, the panel reject the United States' claim for failure to furnish credible evidence, showing that implementation of Article 61 by China leaves out acts of counterfeiting and piracy on a commercial scale from a criminal threshold. The demand by the working party members on the accession of China was precisely to lower the thresholds for criminal responsibility under the practice of Chinese courts to the extent they consider compatible with Article 61 of the TRIPS Agreement. The following section will analyse the extent to which some of the demands on accession countries by working party members were actually beyond what was required by the TRIPS Agreement.

2.2 *Commitments beyond the full implementation of the TRIPS Agreement*

Article 1.1 of the TRIPS Agreement provides for the possibility for member states to provide for IP rights protection more extensive than required by the TRIPS Agreement, provided that such protection does not contravene the provisions of the TRIPS Agreement. It also leaves out the appropriate method of implementation for determination by each country. Members of the working parties established to consider the application for accession sometimes demanded that acceding countries adopt IP rights protection that are more extensive than required by the TRIPS Agreement. Since the provisions of the TRIPS agreement may be interpreted differently, acceding countries have been requested in some cases to follow a certain interpretation and method of implementation favoured by the members of the respective working party. The paragraphs of the working party reports that pertain to more extensive protection of IP rights than required by the TRIPS Agreement are discussed below.

2.2.1 Protection of Undisclosed pharmaceutical and agro-chemical test data

Article 39 of the TRIPS Agreement (see Box 4.2) provides the minimum standards for the protection of undisclosed information and data submitted to government agencies for approval of pharmaceutical and agricultural chemical products that uses new chemical entities. In accordance with Article 39.2, legitimate holders of undisclosed information shall have the possibility of preventing others from acquiring or using the undisclosed information without their consent in a manner contrary to honest commercial practices. The legitimate holders should also have the possibility of preventing the information from being disclosed to others without their consent in a manner contrary to honest commercial practices. Protection is available with respect to information that, when secret, possesses a commercial value and where reasonable steps, under the circumstances, have been taken to be keep it secret.

WTO members are required by Article 39.3 to protect undisclosed pharmaceutical and agricultural chemical test or other data against unfair commercial use and disclosure. The obligation to protect such data from 'unfair commercial use' and disclosure is on the condition that (1) the origination of the data involves considerable effort, (2) the data concern pharmaceutical or agricultural chemical products which utilize new chemical entities and (3) the data are submitted to fulfil a requirement of procedures on the approval of the marketing of pharmaceutical or of agricultural chemical products in the member state concerned.

WTO members do not have an obligation to protect undisclosed pharmaceutical and agricultural/chemical test or other data if such data are

BOX 4.2 ARTICLE 39 OF THE TRIPS AGREEMENT

1. In the course of ensuring effective protection against unfair competition as provided in Article 10bis of the Paris Convention (1967), Members shall protect undisclosed information in accordance with paragraph 2 and data submitted to governments or governmental agencies in accordance with paragraph 3.
2. Natural and legal persons shall have the possibility of preventing information lawfully within their control from being disclosed to, acquired by, or used by others without their consent in a manner contrary to honest commercial practices* so long as such information:
   (a) is secret in the sense that it is not, as a body or in the precise configuration and assembly of its components, generally known among or readily accessible to persons within the circles that normally deal with the kind of information in question;
   (b) has commercial value because it is secret; and
   (c) has been subject to reasonable steps under the circumstances, by the person lawfully in control of the information, to keep it secret.
3. Members, when requiring, as a condition of approving the marketing of pharmaceutical or of agricultural chemical products which utilize new chemical entities, the submission of undisclosed test or other data, the origination of which involves a considerable effort, shall protect such data against unfair commercial use. In addition, Members shall protect such data against disclosure, except where necessary to protect the public, or unless steps are taken to ensure that the data are protected against unfair commercial use.

---

* For the purpose of this provision, 'a manner contrary to honest commercial practices' shall mean at least practices such as breach of contract, breach of confidence and inducement to breach, and includes the acquisition of undisclosed information by third parties who knew, or were grossly negligent in failing to know, that such practices were involved in the acquisition.

ARTICLE 10BIS OF PARIS CONVENTION (1967) ON UNFAIR COMPETITION

(1) The countries of the Union are bound to assure to nationals of such countries effective protection against unfair competition.

(2) Any act of competition contrary to honest practices in industrial or commercial matters constitutes an act of unfair competition.

(3) The following in particular shall be prohibited:
  - (i) all acts of such a nature as to create confusion by any means whatever with the establishment, the goods, or the industrial or commercial activities, of a competitor;
  - (ii) false allegations in the course of trade of such a nature as to discredit the establishment, the goods, or the industrial or commercial activities, of a competitor;
  - (iii) indications or allegations the use of which in the course of trade is liable to mislead the public as to the nature, the manufacturing process, the characteristics, the suitability for their purpose, or the quantity, of the goods.

not submitted to government agencies or are submitted for purposes other than marketing approval of a given pharmaceutical or agricultural chemical product. There could be several possibilities for holders of undisclosed pharmaceutical and agricultural chemical test or other data to submit the data to government agencies. The holders may submit the data in promoting a product, during court proceedings, soliciting subsidies or government assistance for research and development or supply of goods and services and other purposes. Where the data are submitted for marketing approval of pharmaceutical or agricultural chemical products, Article 39.3 does not apply if the data concern or use chemical entities that are already known or used. Even where the data concern or use new chemical entities, there is no obligation to protect such data against commercial use, if the generation of the data do not require 'considerable effort'. All cases of pharmaceutical and agricultural chemical test or other data that do not entail obligation for protection against unfair commercial use and disclosure under Article 39.3, do not necessarily exclude the same data from protection under Article 39.2 as 'undisclosed information' provided that the data are secret, possess commercial value and have been subject to reasonable steps, under the circumstances, to be kept secret.

Where the pharmaceutical and agricultural chemical test or other data fulfil all the requirements of Article 39.3, they shall be protected against 'unfair commercial use' and 'disclosure'. There is no definition of the minimum standards of protection of data against 'unfair commercial use' under Article 39.3 of the TRIPS Agreement, unlike the definition provided for acquisition, disclosure or use of undisclosed information in 'a manner contrary to honest commercial practices' under Article 39.2. Obviously the protection relates only to 'commercial' use of data, permitting non-commercial use by the government agency or third parties.

An early draft of the Article 39.3 used the phrase 'unfair exploitation by competitors'. It further stated that the 'protection shall last for a reasonable time commensurate with the efforts involved in the origination of the data, the nature of the data, and the expenditure involved in their preparation, and shall take account of the availability of other forms of protection' (MTN.GNG/NG11/W/76, of 23 July 1990). A subsequent draft of the provision stated that members shall

> [protect such data against unfair commercial use. Unless the person submitting the information agrees, the data may not be relied upon for the approval of competing products for a reasonable time, generally no less than five years, commensurate with the efforts involved in the origination of the data, their nature, and the expenditure involved in their preparation. In addition, PARTIES shall protect such data against disclosure, except where necessary to protect the public.] (MTN.TNC/W/35/Rev. 1, 3 December 1990).

The latter version indicates interest in preventing third parties from a defined commercial use relying on the data submitted for the approval of competing products. Both earlier versions anticipated that the protection against relying upon the data for approval of competing products should last over a period of time. The final version, however, completely removed reference to reliance on the data for approval of competing products as 'unfair commercial use' and a specific period of protection. The interpretation of the provision was disputed in *Argentina – Patent Protection for Pharmaceuticals and Test Data Protection for Agricultural Chemicals* (WT/DS171/1, 6 May 1999), which was not considered by a panel. In an unrelated case pending before a panel in *China – Measures Affecting the Protection and Enforcement of Intellectual Property Rights*, some members have submitted their understanding of 'unfair commercial use' upon the request of the panel. Australia considered the phrase within the meaning of Article 39.3 to refer to 'the use by competitors of test or other data, relating to new chemical entities utilised in pharmaceutical or agricultural chemical products submitted to a government or its agent, in a manner which diminishes the financial rewards in a market place that would otherwise flow to the data's originator' (WT/DS362, Australian Responses to Questions from the Panel, 8).

The commitments of China, Ukraine, Cambodia and Tonga reflect the intention of their respective working parties to introduce in the domestic legislations of these acceding countries substantive legal aspect of unfair commercial use of data that is not explicitly provided under Article 39.9. The Commitment of China reads as follows:

> . . . China further confirmed that China would, in compliance with Article 39.3 of the TRIPS Agreement, provide effective protection against unfair commercial use of undisclosed test or other data submitted to authorities in China as required in support of applications for marketing approval of pharmaceutical or of agricultural chemical products which utilized new chemical entities, except where the disclosure of such data was necessary to protect the public, or where steps were taken to ensure that the data are protected against unfair commercial use. This protection would include introduction and enactment of laws and regulations to make sure that *no person, other than the person who submitted such data, could, without the permission of the person who submitted the data, rely on such data in support of an application for product approval for a period of at least six years from the date on which China granted marketing approval to the person submitting the data.* During this period, any second applicant for market authorization would only be granted market authorization if he submits his own data (WT/ACC/CHN/49, 284). (*Emphasis added*)

Ukraine committed to clarify in its regulations related to the Law 'On Medicines' that the term 'to use the registration information' would include 'relying upon, referring to, or otherwise using information' (WT/ACC/UKR/152, 433). In the commitment of Tonga and Cambodia, the period of protection is five years from the date of grant of marketing approval to the person that produced the data. Ukraine committed for a period of protection lasting five years for pharmaceutical products and ten years for agricultural chemical products. Ukraine went further by agreeing to introduce procedures of notification concerning existing registration or submission of data for registration of medicines with the 'same or similar active ingredients'. The purpose of the notification is to provide to the prior applicant an opportunity to provide information on whether the subsequent applicant had permission to use the first applicant's data (WT/ACC/UKR/152, 425). In the absence of consent by the prior applicant, any subsequent application for marketing approval or registration would not be granted, unless the subsequent applicant submitted his own data meeting the same requirements as the first applicant (WT/ACC/UKR/152, 433).

China agreed that the protection of data would be 'available to all pharmaceutical and agricultural products which utilize new chemical entities, irrespective of whether they were patent-protected or not'. Here, the working party considering China's accession to the WTO wished to clarify that data protection would be independent from the patent status of the product. However, the commitments of Tonga, Cambodia and Ukraine included elements beyond those reflected in Article 39.3. These countries were required to establish a linkage between marketing approval of pharmaceutical and agro-chemical products and patents and patent applications regarding those products.'

> . . . Prior to the issuance of marketing approval of any pharmaceutical and agricultural chemical products, the relevant Ministries in Tonga would determine the existence of a patent covering a product for which an application for marketing approval had been filed by a party other than the patentee, and would not approve such application for marketing approval until the date of the expiration of such patent (WT/ACC/TON/17, 167 and WT/ACC/KHM/21, 205).

Going far beyond issues related to IP protection of undisclosed pharmaceutical and agro-chemical data, Ukraine made a commitment to ensure that a subsequent applicant for marketing approval of pharmaceutical products will also be required to meet the same requirements as a first applicant even where the subsequent applicant relies on his own data (WT/ACC/UKR? 152, 433).

At the heart of these commitments on pharmaceutical and agro-chemical test and other data lies the question of the regulation of the entry into market by generic pharmaceutical and agro-chemical producers. Patents confer exclusive rights over the use of an invention for the right-holder for a period of 20 years. At the expiry of the patent, any other market player, in particular generic manufacturers, can use the invention for manufacturing and supply of the product that was covered by the patent.

Countries can encourage generic manufacturing by simply not requiring marketing approval where the generic product is chemically the same as the original product. Where a country decides to require safety and efficacy of the product based on pharmaceutical and agro-chemical test data, generic producers could utilize the original data for approval purposes. However, the commitments entered by China, Ukraine, Tonga and Cambodia provide for a 'data exclusivity' requirement for five or more years, during which the authorities cannot rely on the original data for marketing approval purposes of generics. The data exclusivity approach is followed by many advanced nations and by developing countries that have entered into bilateral agreements with the advanced nations (Weissman, 2006 p. 114). In this case, the generic manufacturer does not have any choice except to acquire a 'reference right' from the originator of the data submitted for the approval of the drug or to itself undertake the clinical trials all over again.

The additional 'linkage requirements' between marketing approval and application and registration of patent essentially require authorities to enforce patent rights (which are of a private nature) on behalf of the patent holder, irrespective of any question as to the validity of the invoked patents and all other legal means for the private right-holder to enforce his/her right before a court of law. The patent-registration linkage goes even beyond the standards applied in developed countries. In Europe, for instance, there is complete independence between IP protection and registration of pharmaceuticals (Correa, 2004). The commitments on undisclosed pharmaceutical and agro-chemical test data are a clear disadvantage for countries that have limited industrial innovation capacity in chemicals.

2.2.2 Result-based IP enforcement obligation

China, Chinese Taipei, Ukraine, Viet Nam, Nepal, Cambodia and Tonga have entered into various commitments that focus on the level of results to be achieved or maintained and on measures for enforcement of IP rights. The basic obligation of WTO members under the TRIPS Agreement is 'to make available' effective civil, and administrative and border measures, and to provide for criminal procedures and remedies for specified types of infringement.

Cambodia, Nepal, and Cape Verde, all LDCs, committed to ensuring that existing rates of infringement would not increase significantly over the transition period and that 'any infringement' of IP rights would be addressed immediately in cooperation with and with assistance from affected right-holders. Tonga has also agreed to a similar commitment stating that 'existing rates of infringement would not in his [the representative of Tonga to the Working Party] view increase significantly over this transition period' (WT/ACC/TON/17, 168). The working parties are interested not only in the availability of effective procedures for enforcement of IP rights as required under the TRIPS Agreement but also in the performance of the acceding countries in controlling existing rates of infringement. LDCs are required to ensure that the existing rate of infringement will not significantly increase during the transition period and to immediately address 'any infringement' of IP rights. These commitments are not based on a specific provision of the TRIPS Agreement. Whether infringements occur or significantly increase is not the subject matter addressed under the TRIPS Agreement. The TRIPS Agreement under Part III only deals with the availability of effective legal means (the procedures, relevant authority and competence) when infringement of IP rights takes place. The role of the government to actually enforce IP rights upon its own initiative is limited to infringement that reaches a criminal threshold in accordance with Article 61 of the TRIPS Agreement and to prima-facie cases of importation of counterfeit trademark or pirated copyright goods in accordance with Article 51 of the TRIPS Agreement. Cambodia, Nepal and Cape Verde can be said to have committed to a standard well beyond what is required under the TRIPS Agreement applicable during the transition period.

The commitment of China represents the interest in pushing more on the kind of police measures, especially police crackdown, closure of factories and shops, considered important for enforcement of IP rights irrespective of the steps that need to be taken by the right-holders to enforce their private rights:

> Some members of the Working Party further urged China to ensure the vigorous application by Chinese authorities of the enforcement legislation in order to considerably reduce the existing high levels of copyright piracy and trademark counterfeiting. Action should include the closure of manufacturing facilities as well as markets and retail shops that had been the object of administrative convictions for infringing activities. The representative of China stated that the measures for cracking down on intellectual property piracy were always severe in China. In judicial aspects, courts at all levels were continuously paying attention to the trial of IPR cases. As for administration aspects, the administrative authorities at all levels were putting emphasis on strengthening anti-piracy work. In addition, the administrative authorities were also enhancing the legal publication and education of the general public in a bid to ensure that the legal environment of China would be able to meet the requirements for enforcing the TRIPS Agreement. The Working Party took note of these commitments.

The commitment by Chinese Taipei concerns specific products: alcohol and tobacco. Chinese Taipei committed to destroy or otherwise dispose of what is described as 'contraband smuggled or counterfeit imports of' alcohol and tobacco products, taking into account the practices of WTO members in a similar situation. Control of contraband and smuggling of products using procedures for IP enforcement is not anticipated by the TRIPS Agreement. Chinese Taipei committed further to taking additional efforts unrelated to IP:

> In this regard, Chinese Taipei would ensure that certain alcoholic beverage imports would be accompanied by a certificate of origin similar to that issued by the regulatory authorities in the country of origin in order to combat counterfeiting. The Working Party took note of these commitments (WT/ACC/TPKM/18, 208).

The commitment to require certificate of origin for imports of certain alcoholic beverages may support the enforcement of IP rights where the domestic regime on exhaustion of IP rights prevents parallel importation of the product covered by IP rights. The TRIPS Agreement, however, requires only the availability of the legal means for right-holders to suspend the release of imports.

Another distinct commitment on enforcement made by Viet Nam related to the acquisition, use and management of software by government agencies, and requiring cable television broadcasters to broadcast only 'fully licensed products to their customers' (WT/ACC/VNM/48, 403). These commitments responded to complaints by some members of the working party that some government agencies and state-owned enterprises used computer software that had not been authorized by the right-holder and were providing unlicensed cable television programming:

> Some Members observed that it had been brought to their attention that some agencies of the Government of Viet Nam used computer software that had not been authorized by the right holder. These Members also noted that an agency of the Government of Viet Nam and a State-owned enterprise were providing unlicensed cable television programming to Vietnamese customers. They requested such a practice should be eliminated by Viet Nam in the context of its accession to the WTO and the implementation of the obligations in the WTO Agreement on TRIPS. The representative of Viet Nam confirmed that prior to the date of accession, Viet Nam would issue appropriate legal instruments mandating that all government agencies use only legitimate computer software and not infringe the copyright of such software. Such measures would regulate the acquisition and management of all software for use by government agencies. The representative of Viet Nam also confirmed that prior to the date of accession, Viet Nam would issue appropriate legal instruments mandating that all cable television purveyors provide only fully licensed products to their customers. The Working Party took note of these commitments (WT/ACC/VNM/48, 403).

These commitments favour performance-based enforcement of IP rights measures required for specific products, such as beverages and software, and demonstrate the interest in using accession procedures to advance the interest of right-holders in some members of the working parties, without the trouble of going through the domestic procedures for enforcement of IP rights.

2.3 *Less than full-implementation and stand-still obligation? Least-developed countries and IP rights issues in accession*

The transition period was much more important to LDCs considering their weak foundation for innovation. LDCs were not required to apply the provisions of the TRIPS Agreement for a period of ten years from the date of application as defined under paragraph 1 of Article 65, that is, until 1 January 2006. This period was extended by the Decision of the Council for TRIPS of 29 November 2005. In accordance with this Decision, LDCs shall not be required to apply the provisions of the Agreement, other than Articles 3, 4 and 5, until 1 July 2013, or until such time as they cease to be an LDC, whichever date is earlier. Moreover, in the case of pharmaceutical patents and test data, the Decision of the Council for TRIPS of 27 June 2002 extended the transitional period for LDCs until 2016.

There are only three LDCs that have been able to accede to the WTO to date: Nepal, Cambodia and Cape Verde. Although Tonga is not an LDC, it acceded with a status that fully considers its small-sized economy. The category of 'small and vulnerable economies' is already emerging in the WTO system in addition to those of developed countries, transition economies, developing countries and LDCs. LDCs are the only countries with defined factors for determination of their status based on United Nations criteria.

Nepal and Cambodia acceded in 2004 – before the Decision of the Council for TRIPS of 29 November 2005 extending the transition period until 2013. The working group parties on the accessions of both Nepal and Cambodia took note of the commitments of the two countries to fully implement the TRIPS Agreement by 1 January 2007. This would have confirmed one additional year of transition period for the two countries beyond the first period of transition for LDCs, which expired on 1 January 2006 in accordance with Article 66.1 of the TRIPS Agreement. Since the Decision of the Council for TRIPS of 29 November 2005 extending the transition period until 2013 is applicable to all LDCs, Nepal and Cambodia will not be expected to fully implement the TRIPS Agreement before 2013. The Working Party Report of Cape Verde also accorded a transition period ending in 2013 for Cape Verde's full implementation of the TRIPS Agreement. Tonga, which acceded in July 2007, was accorded a transition period expiring on 30 June 2008. During the transition period, LDCs are required to comply with the national treatment and most-favoured-nation treatment provisions of the TRIPS Agreement. The Decision of the Council for TRIPS of 29 November 2005, which extended the transition period for LDCs until 2013, introduced the stand-still principle of Article 65.5 of the TRIPS Agreement and requires that:

> Least-developed country Members will ensure that any changes in their laws, regulations and practice made during the additional transitional period do not result in a lesser degree of consistency with the provisions of the TRIPS Agreement (IP/C/40, 5).

The applicability of the stand-still principle to LDCs is open to dispute. Article 66.1 of the TRIPS Agreement provides only the mandate for the TRIPS Council to accord an extension of the transition period: 'The Council for TRIPS shall, upon duly motivated request by a least-developed country Member, accord extensions of this period'. This does not authorise the Council to impose additional terms and conditions or substantive provisions to the extension of the transition period.

All LDCs and Tonga that were allowed to benefit from a transition period also agreed to the stand-still principle. However, the working party reports of Cambodia and Tonga expanded the stand-still principle to include additional terms for the transition period. Accordingly, Cambodia and Tonga will not grant patents, trademarks, or copyrights, or marketing approval for pharmaceuticals or agricultural chemicals inconsistent with the provisions of the TRIPS Agreement during the transition period (WT/ACC/KHM/21, 204 and WT/ACC/TON/17, 167). This commitment basically requires Cambodia and Tonga to be TRIPS-consistent during the transition period with respect to domestic procedures and practices in granting patents, trademarks or copyright or marketing approval for pharmaceuticals or agricultural chemicals. In accordance with Article 62.2 of the TRIPS Agreement, the procedures to grant or register IP rights as a condition of validity should permit the granting or registration of the right within a reasonable period of time so as to avoid unwarranted curtailment of the period of protection. The commitments by Cambodia and Tonga do not prevent the application of or change the domestic substantive rules existing on the date of accession for acquisition of IP rights. The commitments also do not apply to related rights in copyright, industrial designs, geographic indications, layout designs and trade secrets other than marketing approval pertaining to pharmaceutical and agricultural chemicals.

Furthermore, the working party groups for the accession of Nepal, Cambodia, Cape Verde (see Box 4.3) and Tonga secured additional commitment as part of the stand-still principle that could be construed well beyond what is required under the TRIPS Agreement. Such commitments include the following:

1. During the transition period Cape Verde would ensure that its IP rights regime would not result in a lesser degree of enforcement (WT/ACC/CPV/30, 245).
2. Cambodia, Nepal, and Cape Verde further committed to result-based IP enforcement in which the existing rate of infringement will not substantially increase as discussed in Section 2.2.2;
3. Cambodia, Nepal, Cape Verde and Tonga committed to make available all legislation in draft and promulgated form to WTO members for circulation and review, to implement an action plan and time frame for promulgations of IP laws to implement the TRIPS Agreement, for membership in international IP treaties, capacity building and training

BOX 4.3 COMMITMENTS OF CAPE VERDE

WTO, Report of the Working Party on the Accession of Cape Verde to the World Trade Organization, Working Party on the Accession of Cape Verde, WT/ACC/CPV/30, 6 December 2007

244. The representative of Cape Verde stated that, for the reasons given above, the Government of Cape Verde requested that the WTO grant a transitional period until 1 January 2013 to obtain technical assistance and equip the administration to implement fully the obligations of the TRIPS Agreement. For the obligations covered by Sections 5 and 7 of Part II of the TRIPS Agreement or to enforce rights provided for under these Sections Cape Verde requested the WTO to recognize its right to an additional transitional period in respect of these obligations, until 1 January 2016, in light of paragraph 7 of the Doha Declaration on the TRIPS Agreement and Public Health. The representative of Cape Verde confirmed that should a transition be granted for the implementation of the WTO Agreement on TRIPS, Cape Verde was prepared to fully apply Articles 3, 4 and 5 of the TRIPS Agreement that provide for, inter alia, national treatment and MFN treatment under current legislation in place during any transition period granted. To this end, Cape Verde would amend its legislation on the fees charged to applicants to ensure full national and MFN treatment upon accession. Cape Verde would also ensure that any change made in its laws and regulations during this period would not result in a lesser degree of consistency with the provisions of the TRIPS Agreement.

245. The representative of Cape Verde further confirmed that, should a transition be granted, his Government would ensure that Cape Verde's intellectual property rights regime would not result in a lesser degree of enforcement during any transition period granted; that existing rates of infringement would not significantly increase; and that any infringements of intellectual property rights in this period would be addressed immediately in cooperation with affected right holders. He added that Cape Verde would seek out all available technical assistance to ensure that its capacity to fully enforce its TRIPS-consistent legal regime upon expiration of the transition periods is assured and that Cape Verde would make

available TRIPS legislation in draft and promulgated form to the WTO Secretariat for circulation to interested WTO Members. In response to requests from delegations for more specificity, the representative of Cape Verde presented an Action Plan in Table 12 setting out details of the steps that still remained to be taken in order to achieve this objective and a timetable for each step.

246. The representative of Cape Verde confirmed that Cape Verde would apply the Agreement on Trade-Related Intellectual Property Rights by no later than 1 January 2013 according to the action plan in Table 12 with the understanding that for the obligations covered by Sections 5 and 7 of Part II of the TRIPS Agreement or to enforce rights provided for under these Sections, Cape Verde would apply the TRIPS Agreement in respect of these obligations no later than 1 January 2016, in light of paragraph 7 of the Doha Declaration on the TRIPS Agreement and Public Health. During this period, protection for intellectual property rights as described in paragraphs 244 and 245 would be applied in Cape Verde. The Working Party took note of this commitment.

of personnel, and enhancing public awareness on the protection of IP rights in their respective territory during the transition period.

The Decision of the Council for TRIPS of 29 November 2005 does not require an action plan and time frame for the LDCs to take steps in implementing the TRIPS Agreement during the transition period. It can be argued that WTO member states can insist on actual progress on the part of LDCs benefiting from a transition period to take agreed steps for the full implementation of the TRIPS Agreement. However, the action plans for participation in international convention on IP rights, such as the Geneva Convention for the Protection of Producers of Phonograms against Unauthorized Duplication of their Phonograms, 1971, the Brussels Convention Relating to the Distribution of Programme-carrying Signals Transmitted by Satellite and the Patent Cooperation Treaty (by Cambodia) are not required by the TRIPS Agreement.

Unlike Cambodia and Tonga, Nepal has not entered into a commitment on implementation and enforcement of pharmaceutical product patent and protection of test data during the transition period. Cape Verde actually asserted its right to the transition period (WT/ACC/

CPV/30, 244 and 246). One important question is the consistency of the commitment by Cambodia with the transition period for LDCs expiring in 2013 and the transition period with respect to pharmaceutical product patents and test data expiring on 1 January 2016. Paragraph 6 of the Decision of the Council for TRIPS of 29 November 2005 has made it clear that the transition period expiring in 2013 is without prejudice to the transition period expiring in 2016 with respect to the implementation and enforcement of pharmaceutical product patent and protection of test data during the transition period. Tonga, however, needs to implement its commitment during the transition period since it is not an LDC that can benefit from the Decision of the Council for TRIPS of 29 November 2005.

In sum, LDCs that acceded to the WTO have to comply with additional terms and conditions during the transition period unlike LDCs that were original members of the WTO. As discussed above, these include (1) the requirement to comply with the TRIPS Agreement in granting patents, trademarks, copyright and marketing approval for pharmaceutical and agricultural chemicals during the transition period; (2) a more robust stand-still principle that includes the obligation to prevent a significant increase in the rate of infringement during the transition period and to address immediately 'any infringement' of IP rights; and (3) to ratify international treaties not required by the TRIPS Agreement.

3. Legislative practice, and administration of IP rights

The commitments of acceding countries on IP-related issues also appear in other sections of the working party reports, in particular in paragraphs dealing with the framework of policy-making, transparency and notification of laws and regulations. The commitments concern administration and IP policy-making, and legislative practices, as well as review and right of appeal against administrative decisions.

3.1 Legislative practices and administration of laws

The institutional aspects of policies, laws and regulations were addressed in a number of commitments concerning uniform administration, transparency in legislation and publication of laws. China has made a commitment which is reflected in its accession protocol concerning uniform, impartial and reasonable administration of laws. China is committed to apply and administer in a uniform, impartial and reasonable manner all its laws, regulations and other measures of the central government as well as local regulations, pertaining to or affecting trade in goods, services, TRIPS or the control of foreign exchange.

The commitments on legislative practice concern consultation with interest groups on draft legislation, translations, publications, date of entry into force and other matters. They include:

1. Commitments indicating that no law or regulation related to international trade/intellectual property would become effective prior to publication (WT/ACC/SAU/61, 305 and WT/ACC/TPKM/18, 331, WT/ACC/VNM/48, 518). In the case of Cambodia and China, the commitment on the publication of laws, regulations and other measures would also include, where appropriate or possible, the list of the products and services affected by the particular measure, identified by appropriate tariff line and classification (WT/ACC/KHM/21, 217 and WT/ACC/CHN/49, 331);
2. Commitment for prompt or expedited publications: China, Nepal, Saudi Arabia, and Chinese Taipei made a commitment that the publication of laws would be 'prompt', unlike the TRIPS Agreement, which only requires publication without additional qualification;
3. China, Saudi Arabia, and Cambodia committed that only those laws, regulations and other measures pertaining to or affecting trade in goods, services, TRIPS or the control of foreign exchange that are *published* and *readily available* to other WTO members, individuals and enterprises, shall be enforced (China's accession protocol 2(C)(1));
4. Commitment by Cambodia, China and Chinese Taipei for translations into one or more of the official languages of the WTO all laws, regulations and other measures before they are implemented or enforced, but in no case later than 90 days (60 days in the case of Chinese Taipei after they are implemented or enforced) (WT/ACC/TPKM/18, 331 and WT/ACC/TPKM/18, 219);
5. Commitment for the establishment of enquiry points, or information centres on TRIPS or generally on intellectual property rights, commitment to circulate legislation to WTO Members for comment within specified time limits, and to establish or designate an official journal or website, published or updated on a regular basis and readily available to WTO Members, individuals and enterprises, dedicated to the publication of all regulations and other measures pertaining to or affecting trade in goods, services, and TRIPS (WT/ACC/KHM/21, 217 and WT/ACC/UKR/152, 499 for Ukraine).

3.2 Review of administrative decisions and right of appeal to court of law

Additional commitments on the review of administrative decisions and the availability of right of appeal to court of law against administrative decisions have been undertaken by China. It committed that

> . . . administrative actions related to the implementation of laws, regulations, judicial decisions and administrative rulings of general application referred to in Article X:1 of the GATT 1994, Article VI of the GATS and the relevant provisions of the TRIPS Agreement including those relating to the implementation of national treatment, conformity assessment, the regulation, control, supply or promotion of a service, including the grant or denial of a licence to provide a service and other matters, would be subject to the procedures established for prompt review under Section 2(D)(2) of the Draft Protocol, and information on such procedures would be available through the enquiry point that China would establish upon accession. The Working Party took note of these commitments (WT/ACC/CHN/49, 79).

The protocol of accession (Section 2(A) and (D)(2)) imposes four further requirements on China:

1. *Uniform application of laws as subject matter for administrative action*: China is required to establish a mechanism under which individuals and enterprises can bring to the attention of the national authorities cases of non-uniform application of the trade regime;
2. *Independence and impartiality*: The tribunals for the prompt review of all administrative actions shall be impartial and independent of the agency entrusted with administrative enforcement and shall not have any substantial interest in the outcome of the case;
3. *Right of appeal to court of law*: The procedures for review of administrative actions should include the opportunity for appeal, without penalty, by individuals or enterprises affected by any administrative action subject to review;
4. *Reasons for decision to be given in writing*: The decision on appeal shall be given to the appellant and the reasons for such decision shall be provided in writing and finally the appellant shall also be informed of any right to further appeal.

In the case of China, the Working Party further took note that 'laws adopted by the National People's Congress and administrative regulations, including implementing rules, issued by the State Council were applied and enforced by the People's courts' (WT/ACC/CHN/49, 252). In a country where law and law enforcement follows a different legal tradition and constitutional structure, it would make sense to request that relevant laws and regulations are indeed enforceable before a court of law. Russia is also expected to make similar commitments.

The commitments on legislative practices and administration of laws show the result of efforts by WTO members to induce changes in domestic laws and institutions so as to ensure that the acceding country maintains stable and credible institutions as a WTO member.

4. Legal status of commitments made under accession process on IP rights: can they be enforced before WTO dispute settlement panels?

The WTO rules are based on agreements negotiated and agreed upon among members and separate custom territories. The agreements are not implementated and enforced by collective action or an independent body. They are basically enforced through the complaints by one or a group of members against another member under the dispute settlement procedure. This suggests the notion that the obligations arising from WTO agreements are reciprocal and bilateral rather than multilateral. For example, these agreements are approved by Congress in the United States as executive agreements and not as treaties (Grimmett, 2008).

In the WTO, what is a consistent or inconsistent domestic measure depends on the possible findings a dispute settlement panel or the Appellate Body requested to make such determinations. The Understanding on Rules and Procedures Governing the Settlement of Disputes governs only disputes brought pursuant to the consultation and dispute settlement provisions of a specific list of covered agreements (Article 1 of the Understanding). The covered agreements are:

(A) Agreement Establishing the World Trade Organization
(B) Multilateral Trade Agreements, including Annex 1A: Multilateral Agreements on Trade in Goods, Annex 1B: GATS, Annex 1C: TRIPS Agreement and Annex 2: Understanding on Rules and Procedures Governing the Settlement of Disputes;
(C) Plurilateral Trade Agreements contained in Annex 4 to the extent the parties to the agreements agreed.

The accession of a country to the WTO depends upon a decision of the General Council acting on behalf of the Ministerial Conference of the WTO. The decision incorporates the Protocol of Accession that contains reference to the commitments of the acceding country. The decisions typically conclude by stating that the country that concluded the accession negotiations 'may accede to the WTO Agreement on the terms and conditions set out in the Protocol annexed to this Decision'. Each of the protocols of accession in turn states that the Protocol, which includes the commitments under the Working Party Report 'shall be an integral part of the WTO Agreement'. The basis for these lies in Article XII of the Agreement establishing the WTO which states that:

> 1. Any State or separate customs territory possessing full autonomy in the conduct of its external commercial relations and of the other matters provided for in this Agreement and the Multilateral Trade Agreements may accede to

> this Agreement, on terms to be agreed between it and the WTO. Such accession shall apply to this Agreement and the Multilateral Trade Agreements annexed thereto.
> 2. Decisions on accession shall be taken by the Ministerial Conference. The Ministerial Conference shall approve the agreement on the terms of accession by a two-thirds majority of the Members of the WTO.

The provision only states that accession is on 'terms to be agreed'. It does not stipulate that the terms of accession shall be an integral part of the Agreement establishing the WTO. Furthermore, the agreement on terms of accession is between the acceding country and the 'WTO' as an organization. The status of the final agreed schedule of commitments for goods is clarified by Article II:7 of the GATT that declares the schedules to be an integral part of the Agreement. Other provisions of various WTO agreements also stipulate that their respective annexes form an integral part of the agreement concerned (see Article II(2) of the Agreement Establishing the WTO, Article XXIX of GATT, Article 21(2) of the Agreement on Agriculture, and Article 1 of the Final Act). Article 3 of the Agreement on Agriculture further integrates commitments on domestic support and export subsidy in each member's schedule of commitment. The Agreement on Rules of Origin that anticipate harmonization also provides under Article 9 that the results of the harmonization of rules would be an integral part of the agreement.

The panel in *China – Measures Affecting Imports of Automobile Parts* was the first to consider the status of commitments arsing from the working party reports. When considering the claims raised by Canada and the United States under paragraph 93 of China's Accession Working Party Report, the panel stated:

> All parties agree that China's commitments under its Working Party Report are enforceable in WTO dispute settlement proceedings. The Accession Protocol is an integral part of the WTO Agreement pursuant to Part I, Article 1.2 of the Accession Protocol. In turn, paragraph 342 of China's Working Party Report incorporates China's commitments under its Working Party Report, including paragraph 93, into the Accession Protocol. Therefore, China's commitment in paragraph 93 of the Working Party Report is also an integral part of the WTO Agreement.
>
> Accordingly, the Panel will interpret China's commitment under paragraph 93 of the Working Party Report in accordance with the interpretative rules of the *Vienna Convention* to determine whether China has acted inconsistently with commitments under paragraph 93 of the Working Party Report (Panel Reports, 7.740 and 7.741, footnotes omitted).

The conclusion of the panel confirmed the binding nature of the commitments in the working party report. The appellate body specifically drew its attention to this conclusion of the panel and remarked that the conclusion has not been disputed at any point in the appellate proceedings (WT/DS339/AB/R, WT/DS340/AB/R, WT/DS342/AB/R, 214).

The ruling in *China – Measures Affecting Imports of Automobile Parts* demonstrates that the enforceability of accession protocols and commitments is based on Article XII of the Agreement establishing the WTO independently of any of the covered agreements. The panel made an independent finding of China's violation of its commitment under paragraph 93 of China's Working Party Report, which is an integral part of the WTO Agreement (Panel Reports, 7.758). Countries that entered into commitments on IP rights issues in acceding to the WTO may face legal challenges based on commitments under the accession protocol independently and separately from the TRIPS Agreement. This is due to Article 1.1 of the Dispute Settlement Understanding, which states:

> The rules and procedures of this Understanding shall also apply to consultations and the settlement of disputes between Members concerning their rights and obligations under the provisions of the Agreement Establishing the World Trade Organization (referred to in this Understanding as the 'WTO Agreement') and of this Understanding taken in isolation or in combination with any other covered agreement.

The enforceability of the accession protocol and commitment would, however, be subject to problems of interpretation of paragraphs of commitments (Abbott and Correa, 2007, p. 5).

Bibliography

Abbott, Frederick M. and Correa, Carlos M., 'World Trade Organization Accession Agreements: Intellectual Property Issues', *Global Economic Issues*, Quaker United Nations Office, Geneva, 2007.

Correa, Carlos M., 'Bilateralism in Intellectual Property: Defeating the WHO System for Access to Medicines', *Case Western Reserve Journal of International Law*, 36(1), Winter, 2004.

Grimmett, Jeanne J., 'Why Certain Trade Agreements are Approved as Congressional-Executive Agreements rather than as Treaties', Legislative Attorney, American Law Division, Congressional Research Service Report for Congress, Order Code 97-896, updated 3 January 2008.

MSCI Index Country Membership, available at http://www.mscibarra.com/index.jsp, last visited on 31 December 2008.

The Economist, Economic and Finance Indicators, 30 December 2008.

UN Office of the High Representative for the Least Developed Countries, Landlocked Developing Countries and Small Island Developing States, List of Least-developed Countries, available at http://www.unohrlls.org/, last visited on 31 December 2008.

Weissman, Robert, 'Public Health friendly Options for protecting pharmaceutical registration data', *Int. J. Intellectual Property Management*, 1(1/2), 2006, Inderscience Enterprises Ltd., 113, available at http://www.essentialaction.org/access/uploads/IJIPM11-2Paper08.pdf, last visited on 31 December 2008.

World Bank, Ease of doing business index, 2008.

WTO, *China – Measures Affecting the Protection and Enforcement of Intellectual Property Rights,* WT/DS362, First Submission of the United States of America, Geneva, 30 January 2008.

WTO, *China – Measures Affecting Imports of Automobile Parts*, WT/DS339/R, WT/DS340/R, WT/DS342/R, and Add.1 and Add.2, Report of the Panel, 18 July 2008.

WTO, *China – Measures Affecting the Protection and Enforcement of Intellectual Property Rights*, WT/DS362, Australian Responses to Questions from the Panel, 5 May 2008.

WTO, *China – Measures Affecting the Protection and Enforcement of Intellectual Property Rights,* WT/DS362/R, Report of the Panel, 26 January 2009.

WTO, *Japan – Measures Affecting Agricultural Products,* WT/DS76/R, expert testimony.

WTO, *Canada – Patent Protection of Pharmaceutical Products*, WT/DS114/R, 17 March 2000.

WTO, Accessions, Protocols of Accession for new members since 1995, including commitments in goods and services, available at http://www.wto.org/english/thewto_e/acc_e/completeacc_e.htm, last visited on 31 December 2008:

- Report of the Working Party on the Accession of Ecuador, 14 July 1995, WT/L/77.
- Report of the Working Party on the Accession of Mongolia, 27 June 1996, WT/ACC/MNG/9.
- Report of the Working Party on the Accession of Bulgaria, 20 September 1996, WT/ACC/BGR/5.
- Report of the Working Party on the Accession of Panama, 20 September 1996, WT/ACC/PAN/19.
- Report of the Working Party on the Accession of Kyrgyz Republic, 31 July 1998, WT/ACC/KGZ/26.
- Report of the Working Party on the Accession of Latvia to the World Trade Organization, 30 September 1998, WT/ACC/LVA/32.
- Report of the Working Party on the Accession of Estonia to the World Trade Organization, 9 April 1999, WT/ACC/EST/28.
- Report of the Working Party on the Accession of Georgia to the World Trade Organization , 31 August 1999, WT/ACC/GEO/31.
- Report of the Working Party on the Accession of Jordan to the World Trade Organization, 3 December 1999, WT/ACC/JOR/33 (also reproduced under number WT/MIN(99)/9).
- Report of the Working Party on the Accession of Croatia to the World Trade Organization, 29 June 2000, WT/ACC/HRV/59.
- Report of the Working Party on the Accession of Albania to the World Trade Organization, 13 July 2000, WT/ACC/ALB/51.
- Report of the Working Party on the Accession of Oman to the World Trade Organization, 28 September 2000, WT/ACC/OMN/26.
- Report of the Working Party on the Accession of Lithuania to the World Trade Organization, 7 November 2000, WT/ACC/LTU/52.
- Report of the Working Party on the Accession of Moldova, 11 January 2001, WT/ACC/MOL/37.
- Report of the Working Party on the Accession of China to the World Trade Organization, 1 October 2001, WT/ACC/CHN/49.
- Report of the Working Party on the Accession of the Separate Customs Territory of Taiwan, Penghu, Kinmen and Matsu (Chinese Taipei), 5 October 2001, WT/ACC/TPKM/18.
- Report of the Working Party on the Accession of the Former Yugoslav Republic of Macedonia, 26 September 2002, WT/ACC/807/27.
- Report of the Working Party on the Accession of Armenia to the World Trade Organization, 26 November 2002, WT/ACC/ARM/23.
- Report of the Working Party on the Accession of Cambodia to the World Trade Organization, 15 August 2003, WT/ACC/KHM/21.

- Report of the Working Party on the Accession of the Kingdom of Nepal to the World Trade Organization, 28 August 2003, WT/ACC/NPL/16.
- Report of the Working Party on the Accession of the Kingdom of Saudi Arabia to the World Trade Organization, 1 November 2005, WT/ACC/SAU/61.
- Report of the Working Party on the Accession of Tonga to the World Trade Organization, 2 December 2005, WT/ACC/TON/17 (also reproduced under document number WT/MIN(05)/4).
- Report of the Working Party on the Accession of Viet Nam, 27 October 2006, WT/ACC/VNM/48.
- Report of the Working Party on the Accession of Cape Verde to the World Trade Organization, 6 December 2007, WT/ACC/CPV/30.
- Report of the Working Party on the Accession of Ukraine to the World Trade Organization, 25 January 2008, WT/ACC/UKR/152.

WTO, Working Party on the Accession of the Russian Federation, Accession of the Russian Federation, List of Adopted and Pending Major Normative Legal Acts Related to the Process of Russia's Accession to the WTO, WT/ACC/RUS/55, 14 August 2007.

WTO, Draft Final Act Embodying the Results of the Uruguay Round of Multilateral Trade Negotiations, Revision, Trade-related Aspects of Intellectual Property Rights, Including Trade in Counterfeit Goods, MTN.TNC/W/35/Rev. 1, 3 December 1990.

WTO, Chairman's report to the Group of Negotiation on Goods, document MTN.GNG/NG11/W/76, of 23 July 1990.

WTO Legal Texts, available at http://www.wto.org/english/docs_e/legal_e/legal_e.htm, last visited on 31 December 2008:

- Marrakesh Declaration of 15 April 1994, Marrakesh, 15 April 1994.
- Final Act Embodying the Results of the Uruguay Round of Multilateral Trade Negotiations, Marrakesh, 15 April 1994.
- Agreement Establishing the World Trade Organization, Marrakesh, 15 April 1994:
  - Multilateral Agreements on Trade in Goods, Annex 1A.
    - General Agreement on Tariffs and Trade 1994.
    - Agreement on Agriculture.
  - General Agreement on Trade in Services and Annexes, Annex 1B.
  - Agreement on Trade-related Aspects of Intellectual Property Rights, Annex 1C.
  - Understanding on Rules and Procedures Governing the Settlement of Disputes, Annex 2.

WTO, Handbook on Accession to the WTO, available at http://www.wto.org/english/res_e/reser_e/handbook_acc_e.htm, last visited on 31 December 2008.

WTO, Extension of the Transition Period under Article 66.1 of the TRIPS Agreement for Least Developed Country Members for Certain Obligations with respect to Pharmaceutical Products', IP/C/25, 2002.

WTO, Extension of the Transition Period under Article 66.1 for Least-developed Country Members, Decision of the Council for TRIPS of 29 November 2005, IP/C/40.

WTO, Ministerial Conference of the WTO Declaration on the TRIPS Agreement and Public Health, WT/MIN(01)/DEC/2, 20 November 2001.

WTO, Doha Round of Trade negotiation, WT/MIN(01)/DEC/1, 14 November 2001.

WTO, Press release, PRESS/3, 31 January 1995.

5 The WTO dispute on trademarks and geographical indications: some implications for trade policy-making and negotiations

*David Vivas-Eugui and María Julia Oliva**

1. Introduction

The World Trade Organization (WTO) dispute on European Communities – Protection of Trademarks and Geographical Indications for Agricultural Products and Foodstuff (EC – GIs) has captured the attention of policy-makers, negotiators, academia and agricultural and food producers around the world. As a chapter in the long-standing conflict over the use and control of certain geographical names over agricultural and food stuff between European countries and what are termed the 'new world' countries (United States, Australia, Argentina, Chile, and South Africa, among others), both the backdrop and implications of the EC – GIs dispute extend far beyond the specific case. As a result, an analysis of the context of the case, the findings of the Panel, and the potential impact of the decision – far from an academic exercise – provide significant lessons for the ongoing implementation and negotiation of geographical indications (GIs) in the framework of the Agreement on Trade-related Aspects of Intellectual Property Rights (TRIPS Agreement).

In the EC – GIs case, the United States and Australia challenged some aspects of the EU regulation on GIs in force at that time (EC Council Regulation No. 2081/92 of 14 July 1992) as inconsistent with the provisions of the TRIPS Agreement and the General Agreement on Tariffs and Trade (GATT) of 1994. At stake more generally, however, were inherently different perspectives on the objectives and characteristics of distinctive signs, which had already led to a fragile compromise and a built-in agenda for negotiations on GIs in the context of the TRIPS Agreement. The EC – GIs case does not resolve the fusion between these different perspectives,

* The views expressed in this chapter are those of the authors and do not necessarily reflect those of ICTSD, the Union for Ethical BioTrade or any related institutions. The authors would like to thank Christophe Spennemann for his valuable comments and input.

but – by addressing issues such as national treatment with regard to GIs and the relationship between GIs and trademarks – it offers significant lessons. These lessons are particularly important for developing countries, who often find themselves in the middle of opposing views and strategies regarding the implementation of the relevant provisions of the TRIPS Agreement, as well as regarding the Doha Round negotiations on a multilateral register of GIs and on the extension of higher levels of protection to products other than wines and spirits.

The objective of this chapter is to analyse the main findings of the EC – GIs ruling and to identify some of the pertinent lessons for implementation of the TRIPS Agreement and for ongoing international and regional negotiations. For that purpose, this note will look at the legal and political situation that triggered the case, the main legal issues raised in the context of the case, and its implications for the implementation of TRIPS Agreement obligations on GIs and for the current negotiations in the WTO on a multilateral register for wines and spirits and on the so-called GIs extension.

2. The TRIPS Agreement: accommodating different approaches to GI protection

Identifiers of the geographical origin of goods have long been protected against commercial misuse.[1] The common law doctrine of passing off, based on protection against the tort of unfair competition, was used to protect merchants against deceptive geographic claims.[2] In US and UK law, for example, geographic origin has been protected by collective marks and certification marks.[3] In civil law jurisdictions, the appellation of origin, unfair competition law and consumer law were used to protect against false claims of geographic origin. Moreover, laws regulating international trade typically required importers to identify the geographic origin of goods to allow for the appropriate application of customs duties, quota regulations and so forth.[4]

---

1 See Document SCT/6/3 Rev, 2 April 2002. On Geographical Indications: Historical Background, Nature of Rights, Existing Systems for Protection and Obtaining Protection in Other Countries, Prepared by the Secretariat, WIPO Standing Committee on the law of Trademarks, Industrial Designs and Geographical Indications, SCT/8/4, 2 April 2002.

2 On the common law doctrine of passing off, see Cornish (1999), at chapter 16.

3 In the UK, for example, Stilton cheese and Harris Tweed are protected by certification trademarks. The Harris Tweed mark was first registered in 1909, and is now owned by the Harris Tweed Authority, which was established by a 1993 Act of Parliament.

4 See Resource Book on TRIPS and Development (2004).

At the multilateral level, however, it was only with the TRIPS Agreement that geographical indications[5] – as we understand this designation today – became a global issue. Several World Intellectual Property Organisation (WIPO) treaties[6] addressed geographical names, but the protection provided was limited. The TRIPS Agreement provided a definition of GIs and minimum levels of protection – an attempt to bring coherence to an unsettled area. Nevertheless, the TRIPS Agreement provides – in comparison with other categories of intellectual property – a limited degree of harmonization of GIs protection. Indeed, the TRIPS Agreement system for GI protection would still in some ways appear to be 'under construction'. This is, in large part, the result of the difficulties of balancing different interests and approaches in relation to the protection of geographical names.

The main features of the GI protection in the TRIPS Agreement[7] include:

- consideration of GIs as a distinct form of intellectual property (Article 1);
- an agreed definition of a GI (Article 21.1). They are defined in Article 22.1 as 'indications which identify a good as originating in the territory of a Member, or a region or locality in that territory, where a given quality, reputation or other characteristic of the good is essentially attributable to its geographical origin';
- a general level of protection for all GIs except those for wines and spirits (Article 22.2), which obligates WTO Members to provide interested parties with the legal means to prevent:
    - designation of a good that misleads the public as to the geographical origin (Article 22.2(a));[8] and
    - use of a GI that constitutes an act of unfair competition within

---

5 'Geographical indications (GIs) are defined in Article 22.1 TRIPS as: 'indications which identify a good as originating in the territory of a Member, or a region or locality in that territory, where a given quality, reputation or other characteristic of the good is essentially attributable to its geographical origin'.

6 Paris Convention (1889), Madrid Agreement (1891) and Lisbon Agreement (1958).

7 For a detailed analysis and explanation of potential interpretations of the TRIPS Agreement see Resource Book (2004).

8 See Article 22.2(a) TRIPS: '2. In respect of geographical indications, Members shall provide the legal means for interested parties to prevent: (a) the use of any means in the designation or presentation of a good that indicates or suggests that the good in question originates in a geographical area other than the true place of origin in a manner which misleads the public as to the geographical origin of the good'.

the meaning of Article 10bis of the Paris Convention for the Protection of Industrial Property (Article 22.2(b));

- a higher level of protection for wines and sprits by requiring WTO Members to provide legal means to prevent the use of a geographical indication identifying wines not originating in the place indicated by the geographical indication in question or identifying spirits for spirits not originating in the place indicated by the geographical indication in question, even where the consumer is not misled as to the true origin of the product (Article 23.1);
- specific exceptions for wines, such as homonymous names for wines and, grape varieties (Article 23.3);
- a built-in mandate to negotiate a register and notification system for wines and sprits (Article 23.4);
- a mandate to review the application of the GIs section (Article 24.2);
- a stand-still clause in relation to applicable levels of protection (Article 24.3);
- general exceptions, including previous use, trademarks previously applied in good faith, genericness, personal names, and lack of national protection (Articles 24.3 to 24.9).

Many of these provisions, including the higher level of protection granted to wines and spirits, the long and explicit list of exceptions, and the built-in mandate for further negotiations, reflect the difficulties faced by WTO Members in coming to terms with the different trade interests related to GIs and in agreeing to their protection in the context of the TRIPS Agreement. In fact, the incorporation of GIs in the TRIPS Agreement was one of the 'trade-offs' in the final package of the Uruguay Round. These trade-offs often exceeded the traditional realm of trade, involving such issues as the opening of markets for agricultural and industrial products against a deeper and wider set of the intellectual property categories under the GATT and more specifically the TRIPS Agreement.

The negotiations on the protection of GIs in the TRIPS Agreement were – and have remained since – quite intense and controversial. Two of the main reasons for a significant display of legal argument and political statements are:

- *Tradition and consumer perception* The recognition of and value placed on the use of geographical names as a sign of reputation and quality of a particular product differs significantly among WTO Members. In Europe, the protection of GIs is widely appreciated and well-established. Such protection has existed in internal trade practice and marketing of products for centuries, especially in the agricultural sector. The concept of 'terroir' (geographical origin – particularly with reference to the land and related environmental conditions[9]), as well as traditional practices and know-how relating to products of certain regions or localities, have been widely recognised and used. Outside Europe, however, while the protection of GIs exists with often similar features, it has never reached the same level of recognition and value.

- *Economic interests and production systems* The economic importance of GIs is also particularly significant in Europe. There are about 4800 GIs registered at the national level, of which more than 600 are protected at the European level.[10] These GIs reflect important economic interests. France's GIs, for example, generate about 19 billion euro per year and constitute the lifeline of 138 000 agricultural outfits. (France has 466 GIs for wines and spirits, which are worth 16 billion euro per year, and 127 other products). Similarly, Italy's GIs generate 12 billion euro per year (300 GIs for wines and spirits – which are worth 5 billion euro – and 120 GIs for other products), and give employment to more than 300 000 citizens. In Spain, 123 GI products generate some 3.5 billion euro of income.[11]

  There are some historical geographical names in other countries that have equally important economic value, such as Café Colombia or Antigua Guatemala, Thai silk, Darjeeling tea, Napa Valley wines and Habanos from Cuba. Their protection under a European-style GI system or through certification trademarks, though, is relatively recent. Moreover, their economic value is linked more to marketing strategies based on trademarks than on the use of GIs. As noted below, Café de Colombia is the first foreign GI that requested, and obtained, internal EU recognition.

  GIs are also correlated to a particular type of production systems, in which limited production, common standards and a restricted geographical scope are essential characteristics. Intensive and undifferentiated productions schemes (focusing on commodities), on the other hand, usually rely on trademarks for consumer awareness and product differentiation. Indeed, some agricultural exporters

---

[9] For a better understanding of the concept of 'terroir', see Rangnekar (2003), and Josling (2006).

[10] Of the total number of registered GIs, 4200 are for wines and spirits; 600 for other products.

[11] EU Commission (2003), Spain's wines and spirits are worth 2.8 billion euro and other products account for the remaining economic value.

relying on the trademark system consider GIs as a protectionist tool by which certain producers 'capture' the value of the reputation of the identifier, which is sometimes well known or widely used even outside the country of origin.

These different needs and approaches with respect to GIs are reflected in the varying legal systems applied for their protection. In Europe, the recognition of the linkages between origin, quality, and reputation has been incorporated into the law and transformed, by tradition and incremental legal reform, into a system that grants exclusive rights over geographical indications/appellations of origin in relation to products produced in a particular geographical area that fulfil requirements established by regulations and producers. GIs are, in this system, a mix of public and private rights that make them a very special category of intellectual property. GI regulations include legal definitions; filing, opposition, and declaration procedures; labelling requirements; exclusive rights in the market; and rules on the relationship with trademarks and systems of verification among others. Criteria established by producers include harmonised production methods in the form of standards, labelling schemes and internal systems of technical verification. Such structures are justified by the need to provide accurate product information to consumers, as well as to promote market differentiation of GI-protected products and rural development. The European Communities (EC) Regulation No. 2081/92 of 14 July 1992 (from now on, EC GI Regulation of 1992) is an example of legislation with such objectives and approach.

Other countries have not developed or needed such systems of protection for GIs. Trademarks, and more specifically certification and collective trademarks, have been used to provide what these countries consider is an equally adequate protection. As part of broader and widely recognized trademarks systems, these are private rights based on registration systems. Trademarks tend to identify the business and industrial origin of a good and protect their reputation in the market. They can also certify the origin (business or geographical) and quality of the product (such as physical aspects or materials), as well other features such as production methods.

The need to accommodate these different traditions, economic interests and legal approaches explains the low ambition of the TRIPS Agreement in terms of minimum standards for GIs protection. It also accounts for the unresolved issues left to implementation or further negotiation. These issues, in turn, provided fertile ground for the EC – GIs dispute, and continue to come up in ongoing international discussions on GI protection.

3. Tensions over the built-in agenda and implementation issues in the TRIPS Agreement: a fertile ground for disputes

As we can see from the previous section, important political and legal gaps remain in the TRIPS Agreement provisions on GI protection. These gaps relate to unsettled questions regarding the international protection of GIs on specific products, as well as to broader issues of a systemic nature. To some degree, the built-in agenda for negotiations[12] in the TRIPS Agreement aims to address existing gaps. The built-in agenda set several mandates for review or follow-up negotiations on the unfinished issues of the Uruguay Round. This agenda forms part of the Doha Round discussions and includes the negotiations on an international notification and registration system on GIs for wines and spirits – TRIPS Article 23.4 – and the general review of the GIs chapter (TRIPS Articles 24.1, 2 and 3).[13]

Differences over the status of the built-in agenda, as well as on the implementation following from GIs of the TRIPS Agreement, have generated a heated debate in the TRIPS Council. The debate is largely shaped by the positions of the main interested countries – the EC on one side and the United States and Australia on the other. The EC's main objective is to obtain international levels of GIs protection comparable to its domestic system, through multilateral, regional and bilateral negotiations.[14] Advancing the protection of European GIs is part of a strategy to maintain European market shares throughout the world, eventually in exchange for commitments to provide more market access and to reduce export and domestic subsidies for EU farmers.[15] In particular, EU negotiating objectives in ongoing discussions linked to the built-in agenda and other GI topics are primarily:

- the establishment of a multilateral register for GIs; and
- the extension of the protection currently available for GIs relating to wines and spirits to other agricultural products.

---

12 Unfinished business of the Uruguay Round subject to negotiations or reviews depending on the level of consensus surrounding the issue.

13 See EU Commission (2003).

14 See Vivas-Eugui and Spennemann (2008).

15 While the EU considers this strategy a shift from protectionism to competition ('compete internationally on quality rather than quantity') (see EU Commission, 2003), others regard this as just another form of protectionism (see S. Laing, 'EU on GIs: Free Trade or Protectionism?', Trade Law Centre for Southern Africa (tralac) Trade Briefs 2003, available at: <http://www.tralac.org/scripts/content.php?id=1999>.

On the other hand, the United States and Australia, among others, have been reluctant to increase the level of GI protection at the multilateral level. Their careful engagement in discussions on the built-in agenda is geared towards avoiding any new commitments on the matter. In a statement related to these discussions, the US trade representative (at the time, Robert Zoellick) indicated: 'For GIs other than wines and spirits, the Doha mandate does not call for negotiations. We believe the current system works well, and we share the concerns of many in the developing world that we don't need to burden everyone with a large and costly new framework, as some have suggested. We need to make sure that we maintain the right balance – protecting against unauthorized use of geographic terms, without upsetting the current efficient and non-burdensome system.'[16] From the US perspective, the current TRIPS Agreement obligations in regards to GIs are sufficient, so that priority should be placed, instead, on Members meeting current obligations.[17]

The interests of developing countries in the polarity between implementing existing obligations on GIs and negotiating new ones, as in many other areas of intellectual property, is less clear. There are many products that could potentially benefit from GI protection, including tea, coffee, cocoa, vanilla, rice, oils and other food products, as well as handicrafts. In many cases, though, such products are still not protected at the national level, and formal production processes are still in the making. There might also be significant downsides from higher GI protection, such as the displacement of products that already have recognition and markets, especially dairy and meat products in former European colonies. Nevertheless, some developing countries have taken an active stand in the GI debate in the WTO. Several developing country Members, for example, including India, Thailand, Peru, Morocco and Sri Lanka, have supported the extension of the higher level of GI protection to products other than wines and spirits.[18]

The debate on GIs in the TRIPS Council is far from over. It seems, in fact, to be spreading to other negotiations, including those linked to bilateral and regional trade agreements. The EC – GIs case – the only case in WTO jurisprudence on the issue – is relevant not only as a clear reflection of the various views and interests in this debate, but also as a source of

16 United States Mission, Geneva (2002).

17 USTR (2005).

18 This issue is part of the so-called 'implementation issues' of the Doha Round and is thus considered by many as outside the possible single undertaking emerging from the negotiations of the Doha Round.

important lessons to feed into the continuing discussion of GI protection in the WTO.

4. Contours and main findings of EC – GIs case

The EC – GIs case dates back to 1999, when the United States first requested consultations with the EC regarding the protection of trademarks and GIs for agricultural products and foodstuffs.[19] The United States claimed the EC Regulation 2081/92 did not provide national treatment – a key WTO discipline – with respect to GIs, discriminating against foreign products and producers. The United States also argued that the EC regulation did not provide sufficient protection to pre-existing trademarks that are similar or identical to a GI, as required by the TRIPS Agreement.

The issues in the EC – GIs case must be understood in the context of the continuing tensions with respect to the protection of GIs between the United States, as well as other 'New World' countries, and the European Union. Indeed, the case has been described as a 'more aggressive step' in the broader international conflict over GIs.[20] Nevertheless, the US claims mentioned above – which would become the core of the case – have specific legal relevance. The lack of compliance with the national treatment discipline, for instance, is seen by some WTO Members as a way of compelling other countries to adopt an 'EC-style' GIs system in order to achieve protection.[21] Similarly, by limiting the protection of trademarks in favour of that of GIs, the EC regulation was also undermining the trademark-based system of protection, which the United States and other countries that have adopted it consider grants access to GI protection on a non-discriminatory basis and in a manner that fully protects the rights of trademark owners.[22]

In 2003, after additional consultations requested by the United States failed,[23] as did consultations taking place at the request of Australia, the matter of the WTO consistency of the EC regulation on GIs was submitted to a panel. A range of countries reserved their rights as third parties

---

[19] IP/D/19, WT/DS174/1.

[20] Handler (2006).

[21] USTR, Dispute Settlement Update, 24 October 2008. Australian Trade Minister Mark Vaile stated that 'The key concern we had with the EU's rules was that they required Australia to protect all EU GIs before any Australian GIs could be protected within the EU'.

[22] USTR (2005).

[23] The request for additional consultations did not replace but rather supplemented the 1999 request.

to the proceeding, highlighting the wide-ranging impacts the issue was deemed to have.[24] The panel issued its reports in March 2005 – agreeing to separate its analysis and findings in the two cases, given that Australia and the United States had made similar but not identical claims. The panel reports found that the EC regulation on GIs, EC Regulation 2081/92, was inconsistent with the EC's national treatment obligations under the TRIPS Agreement and the GATT 1994. The panel nevertheless rejected an infringement of the obligation to protect trademarks under TRIPS Agreement. Since the panel report, a new EC regulation has come into force in which the EC claims to have complied with all the recommendations and rulings of the EC – GIs case.[25] Australia and the United States disagreed and have continued to review the implementation of the EC – GIs system.

4.1 National treatment

Findings under the TRIPS Agreement

The national treatment obligation in the TRIPS Agreement requires each WTO Member to accord to nationals of other Members treatment no less favourable than it accords to its own nationals with regard to the protection of intellectual property.[26] In the EC – GIs case, the United States and Australia claimed that EC Regulation 2081/92 violated this obligation by treating foreign nationals less favourably in everything from the availability of GI protection to the procedures of application, objection and inspection in relation to GIs.

It was not disputed that the EC Regulation 2081/92 established a separate set of procedures for the protection of agricultural products or foodstuffs from a country outside the European Union.[27] These provisions included several conditions linked to the availability of protection – such as requiring inspection and objection arrangements equivalent to those in the EU system and EU-style GI protection for EU products. They also imposed requirements specific for foreign GIs in the application, objection and inspection procedures.

The EC argued that a specific set of conditions did not per se mean less

---

24 Argentina, Brazil, Canada, China, Colombia, Guatemala, India, Mexico, New Zealand, Norway, Chinese Taipei and Turkey reserved their third-party rights, as well as the two complainants in each other's case.

25 EC regulation 510/2006.

26 Article 3.1 of the TRIPS Agreement.

27 There was a question, however, as to whether the set of procedures for foreign GIs applied to other WTO Members. The Panel found that it did.

favourable treatment.[28] The claimants, however, considered that national treatment allowed no such conditions, as it required WTO Members to protect the intellectual property of other Members' nationals regardless of how those other Members treat their own nationals. Moreover, they noted that 'there is a wide variety of mechanisms used to implement the GI obligations' and that a particular method of implementation could not be required as a condition for protecting the GI rights of other Members' nationals.[29] Article 1.1 of the TRIPS Agreement, which says Members are free to determine the method of implementation, was thought to underscore this point.

The Panel examined the parties' arguments under the standard established by WTO jurisprudence, which stated that treatment no less favourable called for 'effective equality of opportunities' – in this case with regard to the protection of intellectual property. As a result, the Panel noted it was not sufficient to prove that the EC Regulation contained different conditions for foreign GIs or even that those conditions are unfavourable – it is necessary to demonstrate that the conditions modify the effective equality of opportunities. Given that the EC Regulation provided no protection for foreign GIs unless third countries met the established conditions, the panel did find that the equivalence (requirement that the government of foreign GIs' owners provides a domestic GI system of protection equivalent to the EU system) and reciprocity (requirement imposed on a country seeking registration in the EU to offer similar guaranties regarding the examination/screening of applications for the registration as those carried out by EU authorities) conditions modified the effective equality of opportunities with respect to the availability of GI protection. The provision was found to grant less favourable treatment to foreign GIs and thus to be inconsistent with the national treatment obligations of the TRIPS Agreement.

The Panel also found that conditions for third country producers with respect to the EU procedures for application for GI registration, the procedures for objection to such registration and the establishment of inspection structures for monitoring the quality of GI-protected goods constituted undue 'extra hurdles'. EC Regulation 2081/92, for example, required applications for the registration of a foreign GI to be accompanied by a description of the inspection procedures in place, which were to be equivalent to those in the EU. The United States argued that while

---

[28] The EC noted, moreover, that none of the conditions to obtain protection of a foreign GI in Europe depended on the nationality of the persons requesting such protection, but the Panel found that GIs inherently linked persons, the territory of a Member and the availability of protection.

[29] EC – GIs, WT/DS/174/R, para. 7.104.

EC Member States have an obligation to establish such procedures – so that EC nationals automatically have a qualifying inspection structure – other WTO Members do not. Moreover, even if inspection structures exist, other countries would not be in a position to assess whether these structures are indeed equivalent to those in the EU. All of these procedures were thus found to violate the national treatment obligation in the TRIPS Agreement.

Findings under the GATT 1994

Perhaps even more significantly, several of the EU procedures were also found to violate the national treatment obligation under the General Agreement on Trade and Tariffs (GATT) 1994. Under WTO rules, any particular measure may be challenged and be found inconsistent in relation to provisions of various WTO agreements. Nevertheless, the link between the TRIPS Agreement and other WTO agreements has always been complex, which is why the finding that intellectual property, and more specifically GI regulations, can affect the sale, offering for sale, distribution or use of products is noteworthy.

In the EC – GIs case, the Panel found that the EC regulation accorded less favourable treatment to imported products not only in a manner inconsistent with the TRIPS Agreement, but also in violation of the national treatment obligation as imposed by Article III:4 of the General Agreement on Trade and Tariffs (GATT) 1994. Such was the finding in respect of three aspects of the EC regulation: the availability of protection, the application procedures and inspection procedures. The Panel found equivalence and reciprocity requirements to be extra hurdles in obtaining the advantage of registration. It also indicated that failure to transmit applications by governments and government participation in inspection structures, while required for GIs originated in the EU, would lead to the failure of products from third countries to obtain benefits set in the regulation.

The Panel found that the GATT 1994 was applicable to the EU regulation insofar as it established requirements concerning the use of certain names in the presentation for sale of agricultural products and foodstuffs. It was therefore considered a regulation affecting the internal sale and offering for sale of products within the meaning of Article III:4 of GATT 1994. Indeed, the regulation on the use of geographical names ultimately affects the provision of certain market advantages, such as protection against unfair competition as well as other legal benefits (for example, protection against genericness). In that sense, the EU regulation allows the removal from sale of products that bear an indication falling within a protected GI, which is a substantive advantage in the competition between relevant products. The Panel noted: 'This is not altered by the fact that the Regulation is also an intellectual property measure covered by the TRIPS Agreement since GATT 1994 and the TRIPS Agreement apply cumulatively'.[30]

4.2 Protection of pre-existing trademarks

Another central aspect of the EC – GIs case was the challenge to the provisions of the EC Regulation 2081/92 allowing the coexistence of GIs with pre-existing trademarks. While the EC system required the refusal of a trademark where its use would infringe the rights of an already registered GI, a prior trademark might not impede the registration of a GI. The complainants argued that such an approach violated Article 16.1 of the TRIPS Agreement, which grants the owner of a registered trademark the right to prevent all third parties from using identical or similar signs – including GIs – if such use would result in a likelihood of confusion. The EC countered that, since the registration of a GI would not be possible 'where, in light of a trademark's reputation and renown and the length of time it has been used, registration is liable to mislead the consumer as to the true identity of the product',[31] there were no inconsistencies with the TRIPS Agreement.

The Panel found the EC Regulation did violate Article 16.1 of the TRIPS Agreement. Article 14(3) of the EC Regulation, quoted above, was limited to a subset of trademarks – it excluded, at a minimum, trademarks with no reputation, renown or use – and applied in a narrower set of circumstances than the trademark owner's right to prevent use that would result in a likelihood of confusion. Moreover, the Panel considered there was no evidence to show that it would be possible to identify, at the time of the proposed GI registration, all the potential uses of the proposed GI that could subsequently result in a likelihood of confusion.

The EC argued that Article 24.5 of the TRIPS Agreement, which states that the validity or right to use a prior, good-faith trademark cannot be denied on the basis of it being identical with, or similar to, a geographical indication, implied that other limitations on the trademark owner's rights – such as preventing confusing uses – were in fact acceptable. The Panel, however, considered it inappropriate to read Article 24.5 to imply *either* the right to prevent confusing uses – which would mean priority for the trademarks – or the limitation on such right – which would mean the coexistence of trademarks and GIs. The Panel noted that Article 24.5

30 IP/D/19, WT/DS174/1, at para. 7.227.
31 Article 14(3), EC Regulation 2081/92.

established an exception to GIs, and did not in fact address the potential conflict between different private parties wishing to use an individual sign as a trademark and as a GI. As a result, the Panel found it inapplicable in the EC – GIs case.

The Panel did find, however, that the EC provision on the coexistence of GIs and pre-existing trademarks was justified by Article 17 of the TRIPS Agreement. Article 17 states that WTO Members may provide 'limited exceptions to the rights conferred by a trademark', as long as such exceptions take account of the 'legitimate interests of the owner of the trademark and of third parties'. The Panel found that the EC Regulation was indeed a narrow exception that permitted only a small diminution of rights. The Panel noted, for instance, that the Regulation curtails the trademark owner's right to prevent the use of the trademark only in respect of certain goods, third parties and signs. Similarly, the Panel found that the exception would likely have little negative impact on the legitimate interests of trademark owners or third parties. The EC had also stated that the balancing of interests in Article 17 required taking account of the fact that trademarks are arbitrary and much easier to create than GIs, but the Panel did not refer back to this argument.

5. The implementation of the Panel findings: the new EU regulation of 2006

In reaction to the Panel decision, the EU on 20 March 2006 adopted Regulation 510/2006 on the Protection of Geographical Indications and Designations of Origin for Agricultural Products and Foodstuffs,[32] replacing EC Regulation 2081/92. Later the EU reported to the Dispute Settlement Body (DSB) in early 2006 that they had fully implemented the DSB's recommendations and rulings by adopting a new regulation which entered into force on 31 March 2006.

As far as GI protection in the EU for third country producers is concerned, the new regulation differs from the 1992 regulation in various aspects, in particular:

Availability of GI protection The new regulation no longer differentiates between EU-based producers and producers based in third countries (see Article 5.9 of Regulation 510/2006). Applications by third country producers have to contain the same information as those by EU-based

---

[32] Official Journal of the European Union L 93/12 of 31 March 2006 (available at <http://europa.eu.int/eur-lex/lex/LexUriServ/site/en/oj/2006/l_093/l_09320060331en00120025.pdf>).

producers, plus a proof that the respective name already enjoys protection in its country of origin (Article 5.9). There is no longer any requirement of a European Commission approval of third country GI protection being equivalent to that in the EU.

Application and objection procedures The new regulation does not require third country authorities to participate in these procedures. Instead, third country producers may send their application directly to the EC Commission (Article 5.9). In such a case, they will have to provide standard requirements, such as fulfilment of the definition, presentation of specifications and proof of the linkages between the product and the geographical environment/origin, plus evidence that the name in question is protected in the country of origin. The applicant may also lodge directly with the Commission their objection to GI registrations. The commission scrutinises all applications directly.

Verification of compliance In relation to GI originating in third countries, the verification of compliance with technical specifications shall be done by public authorities designated by the third country or product certification bodies (Article 11.2 of the regulation).

Inspection structures As opposed to Regulation 2081/92, Regulation 510/2006 does not make the availability of GI protection dependent on the existence, in the respective third country, of inspection bodies.[33] Instead, the new legislation requires the existence of such inspection structures for the marketing in the EU of a GI-protected product, both for EU products and third country products. The Panel had ruled that it was a national treatment violation to make the availability of GI protection dependent on the government participation in inspection bodies in the country of origin of the respective products. As EU Member States are obligated under EU law to establish such inspection bodies, but third countries are not, third country producers might not be able to meet this requirement for GI registration (that is, if their government refuses the establishment of inspection bodies). Under the new legislation, third country producers still face the problem that their domestic authorities might not be willing

---

33 Such bodies monitor the compliance of a given product with a particular product specification. The product specification usually includes the name and a description of the product for which protection is sought, the definition of the relevant geographical area, evidence of the product's origin in that area, as well as details concerning, inter alia, the link between the geographical area and certain characteristics of the product. See Article 4 of EU Regulation 510/2006.

to establish the inspection structures required. This will, however, not affect the availability, acquisition, scope, maintenance and enforcement of GIs, as required for a national treatment violation under Article 3, TRIPS Agreement. Third country producers will be able to have their GIs registered and enforced in the EU. What they might not be able to do is actually to put the protected products on the EU market. The question arises whether this would affect the 'use' of intellectual property as required for a national treatment violation under the footnote to Article 3, TRIPS Agreement. The use of the intellectual property (in this case, third country GIs) needs to be distinguished from the use of the protected products as such. Like other IPRs, GIs are negative rights, excluding others from using the protected indications on their products. This right comes into existence upon registration of the GI, irrespective of whether any inspection structures are in place in the third country. On the other hand, the Commission, if it takes the view that compliance of a protected product with a specification is no longer ensured, must initiate the cancellation of the GI (Article 12.1 of Regulation 510/2006).

Australia and the United States have not directly complained about the new EU legislation, but have indicated to the DSB that they will closely monitor its implementation.

6. Some lessons for policy-making and international negotiations

As mentioned, the impact of the EC – GIs case extends beyond the new European regulation on the protection of GIs and designations of origin. The arguments of the parties and findings of the Panel in the case touched upon key issues for the implementation and further negotiation of commitments related to GIs under the TRIPS Agreement and in other bilateral, regional and multilateral fora. In particular, the EC – GIs case, insofar as it addressed the WTO consistency of some strategies to promote an 'EC-style' GIs system, is relevant to ongoing international discussions. The following conclusions could be drawn from the EC – GIs case, and should be considered by policy makers currently considering the protection of GIs:

> *The panel findings facilitate the registration of foreign GIs in Europe and can be understood as safeguarding WTO Members' flexibility in implementing GI protection.*

The findings of the panel have improved the opportunities for protection of non-EU GIs names in the EU internal market. The new EU regulation (Regulation 510/2006) resolves the problems of availability, application and objection procedures in GI registration and sets clearer rules in relation to verification and inspection procedures. In 2007, the first foreign GI – Café de Colombia – was added to the European register of protected GIs. While encouraging, Café de Colombia remains an isolated and quite unique case. Café de Colombia represents more than 566000 producers and is extremely well organized. It has outstanding marketing and branding strategies. To what extent the new registration process will be suitable and economically affordable for other newcomers, especially for less economically significant products, remains to be seen.

The wider implications of these findings, however, derive from the rejection of the notions of equivalence and reciprocity imposed by the challenged EU regulation. These requirements were considered by many as a legal attempt by the EU to impose their standards of GI protection of foodstuff throughout the world.[34] The Panel found that they granted less favourable treatment to foreign GIs and were inconsistent with WTO rules.

The finding of applicability of all WTO Agreements for goods under IP protection raises new questions.

As mentioned above, the Panel found that intellectual property regulations – and more especially GI regulations – can affect the sale, offering for sale, distribution or use of the imported products using a GI name.[35] This implies that intellectual property regulations must comply not only with TRIPS Agreement provisions, but also with GATT principles such as national treatment.

Now that it is clear that intellectual property regulations can affect internal trade, it would be interesting to explore how they can also affect the obligations for the elimination of quantitative restrictions in cross-border trade. Questions arise in relation to parallel imports under trademark, copyrights and patent provisions. Can the choice of the exhaustion regime and requirements to obtain the consent of the title holder when importing goods be considered a quantitative restriction exercised by a private party in light of intellectual property regulations? Arguments can be made for both the positive or negative answer. Nevertheless, the fact that one regulation might fulfil the requirements of the TRIPS Agreement and not those of the GATT – and vice versa – may generate provocative interpretations. The different nature of trade rules facilitating flows of goods and

---

34 Handler (2006).

35 See EC – GIs, WT/DS/174/R, para. 7.219 and para. 7.231.

services versus exclusive rights generated by intellectual property in terms of imports and exports constitutes fertile ground for future debate.

The panel provided some additional but limited guidance on the GI–trademark relationship: the coexistence of GIs and pre-existing trademarks.

The Panel provided only limited guidance on the relationship between GIs and prior trademarks. The legal analysis in the panel report focuses on a general piece of legislation (that is, the EU regulation), rather than on a specific case of one particular GI and one particular trademark. The reason why the EU regulation was saved under Article 17 was that it did not impose the coexistence of GIs and prior trademarks in general, but conceded trademark priority in at least some cases. It has been observed that the analysis might come to a different result when considering one particular GI affecting the exclusive rights under a particular, prior trademark: would this still be considered a 'limited' exception in terms of Article 17 of the TRIPS Agreement?

The decision does provide guidance on some complex issues in the TRIPS Agreement, such as:

- In general, trademark holders have the right under Article 16 of the TRIPS Agreement to prevent the use of similar, subsequent GIs (subject to the further requirements in this article);
- By expressly considering the trademark exception in the TRIPS Agreement as less restrictive than its counterparts on patents and copyright, the Panel decision complements WTO jurisprudence on patent[36] and copyright exceptions.[37]

A less polluted environment for negotiations was encouraged in the WTO.

Many observers[38] consider the genesis of the dispute to be the current negotiations in the TRIPS Council on a multilateral register for wines and

---

[36] See Canada – Patent Protection of Pharmaceutical Products, WT/DS114/R of 17 March 2000.

[37] See United States – Section 110(5) of the US Copyright Act, WT/DS160/R of 15 June 2000.

[38] Several authors, including Handler (2006), Charlier and Ngo (2006) and Cortes (2004). See Bibliography below.

spirits, as well as proposals for extending the higher level of GI protection to other products. While not directly addressing – much less solving – the differences between the EU and new world countries, including the complainants, on these issues, the Panel in the EC – GIs case did reduce political tensions. It was able to point out the WTO inconsistencies of the EU legislation while at the same time safeguarding some key EU political positions, such as the need for verification procedures and inspection structures and for provisions allowing the coexistence of GIs with pre-existing trademarks. Indeed, after the release of the panel report, claims of victory were made by all sides.

As a result, the Panel has, at least in the short term, contributed to a less polluted environment for international discussions on GIs. It has allowed the countries involved in the debate to focus more on the negotiations and discussions and less on the application and implementation of EU regulations on GIs. Many third countries possessing GIs that could benefit from international protection feel more comfortable in directly negotiating trade-offs with the EU. For example, a July 2008 proposal[39] by more than 100 WTO Members reflected a historical compromise between proposals on GIs registration, disclosure of origin requirements and the extension of higher levels of GI protection. Nevertheless, it should be noted that new world countries remain opposed to such a deal, including the two complainants in the EC – GIs dispute. In this regard, the EC – GIs case was merely an incident in a broader and still unclear ongoing debate.

Bibliography

Bullbrook, Jane. 'Geographical Indications within the GATT'. *Journal of World Intellectual Property*, 7(4) 2004.

Charlier, Christophe and Ngo, Mai-Anh, 'An Analysis of the Dispute European Communities – Protection of Trademarks and Geographical Indications for Agricultural Products and Foodstuffs'. *IDEAS* (2006). Last accessed May 2006.

Cornish, W.R., *Intellectual Property: Patents, Copyright, Trade Marks and Allied Rights*. Thompson /Sweet and Maxwell, 1999.

Cortez, Marin, Jose Manuel, 'The WTO Trips Agreement: The Battle between the Old and the New World over the Protection of Geographical Indications'. *Journal of World Intellectual Property*, 7(3), 2004, 287–326.

European Commission, 'Why do Geographical Indications Matter to Us?' *External Trade*, 30 July 2003. Available at http://ec.europa.eu/trade/issues/sectoral/intell_property/argu_en.htm.

Handler, Michael, 'The WTO Geographical Indications Dispute'. *Modern Law Review*, 2006.

Josling, Tim. 'War on Terroir: Geographical Indications as a Transatlantic Trade Conflict'. *Journal of Agricultural Economics*, 57(3), June 2006.

---

[39] See WTO JOB(08)/80 of 17 July 2008.

Laing, Suzaan and Erasmus, Gerhard, 'Geographical indications: quo vadis?', *Journal of Law and Economics in International Trade*, 1(1), January, 2004.

Rangnekar, Dwijen. 'Geographical Indications – A Review of Proposals at the TRIPS Council: Extending Article 23 to Products other than Wines and Spirits', UNCTAD-ICTSD, Issue Paper No. 4, Geneva, 2003.

Resource Book on TRIPS and Development, *UNCTAD/ICTSD project on IPRs and Sustainable Development*, Cambridge, UK: Cambridge University Press; 2004. Available at http://www.cambridge.org/uk/catalogue/catalogue.asp?isbn=0521850444.

United States Mission, Geneva. 'US and Other Trade Partners Present Positions and Proposals to Prevent Unauthorized Use of Geographic Names'. Press Release, 20 September 2002. List of US Mission Press releases, last accessed in May 2009. See http://geneva.usmission.gov/press2002.html.

USTR 'United States Wins "Food Name" Case in WTO against EU; WTO says EU System Discriminates against US Producers and Products', Press release, 15 March 2005. Available at http://www.ustr.gov/Document_Library/Press_Releases/2005/March/United_States_Wins_Food_Name_Case_in_WTO_Against_EU.html. Last accessed May 2009.

Vivas-Eugui, David and Christoph Spennemann, 'The Evolving Regime for Geographical Indications in WTO and in Free Trade Agreements' in Carlos M. Correa and Abdulqawi A. Yusuf (eds), *Intellectual Property and International Trade: The Trips Agreement*, 2nd revised edition. Kluwer Law, 2008.

WIPO documents

SCT/6/3 Rev, 2 April 2002.
SCT/8/4, 2 April 2002.

WTO documents

IP/D/19.
WT/DS174/1.
JOB(08)/80, 17 July 2008.
WTO TN/IP/W/10/Rev.2, 24 July 2005.
WT/DS160/R, 15 June 2000.
WT/MIN(01)/DEC/1, 20 November 2001.
WT/DS114/R, 17 March 2000.

6 United States – Section 110(5) of the US Copyright Act: summary and analysis

Dalindyebo Shabalala

1. Introduction

That this was the first TRIPS Copyright case is reason enough to pay attention. It was however, also the first case to interpret the three step test as embodied in Article 13 of the Agreement on Trade-related Intellectual Property Rights (TRIPS), a test of the fundamental international bargain presented by the TRIPS Agreement. For copyright people, the additional significance lies in that it was the first interpretation by a tribunal of the three-step test that had its roots in the Berne Convention, which was added in the 1967 Stockholm revision. The case had the potential to transform the ways in which domestic legislators balanced public welfare against the interests of rights holders. Subsequent scholarship since the case, and the fact that there has not been a follow-up case suggest that, far from clarifying, or establishing a significant precedent, the Panel in the case did little to address the problems of clarity, while adding several more confusing elements. This chapter examines the case in the light of that subsequent scholarship, by providing an analysis of the case that focuses on the litigation choices of the parties, and the methodology and reasoning of the Panel in analyzing the test. It then discusses some of the reactions to the Panel decision and what the Panel decision may mean for developing country policies in this area. The key conclusion that can be drawn is that the various failures of the Panel, the specific context and subject matter of the case, as well as the lack of an appellate body statement of the test all suggest that the interpretation of the three-step test remains an open subject, on which state practice may still have a significant influence.

2. History of the case: who brought it and why?

Ostensibly, the complainant was the European Communities. On 4 February 1999, the European Communities communicated a request for consultations to the Dispute Settlement Body (DSB).[1] The complaint was targeted at recent amendments to US copyright law that had been made by the Fairness

[1] 'United States – Section 110(5) of US Copyright Act – Request for Consultations by the European Communities and their Member States', WT/

in Music Licensing Act (FMLA) of 1998.[2] The Act took exceptions that had occurred largely in US common law and codified them for certain retail, eating and drinking establishments so that they could play broadcasts to their patrons. Several kinds of copyright-related acts are implicated here, including public communication by loudspeaker, as well as public performance over the radio or otherwise. While this is not a legal definition of the targeted actions, the thinking behind the Act was to ensure that restaurants and bars could broadcast games and music over the radio, or play televisions for their patrons, and retail stores could play music in the background for their shoppers. Such actions raise questions of what consists of normal activity, including music or television being played in the background or as part of some broader activity. It raises the question of normal social activity and when it crosses the line into commercial activity, such as a sports bar enabling patrons to watch a hockey game on their big screen television. There is a fundamental question as to from whom copyright holders may legitimately expect to receive remuneration, and with whom such a balancing decision should rest: a representative legislature or a multilateral judicial process. It is also important that this issue is raised in the context of a dispute between two competing commercial public policy concerns and the interests of small business and establishment versus those of rights holders.

What was it exactly that the Fairness in Music Licensing Act (FMLA)[3] did? First of all, it amended the copyright law of the US to provide, legislatively, for particular exceptions to licensing practices that the Congress deemed inappropriate. It provided exceptions to the following rights:[4]

1. public performances of 'literary, musical, dramatic, and choreographic works, pantomimes, and motion pictures and other audiovisual works';[5]

DS160/1 (4 February 1999). Available at: http://www.wto.org/english/tratop_e/dispu_e/cases_e/ds160_e.htm.

[2] 'United States – Section 110(5) of US Copyright Act – Request for Consultations by the European Communities and their Member States', WT/DS160/1, p. 1 (4 February 1999). Available at: http://www.wto.org/english/tratop_e/dispu_e/cases_e/ds160_e.htm.

[3] Fairness in Music Licensing Act of 27 October 1998, Pub. L. 105th-298, 112 Stat. 2830, 105th Cong., 2nd Session (1998).

[4] This is a less detailed representation. For the full subject matter of the rights, see World Trade Organization (2000), 'United States – Section 110(5) of US Copyright Act – Report of the Panel', WT/DS160/R, paragraph 2.1, available at http://www.wto.org/english/tratop_e/dispu_e/cases_e/ds160_e.htm (accessed 26 May 2009).

[5] Section 106 of the 1976 Copyright Act.

2. public display of the work.

The definition of 'public performance' and 'public display' are fundamental to the case, and conveniently, Section 101 of the US Copyright Act defines what is encompassed by these phrases.[6] Most relevant to the case is that a 'performance' includes 'rendering' by means of a 'device' and to 'perform' or 'display' it 'publicly means to any place open to the public or a large number of people outside family or social circle'. It also includes transmission or communication in public or to the public.

What the FMLA did, therefore, was to take certain public performances, displays and communications and exempt them from being subject to payment for authorized permission. The exception is quite specific about who the beneficiaries of the exceptions should be, the extent to which those exceptions should be exercised and through what means and the purposes for which the exceptions should be exercised.

Section 110(5) states:

> § 110. Limitations on exclusive rights: Exemption of certain performances and displays
> Notwithstanding the provisions of section 106, the following are not infringements of copyright:
> . . .
> (5)(A) except as provided in subparagraph (B), communication of a transmission embodying a performance or display of a work by the public reception of the transmission on a single receiving apparatus of a kind commonly used in private homes, unless –
>
> (A) a direct charge is made to see or hear the transmission; or
> (B) the transmission thus received is further transmitted to the public;
>
> (B) communication by an establishment of a transmission or retransmission embodying a performance or display of a nondramatic musical work intended to be received by the general public, originated by a radio or television broadcast station licensed as such by the Federal Communications Commission, or, if an audiovisual transmission, by a cable system or satellite carrier, if –
>
> (i) in the case of an establishment other than a food service or drinking establishment, either the establishment in which the communication occurs has less than 2,000 gross square feet of space (excluding space used for customer parking and for no other purpose), or the establishment in which the

---

6 See World Trade Organization (2000), 'United States – Section 110(5) of US Copyright Act – Report of the Panel', WT/DS160/R, para. 2.1, available at http://www.wto.org/english/tratop_e/dispu_e/cases_e/ds160_e.htm (accessed 26 May 2009).

communication occurs has 2,000 or more gross square feet of space (excluding space used for customer parking and for no other purpose) and –

(I) if the performance is by audio means only, the performance is communicated by means of a total of not more than 6 loudspeakers, of which not more than 4 loudspeakers are located in any 1 room or adjoining outdoor space; or
(II) if the performance or display is by audiovisual means, any visual portion of the performance or display is communicated by means of a total of not more than 4 audiovisual devices, of which not more than 1 audiovisual device is located in any 1 room, and no such audiovisual device has a diagonal screen size greater than 55 inches, and any audio portion of the performance or display is communicated by means of a total of not more than 6 loudspeakers, of which not more than 4 loudspeakers are located in any 1 room or adjoining outdoor space;

(ii) in the case of a food service or drinking establishment, either the establishment in which the communication occurs has less than 3,750 gross square feet of space (excluding space used for customer parking and for no other purpose), or the establishment in which the communication occurs has 3,750 gross square feet of space or more (excluding space used for customer parking and for no other purpose) and –

(I) if the performance is by audio means only, the performance is communicated by means of a total of not more than 6 loudspeakers, of which not more than 4 loudspeakers are located in any 1 room or adjoining outdoor space; or
(II) if the performance or display is by audiovisual means, any visual portion of the performance or display is communicated by means of a total of not more than 4 audiovisual devices, of which not more than one audiovisual device is located in any 1 room, and no such audiovisual device has a diagonal screen size greater than 55 inches, and any audio portion of the performance or display is communicated by means of a total of not more than 6 loudspeakers, of which not more than 4 loudspeakers are located in any 1 room or adjoining outdoor space;

(iii) no direct charge is made to see or hear the transmission or retransmission;
(iv) the transmission or retransmission is not further transmitted beyond the establishment where it is received; and
(v) the transmission or retransmission is licensed by the copyright owner of the work so publicly performed or displayed . . .

One common thread to note is that a prerequisite for use of the exceptions is that no direct charge is made for the performance, display or communication of the work. Thus no direct commercial competition with the rightsholder is envisaged.

In terms of scope, Section 5A is limited to public display or performance as received on a 'homestyle' apparatus such as a radio or television, hence the term 'homestyle' exception. This essentially covers such establishments as bars and restaurants, playing music on a small loudspeaker or playing television in a corner of a restaurant or bar or other establishment.

Part B is the more extensive part, with quite a few sub-clauses. It is thus both more specific but also covers more situations. There are clear attempts to impose limits by specifying the size of establishment that generally may be eligible, with somewhat more space allocated to eating and drinking establishments. If the establishment is larger than the prescribed size, there are also clear attempts to limit the number of devices on which such a public performance, display or communication can be shown or played. The overall impression is of a very narrowly crafted exception designed to benefit a relatively small and narrow interest group whose primary activity does not involve direct monetary benefit from these specific uses of the works. In characterizing this exception, the Panel chooses to call it the 'business' exception, which it views as a neutral descriptor but, from a normative point of view, suggests that the subjects of the exception may be less deserving of consideration because they are businesses.

Of the two parts of Section 110(5), part B is the newer, as part A comprises only a slight alteration of a pre-existing exception from 1976. Thus we have an exception that, in scope and conception, predates the inclusion of the Berne Convention in the TRIPS Agreement and one that was enacted afterwards.

There is also an important difference in the subject matter covered by parts A and B. From the wording and as agreed by the parties, part B only applies to non-dramatic musical works, that is, music not linked to a play, film or other dramatic work. Conversely, because of the wording of part A, all works except for non-dramatic musical works are covered in part A.[7] In combination, therefore, the broader exception limits itself to a much narrower subject matter, not applying to television shows and other audiovisual transmissions. The structure of the section almost requires the EU to therefore challenge both parts if it is to achieve its goal of ensuring remuneration for its companies, since the subject-matter scope of part A is so much broader.

The Panel, in framing its approach to the legislation, pointed to the

---

[7] 'First Written Submission of the European Communities and their Member States', at para. 31, available as Attachment 1.1 to World Trade Organization (2000), 'United States – Section 110(5) of US Copyright Act – Report of the Panel', WT/DS160/R, available at http://www.wto.org/english/tratop_e/dispu_e/cases_e/ds160_e.htm (accessed 26 May 2009).

rationale underlying the original homestyle exception as passed in 1976. It points to a House Report ('House Report') and the Conference report to note that the aim of the legislation was to exempt *de minimis* actions.[8] A House Report is produced by the House of Representatives of the US Congress to describe the legislative history and rationale for a particular bill. A Conference report is produced by the body that meets to reconcile the differing versions of the same legislation produced by the House of Representatives and the Senate.

US jurisprudence lends significant weight to such reports, although significant legal controversy remains as to their use, as some judicial schools of thought (as exemplified by Supreme Court Justice Antonin Scalia) argue that legislation should be read on its face and for plain meaning. In addition to such reports, the reported rationales and justifications of the sponsors of the legislation have great weight, as well as studies conducted by various stakeholders to support or oppose the legislation. US courts struggle in many cases to reconcile the multiple and sometimes conflicting rationales provided in such statements and reports. In addition, US courts struggle to distinguish between the strengths and weaknesses of various studies, their scientific and methodological validity and the limits of the conclusions that may be drawn from them. Such studies and expert testimony are the subject of significant jurisprudential controversy in the US, and experts from both sides, especially during court cases, are brought to bear. Understanding this, a Panel would do well to exercise caution, in the absence of consensus, in relying on data and studies provided by interested parties, at the least, ensuring that they are methodologically sound and that valid conclusions can be drawn from them.

In considering interest groups, while the case is characterized as an EU versus US case, there existed strong interest groups in the United States, in particular the collective management agencies responsible for collecting royalties and distributing a portion of the proceeds to music and audiovisual companies who would then distribute a portion to artists. However, there were also, of course, a significant number of interested European artists, in particular Irish musicians whose music is particularly popular in the many bars, taverns and other establishments in cities such as Boston where there are large populations of Irish descent. Such venues are popular live and recorded music venues. The initial complaint was

[8] See World Trade Organization (2000), 'United States – Section 110(5) of US Copyright Act – Report of the Panel', WT/DS160/R, para. 2.5, available at http://www.wto.org/english/tratop_e/dispu_e/cases_e/ds160_e.htm (accessed 26 May 2009).

therefore made by the Irish Music Rights Organization, calling on the EC to bring a case.[9]

3. The landscape leading up to the Panel

The EU's legal case in its request for consultations rested on the argument that such activities contravened Article 11bis(1), and Article 11(1), of the Berne Convention (amended by the Paris Act of 1971). Article 11 (1) states:

> (1) Authors of dramatic, dramatico-musical and musical works shall enjoy the exclusive right of authorizing:
>
> > (i) the public performance of their works, including such public performance by any means or process;
> > (ii) any communication to the public of the performance of their works.

Article 11bis (1) states:

> (1) Authors of literary and artistic works shall enjoy the exclusive right of authorizing:
>
> > (i) the broadcasting of their works or the communication thereof to the public by any other means of wireless diffusion of signs, sounds or images;
> > (ii) any communication to the public by wire or by rebroadcasting of the broadcast of the work, when this communication is made by an organization other than the original one;
> > (iii) the public communication by loudspeaker or any other analogous instrument transmitting, by signs, sounds or images, the broadcast of the work.

Thus, while trying to stay broad, the complaint was particularly targeted at activities covered by part (iii) of the Article.

However, Article 11bis also states:

> (2) It shall be a matter for legislation in the countries of the Union to determine the conditions under which the rights mentioned in the preceding paragraph may be exercised, but these conditions shall apply only in the countries where they have been prescribed. They shall not in any circumstances be prejudicial to the moral rights of the author, nor to his right to obtain equitable remuneration which, in the absence of agreement, shall be fixed by competent authority.
> (3) In the absence of any contrary stipulation, permission granted in accordance with paragraph (1) of this Article shall not imply permission to record, by

[9] Brennan, D.J. (2002), 'The Three-step Test Frenzy – Why the TRIPS Panel Decision Might be Considered Per Incuriam', *Intellectual Property Quarterly*, **2**, 6, available at http://ssrn.com/abstract=299543 (accessed 26 May 2009).

> means of instruments recording sounds or images, the work broadcast. It shall, however, be a matter for legislation in the countries of the Union to determine the regulations for ephemeral recordings made by a broadcasting organization by means of its own facilities and used for its own broadcasts. The preservation of these recordings in official archives may, on the ground of their exceptional documentary character, be authorized by such legislation.

Much like other parts of the Berne Convention, the rights on which the EU complaint is based are also hedged about with exceptions and limitations. As in paragraph 2, they explicitly recognize the necessity for some balancing of interests to be carried out at the national level. In citing the Berne Convention, the EU was therefore tapping into a long history of state practice and scholarship related to exceptions and limitations surrounding the Berne Convention, a history which was known and recognized at the time that the Berne Convention was incorporated into the TRIPS Agreement. A major element of the dispute would then revolve around the extent to which those exceptions were incorporated into the TRIPS Agreement, and whether the TRIPS Agreement[10] Article 13 should be applied to retroactively limit or alter the Berne Convention jurisprudence and whether new domestic constructions regarding Berne Convention rights should be subject to Article 13 of TRIPS or the Berne Convention.

The EU's request for consultation was soon joined by third-party requests to reserve their rights from Australia,[11] Switzerland,[12] and Canada.[13] Japan and Brazil also joined. Either because there was no belief that there would be an issue regarding the interpretation of Article 13, or because of the relationship between the TRIPS Agreement and the Berne Convention, no other developing countries besides Brazil expressed interest as third parties in the case. That lack of interest may also have lain in erroneous assumptions that standards or decisions in one case would not set precedents for other cases. While it is true that Panel and Appellate body decisions have no formal precedential value, it has turned out that the Appellate Body has actively pursued consistency from case to case, especially in setting criteria and guidelines for interpretation. Canada's request pointed to the use of Canadian works in the US, given the shared

---

[10] Article 13 states: 'Members shall confine limitations or exceptions to exclusive rights to certain special cases which do not conflict with a normal exploitation of the work and do not unreasonably prejudice the legitimate interests of the right holder'.

[11] WT/DS160/2.

[12] WT/DS160/4.

[13] WT/DS160/3.

border and language; Switzerland provided no justification. A Panel was established 26 May 1999,[14] suggesting that consultations were short-lived. In fact, only one set of formal consultations was held, on 2 March 1999.[15]

4. The written submissions and responses

4.1 The EU's first submission[16]

The EU's complaint challenged both exemptions in Section 110(5).

4.1.1 Factual basis

In describing their concerns about the homestyle exception, the EC complaint began by noting that the scope of device limitation, that is, 'a single receiving apparatus of a kind commonly used in private homes', has been continuously expanded by virtue of the advance of technology, such as portable radio players, MP3 players, computers and computer networks.[17] The EC also argued that there had been legal evolution of the exception such that it had been interpreted broadly despite what was initially narrow guidance from the legislative history.[18] In addition to inconsistency of application and extension of the original homestyle exception, the EC also pointed to the motivations for the legislation being lobbying by retail outlets and other businesses to ensure that the interpretation of the homestyle exception would include them or at least an exception would be carved out for them. The EC maintains that therefore the legislation essentially ratified the expanded interpretations of the homestyle exception.

The EU was particularly concerned by what it called the extension, in

---

[14] World Trade Organization, 'Summary US – Section 110(5) Copyright Act (DS160)', available at http://www.wto.org/english/tratop_e/dispu_e/cases_e/1pagesum_e/ds160sum_e.pdf (accessed 26 May 2009).

[15] World Trade Organization (2000), 'United States – Section 110(5) of US Copyright Act – Report of the Panel', WT/DS160/R, para. 1.2, available at http://www.wto.org/english/tratop_e/dispu_e/cases_e/ds160_e.htm (accessed 26 May 2009).

[16] Attachment 1.1 (p. 74) World Trade Organization (2000), 'United States – Section 110(5) of US Copyright Act – Report of the Panel', WT/DS160/R, para. 2.5, available at http://www.wto.org/english/tratop_e/dispu_e/cases_e/ds160_e.htm (accessed 26 May 2009).

[17] 'First Written Submission of the European Communities and their Member States', at para. 21 available as Attachment 1.1 to World Trade Organization (2000), 'United States – Section 110(5) of US Copyright Act – Report of the Panel', WT/DS160/R, available at http://www.wto.org/english/tratop_e/dispu_e/cases_e/ds160_e.htm (accessed 26 May 2009).

[18] *Id.* at paras 25, 26.

part B, and only in part B, of the exception to 'retransmission' rights. The right to retransmit is one of those related rights that lives in the penumbra around other related rights such as the right to authorize a transmission. Generally speaking, it involves situations where someone receives a 'communication' and uses a device to retransmit it to another device or to the public. The EU's particular concern was that the ability of computers to retransmit the performance or display meant that each individual computer receiving in an establishment could potentially retransmit to millions of other computers. The reality of that possibility and the potential application of the exceptions to such activities remains hypothetical and does not seem to have been in the original conception of the exemption. Why was this provision on retransmission included? One reason is that in a large establishment, it may be necessary to retransmit along wires or over wireless the original display or performance received on an instrument.

Another concern of the EU was the definition of the establishments to which the exceptions would apply.[19] In particular, they argued that using a store-by-store definition ignored the multiple uses by a single corporate entity embodied by the owners of multiple chain stores. The EU was appealing to a normative sense of fairness, rather than as to whether the exception should really be applied on a store-by-store basis when a large 'undeserving' corporation might be making a significant profit.

The EU dismisses the argument that since the exemptions require that there be no direct charge for listening, there is no royalty per se.[20] The EU's argument essentially asks us to believe that benefits accrue from the goods and products sold through a process of amortization. The goods and products would not otherwise have been sold in the absence of the public performance or display. However, we get no economic analysis of whether and how such benefits actually accrue.

In large part, the EU's original argument therefore rests on the idea that there are no 'meaningful' limits on the exceptions as they would cover retransmissions to new audiences and would cover what they believe to be a significant portion of US business.

To underpin its arguments with factual evidence, the EU cites Dun and Bradstreet reports on the number of businesses above a certain size that would qualify for the exemptions.[21] They cite this as the data that the Congressional Research Service used in making its calculations about exempted users in 1995.

---

19 *Id.* at para. 42.
20 *Id.* at para. 43.
21 *Id.* at para. 49.

4.1.2 Legal basis

The EU's key argument revolves around Article 9(1) of TRIPS, which incorporates the substantive articles of the Berne Convention, in this case specifically addressing Article 11bis(1) and Article 11(1).

The most complex and difficult basis for the case was the issue of 'minor exceptions' or 'minor reservation' in the Berne Convention and whether and how they were incorporated into the TRIPS regime. The US asserted in defence that Section 110(5) A and B were covered exceptions under the minor exceptions in the Berne Convention. They also argued that TRIPS Article 13 was the standard by which such exceptions should be judged. The EU, in its first submission, therefore argued that it did not have to make any further arguments on this issue but would respond to US arguments as to why the exceptions applied.

4.2 The US's first submission

4.2.1 The factual basis

The US first addresses the homestyle exception. The US's first argument rests on what the FMLA actually did. In looking at existing licensing practices, the US argued that the Act, especially the newer part B, only codified existing practices by licensing organizations who saw little or no benefit in collecting from the covered organization given the high transaction costs of doing so.[22]

The US submission focuses less on the scope of the rule and more on what the actual effect of the provision has been when challenged. The US argues that the homestyle exception has been very narrowly interpreted by courts and has been used sparingly.[23]

The US also points to the fact that since the homestyle exception no longer even covers non-dramatic musical works, it is even narrower than it has historically been, and now only covers subject matter for which no formal licensing mechanisms exist to begin with. Given that no such mechanism exists, the US argues there is no 'market' as such to be affected.[24]

What is interesting to note is that, tactically, the US seems to have decided to shift as much of the burden of the case to part B, having calculated that they had a strong case on part A. The fundamental factual conflict with respect to part A is whether or not courts have interpreted the provision much more broadly than initially intended and that the practice

---

22 *Id.* at para. 6.
23 *Id.* at para. 7.
24 *Id.* at para. 9.

over more than two decades had shifted so much that part A codified that new scope rather than the original scope.

With respect to part B, the US characterized it as a response to complaints about abuses, or more precisely 'shakedowns' from licensing bodies.[25] The practice of demanding royalty payments with a threat to sue had forced many establishments, especially small business owners running franchises of larger brands, to settle rather than run the risk of escalating legal bills.

On a key testimonial issue, that is, the testimony of the Registrar of Copyright before Congress as reported in the Conference and other reports of the legislation, the US contends that the EU cited comments not about the final legislation as it was passed, but on an original and much broader proposal put forward by business coalitions seeking an exception. This factual dispute is important as it has a direct bearing on the Panel's ability to examine and make factual findings and evaluations in given testimony in front of it.

The US also applies its codification argument to part B, as it notes that section B is almost identical to the negotiated exemptions in a 1995 voluntary agreement between a major US colleting licensing organization and a major small business owner group in the US, thus arguing that the act essentially codified the existing practice as viewed by the relevant US stakeholders.[26] The relevance of this argument goes to factual arguments about the effect on the market but does not, of course, necessarily represent the interests of foreign rightsholders.

Finally, the US submission takes particular exception to the EU assertion that either exemption would apply to transmission over the internet.[27] In the US, copies made in the process of internet transmission are covered by the reproduction right, and the US argues that the section only covers the performance right. The US argues that such rights would require separate permissions under US law and practice.

4.2.2 The Legal basis

The core of the US argument is its assertion of the application of Article 13 of the TRIPS Agreement. The US argues very clearly that the minor exceptions in the Berne Convention must be interpreted under TRIPS Article 13.[28] In particular, the US states that Article 13 is based on the language in Article 9(2) which states:

---

25 *Id.* at para. 10.
26 *Id.* at para. 13.
27 *Id.* at para. 15.
28 *Id.* at para. 18.

> It shall be a matter for legislation in the countries of the Union to permit the reproduction of such works in certain special cases, provided that such reproduction does not conflict with a normal exploitation of the work and does not unreasonably prejudice the legitimate interests of the author.

This standard applies to the reproduction right, the core right under the Berne Convention and therefore the most restrictive of the exceptions. The reliance on Article 13 therefore results in applying a strict reproduction right standard to the performance right, which is a related and subsidiary right.

The standard that actually applies under the minor exceptions doctrine is actually quite different from that enunciated in Article 9(2) of Berne and yet the US chooses to focus directly on how the standard in Article 13 should be articulated. Thus, the US argues that Article 13 should be read as a cumulative requirement that all three elements of Article 13 must be met to qualify for an exception and that failure of any of them invalidates the exception.[29] Thus the US divests itself of a potentially strong argument that the provisions could be interpreted as co-equal elements, or in a different sequence beginning with the third step first.

The US also argues that the provision should be read in line with the Vienna Convention on the Law of Treaties (VCLT), especially Article 31 stating that 'A treaty shall be interpreted in good faith in accordance with the ordinary meaning to be given to the terms of the treaty in their context and in the light of its object and purpose'.[30] In arguing for this, the US also therefore asks the Panel to ignore the long history and practice underlying Article 9(2) of Berne in favour of dictionary plain meanings. It seems reasonable to argue that since TRIPS Article 9(2) of Berne was the basis of TRIPS Article 13, then the negotiators were aware of the existing state practice and interpretations under the Berne Convention and would therefore interpret TRIPS Article 13 in light of that. Given the broad range of exceptions available at the time of the signing of these provisions of the Berne Convention and also the ensuing state practice, it may be that the concept of what is 'normal' under Article 13 would be interpreted in reference to that state practice rather than simple recourse to plain meaning. This may be especially true in those cases of treaties covering the same or similar subject matter. The US failure to raise this argument is a crucial part of the consequences of this case.

---

29 *Id.* at para. 19.

30 *India – Patent Protection for Pharmaceutical and Agricultural Chemical Products*, WT/DS50/AB/R, 18 AB Report, 18 December 1997 (citing Vienna Convention, done at Vienna, 23 May 1969, 1155 UNTS 221; 8 International Legal Materials 679 (1969)).

The rest of the US case argues that the provisions meet the criteria of TRIPS Article 13, in particular the three-step test, relying on a two-pronged approach. The first is to argue for the meaning of the standard and then to argue that under the facts of the case, Section 110(5) meets the standard. This allows the US to argue for a relatively narrow and strict interpretation of Article 13, while also defending its legislation specifically and some of the facts on which the EU has relied. Looking at the three steps, several areas are important to note.

Under 'certain special cases', the US argues for a standard that requires that the exception be clearly delineated rather than vague and open ended.[31] In support, the US only cites an article by an academic, discussing the drafting history of the TRIPS Agreement rather than any precedents from the Berne Convention practice. Factually, the US points to the specificity and clarity of the provisions and the clearly understood limits as meeting the requirement.

What is striking in this submission is the paucity of any substantial legal argument or factual dispute surrounding this portion of the argument.

Under 'does not conflict with normal exploitation', the US argues for a standard that must include permissible exceptions as part of what is 'normal'.[32] The US argues that the standard should be based on 'the ways in which an author might reasonably be expected to exploit his work in the normal course of events'.[33] This is language based on Ricketson's analysis of the meaning of the phrase under the Berne Convention, one of the few such references by the US. Thus the full range of potential exploitation must be viewed (looking at the whole bundle of copyright and related rights) and the particular provision examined on how much of that range of exploitation rights is affected. The implication is that if only a small element of the whole bundle of rights is affected, then this should not be seen as affecting normal exploitation. Factually, this means that an exception that only affects the secondary performance right and not the primary performance right is not a normal exploitation. Legally, however, the US is again making the argument for an essentially *de minimis* standard rather

---

[31] 'First Written Submission of the European Communities and their Member States', at para. 24, available as Attachment 1.1 to World Trade Organization (2000), 'United States – Section 110(5) of US Copyright Act – Report of the Panel', WT/DS160/R, available at http://www.wto.org/english/tratop_e/dispu_e/cases_e/ds160_e.htm (accessed 26 May 2009).

[32] *Id.* at para. 27.

[33] Ricketson, S. (1987), *The Berne Convention for the Protection of Literary and Artistic Works: 1886-1986,* 483, Kluwer. This language refers to the use of the phrase 'normal exploitation' in the context of Berne Article 9(2).

than for a broader standard. The US position is still based on the assumption that while exceptions are normatively part of normal exploitation, the rights holder still has a right to each and every potential royalty from exercising the right. It fails to make the normative argument that, under the exceptions doctrine, there are some markets from which a rights holder cannot expect to earn significant royalties due to public interest, equity and other considerations, not just quantitative or based on the capacity to collect royalties.[34]

The US also argues that 'normal' does not also cover those situations where the rights holder would not expect to have collected a fee, again citing Ricketson's work on Berne.[35] The US argues that this means that if a right is not 'capable' of being exploited in the relevant market that should not be included in the concept of normal exploitation. The US seems to elide any element of a normative element to the right other then noting that the existence of exceptions must be included.

With respect to 'unreasonable prejudice to the legitimate interests of the rights holder', the US argues that while the second step of the three-step test is about 'market displacement', that is, whether the exception substitutes for the rights holder in a relevant market, the third step is about the level of harm or losses in that market.[36] That harm, the US argues, must rise to the level of being unreasonable. In making its argument for 110(5), the US goes on to treat this as a purely economic test, one that would measure earnings against losses and look at how high some of those losses may be. Again, the US fails to reach for the stronger argument that 'legitimate' may have some normative content beyond the quantitative, and that there may even be circumstances where, legitimately, the entirety of the rights holders' earnings may be prejudiced if the public interest is sufficiently strong.

Thus, in applying the standard to Section 110(5), the US argues that part A has no real economic relevance now that it excludes non-dramatic musical works and codifies a practice whereby rightsholders had never had any significant income from the collection of such royalties in the US.

---

[34] See Hugenholtz, P.B. and R.G. Okediji (2008), 'Conceiving an International Instrument on Exceptions and Limitations to Copyright,' available at http://www.ivir.nl/publicaties/hugenholtz/finalreport2008.pdf (accessed 26 May 2009).

[35] 'First Written Submission of the European Communities and their Member States', at para. 30, available as Attachment 1.1 to World Trade Organization (2000), 'United States – Section 110(5) of US Copyright Act – Report of the Panel', WT/DS160/R, available at http://www.wto.org/english/tratop_e/dispu_e/cases_e/ds160_e.htm (accessed 26 May 2009).

[36] *Id.* at para. 34.

With respect to part B, the US argues that the EC errs in asking the Panel to count the harm by asking it to look only at the potential establishments covered by the square footage. The US argues that lost revenue should be based on estimates of actual usage of such music rather than simply pointing to the fact that all establishments above a certain size might be able to use the exception. In particular, it notes that the EC over-counts because it presumes that all establishments above a certain size do play music, do play it from radio broadcasts rather than CDs etc., do not pay for licences already.[37] In particular, the US argues that without a proper estimate of the actual loss of income, the EC cannot assert that there has been unreasonable prejudice compared to the estimate of potential income.[38]

What is significant about the US argument is the relative shortness of its first submission coupled with the relative paucity of legal arguments to defend its position. As a major copyright holder country, the US may have felt that it needed to defend its interests in the legislation. However, understanding what an influential lobby group rights holder groups in the US are, especially in the motion picture and sound recording industry, the US argument was fundamentally constrained by being unable to make arguments that might later be used to effectively limit the interests of such influential rights holder groups in the US. This points to a major element of this case: the US could not be relied upon to make arguments that would effectively protect the interests and interpretations favoured by developing countries or public interest organizations. This highlights the importance of third-party participation and of amicus curiae briefs which may raise such issues and enable the court to take on board other arguments. In this case, there were no amicus curiae briefs from public interest organizations as there had been in the trade and environment cases such as *US – Shrimp Turtles*, and the third-party submissions did not go beyond those arguments already made by the US and the EC.

The submissions were followed by oral statements at hearings, second submissions in response to first submissions and responses to questionnaires sent out by the Panel. The fact finding in this case was quite extensive, with the Panel requiring more information and data from both the EC and the US. The Panel also sent a letter to WIPO requesting information and input regarding the Berne Convention, to which both parties responded. The next section looks at some issues raised in these exchanges but does not elaborate on them beyond pointing to them as issues that the Panel would have to consider in its decision.

---

[37] *Id.* at para. 37.

[38] *Id.* at para. 38.

4.3 The subsequent submissions and arguments

4.3.1 The Oral hearings and questions from the Panel

At the first hearing, the EC took issue with the statement that there are minor exceptions in the Berne Convention that can be applied to the public performance and communication right. It notes that these rights are covered by Article 11 in the Berne Convention which they argue foresees no exceptions to the rights. Article 9(2) covers exceptions to the reproduction right and Articles 10 and 10bis cover free uses more generally, including of broadcasts, and communications to the public by wire. The EC essentially argued that Articles 10 and 10bis do not apply to Article 11 rights.[39] The EC acknowledged that Article 11bis(2) leaves states free to determine the conditions under which the affected 11bis(1) rights are exercised, but it argues that the failure to provide equitable remuneration renders Section 110(5) invalid.[40]

Finally, while it acknowledges the possible existence of minor reservations discussed during the Brussels and Stockholm revisions of the Convention, the EC argued that such discussions did not conclude anything definitive and in any case, any such exceptions were of a very narrowly limited non-commercial nature and applied only to such situations as 'religious ceremonies, military bands and the needs of the child and adult education'.[41]

With respect to Article 13 of TRIPS, the EC took issue with its ability to support any new exceptions and limitations not covered by the Berne Convention. The EC first argued that Berne Convention member countries cannot enter into treaties that would reduce protection under the Berne Convention and thus Article 13 cannot be seen to grant the right to formulate new exceptions and limitations applicable to Berne Convention rights.[42] In addition, the EC argued that Berne Convention exceptions should not be interpreted by TRIPS Article 13, but if they are, in this case, the failure to ensure equitable remuneration would make Section 110(5) fail the test of Article 11bis(2).

---

39 'Oral Statement of the EC and its member states at the First meeting with the Panel', at para. 49, available as Attachment 1.2 to World Trade Organization (2000), 'United States – Section 110(5) of US Copyright Act – Report of the Panel', WT/DS160/R, available at http://www.wto.org/english/tratop_e/dispu_e/cases_e/ds160_e.htm (accessed 26 May 2009).

40 *Id.* at para. 51.

41 *Id.* at para. 52.

42 *Id.* at para. 53.

The EC also argued that Section 110(5) does not meet the three-step test. Important elements of the argument are that:

- the US did not make any argument that the exception applies only to special cases. The fact that potentially the majority of business establishments in the US might be covered by the exceptions make it the rule rather than the exception;[43]
- an examination of normal exploitation must look at each individual right rather than the bundle of rights associated with copyright;[44]
- an interpretation of normal exploitation must include anything that provides an economic benefit to the user, thus all commercial uses would not be covered by exceptions;[45]
- the standard for 'legitimate interest' should include 'being able to prevent all instances of a certain use of his work protected by a specific exclusive right done by a third party without his consent'.[46] This again presumes that a copyright holder has a right to *all* possible economic benefits from the right.

In its oral statement, the US addressed some of the contentions regarding the applicability of Article 11bis(2). In particular, it notes that there is a difference between exceptions on the one hand and compulsory licences on the other. Article 11bis(2), it argued, allows states to substitute compulsory licences instead of an exclusive right, but does not address itself to exceptions where a state decides to allow for exclusive rights.[47] Thus the issue of equitable remuneration under 11bis(2) does not apply to the Section 110(5) exceptions. The exceptions, the US argued, must be reviewed under the doctrine of minor reservations rather than the standard of equitable remuneration.[48] The US reiterated its TRIPS Article 13 arguments.

At the first hearing, both parties also responded to a set of written questions from the Panel, one set addressed to each individually and another for both to answer. The questions directed to the EU asked for more factual information regarding actual licensing royalties in the EU and actual estimated losses.[49] In its replies, the EC has few answers, and where

---

43 *Id.* at para. 67.
44 *Id.* at para. 69.
45 *Id.* at para. 70.
46 *Id.* at para. 72.
47 *Id.* at para. 10.
48 *Id.*
49 See 'Responses of the European Communities and their Member States to

it does, it relies on numbers produced by the major EU complaining organization, the Irish Music Rights Organization, an Irish collecting society. On the legal questions, the EU responses to questions regarding the minor reservations doctrine under Berne confirmed that they argued that TRIPS Article 13 only applied to the new rights in TRIPS and did not apply to Berne, which had its own jurisprudence on exceptions and was intended to maintain existing (and, they argued, very minor *de minimis*) exceptions at the time of the Brussels and Stockholm revisions. The EU argued that under Berne, there was no intention that new exceptions to Berne rights would be developed and that TRIPS was not meant to enable new exceptions to Berne Convention rights.[50] The EC concludes that, in any case, since Section 110(5) and its precursors post-date the Berne Convention changes of the revisions in 1967, they would not apply to Section 110(5).

The questions to the US also focused primarily on the actual number of businesses that qualify, to which the US also had few answers beyond the numbers already cited. In its response to questions on legal issues, the US stated that it 'does not claim that TRIPS Article 13 permits exceptions or limitations that would not be allowed by the Berne Convention'.[51] Instead, it argued that the standard by which Berne Convention exceptions should be judged is TRIPS Article 13. What is interesting to note is that, while the US argues for the applicability of the Berne Convention minor reservations doctrine, it does not make the argument that (1) all countries were free to maintain, preserve and implement exceptions extant in member states at the time of the signing of the most recent revision of the Berne Convention and (2) exceptions not covered by the reproduction right should reasonably be judged under the Berne Convention under a less

---

Footnote 49 (*cont.*)
Written Questions from the Panel – First Meeting', available as Attachment 1.3 to World Trade Organization (2000), 'United States–Section 110(5) of US Copyright Act–Report of the Panel', WT/DS160/R, available at http://www.wto.org/english/tratop_e/dispu_e/cases_e/ds160_e.htm (accessed 26 May 2009).

[50] See 'Responses of the European Communities and their Member States to Written Questions from the Panel–First Meeting', Question 11 at 111, available as Attachment 1.3 to World Trade Organization (2000), 'United States – Section 110(5) of US Copyright Act – Report of the Panel', WT/DS160/R, available at http://www.wto.org/english/tratop_e/dispu_e/cases_e/ds160_e.htm (accessed 26 May 2009).

[51] See 'Responses of the United States to Written Questions from the Panel – First Meeting', available as Attachment 2.3 to World Trade Organization (2000), 'United States – Section 110(5) of US Copyright Act – Report of the Panel', WT/DS160/R, available at http://www.wto.org/english/tratop_e/dispu_e/cases_e/ds160_e.htm (accessed 26 May 2009).

strict standard than that for the reproduction right (Article 9(2)) which is replicated by TRIPS Article 13. By insisting that TRIPS Article 13 be the standard by which *all* Berne exceptions should be judged, the US tied its own hands in the argument, by opting for a much stricter standard of review than might otherwise have been available under a more expansive view of the minor reservations doctrine.

4.3.2 The Second submission

In its second submission, the EC directly addressed the issue of minor reservations again. It made several points. The first was that there is no ordinary meaning in the Berne Convention that would allow for minor reservations and therefore no need, under the VCLT Article 31, to seek out further guidance. In any case, the general reports of the Brussels and Stockholm Diplomatic conferences may constitute preparatory materials (Article 31(3) of the Vienna Convention), which may provide some guidance on meaning, but that it is not supportive of 'minor reservations' of any significant scope.[52]

In particular, the EC argued that the scope of the doctrine only covers religious ceremonies, military bands and child and adult education, citing some existing exceptions mentioned in the report of the Brussels Conference of the revision of Berne Conventions.[53] The EC considers these mentions to be exhaustive of the existing exceptions at the time, or at most, pointing to the purely non-commercial nature of the permitted exceptions. In either case, it argues, Section 110(5) is not covered.

With respect to the interpretation of TRIPS Article 13, the EC argued that Berne Article 11bis(2), which requires equitable remuneration for compulsory licences, is an additional and applicable standard.[54] In looking at how to apply TRIPS Article 13, the EC argued that it is meant to reduce or eliminate new and existing exceptions, given what it believes is the objective of the TRIPS Agreement to raise intellectual property protection.[55]

The US Second Submission also focuses more concretely on legal questions, although it reiterates some of the factual and evidentiary background. On the issue of the applicability of TRIPS Article 13, the US

---

[52] 'Second Written Submission of the European Communities and their Member States', at para. 17, available as Attachment 1.5 to World Trade Organization (2000), 'United States – Section 110(5) of US Copyright Act – Report of the Panel', WT/DS160/R, available at http://www.wto.org/english/tratop_e/dispu_e/cases_e/ds160_e.htm (accessed 26 May 2009).

[53] *Id.* at para. 22.

[54] *Id.* at para. 26.

[55] *Id.* at para. 27.

argues that the article is simply an articulation of the 'minor reservations' doctrine, which has a long-standing history and practice in the Berne Convention.[56] The US argues that subsequent state practice and the existence of similar exceptions in other member countries should be dispositive under Vienna Convention Article 31(3).

With respect to the argument that the EC made that after 1967 no further exceptions other than those already existing were allowed, the US argued that this would be manifestly absurd and unfair to developing countries, many of whom only developed full copyright laws after 1967 and would be deprived of any option to have exceptions of any kind.[57]

The US devoted a significant amount of time to the factual discussion needed to determine unreasonable prejudice, essentially using an economic analysis to argue that the effect of Section 110(5) is *de minimis*. By setting itself such a high standard, it had to work very hard to argue that actual costs rather than potential costs should be the measure of harm and that harm is minimal in comparison to the size of the market.

Finally, the Panel sent a letter of request to the WIPO Secretariat requesting information, to which both parties responded.[58] The letter requested factual information regarding the negotiating history of the Berne Convention, and factual information regarding the status of the minor reservations doctrine. It is difficult to understand quite what 'factual' information might be provided regarding the legal status of minor reservations doctrine, since this would seem to call for some description or presentation of legal analyses. In addition, given critiques of WIPO's historical bias in favour of rights holders,[59] the nature of the facts communicated may need to be approached with caution. The response from the World Intellectual Property Organization (WIPO) was a note on 'Certain Questions Regarding the Berne Convention raised by the World Trade Organization'.[60] Aiming at 'neutrality', the note first tries to provide text

---

56 *Id.* at para. 8.

57 *Id.* at para. 22.

58 'Letter from the Chair of the Panel to the Director General of WIPO', available as Attachment 4.1 to World Trade Organization (2000), 'United States – Section 110(5) of US Copyright Act – Report of the Panel', WT/DS160/R, available at http://www.wto.org/english/tratop_e/dispu_e/cases_e/ds160_e.htm (accessed 26 May 2009).

59 Shabalala, D.B. (ed.) (2007), *A Citizen's Guide to WIPO*, Geneva: CIEL, available at http://www.ciel.org/Publications/CitizensGuide_WIPO_Oct07.pdf (accessed 26 May 2009).

60 'Letter from the Director General of WIPO to the Chair of the Panel', available as Attachment 4.2 to World Trade Organization (2000), 'United States – Section 110(5) of US Copyright Act – Report of the Panel', WT/DS160/R,

regarding the negotiating history of Articles 11 and 11bis. With respect to the minor reservations doctrine, the note refers simply to the materials it presented on the negotiating history. The note also provided materials regarding the negotiating history of Article 9(2), the Berne exception on which TRIPS Article 13 was based. In each case, the secretariat refused to analyse or present materials on subsequent practice, pleading that it was too extensive and broad a question to answer.[61] However, it is that subsequent practice which may potentially point to the core understanding of the questions raised in the case on Berne Convention practice and might give a full sense of the actual scope and exercise of exceptions under Berne. That 'factual' omission in the submission by WIPO to a Panel that had done little or no fact finding of its own was crucial in the interpretation of the minor reservations doctrine and its incorporation into TRIPS Article 13.

In response to the letter, both parties argued that the materials presented supported their position.[62]

4.4 Third-party submissions

As previously noted, no developing countries, other than Brazil, made representations to the Panel. Several developed countries did, however, make submissions. The importance of such submissions cannot be overstated given the fact that the US did not raise several kinds of arguments that might have led to a more flexible and open interpretation of the relationship between TRIPS and Berne as well as the proper standards for meeting the three-step test of Article 13.

Australia's submission was one of the more extensive.[63] It argues that the TRIPS Agreement was directed at achieving a balance of rights and

---

available at http://www.wto.org/english/tratop_e/dispu_e/cases_e/ds160_e.htm (accessed 26 May 2009).

[61] *Id.*

[62] 'Comments from the European Communities and their Member States on the Letter from the Director General of WIPO to the Chair of the Panel', available as Attachment 1.7 and 'Comments on the Letter from the Director-General of WIPO to the Chair of the Panel', available as Attachment 4.7 to World Trade Organization (2000), 'United States – Section 110(5) of US Copyright Act – Report of the Panel', WT/DS160/R, available at http://www.wto.org/english/tratop_e/dispu_e/cases_e/ds160_e.htm (accessed 26 May 2009).

[63] 'Written Submission of Australia', available as Attachment 3.1 to World Trade Organization (2000), 'United States – Section 110(5) of US Copyright Act – Report of the Panel', WT/DS160/R, available at http://www.wto.org/english/tratop_e/dispu_e/cases_e/ds160_e.htm (accessed 26 May 2009).

obligations as noted in Article 7.[64] This is in contrast to the US and the EU's apparent agreement that the purpose of the TRIPS Agreement was to increase intellectual property protection. Australia argued that there was no contradiction between Article 11bis standards for exceptions and the TRIPS Article 13 standard for exceptions. Both must be met, but Article 11bis2, as a specific provision, must guide the interpretation of Berne. In any event, there must be equitable remuneration, as required by Article 11bis(2).[65] Australia also supports the EU argument that minor reservations were purely for public interest objectives or use in private settings.[66] Thus the provisions in this case would not qualify, because of their commercial nature and scope.[67]

Brazil limited its interventions to an oral statement at the first hearing. The statement explicitly noted that it was concerned about the systemic implications of the case for the TRIPS Agreement, as well as the protection of the interests of Brazilian artists and composers.[68] Brazil argued that Section 110(5) is incompatible with the TRIPS Agreement and bases its arguments on the incompatibility of Section 110(5) with Berne Article 11bis(2), concurring with the Australian argument that they are concurrent obligations, in which Article 11bis(2) is a special application (*lex specialis*) of the general rule embodied by TRIPS Article 13.[69] Brazil also concurred that the minor reservations doctrine covers exceptions of a non-commercial nature, thus limiting the bases on which public interest and public policy justifications could be made.[70]

Canada's written submission consisted of three lines expressing interest in viewing the arguments made.[71]

Japan's written submission agreed that the relevant analysis should be carried out under the minor reservations doctrine and Article 11bis, but argued that TRIPS Article 13 helps to clarify the meaning of minor

---

64 *Id.* at para. 12.

65 *Id.* at Synopsis.

66 *Id.*

67 *Id.* at para. 5.3.

68 'Brazil: Oral Statement at the Third Party Hearing', available as Attachment 3.2 to World Trade Organization (2000), 'United States – Section 110(5) of US Copyright Act – Report of the Panel', WT/DS160/R, available at http://www.wto.org/english/tratop_e/dispu_e/cases_e/ds160_e.htm (accessed 26 May 2009).

69 *Id.*

70 *Id.*

71 'Canada: Written Submission', available as Attachment 3.3 to World Trade Organization (2000), 'United States – Section 110(5) of US Copyright Act – Report of the Panel', WT/DS160/R, available at http://www.wto.org/english/tratop_e/dispu_e/cases_e/ds160_e.htm (accessed 26 May 2009).

reservations, supporting the US position.[72] It also argues that under the three-step test, Section 110(5) meets the standard required.[73]

Switzerland both made an oral statement and responded to questions from the Panel.[74] It substantively agreed with the EC submission and arguments.[75] However, it argued that TRIPS Article 13 must be the standard by which *all* exceptions are measured, especially since it limits the scope of any such exceptions, including any minor reservations, and that in addition, exceptions to Article 11bis(1) must comply with Article 11bis(2).[76] Interestingly, Switzerland is the only one who argued that Article 7's obligation on a balance of rights and obligations is subordinate to the more specific provision of Article 13 which, it argues, applies that exhortation in a specific case.[77]

5. The Panel decision

The Panel faced a difficult fact-finding and legal challenge, requiring significant engagement with a pre-existing body of law, as well as several factual and evidentiary issues. With those difficulties in mind, it is interesting to note what evidence and facts the Panel seems to accept as part of the factual basis of the case. The Panel primarily cites the 1976 House and Conference reports on the scope and purpose of the original Section 110(5) in the 1976 Copyright Act.[78] In addition, it only rarely refers to the materials from the negotiating history, preferring instead to rely on dictionary meanings.

---

[72] 'Japan: Written Submission', available as Attachment 3.4 to World Trade Organization (2000), 'United States – Section 110(5) of US Copyright Act – Report of the Panel', WT/DS160/R, available at http://www.wto.org/english/tratop_e/dispu_e/cases_e/ds160_e.htm (accessed 26 May 2009).

[73] *Id.* at para. 5.

[74] 'Switzerland: Oral Statement at the Third Party Hearing', available as Attachment 3.5 to World Trade Organization (2000), 'United States – Section 110(5) of US Copyright Act – Report of the Panel', WT/DS160/R, available at http://www.wto.org/english/tratop_e/dispu_e/cases_e/ds160_e.htm (accessed 26 May 2009).

[75] *Id.* at para. 3.

[76] *Id.* at para. 6.

[77] *Id.* at para. 8.

[78] World Trade Organization (2000), 'United States – Section 110(5) of US Copyright Act – Report of the Panel', WT/DS160/R, para. 2.5, available at http://www.wto.org/english/tratop_e/dispu_e/cases_e/ds160_e.htm (accessed 26 May 2009).

5.1 Applicability of the three-step test

As an initial matter, the Panel rejected without much explanation any contention that the TRIPS Agreement is a subsequent treaty to Berne for the purposes of the Vienna Convention. This would therefore require the application of VCLT Article 30, the relevant provisions of which state:

> 2. When a treaty specifies that it is subject to, or that it is not to be considered as incompatible with, an earlier or later treaty, the provisions of that other treaty prevail.
> 3. When all the parties to the earlier treaty are parties also to the later treaty but the earlier treaty is not terminated or suspended in operation under article 59, the earlier treaty applies only to the extent that its provisions are compatible with those of the later treaty.
> 4. When the parties to the later treaty do not include all the parties to the earlier one:
> (*a*) as between States Parties to both treaties the same rule applies as in paragraph 3;
> (*b*) as between a State party to both treaties and a State party to only one of the treaties, the treaty to which both States are parties governs their mutual rights and obligations.

Thus under VCLT Article 30(2), the incorporation of the Berne Convention would arguably be an explicit statement making TRIPS subject to Berne and thus ensuring that Berne Convention standards would prevail. Under VCLT Article 30(3) and 30(4), the Berne Convention would prevail only if both states were members of the Berne Convention. However, where the US is not a member of the Berne Convention, the Berne Convention provisions incorporated by reference would be considered as applicable and in force from the date of their incorporation into TRIPS and not prior to that.

The Panel, however, does not address or make any of these arguments. It argues that all provisions of the TRIPS Agreement, including those of the Berne Convention incorporated by TRIPS, came into force at the same time.[79] The logic of that position remains questionable, especially without further legal justification. It is especially significant since the US has been a party to the Berne Convention since 1989, thus potentially making VCLT Article 30(4)(a) applicable and providing a stronger argument for applying and doing a conflict analysis between the TRIPS Agreement and the Berne Convention.

The Panel outlines the primary dispute in this case as that regarding TRIPS Article 13, noting that the entirety of the US defence rested on it.[80]

---

79 *Id.* at para. 6.41.
80 *Id.* at para. 6.30.

In looking at the applicability of the three-step test, the Panel first aims to determine the status of the minor exceptions doctrine under the TRIPS Agreement. This involved establishing its status as part of the Berne body of law and interpretation (Berne Acquis) and then, if it is part of the Berne Acquis, whether it has been incorporated by the TRIPS Agreement. If so, only then can the Panel decide what the proper relationship is between TRIPS and the minor reservations doctrine.[81]

In addressing the status of the minor reservations doctrine, the Panel looks to the Vienna Convention and tries to establish the ordinary meaning of the words of the treaty, but in the context of the purposes and objectives of the treaty.[82] They emphasize that the context would include any agreement made between the parties in connection with the conclusion of the treaty, and that 'uncontested' interpretations by the chair of a party conference might also constitute agreement.[83] This is important because of the Reports of the Brussels conference which contained a statement from the chair that the minor exceptions were only 'lightly pencilled in'. In applying this standard, the Panel views that statement as evidence of an agreement between the parties that the minor reservations doctrine was part of the Berne Convention.[84] However, their conclusions with regard to the scope of the doctrine place some severe limits on the understanding of the minor reservations doctrine.

The EC had noted that the examples cited in the Brussels Report were exhaustive. The Panel rejects that argument. Given the subsequent history, as well as references from the Stockholm Conference report, the Panel concluded that the references were illustrative not exhaustive.[85] In addition, the Panel notes that they cannot have been exclusively non-commercial as the examples of child and adult education could include for profit educational institutions. In any case, they could not conclude that the doctrine excluded all possible commercial activities.[86] As far as the Panel is concerned, the key question for the exception is whether it is 'minor' rather than commercial.

The Panel also rejects the EC's argument that only exceptions in existence before the 1967 Stockholm Conference were covered by the doctrine. However, it does not elaborate on why.[87] One possible rationale is that

---

81 *Id.* at para. 6.42.
82 *Id.* at para. 6.44.
83 *Id.* at para. 6.46.
84 *Id.* at para. 6.53.
85 *Id.* at para. 6.57.
86 *Id.* at para. 6.58.
87 *Id.* at para. 6.59.

subsequent state practice following the Stockholm Convention shows states putting in place such exceptions without objection from other member states.

The Panel then looks at the issue of the status of the minor exceptions doctrine under the TRIPS Agreement, that is, whether it was incorporated under Article 9(1). The Panel first points out that the doctrine has not been explicitly excluded by 9(1).[88] Thus there was no explicit intention to exclude minor exceptions and the implications of subsequent practice. The Panel notes that since some of these exceptions were mentioned during the TRIPS negotiations, parties were aware of these as part of existing international standards and yet did not specifically choose to exclude them, thus supporting their conclusion that the minor exceptions doctrine was incorporated into TRIPS.[89]

Finally, the Panel reviewed whether TRIPS Article 13 can be applied to the minor exceptions to Berne Article 11(1) and 11(1)bis. The US argued that it should be and the EC argued that it only applied to new rights within TRIPS.

The Panel first notes that while based on Article 9(2), TRIPS Article 13 is not limited to the reproduction right.[90] It states its view that TRIPS Article 13 cannot be viewed as applying only to the new rights enunciated in the TRIPS Agreement.[91] In concluding thus, it rejects the EC's arguments regarding the aim of the TRIPS Agreement as aimed only at increasing protection, and that Berne Article 20 prevents countries from entering into agreements that reduce protection. In its reasoning, the Panel argues that the application of TRIPS Article 13 need not lead to a different standard for interpreting Berne rights, given that those standards and background are incorporated into TRIPS. The Panel agreed with the US that Article 13 could not be interpreted in a way that would be inconsistent with Berne standards, but that it articulates such standards.[92] This is an important part of the argument because it follows that in understanding the scope of how to apply the three-step test in the analysis that follows, the Panel should give deference to existing interpretation and guidance under the Berne Convention, including subsequent practice and acceptable limitations and exceptions.

Finally, the Panel looks at the scope of 11bis(2) as incorporated into the TRIPS Agreement and whether it is the applicable standard. If it was,

---

88 *Id.* at para. 6.61.
89 *Id.* at para. 6.64.
90 *Id.* at para. 6.74.
91 *Id.* at para. 6.80.
92 *Id.* at para. 6.82.

as the EC argued, the failure to provide adequate remuneration would automatically doom Section 110(5) under any analysis, including one that applied TRIPS Article 13. The Panel notes that the article has generally been understood to refer to the substitution of exclusive rights with compulsory licences.[93] In support, they cite the WIPO Guide to the Berne Convention, but no other learned authority, nor do they suggest that there might be legal or academic disagreement on that point. The Panel argues that under the EC position, there would be no way to give full effect to Article 13, the minor exceptions doctrine and Article 11bis(2) because there would be no circumstances under which free uses would be allowed, despite the clear intention of the minor reservations doctrine and TRIPS Article 13. Only by limiting Article 11bis(2) to situations of substitution by compulsory licensing do you give full effect to the provision, while allowing the others to also have effect.[94] The Panel concludes that Article 11bis(2) is not relevant for the case at hand.

An overview of this section shows that the EC lost its argument on every substantive point and that the Panel adopted the arguments of the US, leaving a very narrow path for a defence. One possible area left open was what role the history of the interpretation of Article 9(2) under the Berne Convention would play. The reproduction right is normally the right to which exceptions are most restricted, as it is the primary right. Related rights to that do not normally achieve the same level of deference. The argument is whether Article 13 applies the exact same standard to other rights as applies to the reproduction right, and whether practice and interpretation under Berne should guide any interpretation of TRIPS Article 13.

5.2 Interpretation of the three-step test

The Panel begins by setting out how the article should be read. First, all provisions must be given utility and meaning. Secondly, all provisions must be satisfied for an exception to be acceptable. The Panel also notes that the article must be construed narrowly and in a limited way, given that it was based on Article 9(2) of the Berne Convention and was not meant to be read broadly.[95]

The Panel then plunges into an analysis of each step of the test, without going into any discussion of how it will review and apply any Berne exceptions and practice as guidance.

---

93 *Id.* at para. 6.84.
94 *Id.* at para. 6.90.
95 *Id.* at para. 6.97.

5.2.1 Certain Special Cases

The Panel states its intention to interpret the words and terms according to ordinary meaning.[96] The Panel therefore states its intention to ignore any previous elucidations of the meaning of these particular terms of art which had been developed in many academic and national practices. It is particularly interesting that having determined that the entire Berne Acquis was incorporated into the TRIPS Agreement, the Panel would not look to practice and interpretation of Article 9(2) to inform its interpretation of TRIPS Article 13. In an extraordinary misapplication of the Vienna Convention, the Panel used the *New Shorter English Oxford Dictionary*, on its own, to find a meaning for what is meant by 'certain', so as to mean clearly defined. Thus, in addition to misapplying the Vienna Convention, the Panel also misread the juxtaposition of the terms 'certain' and 'special'. A plain language analysis suggests that the analysis would have been correct had there been a comma between the terms, but without the comma, the term 'certain' means particularized or one of a limited set or number: a subtle difference in English. More accurately, this language plainly read should be better read as 'one of a limited set' and meant to refer to the treatment of exceptions generally. This double misuse of the Vienna Convention and the *Dictionary* already compounds the failure to treat the terms as special legal terms of art with a distinct meaning within the Berne Acquis, separate from the ordinary everyday meaning of the terms.

In this case, this approach leads the Panel to decide that 'certain' means that each exception must be clearly defined. In deciding what is 'special', the Panel again refers to the *Oxford English Dictionary* and decides that it must require that each exception be limited in scope, both quantitatively and qualitatively.

The Panel rejects any suggestion that the public policy objective of an exception should be part of the qualitative analysis, basing its argument on the fact that the Appellate Body has rejected such attempts in the context of GATS and GATT cases.[97] In this case, they note that they do not wish to equate special purpose with special case, thus rejecting the guidance of Samuel Ricketson's analysis of Article 9(2). They argue that they are reluctant to use a definition and teaching developed only for an article extending the reproduction right to one that addresses broader sets of rights.[98] However, the Panel could clearly have relied on Ricketson's analysis to set the outer boundary of what could be applied to the most important of the

---

[96] *Id.* at para. 6.107.
[97] *Id.* at para. 6.111.
[98] See *id.* at para. 6.111, footnote 114.

copyrights, the reproductive right. Thus, for other rights, the terms could clearly not be more stringent than for the reproduction right.

The key concluding paragraph of the decision on the standard for certain special cases is paragraph 6.112 and it is worth reproducing it in its entirety:

> In our view, the first condition of Article 13 requires that a limitation or exception in national legislation should be clearly defined and should be narrow in its scope and reach. On the other hand, a limitation or exception may be compatible with the first condition even if it pursues a special purpose whose underlying legitimacy in a normative sense cannot be discerned. The wording of Article 13's first condition does not imply passing a judgment on the legitimacy of the exceptions in dispute. However, public policy purposes stated by law-makers when enacting a limitation or exception may be useful from a factual perspective for making inferences about the scope of a limitation or exception or the clarity of its definition.[99]

While seemingly neutral or positive about the public purposes of exception, it leaves out the worst-case scenario which may apply to developing countries in particular; there would also be cases where a clear public policy special purpose was being pursued but which would not meet the standard which they pursued, and their standard would give no special consideration or leeway to such legitimate and strong special purposes. Reasons of public health and the environment, come to mind, for example. Education is at least covered by explicit mention in the minor reservations doctrine.

The Panel then applies this standard to Section 110(5). On part B, the Panel decides that, in terms of equipment and square footage requirements, the exception is clearly defined.[100] The Panel then address whether the exception is sufficiently narrow in scope and reach. The numbers it relies on for this analysis are the Congressional Research Service (CRS) numbers cited by the EC, generated as part of the consideration of the Act in Congress, as well as the follow-up Dun and Bradstreet report based (1998) on the same methodology as the CRS report. The Panel notes that they are not in a position to evaluate the methodology of the Dun and Bradstreet study, but that it seems consistent with the CRS study.[101]

Crucially, the Panel notes that it is the potential number of users rather than the actual number of users that should be the basis for any analysis of the effects, scope and reach of the exception.[102]

---

99 *Id.* at para. 6.112.
100 *Id.* at para. 6.117.
101 *Id.* at para. 6.124.
102 *Id.* at para. 6.127.

Uncritically accepting the CRS number, and noting that 11bis was meant to cover business establishments where people congregate,[103] the Panel therefore argues that they 'fail to see how a law that exempts a major part of the users that were specifically intended to be covered by the provisions of Article 11*bis*(1)(iii) could be considered as a *special* case in the sense of the first condition of Article 13 of the TRIPS Agreement.'[104] The Panel concludes that part B is not a special case under Article 13 TRIPS.

In its analysis of part A, the Panel also relies on the CRS study to conclude that the quantitave effect of the article is much smaller and limited to a minority of establishments. On the specifics of the coverage of what is meant by 'equipment', the Panel concludes that it is sufficiently clear given that there is no need to specify each and every kind of equipment covered, but to determine it by usage criteria.[105] Finally, while the Panel considers the EC's argument that part A could cover internet transmissions, it takes no position on the issue, not having sufficient facts to indicate such uses, but reserves judgment, suggesting that if such transmissions took place, they might not be covered by the exception.

Having decided that part B did not meet the standard but part A did, it seems logical that the Panel would therefore consider the other issues only with respect to part A. However, the Panel argues that because of the close connection between the two parts, it is necessary to consider and apply the other conditions of Article 13 to both sections.[106]

5.2.2 'Not conflict with a normal exploitation of the work'

As with the preceding analysis, the Panel looks first to the ordinary meaning of the words, turning to dictionary meanings. In looking at the definition of 'normal', the key element of this condition, the Panel notes that there is both a normative and empirical element of the meaning. One meaning is to understand what is 'typical or ordinary', the other is what may 'conform to a standard or type'.[107]

The Panel declines to choose between the two but seeks to give full meaning to both.[108] The Panel fails to ask the more pertinent question of which approach to meaning the parties might have intended, especially in light of the Berne Acquis and subsequent practice.

---

103 *Id.* at para. 6.131.
104 *Id.*
105 *Id.* at para. 6.145.
106 *Id.* at para. 6.161.
107 *Id.* at para. 6.166.
108 *Id.* at para. 6.167.

The Panel notes that 'normal' could not be equated with full exclusive use of rights and that exceptions must be part of what is considered normal if Article 13 is to have any meaning.[109] What is to be determined, however, is the extent of those exceptions.

In determining what is normal, the Panel first addresses whether the scope should be the exploitation of the work as a whole,[110] as the US argued, or the specific exclusive right affected. Article 13 refers to the 'work'. This would allow some significant effect on one exclusive right as long as the set of exclusive rights related to a work were largely unaffected, especially as a percentage of potential earnings related to the work. The Panel rejects that argument, noting that 'work' refers to all the exclusive rights in the work and that harm to one right cannot be balanced by benefit in another right. In addition, the Panel notes, these may not be held by the same rights holder.[111]

The Panel then takes up the issue of whether the use or exception in question is part of the normal exploitation. The Panel first addresses the US argument that the primary measure should be quantitave, that is, how much market displacement does the use cause?[112] Thus 'normal' would not include those situations where the author would not normally expect to receive royalties due to existing market conditions or incapacity to collect. While accepting this standard, the Panel argues that it also has to give meaning to the normative, qualitative meaning of 'normal'.[113] In an extraordinary turnaround, the Panel here seeks guidance directly from a study carried out by the Swedish government and the precursor to the WIPO secretariat in preparation for the Stockholm Revisions. The status of these materials as interpretive guidance is never examined nor is it placed in the context of any agreed interpretations of Article 9(2) during the negotiations, nor of subsequent practice or reports of the meetings themselves that referred to Article 9(2) as required by the VCLT Article 31. The Panel instead turns directly to supplementary materials, a second step which is covered by VCLT Article 32. This constitutes significant misapplication of normal practice under the Vienna Convention which places the interpretation under severe scrutiny. From this Swedish study it draws the conclusion that a normative standard would make sure that normal would also include all those activities for which it would be plausible that

109 *Id.* at para. 6.166.
110 *Id.* at para. 6.168.
111 *Id.* at para. 6.173.
112 *Id.* at para. 6.177.
113 *Id.* at para. 6.178.

income might be generated.[114] The Panel finally decides to apply the following standard based on the above reasoning:

> an exception or limitation to an exclusive right in domestic legislation rises to the level of a conflict with a normal exploitation of the work (i.e., the copyright or rather the whole bundle of exclusive rights conferred by the ownership of the copyright), if uses, that in principle are covered by that right but exempted under the exception or limitation, enter into economic competition with the ways that right holders normally extract economic value from that right to the work (i.e., the copyright) and thereby deprive them of significant or tangible commercial gains.[115]

While somewhat circular, the Panel's standard focuses on the concept of competing in the market with the rights holder or have the potential to do so. This is purely an economic test with no room for any normative considerations. In the sequencing, this means that neither the first step nor the second step consider the normative issue of public policy purposes of an exception and thus an exception can be invalidated in these two steps well before any consideration takes place of its public policy purposes.

Applying the standard to part B, the Panel, looking at the CRS numbers as well as the potential for establishments not playing music over speakers to begin doing so, finds that part B conflicts with normal exploitation of the work.

Applying the standard to part A, the Panel, looks directly to the stated public purpose of the exception, which was to exempt from liability somebody just tuning in a regular receiver of a kind in a public place. This is, of course, in direct contradiction to their stating earlier that they would not look at those purposes except as supplementary support. The Panel concludes that the activities are of no significant consequence and could never be of significant economic consequence and thus finds that the homestyle exception does not conflict with normal exploitation of the work.

Both applications of the standard rest on very narrow factual determinations regarding the nature of the potential economic consequences. However, none of this is actually underpinned with any actual economic analysis. In that sense the decision is overly reliant on the economic meaning of 'normal' which was based on a very weak reading of a preparatory conference document whose relevance is questionable. This condition of the step is probably the most crucial and is the weakest part of a generally weak legal analysis. The failure to require more significant economic analysis of 'potential' loss or harm points to a major failure of

---

114 *Id.* at para. 6.181.
115 *Id.* at para. 6.183.

the panel: that they are poor finders of fact, utterly reliant on the facts placed before them by the parties without doing any analysis of the reliability or appropriateness of the measures or information. In addition, they are poor evaluators of whether sufficient facts have been adduced to meet the standard that they themselves enunciate i.e. analysis of the actual or potential market and economic analysis of the level of market displacement or competition that the exception would engender. Finally, they do not actually address whether there was a valid public policy purpose so as to give meaning to the 'normative' element of the step.

5.2.3 'Not unreasonably prejudice the legitimate interests of the right holder'

The Panel begins with what it has to determine. The Panel aims to first determine what are the 'interests' concerned, and what makes them 'legitimate'. The Panel then determines what 'prejudice' would entail and then determines what level of prejudice would be unreasonable.[116]

The key standard here is what is considered a 'legitimate interest'. Again, the Panel goes to the *Dictionary* rather than the TRIPS Agreement itself in the preamble or Article 7. The Panel recognizes that there is a normative aspect regarding justifications for actions to serve a particular end. The Panel reads 'legitimate' to essentially mean the interests that rights holders have in exercising their exclusive rights.[117] The Panel, however, fails to note that legitimacy may also work against a rights holder as there are also potential interests that are not based on exclusive rights but are aimed at achieving greater dissemination, greater creativity, freedom of expression, privacy which exclusive rights are balanced against. The Panel limits the concept of legitimacy only to the right to exercise exclusive rights.

With respect to 'unreasonable prejudice', the Panel simply announces a standard based on dictionary readings that: 'prejudice to the legitimate interests of right holders reaches an unreasonable level if an exception or limitation causes or has the potential to cause an unreasonable loss of income to the copyright owner'.[118] While also being circular, it also seems to replicate the 'significant competition with the economic activity' standard that the Panel established for the second condition. The decision relies on wording from the WIPO Guide to the Berne Convention, a document whose probative value is questionable at best. The Panel again fails to follow the requirement of VCLT Article 31 in carrying out its

116 *Id.* at para. 6.222.
117 *Id.* at para. 6.226.
118 *Id.* at para. 6.229.

interpretation by going directly to supplementary materials rather than exploring agreements or subsequent state practice first.

In applying the standard to part B, the Panel does an in-depth examination of the potential number of establishments covered and takes the numbers presented at face value, while examining the US argument that the effect, potential or otherwise, is *de minimis*. Much of the section focuses on an attempt at making estimates of analysis, based on thin or non-existent analysis or economic modelling. While unable to fully determine the potential losses and whether they are *de minimis*, the Panel decides that since the burden of proof lies with the US, it has not shown that the exception does not unfairly prejudice rightsholders. Thus part B does not meet the standard of the third condition.[119] In the analysis, however, the Panel does seem to accept the US contention that only *de minimis* exceptions should be covered.

In applying the standard to part A, the Panel refers again to the purpose underlying the legislation, as well as the numbers of establishments potentially covered. The Panel concludes, without any economic analysis or much evidence from the US, that the effect of the exception is *de minimis* and is not persuaded that the EU has offered any evidence of unreasonable prejudice.[120] At no point in the analysis does the Panel suggest that other legitimate interests may exist that would allow an exception that had a more than a *de minimis* effect on the income of the rights holder.

6. Post-decision process and compliance

After the Panel report was adopted 27 July 2000, the US did not appeal the decision to the Appellate Body. The Appellate Body which has developed much of the ongoing jurisprudence of the WTO has never had a chance to review the reasoning of the Panel. The US failed to implement the decision within the time allotted by the DSB; the EC was authorized to suspend concessions under the TRIPS Agreement to the value of Euro 1 219 900 per year.[121] Negotiations continued throughout 2001 and 2002 until a temporary and mutually satisfactory solution was found in June 2003. Since the agreement ended, however, the US has continued to file status reports but no movement has been made to amend the legislation to make it compliant. In many ways, the US seems content to pay the relatively small price to maintain its legislation and can clearly afford to do so.

---

119 *Id.* at para. 6.265

120 *Id.* at paras 6.267–6.272.

121 World Trade Organization, 'Summary US – Section 110(5) Copyright Act (DS160)', available at http://www.wto.org/english/tratop_e/dispu_e/cases_e/1pagesum_e/ds160sum_e.pdf (accessed 26 May 2009).

One could argue in fact, that while the business exception was found invalid, on all the fundamental points, the US won and it won in ensuring that the Panel imposed an extremely narrow interpretation of the three-step test, albeit not as narrow as that desired by the EU.

7. Commentaries and critiques of the case and the implications for developing countries

In carrying out the analysis above, this chapter has pointed out several potential flaws and inaccuracies in the Panel's reasoning, as well as some of the problems caused by the particular litigation strategies chosen by the US. These circumstances have consequences for developing countries as to the risk they face in fashioning new exceptions and limitations and in applying older ones. The next section reviews some of the critiques and commentaries of the case and examines the room that the case leaves open for developing countries.

7.1 Fact-finding and legal methodology

The Panel's use of the VCLT has not been a significant element in the criticism of its approach. However, it is difficult to reconcile the wording of VCLT Article 31(1) which requires not just that the Panel use the ordinary meaning of the words but that interpretation must be done 'in accordance with the ordinary meaning to be given to the terms of the treaty in their context and in the light of its object and purpose'. The context and object and purpose are crucial elements of determining ordinary meaning and according to Article 31(2), these include:

> (*a*) any agreement relating to the treaty which was made between all the parties in connection with the conclusion of the treaty;
> (*b*) any instrument which was made by one or more parties in connection with the conclusion of the treaty and accepted by the other parties as an instrument related to the treaty.

In addition under Article 31(3), the Panel is obligated to take into account:

> (*a*) any subsequent agreement between the parties regarding the interpretation of the treaty or the application of its provisions;
> (*b*) any subsequent practice in the application of the treaty which establishes the agreement of the parties regarding its interpretation;
> (*c*) any relevant rules of international law applicable in the relations between the parties.

Other than the first part of Article 31(1), the Panel fails to apply in any systematic way the required interpretive steps outline in VCLT Article

31(1) and 31(2). Article 31 is meant to be applied as a whole, not selectively and there is no hierarchy between dictionary meanings and meanings that can be gleaned from subsequent practice or agreements between the parties. There are other provisions on supplementary materials (VCLT Article 32) which may also apply, but only after interpretation under Article 31 has not succeeded in providing clarity.

While it is possible that the final outcome would not differ significantly, a proper application of interpretive methodology may profoundly affect the level of the standard for the three-step test that they articulated. This fundamental methodological weakness of the Panel suggests that the standard will most definitely have to be revisited if a case is ever brought again. In any case, it suggests that, in forming domestic legislation on exceptions and limitations, little interpretive guidance can be gained from following the Panel's reasoning. The fact that this reasoning has not been tested or reviewed by the Appellate Body provides even less assurance that the case is a reliable source for a standard.[122] Finally, the specific facts of the case, given the highly commercial nature of the establishments concerned and the failure of the US to make all the relevant arguments, suggest that the conclusions drawn by the Panel may be narrowly limited to this case and are likely not going to be applicable in other situations.

However, this is not to say that there have not been commentators approving the Panel's decision,[123] but few have had any issue with the reasoning or found a particular need to defend it against other critiques. However, there is consensus that the case did not necessarily present the best analysis of the three-step test and that further work is needed to ensure that later Panels apply it properly.[124] One of the outcomes of discussions about this issue is a 'Declaration on a Balanced Interpretation of the Three Step Test in Copyright Law' written and supported by copyright scholars from across the full spectrum of approaches to copyright.[125] Kur, while agreeing with the Declaration's principles of a holistic and balanced

---

[122] UNCTAD – ICTSD (2005), *Resource Book on TRIPS and Development*, Cambridge: Cambridge University Press, available at http://www.iprsonline.org/unctadictsd/ResourceBookIndex.htm (accessed 26 May 2009).

[123] See e.g. Landau, Michael (2007), 'Fitting United States Copyright Law into the International Scheme: Foreign and Domestic Challenges to Recent Legislation', *Georgia State University Law Review*, **23**, 847.

[124] See Kur, A. (2008) 'Of Oceans, Islands, and Inland Water – How Much Room for Exceptions and Limitations Under the Three-step Test?', *Max Planck Papers on Intellectual Property, Competition & Tax Law*, Research Paper No. 08-04, 21, available at http://ssrn.com/abstract=1317707 (accessed 26 May 2009).

[125] See http://www.ip.mpg.de/ww/en/pub/news/declaration_on_the_three_step_.cfm.

approach, also notes that the Panel did not do an analysis of public policy justifications and therefore has left wide open the issue of whether an exception with a strong public policy basis would pass muster.[126] She notes in particular the US failure to raise such an argument, something that this chapter has previously described.

7.2 Applicability of the three-step test

Some authors have found fault with the Panel's decision on the proper relationship between the TRIPS Agreement and the Berne Convention. David Brennan argues that the Panel fundamentally misused and misunderstood the secondary material regarding the negotiating history of the Berne Convention.[127] In part, Brennan's analysis relies on his analysis of the way in which the Panel integrated the minor exceptions doctrine and its relationship to Article 11bis(2). In particular, he looks at the Panel's reliance on the Brussels Report, in which the Rapporteur made statements regarding exceptions existing in state law. Brennan notes that the Panel treats this statement as evidence of an agreement amongst states rather than as a statement made in the chair's personal capacity and thus only supplementary material. The Panel uses it to decide that Article 11, which was being referred to, was to be interpreted in light of the minor exceptions doctrine. Brennan, however, points to another explicit statement by the chair of the Panel that directly addresses the application of Article 11bis(2) to the rights in 11bis(1).[128] This statement explicitly notes that

---

[126] Kur, A. (2008) 'Of Oceans, Islands, and Inland Water – How Much Room for Exceptions and Limitations Under the Three-step Test?', *Max Planck Papers on Intellectual Property, Competition & Tax Law*, Research Paper No. 08-04, 30, available at http://ssrn.com/abstract=1317707 (accessed 26 May 2009). She also notes that other Panels addressing similar problems have also failed to address the public policy question.

[127] Brennan, D.J. (2002), 'The Three-step Test Frenzy – Why the TRIPS Panel Decision Might be Considered Per Incuriam', *Intellectual Property Quarterly*, **2**, available at http://ssrn.com/abstract=299543 (accessed 26 May 2009).

[128] 'Pursuant to an observation made by Mr Pilotti, President of the International Institute for the Unification of Private Law, and according to sound legal interpretation, *paragraph (1), with its three separate items, is inseparable from paragraph (2), which makes it a matter for national legislation to determine the conditions under which the rights mentioned in paragraph (1) may be exercised. Those conditions may, as the Nordic and Hungarian Delegations observed, relate to free-of-charge exceptions made for religious, patriotic or cultural purposes*. These possible conditions are placed within a fairly broad framework: they may not in any circumstances be prejudicial to the moral rights of the author or to his right to obtain just remuneration which, in the absence of agreement, is fixed by the competent authority.' *Id.* at p. 14.

these cannot be treated separately from Article 11bis(2), which must apply directly to them.[129] Thus while the Panel's reasoning and use of the chair's statement may be consistent for the Article 11 rights under consideration, they were not correct for the Article 11bis rights under the dispute.[130] We can only share Brennan's confusion that such an explicit statement was overlooked by the Panel. In this instance, regarding the applicability of the minor exceptions doctrine to Berne Article 11bis, the Panel's decision is rendered invalid due to carelessness or by the more proper term, rendered *per incuriam*.[131]

The broader issue that Brennan raises is that the Panel's reasoning appears to reflect faulty reasoning, reflecting after the fact justification for a desired position rather than an examination of the full factual and legal bases underlying one option rather than another. If this element of the Panel's decision-making is so clearly flawed, this places some of its other reasoning under suspicion as well. This is particularly true of the Panel's treatment of secondary and supporting material and its selective and sometimes incorrect application of the Vienna Convention on the Law of Treaties.

However Brennan's concern is that the TRIPS Agreement became the sole standard and, as with other commentators from developed countries, he views the three-step test as too broad. Thus, while Brennan provides a useful challenge to the Panel's method of work, the desired outcome from his reasoning would largely be incompatible with broad readings that would maintain greater flexibility and freedom for developing countries to apply and implement exceptions and limitations. Brennan reiterates the EC's argument that Article 13 was inserted to restrict exceptions and limitations rather than as a tool for implementing the balance between rights and obligations, rights holders and users embodied in Article 7 of the TRIPS Agreement. In any case, his argument for a narrow reading rests only on Article 11bis(2), and may not affect the applicability of the minor exceptions doctrine more broadly. In addition, the minor exceptions doctrine only applies to public performance rights and not to the other rights such as reproduction which have a whole set of practices to which they also relate.[132] Those exceptions are not minor and may not be as subject

---

[129] *Id.*

[130] *Id.*

[131] *Id.* at p. 16.

[132] Ricketson, S. (2003), 'WIPO Study on Limitations and Exceptions Copyright and Related Rights in the Digital Environment', WIPO SCCR/9/7 2003, 34, available at: http://www.wipo.int/meetings/en/doc_details.jsp?doc_id=16805 (accessed 26 May 2009).

to the narrow reading given to exceptions to the pubic performance rights by the Panel. Kur notes that the Panel seems to have taken the standard for the minor reservations doctrine and applied it broadly to all exceptions and limitations.[133] There clearly seems to have been some confusion on the part of the Panel which, in interpreting the standard for the three-step test, applied the essentially *de minimis* test for exceptions to public performance rights,[134] to all exceptions more generally.

From a development viewpoint, it is important that all of the Berne Acquis is imported into the TRIPS Agreement in a manner that recognizes all the subsequent practice that existed under Berne at the time of the TRIPS Agreement. It cannot be the case that countries believed that in signing the TRIPS Agreement they were agreeing that their existing exceptions and limitations would not be included. Given the pattern of subsequent Berne Convention practice, any exceptions and limitations that were acceptable under the Berne Convention's interpretations of Article 9(2) and other exceptions should be acceptable under the TRIPS Agreement.[135] This is especially important in light of the fact that, unlike the Berne Convention, the TRIPS Agreement itself contains no special provisions for developing countries other than the now expired transition period. Least developing countries still have four years for implementation, except for pharmaceutical products, where they have until 2016. Thus, the Berne Acquis contains crucial flexibilities that can influence the way that the TRIPS Agreement is interpreted.

7.3 Interpretation of the three-step test

Commentators have taken issue with various aspects of the Panel's reasoning in analysing the three-step test. Gervais argues that, not only did the Panel's reasoning on 'certain special cases' ignore the history and text of the Convention, but that the conclusion that 'certain' therefore requires an exception that is limited in its field of application is a huge and unjustified

---

[133] Kur, A. (2008) 'Of Oceans, Islands, and Inland Water – How Much Room for Exceptions and Limitations Under the Three-step Test?', *Max Planck Papers on Intellectual Property, Competition & Tax Law*, Research Paper No. 08-04, 43, available at http://ssrn.com/abstract=1317707 (accessed 26 May 2009).

[134] For discussion of the Berne Convention standards for public performance rights, see Ricketson, S. (2003), 'WIPO Study on Limitations and Exceptions Copyright and Related Rights in the Digital Environment', WIPO SCCR/9/7 2003, 35, available at: http://www.wipo.int/meetings/en/doc_details.jsp?doc_id=16805 (accessed 26 May 2009).

[135] UNCTAD – ICTSD (2005), *Resource Book on TRIPS and Development*, 188, Cambridge: Cambridge University Press, available at http://www.iprsonline.org/unctadictsd/ResourceBookIndex.htm (accessed 26 May 2009).

logical leap.[136] Gervais argues that this step is really one aimed at ensuring that there is an actual non-arbitrary public policy.[137]

Like many others, Gervais agrees with the Panel's core economic analysis standard for the second step, but finds significant fault with its analysis of the third step. Gervais argues that the Panel's focus on an economic test essentially conflates the second and third steps.[138] Others have argued that the Panel, in any case, did not truly clarify the normative content of the second step, especially where other public policy concerns exist.[139] Ginsburg accepts the economic analysis that the Panel engages in, but considers it too limited and somewhat circular.[140] Others have also pointed to the fact that subsequent analyses of similar language on patents exceptions by another Panel clearly articulated that one of the normative elements of 'normal' exploitation must be whether the exploitation is directed at meeting the primary public patent policy aims of why the rights exist in the first place.[141] Thus it would not be reasonable to argue, as the Panel did, that a rights holder has the right to earn income from every possible use, except those that are *de minimis*, and that anything that conflicted with that would encroach on normal exploitation. In addition, some have argued that the key problem may be that in reading the second step so narrowly as to exclude non-economic normative considerations, the Panel negated the third step of the test by ensuring that most exceptions would likely fail the second. Koelman argues that the first two steps should be read much less strictly if the third step is to play the role originally envisioned for it as a final evaluation and balancing of interests identified in the first two.[142] Senftleben also argues that while an economic analysis is

---

136 Gervais, D.J. (2005), 'Towards a New Core International Copyright Norm: The Reverse Three-step Test', *Marquette Intellectual Property Law Review*, **9**, 15, available at http://ssrn.com/abstract=499924 (accessed 26 May 2009).

137 *Id.*

138 *Id* at p. 19. See also Senftleben, M. (2006), 'Towards a Horizontal Standard for Limiting Intellectual Property Rights? – WTO Panel Reports Shed Light on the Three-step Test in Copyright Law and Related Rights in Patent and Trademark Law', *International Review of Intellectual Property and Competition Law*, **37**(4), 434.

139 Ginsburg, J.C. (2001), 'Toward Supranational Copyright Law? The WTO Panel Decision and the "Three-step Test" for Copyright Exceptions', *Revue Internationale du Droit d'Auteur* **187**, 14, available at http://ssrn.com/abstract=253867 (accessed 26 May 2009).

140 *Id.*

141 Hugenholtz, P.B. and R.G. Okediji (2008), 'Conceiving an International Instrument on Exceptions and Limitations to Copyright', p. 24, available at http://www.ivir.nl/publicaties/hugenholtz/finalreport2008.pdf (accessed 26 May 2009).

142 Koelman, K.J. (2006), 'Fixing the Three-step Test', *EIPR*, **28**(8), 410.

appropriate as part of the second step, by doing the analysis on a right-by-right basis rather than looking at a broader set of rights, the Panel may artificially inflate the level of conflict by only looking at the effect on rights which in and of themselves bring in very small amounts of income. He argues that it would have been better to look at how such rights are actually exercised as a set of economic activities to get a more realistic sense of income derived relative to exceptions applied.[143]

With respect to the third step, some commentators have also suggested that some normative element was clearly part of the Panel's underlying considerations because of the nature of the beneficiaries of part B of the Section 110(5) exception. Ginsburg characterizes this as a 'pork-barrel exception', aimed at serving the needs of a lobby group, which the Panel may have thought was undeserving.[144] This is in line with the nomenclature chosen by the Panel, which chose to characterize this as a 'business' exception, thus suggesting a purely economic rationale for the beneficiaries. Ginsburg argues that the facts of the case may not translate into other arenas where the 'legitimate' interests of other authors and public welfare issues are concerned.[145] One issue that Ginsburg's analysis emphasizes is that it may be possible to reduce the unreasonableness of an exception by arranging for compensation, such as would be available through a compulsory licence.[146] However, she does not elaborate on how the reasonableness of the level of compensation would be determined, especially if non-economic factors are to be considered.

Senftleben also points out the failure to address the non-economic normative elements of the second step. See Senftleben, M. (2006), 'Towards a Horizontal Standard for Limiting Intellectual Property Rights? – WTO Panel Reports Shed Light on the Three-step Test in Copyright Law and Related Rights in Patent and Trademark Law', *International Review of Intellectual Property and Competition Law*, **37**(4), 425.

[143] Senftleben, M. (2006), 'Towards a Horizontal Standard for Limiting Intellectual Property Rights? – WTO Panel Reports Shed Light on the Three-step Test in Copyright Law and Related Rights in Patent and Trademark Law', *International Review of Intellectual Property and Competition Law*, **37**(4), 427.

[144] Ginsburg, J.C. (2001), 'Toward Supranational Copyright Law? The WTO Panel Decision and the "Three-step Test" for Copyright Exceptions', *Revue Internationale du Droit d'Auteur* **187**, 9, available at http://ssrn.com/abstract=253867 (accessed 26 May 2009).

[145] *Id.*

[146] *Id.* at p. 15; Hugenholtz, P.B. and R.G. Okediji (2008), 'Conceiving an International Instrument on Exceptions and Limitations to Copyright,' p. 15, available at http://www.ivir.nl/publicaties/hugenholtz/finalreport2008.pdf (accessed 26 May 2009).

8. Development implications of the case

8.1 Is the Panel's interpretation of the three-step test reliable?

Given the critiques of commentators, it cannot be said to be a reliable source of interpretation. Ginsburg points out that the Panel's decision has not made future outcomes of cases any more reliable.[147] Unfortunately, the three-step test has now been replicated verbatim in many states' laws, including the EU Information Society Directive[148] and is being interpreted at national level. The Panel decision in this case is providing a source of interpretive guidance to cases in these situations and state practice may already be forming. Two approaches to addressing this question may be to either follow the US in declaring that its existing exceptions all meet the standard of the three-step test, or to begin to interpret the three-step test in domestic legislation, and ensure that public policy objectives are properly included. However, as some commentators have pointed out, a test that was designed as guidance for legislators in formulating exceptions may be less suited to the process of judicial determinations at domestic level, where judges may not be in a position to do the kind of balancing of stakeholder interests best done in a legislature.[149] Unless clear interpretive guidance is given by the legislature, it may be best to use legislation to state how the exception meets the criteria as understood by the drafters. Some commentators view the three-step test as fatally flawed and inappropriate for use by judges, as well as being need in amendment.[150] Given the complexity of the balancing, it may be more appropriate for legislatures to give directions for use of existing patterns of interpretation such as 'fair use' or 'fair dealing' in conjunction with open-ended lists of examples that qualify.

Finally, in terms of interpretation under the Vienna Convention, Kur makes a convincing argument that WTO Panel decisions do not count as a subsequent agreement applicable to all WTO member states or even to the parties involved in the dispute, nor do they constitute subsequent

---

[147] Ginsburg, J.C. (2001), 'Toward Supranational Copyright Law? The WTO Panel Decision and the "Three-step Test" for Copyright Exceptions', *Revue Internationale du Droit d'Auteur* **187**, 16, available at http://ssrn.com/abstract=253867 (accessed 26 May 2009).

[148] Directive 2001/29/EC of the European Parliament and of the Council of 22 May 2001 on the Harmonisation of Certain Aspects of Copyright and Related Rights in the Information Society.

[149] Hugenholtz, P.B. and R.G. Okediji (2008), 'Conceiving an International Instrument on Exceptions and Limitations to Copyright', p. 18, available at http://www.ivir.nl/publicaties/hugenholtz/finalreport2008.pdf (accessed 26 May 2009).

[150] Koelman, K.J. (2006), 'Fixing the Three-step Test', *EIPR*, **28**(8), 408.

practice.[151] However, we should note again that actual state practice in domestic legislation may indeed become evidence of subsequent state practice and thus it is crucial that legislatures and judiciaries in developing countries begin to put together consistent and coherent interpretations of the test for themselves, in ways that meet their domestic circumstances. Simple transposition of the test will be insufficient.

8.2 What is the minimal scope of available exceptions after this case?

8.2.1 Existing and New Exceptions

Some guidance for this can be found in the WIPO Copyright Treaty (WCT) and the WIPO Performances and Phonograms Treaty (WPPT), which were adopted in 1996, three years prior to the Panel. The Agreed Statements to Article 10 (which replicates the three-step test, especially Article 10(2) on how to apply Berne exceptions and limitations to the rights under the WCT, notes:

> It is understood that the provisions of Article 10 permit Contracting Parties to carry forward and appropriately extend into the digital environment limitations and exceptions in their national laws which have been considered acceptable under the Berne Convention. Similarly, these provisions should be understood to permit Contracting Parties to devise new exceptions and limitations that are appropriate in the digital network environment.

As other commentators have noted,[152] this is a crucial re-balancing as it establishes that domestic legislation is free to apply existing exceptions and create new ones, provided that they are consistent with Berne. At least as far as digital content is concerned, the Agreed Statements cabin the three-step test and place it in proper perspective as an open-ended enabling tool for crafting exceptions, without actually pre-determining the scope of those exceptions beyond the Berne Convention.

Despite these statements being raised by the US as evidence of subsequent state practice and evidence of an agreement between the parties as to the meaning and role of the minor exceptions doctrine,[153] the Panel rejected that view, stating:

---

[151] Kur, A. (2008), 'Of Oceans, Islands, and Inland Water – How Much Room for Exceptions and Limitations Under the Three-step Test?', *Max Planck Papers on Intellectual Property, Competition & Tax Law*, Research Paper No. 08-04, 32–3, available at http://ssrn.com/abstract=1317707 (accessed 26 May 2009).

[152] Samuelson, P. (1997), 'The U.S. Digital Agenda at WIPO', *Vanderbilt Journal of International Law*, 369.

[153] World Trade Organization (2000), 'United States – Section 110(5) of US

> We note that the subsequent developments just mentioned do not constitute a subsequent treaty on the same subject-matter within the meaning of Article 30, or subsequent agreements on the interpretation of a treaty, or subsequent practice within the meaning of Article 31(3).

The Panel makes no legal argument as to why this would not be the case, but does point to the WCT as providing some support for inclusion of the minor exceptions doctrine into TRIPS. However, it only notes that it made the exceptions subject to the three-step test, but does not also address the agreed statement that also noted that all exceptions considered acceptable under the Berne Convention prior to the three-step test were carried forward.

Despite the Panel's failure to properly use this evidence of a subsequent agreement, developing countries can feel comfortable relying on the practice to continue formulating their own exceptions and limitations based on the full scope of practice available under the Berne Convention and to continue to make new ones to address digital and internet content. Hugenholtz and Okediji point out that the drafting history of Article 9(2) of the Berne Convention shows that it was also primarily meant as a grandfathering clause, essentially enabling existing exceptions in 1967 to continue.[154]

In addition, some guidance can also be found in the optional list of exceptions described in the EU Information Society Directive, which the EU considers as already covered by the three-step test.[155] However, the EU's approach should not be seen as exhaustive but only descriptive of EU practice under the Berne Convention and the TRIPS Agreement.

8.2.2 Sequencing

One of the key problems of the way that the Panel interpreted the three-step test is the way in which they used a cumulative and step-by-step

---

Footnote 153 (*cont.*)
Copyright Act – Report of the Panel', WT/DS160/R, para. 6.67, available at http://www.wto.org/english/tratop_e/dispu_e/cases_e/ds160_e.htm (accessed 26 May 2009).

[154] See also, Koelman, K.J. (2006), 'Fixing the Three-step Test', *EIPR*, **28**(8), 407; Senftleben, M. (2006), 'Towards a Horizontal Standard for Limiting Intellectual Property Rights? – WTO Panel Reports Shed Light on the Three-step Test in Copyright Law and Related Rights in Patent and Trademark Law', *International Review of Intellectual Property and Competition Law*, **37**(4), 411.

[155] For the full list, see Directive 2001/29/EC of the European Parliament and of the Council of 22 May 2001 on the Harmonisation of Certain Aspects of Copyright and Related Rights in the Information Society.

process to move the consideration of normative public policy issues to the last possible step, while focusing purely on economic effects tests in the first two steps. This means that in almost all cases, a failure to meet the first or the second test cannot be modified by consideration of the public policy justification and legitimate interests of other parties, the state or the public.

Some commentators have noted that the sequencing that the Panel chose is not actually required to sequence the test in that manner.[156] To apply the test, two other options have been suggested.

One is to reverse the sequencing by considering the third, more normative step first.[157] Gervais argues that a reading of the 1967 Stockholm Conference Report clearly treats the 'certain special cases' as the last consideration in the chain, rather than the first.[158] This 'reverse three-step test' could be applied either in domestic judicial interpretation or in the process of drafting domestic legislation.

The second option would be to balance and treat in combination and holistically, the three steps so that public interest elements are addressed co-equally with the narrow economic tests.[159]

8.2.3 Other issues

More generally, the TRIPS Agreement establishes certain principles of which it is crucial to remind developing countries. As Reichmann[160] points out, TRIPS ensures that countries are free to implement the Agreement according to their own legal system and practice; the DSU cannot be used to add more rights than agreed in the treaty, and with respect to

---

156 Hugenholtz, P.B. and R.G. Okediji (2008), 'Conceiving an International Instrument on Exceptions and Limitations to Copyright,' 21, available at http://www.ivir.nl/publicaties/hugenholtz/finalreport2008.pdf (accessed 26 May 2009).

157 See Gervais, D.J. (2005), 'Towards a New Core International Copyright Norm: The Reverse Three-step Test', *Marquette Intellectual Property Law Review*, **9**, available at http://ssrn.com/abstract=499924 (accessed 26 May 2009).

158 *Id.* at 16. See also Hugenholtz, P.B. and R.G. Okediji (2008), 'Conceiving an International Instrument on Exceptions and Limitations to Copyright', 21, available at http://www.ivir.nl/publicaties/hugenholtz/finalreport2008.pdf (accessed 26 May 2009).

159 Koelman, K.J. (2006), 'Fixing the Three-step Test', *EIPR*, **28**(8), 410. See also Kur, A. (2008) 'Of Oceans, Islands, and Inland Water – How Much Room for Exceptions and Limitations Under the Three-step Test?', *Max Planck Papers on Intellectual Property, Competition & Tax Law*, Research Paper No. 08-04, available at http://ssrn.com/abstract=1317707 (accessed 26 May 2009).

160 Reichman, J.H. (2000), 'The TRIPs Agreement Comes of Age: Conflict or Cooperation with the Developing Countries?', *Case Western Reserve Journal of International Law*, **32**, 446.

enforcement, countries are not required to shift resources to IP enforcement in a way that would distort their domestic judicial policy.

However, one cannot discount the influence of unilateral measures and pressure such as the US Section 301 process which lists and threatens withdrawal of preferential trade treatment for countries the US considers 'unfriendly' towards higher intellectual property. It should, however, be noted that even over-compliance with the TRIPS Agreement is no protection from such measures: Canada has recently been listed on the 301 Priority Watch lists, despite being an industrialized country that provides more protection, even in copyright, than the TRIPS Agreement requires.[161]

9. In conclusion

Ten years after the complaint was first instituted, the US Section 110(5) Panel decision begins to look less like the bombshell it first seemed. As a legal matter, it remains a fundamentally flawed and unreliable indicator of what may occur in future cases, or as a guide to legal interpretation at national level. However, the failure to revisit the issue at the WTO over the past ten years has allowed the standard to become the de facto yardstick against which proposals to further or to restrict copyright protection have been made, possibly giving it far more influence than its legal reasoning would deserve. A significant amount of literature was generated at the time the decision came out, but this has gradually dwindled. Given the potentially restrictive influence on national policy-making as the three-step test of Article 13 has been transposed ionto different national laws, it is imperative for developing countries to ensure that subsequent state practice does not point to an adoption of the Panel decision in this case. The key issues with respect to public policy remain to be addressed and, in the meantime, developing countries remain free to pursue a broad range of options in applying exceptions and limitations in the public interest.

Bibliography

Books

Correa, C. (1997), *The TRIPS Agreement – A Guide for the South: The Uruguay Round Agreement on Trade-related Intellectual Property Rights*, Geneva: South Centre, available at http://www.southcentre.org/index.php?option=com_content&task=view&id=87&Itemid=67 (accessed 26 May 2009).

---

161 United States Trade Representative (2009), '2009 Special 301 Report', p. 18, available at http://www.ustr.gov/assets/Document_Library/Reports_Publications/2009/2009_Special_301_Report/asset_upload_file903_15608.pdf.

UNCTAD – ICTSD (2005), *Resource Book on TRIPS and Development*, Cambridge: Cambridge University Press, available at http://www.iprsonline.org/unctadictsd/ResourceBookIndex.htm (accessed 26 May 2009).

Articles and reports

Brennan, D.J. (2002), 'The Three-step Test Frenzy – Why the TRIPS Panel Decision Might be Considered Per Incuriam', *Intellectual Property Quarterly*, **2**, available at http://ssrn.com/abstract=299543 (accessed 26 May 2009).

Dinwoodie, G.B. (2006), 'The International Intellectual Property Law System: New Actors, New Institutions, New Sources', *Marquette Intellectual Property Law Review*, **10**(2), available at http://ssrn.com/abstract=749349 (accessed 26 May 2009).

Dun and Bradstreet (1998) *Dun's Market Identifier Market Profile.*

Engle, E.A. (2002) 'When is Fair Use Fair?: A Comparison of E.U. and U.S. Intellectual Property Law', *Transnational Lawyer*, **15**(187), available at http://ssrn.com/abstract=1020474 (accessed 26 May 2009).

Garza Barbosa, R. (2007), 'Revisiting International Copyright Law', *Barry Law Review*, **8**, 43, available at http://ssrn.com/abstract=987090 (accessed 26 May 2009).

Gervais, D.J. (2005), 'Towards a New Core International Copyright Norm: The Reverse Three-step Test', *Marquette Intellectual Property Law Review*, **9**, available at http://ssrn.com/abstract=499924 (accessed 26 May 2009).

Ginsburg, J.C. (2001), 'Toward Supranational Copyright Law? The WTO Panel Decision and the "Three-step Test" for Copyright Exceptions', *Revue Internationale du Droit d'Auteur* **187**, available at http://ssrn.com/abstract=253867 (accessed 26 May 2009).

Hugenholtz, P.B. and R.G. Okediji (2008), 'Conceiving an International Instrument on Exceptions and Limitations to Copyright,' available at http://www.ivir.nl/publicaties/hugenholtz/finalreport2008.pdf (accessed 26 May 2009).

Hugenholtz, P.B (1997), 'Fierce Creatures–Copyright Exemptions: Towards Extinction?', *Keynote Speech*, IFLA/IMPRIMATUR Conference, *Rights, Limitations and Exceptions: Striking a Proper Balance*, Amsterdam, Netherlands, 30–31 October 1997, available at http://www.ivir.nl/publications/hugenholtz/PBH-FierceCreatures.doc (accessed 26 May 2009).

Koelman, K.J. (2006), 'Fixing the Three-step Test', *EIPR.*, **28**(8), 407–412.

Kur, A. (2008) 'Of Oceans, Islands, and Inland Water–How Much Room for Exceptions and Limitations under the Three-step Test?', *Max Planck Papers on Intellectual Property, Competition & Tax Law*, Research Paper No. 08-04, available at http://ssrn.com/abstract=1317707 (accessed 26 May 2009).

Landau, Michael (2007), 'Fitting United States Copyright Law into the International Scheme: Foreign and Domestic Challenges to Recent Legislation', *Georgia State University Law Review*, **23**, 847.

Netanel, N.W. (2001), 'From the Dead Sea Scrolls to the Digital Millennium; Recent Developments in Copyright Law', *Texas Intellectual Property Law Journal*, **9**, available at http://ssrn.com/abstract=245455 (accessed 26 May 2009).

Okediji, R.G. (2005), 'The International Copyright System: Limitations, Exceptions and Public Interest Considerations for Developing Countries', Geneva, Switzerland: ICTSD available at http://www.iprsonline.org/unctadictsd/docs/Okediji_Copyright_2005.pdf (accessed 26 May 2009).

Reichman, J.H. (2000), 'The TRIPs Agreement Comes of Age: Conflict or Cooperation with the Developing Countries?', *Case Western Reserve Journal of International Law*, **32**, 441.

Ricketson, S. (1987), *The Berne Convention for the Protection of Literary and Artistic Works: 1886–1986,* 483, Kluwer.

Ricketson, S. (2003), 'WIPO Study on Limitations and Exceptions Copyright and Related Rights in the Digital Environment', WIPO SCCR/9/7 2003, available at: http://www.wipo.int/meetings/en/doc_details.jsp?doc_id=16805 (accessed 26 May 2009).

Samuelson, P. (1997), 'The U.S. Digital Agenda at WIPO', *Vanderbilt Journal of International Law*, 369.

Senftleben, M. (2006), 'Towards a Horizontal Standard for Limiting Intellectual Property Rights? – WTO Panel Reports Shed Light on the Three-step Test in Copyright Law and Related Rights in Patent and Trademark Law', *International Review of Intellectual Property and Competition Law*, **37**(4), 407–38.
Shabalala, D.B. (ed.) (2007), *A Citizen's Guide to WIPO*, Geneva: CIEL, available at http://www.ciel.org/Publications/CitizensGuide_WIPO_Oct07.pdf.
Story, A, Darch, C. and Halbert D. (eds.) (2006), 'The Copy/South Dossier: Issues in the Economics, Politics and Ideology of Copyright in the Global South', Copy/South Research Group, available at www.copysouth.org (accessed 26 May 2009).
Sun, H. (2007), 'Overcoming the Achilles Heel of Copyright Law', *Northwestern Journal of Technology and Intellectual Property*, **5**, 265, available at http://ssrn.com/abstract=1021027 (accessed 26 May 2009).
United States Trade Representative (2009), '2009 Special 301 Report,' available at http://www.ustr.gov/assets/Document_Library/Reports_Publications/2009/2009_Special_301_Report/asset_upload_file903_15608.pdf.
World Trade Organization, 'Summary US – Section 110(5) Copyright Act (DS160)', available at http://www.wto.org/english/tratop_e/dispu_e/cases_e/1pagesum_e/ds160sum_e.pdf (accessed 26 May 2009).
World Trade Organization (2000), 'United States – Section 110(5) of US Copyright Act – Report of the Panel', WT/DS160/R, available at http://www.wto.org/english/tratop_e/dispu_e/cases_e/ds160_e.htm (accessed 26 May 2009).
Yu, P.K. (2004), 'The Escalating Copyright Wars', *Hofstra Law Review*, **32**, 907–51, available at http://ssrn.com/abstract=436693 (accessed 26 May 2009).
Yu, P.K. (2006), 'TRIPs and its Discontents,' *Marquette Intellectual Property Law Review*, **10**, 369–410, MSU Legal Studies Research Paper No. 03-03, available at http://ssrn.com/abstract=578577 (accessed 26 May 2009).

7 WTO panel on United States – Section 110(5) of the US Copyright Act

Maximiliano Santa Cruz

Introduction

This dispute between the European Communities and the United States[1] is the only controversy on the issue of copyright that has got to the stage where the Dispute Settlement Body (DSB) of the World Trade Organization (WTO) has adopted a panel report.[2] At issue was the compatibility of certain limitations to the exclusive rights of right holders incorporated in the US Copyright Act[3] with the TRIPS Agreement and the substantive provisions of the Berne Convention.

The exceptions in dispute (known as the homestyle exception and the business exception) except certain food, drinking and retail establishments from paying royalties for the public communication by radio or TV of a broadcast embodying a work.

The parties to the dispute did not disagree on whether the limitations in US law implicated the exclusive rights of communication to the public,[4] but whether they complied with the TRIPS general copyright exception clause, known as the three-step test.

Interestingly, at the same time that this dispute was being litigated, another WTO panel was deciding on the issue of exceptions and limitations, but this time in relation to patent rights. In that case (see Chapter 9, Canada – Patent Protection of Pharmaceutical Products), the respective panel also made an extensive analysis of the (Berne Convention's) three-step test, as the precedent for the general patent exception clause in the

---

1 The report of the Panel is to be found in WTO document WT/DS160/R of 15 June 2000, hereinafter referred to as the Panel Report. Go to http://www.wto.org/english/tratop_e/dispu_e/cases_e/ds160_e.htm, last visited February 18, 2009.

2 In the other two copyright disputes ventilated in the WTO, the US requested the establishment of a panel but later on the parties to the disputes notified that they had reached a mutually satisfactory solution. See dispute DS115 European Communities – Measures Affecting the Grant of Copyright and Neighboring Rights and dispute DS82 – Ireland – Measures Affecting the Grant of Copyright and Neighboring Rights at http://www.wto.org.

3 17 USC §§ 101–810.

4 Panel report 6.27.

TRIPS Agreement, on which Canada based its defense, is precisely that same provision.

The question of limitations and exceptions has always been at the center of the debates in copyright because it goes to heart of the system itself. The purpose of copyright is twofold. First, the granting of temporary exclusive rights to authors is seen as an incentive to create and a possibility for the author to maintain control over its work. Second, the granting of exclusive rights carries benefits not only to authors, but also to society as a whole, as the creation of these new works enriches the body of knowledge and permits unlimited access to, and use of these works once they have fallen in the public domain with respect to copyright.

The law should always seek to balance the interest of right holders with the legitimate expectations of society. In seeking this balance, limitations and exceptions are fundamental to fulfilling the second purpose.

This chapter will describe the main arguments and findings in the dispute, including, first, the provisions in the US Copyright Law that were questioned by the European Communities, and second, the provisions of the TRIPS Agreement and the Berne Convention allegedly violated by the homestyle and business exceptions. After that, it will talk about the importance of the findings, particularly to the use of exceptions and limitations.

The dispute

At issue was whether Section 110(5)(A) and (B) of the US Copyright Act was in violation of TRIPS Article 9.1, which incorporates the substantive provisions of the Berne Convention (1971) into TRIPS, in connection with the Berne Convention's Article 11(1)(ii) and Article 11*bis*(1)(iii), and whether the exceptions in Section 110(5) were justified under the general copyright exception clause of the TRIPS Agreement contained in Article 13.

The European Communities alleged that two exceptions in the US Copyright Act, contained in subparagraphs (A) and (B) of Section 110(5), were inconsistent primarily with Article 11*bis*(1)(iii) (establishing the exclusive right to authorize the public communication by loudspeaker or any analogous instrument transmitting, by signs, sounds or images, the broadcast), and also with Article 11(1)(ii) of the Berne Convention (establishing the exclusive right of authorizing any communication to the public of the performance of their works), as incorporated into the TRIPS Agreement.[5]

The US, on the other hand, argued that the exceptions were justified

---

[5] Panel report 6.17.

under the 'minor exceptions' doctrine, which allows Members of the WTO (and Berne) to provide for minor limitations on exclusive rights. According to the US, TRIPS Article 13 (*limitations and exceptions*) 'clarifies and articulates the scope of the minor exceptions doctrine, which is applicable under the TRIPS Agreement'[6] and 'provides the standard by which to judge the appropriateness of such limitations or exceptions'.[7] TRIPS Article 13 contains the so-called three-step test, a three-prong test setting certain criteria to be followed when crafting exceptions and limitations to copyright.

Because the US did not contest that both subparagraphs (A) and (B) of Section 110(5) implicate Articles 11*bis*(1)(iii) and 11(1)(ii),[8] the focus of the panel fell mainly on whether the exceptions met the criteria in the three-step test. Consequently, the panel reasoned, the ultimate burden of proof of establishing that an exception or limitation is applicable, and that the conditions for invoking it are met, fell on the US.

The United States Copyright Act

Section 106 of the US Copyright Act lays down the exclusive rights in copyrighted works, establishing that the owner of a copyright has the exclusive right to do and authorize the reproduction of the work, the preparation of derivative works, the distribution of copies of the work or phonogram, the public performance and display of the work and in the case of sound recordings, the public performance by means of a digital audio transmission.[9]

---

6 Panel report 6.42.

7 Panel report 3.3.

8 Panel report 6.27.

9 Subject to sections 107 through 122, the owner of copyright under this title has the exclusive rights to do and to authorize any of the following:

(1) to reproduce the copyrighted work in copies or phonorecords;
(2) to prepare derivative works based upon the copyrighted work;
(3) to distribute copies or phonorecords of the copyrighted work to the public by sale or other transfer of ownership, or by rental, lease, or lending;
(4) in the case of literary, musical, dramatic, and choreographic works, pantomimes, and motion pictures and other audiovisual works, to perform the copyrighted work publicly;
(5) in the case of literary, musical, dramatic, and choreographic works, pantomimes, and pictorial, graphic, or sculptural works, including the individual images of a motion picture or other audiovisual work, to display the copyrighted work publicly; and
(6) in the case of sound recordings, to perform the copyrighted work publicly by means of a digital audio transmission.

Amongst the several exceptions and limitations in the US Copyright Act,[10] Section 110 provides for limitations to the exclusive rights of authors, particularly to the exclusive rights to perform and display established in Section 106 of the Copyright Act. Two of the more than ten exceptions incorporated in Section 110 were questioned by the European Communities,[11] namely the so-called homestyle exception and the business exception.

The homestyle exception[12] benefits those establishments communicating a transmission embodying a performance or display of works other than nondramatic musical works, using a single receiving apparatus of the kind commonly used in private homes.

The business exception,[13] in its turn, comprises two types of beneficiaries:

---

[10] See 17 USC 107–22, providing among other, limitations for fair use, for reproduction by libraries and archives, first sale of a copy or phonorecord, for computer programs, architectural works and for blind and other people with disabilities.

[11] 17 USC provides for limitations for performances and displays, among others, for face to face teaching, at places of worship or religious services, for government bodies and organizations in agricultural fairs, for establishments selling phonorecords and for blind or other handicapped persons.

[12] Section 110: 'Notwithstanding the provisions of section 106 the following are not infringements of copyright: [. . .] (5)(A) except as provided in subPanel report (B), communication of a transmission embodying a performance or display of a work by the public reception of the transmission on a single receiving apparatus of a kind commonly used in private homes, unless –

> (A) a direct charge is made to see or hear the transmission; or
> (B) the transmission thus received is further transmitted to the public;

[13] Section 110: 'Notwithstanding the provisions of section 106 the following are not infringements of copyright: [. . .] (5)(B) communication by an establishment of a transmission or retransmission embodying a performance or display of a nondramatic musical work intended to be received by the general public, originated by a radio or television broadcast station licensed as such by the Federal Communications Commission, or, if an audiovisual transmission, by a cable system or satellite carrier, if –

> (i) in the case of an establishment other than a food service or drinking establishment, either the establishment in which the communication occurs has less than 2,000 gross square feet of space (excluding space used for customer parking and for no other purpose), or the establishment in which the communication occurs has 2,000 or more gross square feet of space (excluding space used for customer parking and for no other purpose) and –
>
> > (I) if the performance is by audio means only, the performance is communicated by means of a total of not more than 6 loudspeakers, of which not more

(i) retail establishments and (ii) food service and drinking establishments. On the one hand, retail establishments under 2000 square feet (186 m^2) benefit from the exemption at all event. Over 2000 square feet, they have to comply with specifications on equipment. On the other hand, food service and drinking establishments under 3750 square feet (348 m^2) benefit from the exemption at all event. Over 3750 square feet, they have to comply with specifications on equipment. As opposed to the homestyle exception, the business exception applies to nondramatic musical works.

The homestyle exception had been introduced into the Copyright Act in 1976, having as its precedent the *Aiken* case decided by the United States

---

than 4 loudspeakers are located in any 1 room or adjoining outdoor space; or

(II) if the performance or display is by audiovisual means, any visual portion of the performance or display is communicated by means of a total of not more than 4 audiovisual devices, of which not more than 1 audiovisual device is located in any 1 room, and no such audiovisual device has a diagonal screen size greater than 55 inches, and any audio portion of the performance or display is communicated by means of a total of not more than 6 loudspeakers, of which not more than 4 loudspeakers are located in any 1 room or adjoining outdoor space;

(ii) in the case of a food service or drinking establishment, either the establishment in which the communication occurs has less than 3,750 gross square feet of space (excluding space used for customer parking and for no other purpose), or the establishment in which the communication occurs has 3,750 gross square feet of space or more (excluding space used for customer parking and for no other purpose) and –

(I) if the performance is by audio means only, the performance is communicated by means of a total of not more than 6 loudspeakers, of which not more than 4 loudspeakers are located in any 1 room or adjoining outdoor space; or

(II) if the performance or display is by audiovisual means, any visual portion of the performance or display is communicated by means of a total of not more than 4 audiovisual devices, of which not more than 1 audiovisual device is located in any 1 room, and no such audiovisual device has a diagonal screen size greater than 55 inches, and any audio portion of the performance or display is communicated by means of a total of not more than 6 loudspeakers, of which not more than 4 loudspeakers are located in any 1 room or adjoining outdoor space;

(iii) no direct charge is made to see or hear the transmission or retransmission;
(iv) the transmission or retransmission is not further transmitted beyond the establishment where it is received; and
(v) the transmission or retransmission is licensed by the copyright owner of the work so publicly performed or displayed;

Supreme Court.[14] In the *Aiken* case (*Twentieth Century Music Corp. v. Aiken*, 422 US 151 (1975)), the Supreme Court 'held that an owner of a small fast food restaurant was not liable for playing music by means of a radio with outlets to four speakers in the ceiling; the size of the shop was 1,055 square feet (98 m^2), of which 620 square feet (56 m^2) were open to the public'.[15]

As stated in two House Reports in 1976 the rationale behind the limitation was that the homestyle exception (in its original form) 'applies to performances and displays of all types of works, and its purpose is to exempt from copyright liability anyone who merely turns on, in a public place, an ordinary radio or television receiving apparatus of a kind commonly sold to members of the public for private use'. '[The clause] would impose liability where the proprietor has a commercial "sound system" installed or converts a standard home receiving apparatus (by augmenting it with sophisticated or extensive amplification equipment) into the equivalent of a commercial sound system.' The exemption would cover small commercial establishments 'which [were] not of sufficient size to justify, as a practical matter, a subscription to a commercial background music service'.[16]

In 1998 the Fairness in Music Licensing Act amended the Copyright Act in two ways. First, it incorporated the business exception into Section 110, limiting its application to nondramatic musical works. Second, by confining the application of the business exception to nondramatic musical works, the application of the homestyle exception was narrowed down to works other than nondramatic musical works (that is, 'music that is part of an opera, operetta, musical or other similar dramatic work when performed in a dramatic context'[17]). The legislation would have been 'a *quid pro quo* for the 20-year extension of the copyright term for, among other things, popular music dating back to the 1920s and 1930s'.[18]

In describing the factual aspects of the dispute, the panel noted that 'the types of transmissions covered by both subparagraphs (A) and (B) of Section 110(5) include original broadcasts over the air or by satellite,

---

[14] Panel report 2.6.

[15] Panel report 2.6.

[16] Panel report 2.5 quoting the Report of the House Committee on the Judiciary, H.R. Rep. No. 94-1476, 94th Congress, 2nd Session 87 (1976) and Conference Report of the House Committee on the Judiciary, Subcommittee on Courts and Intellectual Property, H.R. Rep. No. 94-1733, 94th Congress., 2nd Session 75 (1976).

[17] Panel report 2.7.

[18] Gorman, Robert A. and Ginsburg, Jane C., *Copyright Cases and Materials*, University Casebook Series, 6th edition, New York: Foundation press, 2002, p. 602.

rebroadcasts by terrestrial means or by satellite, cable retransmissions of original broadcasts, and original cable transmissions or other transmissions by wire. The provisions do not distinguish between analog and digital transmissions'[19] and the exceptions do 'not apply to the use of recorded music, such as CDs or cassette tapes, or to live performances of music'.[20]

The provisions in the TRIPS Agreement and the Berne Convention

The TRIPS Agreement (Article 9.1) incorporated the substantive provisions of the Berne Convention,[21] meaning that Members of the WTO have to fully comply with Articles 1 to 21 of Berne (except Article 6*bis* on moral rights) and with the Appendix regarding developing countries.

As said before, the European Communities alleged that subparagraphs (A) and (B) of Section 110(5) were inconsistent primarily with Article 11*bis*(1)(iii) 'which covers the communication to the public of a broadcast which has been transmitted at some point by hertzian waves, [and also with Article 11(1)(ii) of the Berne Convention (1971)] to the extent that a communication to the public concerns situations where the entire transmission has been by wire'.[22] The panel noted that while 'rights conferred in Article 11(1)(ii) concern the communication to the public of performances of works in general, Article 11*bis*(1)(iii) is a specific rule conferring exclusive rights concerning the public communication by loudspeaker or any other analogous instrument transmitting, by signs, sounds or images, the broadcast of a work'.[23]

The TRIPS Agreement in relation to the Berne Convention grants authors and right holders exclusive rights to their works. The rights implicated in the case were only two of the several exclusive economic rights (as opposed to moral rights) included in the Berne Convention, such as the right of translation (article 8), the right of reproduction (article 9), the right of public performance of dramatic, dramatico–musical and musical works (article 11, including the exclusive right of authorizing any communication to the public of the performance of their works, questioned by the European Communities), the right of broadcasting and communication to

---

19 Panel report 2.15.

20 Panel report 2.16.

21 TRIPS Article 9(1): 'Members shall comply with Articles 1 through 21 of the Berne Convention (1971) and the Appendix thereto. However, Members shall not have rights or obligations under this Agreement in respect of the rights conferred under Article 6*bis* of that Convention or of the rights derived therefrom'.

22 Panel report 6.26.

23 Panel report 6.25.

the public by wire, by re-broadcasting or (article 11*bis*, which also includes the right of communication to the public by loudspeaker or any other analogous instrument of the broadcast of the work, also questioned by the European Communities), right of public recitation (article 11*ter*), the right of adaptation (article 12), the right of making cinematographic adaptation and reproduction of works, and the right of distribution of the works thus adapted and reproduced (article 14).[24]

The United States did not deny that the two exceptions in Section 110 involved both Articles 11*bis*(1)(iii) and 11(1)(ii). However, it claimed the exceptions were fully consistent with the TRIPS Agreement, incorporating Berne, as the Agreement allows Members of the WTO to place minor limitations on exclusive rights. Article 13 of the TRIPS Agreement, the US asserted, 'provides the standard by which to judge the appropriateness of such limitations or exceptions'.[25]

The minor exceptions doctrine

Before applying the conditions of TRIPS Article 13 to the exceptions in US law, the panel went on to analyze the minor exceptions doctrine because, as said before, the United States argued that TRIPS Article 13 'clarifies and articulates the scope of the minor exceptions doctrine, which is applicable under the TRIPS Agreement'.[26] So the panel first undertook to find whether the minor exceptions doctrine forms part of the Berne Convention *acquis* and second, if it did, whether it applies to TRIPS by virtue of TRIPS Article 9.1 together with Berne Articles 1 to 21. In doing this, the panel analyzed the reports of several revision conferences as supplementary means of interpretation.

There is no explicit or implicit reference to the minor exceptions doctrine in the Berne Convention. However, when the general right of communication to the public (Article 11) was incorporated in the Brussels Act in 1948, it was also proposed to incorporate a general provision under which Members of the Berne Convention would be able to retain minor exceptions existent in their national laws. This idea did not succeed because there was concern that Members would introduce additional exceptions in their domestic legislation. Instead, Members decided to include a statement in the General Report of the Brussels Conference referring to the 'possibility available to national legislation to make what is commonly called minor

[24] See WIPO document, 'International protection of copyright and related rights' (Panel report 10.f, p. 4) at http://www.wipo.int/copyright/en/activities/other.html.

[25] Panel report 3.3.

[26] Panel report 6.42.

reservations. The Delegates of Norway, Sweden, Denmark, and Finland, the Delegate of Switzerland and the Delegate of Hungary, have all mentioned these limited exceptions allowed for religious ceremonies, military bands and the needs of the child and adult education'.[27] According to the panel, 'the choice of these words reflects an agreement within the meaning of Article 31(2)(a) of the Vienna Convention between the Berne Union members at the Brussels Conference to retain the possibility of providing minor exceptions in national law'[28] and that this 'was made in connection with the conclusion of a revision of the Convention introducing additional exclusive rights, including those contained in Articles 11*bis*(1)(iii) and 11(1)(ii), to which these limitations were to apply'.[29]

Reinforcing this idea, the panel noted that reports of the Stockholm Conference (1967) made reference to the agreement between Berne Members that minor exceptions are permitted, *inter alia*, in respect of Articles 11 and 11*bis* of Berne. Also, parties and third parties to the dispute brought to the attention of the panel several exceptions in their domestic legislation, based on the minor reservation doctrine previous to the three Diplomatic Conferences (Brussels, Stockholm and Paris) held by Berne Members and to the date the TRIPS Agreement became applicable to them, confirming a state practise.

The panel rejected claims by the European Communities, stating that the examples of exceptions given in the records of the Brussels and Stockholm conferences (that is, religious ceremonies, military bands and the needs of the child and adult education) were exhaustive and that the doctrine was limited to cases of an exclusively non-commercial character. It also rejected claims by the European Communities that the records of the Stockholm Conference understood the doctrine as allowing countries only to 'maintain' existing national exceptions (grandfathering).

With respect to the claim that the examples given in the Brussels Conference were exhaustive, the panel said that it was 'evident that the given examples are of an illustrative character',[30] giving examples of the views of both the Belgian government and BIRPI (United International Bureaux for the Protection of Intellectual Property), saying that it would be virtually impossible to list all of the pre-existing exceptions as they were too varied. The panel also noted that the examples in the Brussels Report

---

[27] See footnote 61 of the Panel Report citing the Report of the Conference included in Annex XII.1 to the letter from the Director General of WIPO to the Chair of the panel.

[28] Panel report 6.53.

[29] Ibid.

[30] Panel report 6.57.

were given with respect to Article 11(1) of the Berne Convention, but at the same time clarified that exceptions can be provided for other exclusive rights, namely the ones in Articles 11*bis*, 11*ter*, 13 and 14 without giving specific examples, which was another demonstration that they were not exhaustive.

Regarding the claim that the doctrine was limited to cases of exclusively non-commercial character, the panel dismissed the claims, arguing that it wasn't in a 'position to determine that the minor exceptions doctrine justifies only exclusively non-commercial use of works and that it may under no circumstances justify exceptions to uses with a more than negligible economic impact on copyright holders'.[31] The panel observed that the examples of exceptions in the Brussels Conference normally involve minimal uses which are not carried out for profit, but the case of child and adult education is less clear and could even reach a level that has a major economic impact on the right holder. Consequently, the panel concluded that the non-commercial use is not determinative as long as the exceptions are minor.

Finally, the panel simply did not give credit to the European Communities' argument that the word 'maintain' in the reports of the Stockholm Conference would have 'frozen' the coverage of the exceptions existing at that moment in Berne Members.

After concluding that the minor exceptions doctrine forms part of the context of the Berne Convention, particularly of the context of Articles 11*bis* and 11, the panel went to analyze whether or not the minor exceptions doctrine was incorporated into TRIPS through Article 9.1 together with Articles 1 to 21 of Berne.

In this respect, the panel determined that because there was no express exclusion of the doctrine in TRIPS Article 9.1 (as was, for example, the express exclusion of Article 6*bis* of Berne on moral rights), Articles 11 and 11*bis* of Berne have been included in TRIPS with the entire *acquis* of the provisions, including the minor exceptions doctrine.

TRIPS Article 13 – the scope of the three-step test

After concluding that the Berne Convention allows Members to provide for minor exceptions to exclusive rights, primarily concerned with *de minimis* use[32] and not limited to the examples given in the Brussels and

---

31 Panel report 6.58.

32 See Senftleben, Martin, 'Copyright, Limitations and the Three-step Test – An analysis of the Three-step Test in International and EC Copyright Law', The Hague, The Netherlands: Kluwer Law International, 2004, p. 47.

Stockholm Conferences, and that this doctrine was incorporated into the TRIPS Agreement, the panel analyzed the scope of Article 13 of TRIPS and its relation to Articles 11*bis*(1)(iii) and 11(1)(ii) of Berne.

The panel noted that Article 13 of TRIPS is based on similar language in Article 9(2) of the Berne Convention. Article 9(2) of Berne states:

> It shall be a matter for legislation in the countries of the Union to permit the reproduction of such works in certain special cases, provided that such reproduction does not conflict with a normal exploitation of the work and does not unreasonably prejudice the legitimate interests of the author.

The main difference would be that the latter applies only to the reproduction right, whereas the former doesn't have any limitation as to the exclusive rights it would apply to.

One of the main arguments of the European Communities against the application of Article 13 to Articles 11*bis*(1)(iii) and 11(1)(ii) of Berne was that in its opinion it only applies to 'those rights that were added to the TRIPS Agreement, and, therefore, it does not apply to those provisions of the Berne Convention (1971), including its Articles 11(1) and 11*bis*(1), that were incorporated into the TRIPS Agreement by reference'.[33] In the European Communities opinion, parties to Berne cannot agree in another treaty to reduce its level of protection, as Article 20 of the Berne Convention only allows countries of the Union to 'enter into special agreements among themselves, insofar as such agreements grant to authors more extensive rights than those granted by the Convention'. The European Communities also argued that the objective of the TRIPS Agreement was precisely to reduce or eliminate exceptions existing at that time.

Regarding this argument, the panel noted that nothing in Article 13 or any other Article in TRIPS supported the interpretation that the three-step test only applies to rights incorporated into the TRIPS Agreement.

Another argument of the European Communities is that any exception to the exclusive rights in Article 11*bis*(1) of Berne would have to provide an equitable remuneration based on Article 11*bis*(2) of Berne. The US countered, and the panel agreed, that Article 11*bis*(2) was not related to the minor exceptions doctrine. Article 11*bis*(2) simply authorized a party to the Berne Convention to substitute a compulsory license for one of the exclusive rights in Article 11*bis*. The panel noted that if the European Communities argument were to prevail, no exceptions whatsoever would be allowed free of charge, which would amount to adding a fourth requirement to the three-step test.

---

33 Panel report 6.75.

The three-step test of TRIPS Article 13

Once having established that the minor exceptions doctrine applies to the Berne Convention and to the TRIPS Agreement, and that the scope of Article 13 covers both Articles 11*bis* (1)(iii) and 11 (1)(ii), the panel turned its attention to the analysis of the so-called three-step test contained in TRIPS Article 13. The panel then proceeded to apply the three-step test to the exceptions of Section 110(5) of the US Copyright Act in relation to Berne Articles 11*bis*(1)(iii) and 11(1)(ii).

Article 13 of TRIPS on *Limitations and Exceptions* states:

> Members shall confine limitations or exceptions to exclusive rights to certain special cases which do not conflict with a normal exploitation of the work and do not unreasonably prejudice the legitimate interests of the right holder.

The panel noted, and the parties agreed, that the three conditions were cumulative. Therefore all of them should be fulfilled in order for an exception to be valid.

In applying the three conditions of the three-step test to both exceptions of Section 110, the panel first analyzed the first condition of the test in general terms, and then applied it to both exceptions in Section 110. It discussed the business exception of Section 110(5)(B) first because most of the arguments raised by the parties focused on it'.[34] It then followed the same procedure with the other two conditions of the three-step test.

Certain special cases

Regarding the first requisite of the three-step test, both parties were of the opinion, and the panel agreed, that the meaning of 'special cases' was that the exceptions and limitations had to be clearly defined and of limited application. However, the European Communities added that the exception should serve a special purpose, meaning that there should be a legitimate public policy objective justifying the exception. The US countered, saying that there was no requirement in the TRIPS Agreement as to the legitimacy of the exception. At the most, there should be a specific policy objective.

After analyzing the ordinary meaning of the words 'certain' and 'special', the panel concluded that for the first condition of the test to be met, the limitation or exception adopted at domestic level should be clearly defined and should be narrow in scope and reach (that is, narrow in a quantitative as well as in a qualitative sense). With respect to the EC's argument on the legitimacy of the exceptions, the panel concluded that the

---

34 Panel report 6.98.

limitation or exception does not need to serve a special purpose or legitimate public policy objective, as this was hard to reconcile with the words of Article 13 and interpretations of the Appellate Body rejecting 'interpretative tests which were based on the subjective aim or objective pursued by national legislation'.[35]

After examining the first condition in general, the panel examined whether the two exceptions of Section 110(5) were clearly defined and sufficiently narrow in scope and reach.

THE BUSINESS EXCEPTION

As said before, the business exception comprises two types of beneficiaries: (i) retail establishments and (ii) food service and drinking establishments. Retail establishments under 2000 square feet benefit from the exemption at all event. Over 2000 square feet they have to comply with specifications on equipment. On the other hand, food service and drinking establishments under 3750 square feet benefit from the exemption at all event. Over 3750 square feet they have to comply with specifications on equipment.

The US claimed that the business exception complied with the first condition of the three-step test because it was clearly defined in Section 110(5) by square footage and equipment limitations. To the European Communities on its part, footage and equipment requirements were irrelevant when 'the broad scope of the business exception turns an exception into the rule'.[36] The panel noted that the European Communities didn't question whether the exception was clearly defined but whether it constituted a special case given its scope and reach.

The European Communities observed, based on several studies, that 70 percent of food service and drinking establishments and 45 percent of retail establishments were potential users of the business exception. Despite the US asserting that many establishments had to be subtracted from those figures, the panel dismissed those arguments. Among others, the US claimed that there are establishments which do not play music at all; others use different sources, such as CD or live performances, and others would not play music if they became liable.

Finally, the panel noted that if Section 110(5)(B) excepted a major part of the users that were meant to be covered by the introduction of Article 11*bis*(1)(iii) to the Berne Convention, the business exception could not qualify as a *special case*. Indeed, the preparatory work of the 1948 Brussels Conference, where the exclusive rights in question were introduced,

---

[35] Panel report 6.111.
[36] Panel report 6.116.

indicates that the establishments intended to be covered by these rights were precisely those exempted by Section 110(5)(B), among others, restaurants and tea rooms.

Therefore, the panel concluded, the business exception does not meet the requirement of being a certain special case under the three-step test.

The homestyle exception

The beneficiaries of the homestyle exception are those establishments communicating a transmission embodying a performance or display of works other than nondramatic musical works.

The US claimed that the homestyle exception complied with the first condition of the three-step test because it was 'clearly defined in Section 110(5) by requiring the use of a *homestyle receiving apparatus*. The European Communities countered, saying that the expression "single receiving apparatus of a kind commonly used in private homes" was imprecise and may evolve due to technological development'.[37]

The parties, based on a study, did not dispute that 16 percent of all eating establishments, 13.5 percent of all drinking establishments, and 18 percent of all retail establishments were below the square footage (1055 square feet) of the *Aiken* case and therefore could potentially benefit from the exception. Based on these numbers, the panel concluded that from a quantitative point of view, the reach of the exception in respect of potential users was limited to a comparably small percentage of establishments.

With respect to the requirement to use a *single receiving apparatus of a kind commonly used in private homes*, the panel noted that the concept could indeed evolve with technological development, might vary between different countries and could mutate depending on consumer preferences. However, the panel also noted that the concept was sufficiently clear and a 'Member is not required to identify homestyle equipment in terms of exceedingly detailed technical specifications in order to meet the standard of clarity set by the first condition'.[38] The panel recalled that the term '*certain* special cases' suggests 'known and particularized, but not explicitly identified' and that its determinations were limited to what at the time was perceived as homestyle equipment in the US market.

The panel also observed that the coverage of the exception was limited to works other than nondramatic musical works (that is, 'music that is part of an opera, operetta, musical or other similar dramatic work when performed in a dramatic context'). The panel decided that the exception

---

37 Panel report 6.137.
38 Panel report 6.145.

was sufficiently narrow in its scope of application because it was limited to only these types of works. 'Most if not virtually all music played on the radio or television is covered by' the business exception.

Summing up, the panel concluded that the homestyle exception met the requirement of being a certain special case under the three-step test because it was well-defined and limited in its scope and reach in terms of limitations imposed in subsection (A) to permissible equipment and categories of works.

Because the panel concluded that the business exception did not fulfill the requirement of being a *certain special case,* and that the three requirements of TRIPS Article 13 are cumulative, the panel could have stopped its analysis of the business exception. However, given that 'the two subparagraphs are closely related and their respective fields of operation overlap in respects other than the categories of works covered',[39] the panel decided to continue its examination of the two exceptions in light of the other two requirements of the three-step test.

Do not conflict with a normal exploitation of a work

With respect to the second requirement of the three-step test, that the exception does not conflict with a normal exploitation of a work, the panel first looked to interpret the meaning of the words 'normal exploitation'. The panel said that *exploitation* 'refers to the activity by which copyright owners employ the exclusive rights conferred on them to extract economic value from their rights to those works'.[40] Regarding *normal,* the panel noted that the word has two dimensions, an empirical or quantitative one (that is, regular, usual, typical, and ordinary) and a normative one (that is, conforming to a type or standard). It also noted that normal exploitation means something less than full use of an exclusive right.[41]

The US took the view that when examining the second condition of the test, the panel should take into consideration the exception *vis-à-vis* all of the exclusive rights given to the right holder, as well as *vis-à-vis* the exclusive right in question. The exceptions at issue are with respect only to secondary uses of a broadcast, not one of the primary uses where right holders extract many of the gains from. Responding to an argument from the European Communities that all rights are equally important, the US asserted that this did not imply a hierarchy between 'primary' and 'secondary' rights, but it did matter whether an exception affected one or

---

39 Panel report 6.161.
40 Panel report 6.165.
41 Panel report 6.167.

more rights and the extent to which it affected a specific right. The panel agreed with this argument but at the same time said that how an exception or limitation may affect one of the rights cannot be justified by the fact that other rights are not affected. Therefore, it agreed with the European Communities that the conflict with the normal exploitation of a work must be assessed with respect to each exclusive right individually, in this particular case, the rights in Berne Articles 11(1)(ii) and 11*bis*(1)(iii).

The viewpoint of the US was that those areas of the market in which the right holder would not ordinarily expect to receive compensation wouldn't be part of the normal exploitation. The panel agreed with this approach, but only for the empirical dimension of the word *normal*. With regard to the other dimension, the normative approach, the panel concluded that exceptions or limitations that are confined to a scope or degree that does not enter into competition with the non-exempted uses would not conflict with the normal exploitation.

To the European Communities argument that at least all those uses that create an economic benefit to the user should be considered as normal exploitation of the work, the panel replied that 'not every use of a work, which in principle is covered by the scope of exclusive rights and involves commercial gain, necessarily conflicts with a normal exploitation of that work. If this were the case, hardly any exception or limitation could pass the test of the second condition and Article 13 might be left devoid of meaning, because normal exploitation would be equated with full use of exclusive rights'.[42]

Finally, the panel concluded the general analysis of the second requirement by stating that the normal exploitation of a work is not only affected by the actual use of the work without authorization due to an exception or limitation, but also by potential uses.

The business exception

The US argued that the business exception was not in conflict with the normal exploitation of the work for three reasons: first, 'in view of the great number of small eating, drinking and retail establishments, individual right holders or their collective management organizations (CMOs) face considerable administrative difficulties in licensing all these establishments'; second, 'a significant portion of the establishments exempted by the new business exemption had already been exempted under the old homestyle exemption';[43] third, an almost identical exception was avail-

---

42 Panel report 6.182.

43 Panel report 6.190.

able under agreements with the collective societies. For these reasons, the US argued that even before the 1998 amendment, right holders would not normally have expected to obtain fees from these establishments.

With respect to the first argument, the European Communities responded that administrative difficulties in licensing did not justify the non-recognition of a right. Additionally, that if there were such difficulties, then the exception should also have covered recorded music, because it should apply independent of the medium used. The panel agreed with this argument because it did not see a logical reason for differentiating between broadcast and recorded music when examining what is a normal exploitation of a work.

With regard to the second argument, the panel agreed with the estimates given by the US indicating a relatively low level of licensing of restaurants likely to play music. However, it did 'not find the argument compelling, according to which an exception that codifies an existing practice by the CMOs of not licensing certain users should be presumed not to conflict with normal exploitation, as it would not affect right holders' current expectations to be remunerated'.[44] In other words, the panel said, 'licensing practices of the CMOs in a given market at a given time do not define the minimum standards of protection under the TRIPS Agreement'.

Regarding the third argument, that establishments could avail themselves of an almost identical exception under agreements with the CMOs, the panel recognized similarities between those agreements and the business exception; however, it did not find this argument compelling. The panel noted that right holders are free to exercise their rights in whichever manner they want, even choosing not exploit them. Another thing was to enact legislation that prevents the exercise of a right which a country is obliged to respect by virtue of the TRIPS Agreement.

Finally, the panel reasoned that right holders would expect to be in a position to authorize the broadcast of their musical works, and receive compensation for it, by many of the establishments covered by the business exception. Consequently, the panel concluded, the business exception conflicted with the normal exploitation of the work.

The homestyle exception

In its analysis of the homestyle exception, in light of the first requirement of the three-step test (that the exceptions and limitations must be limited to certain special cases) the panel had concluded that from a quantitative point of view the reach of the exception in respect of potential users was

---

[44] Panel report 6.198.

limited to a comparably small percentage of establishments (16 percent of all eating establishments, 13.5 percent of all drinking establishments, and 18 percent of all retail establishments). Based on this finding, and on the fact that right holders 'do not normally license or attempt to license the public communication of transmissions embodying dramatic renditions of "dramatic" musical works in the sense of Article 11*bis*(1)(iii) and/or 11(1)(ii)', the panel concluded that the homestyle exception did not conflict with a normal exploitation of a work.

Not unreasonably prejudice the legitimate interests of the right holder

As it had done with the other two requirements of the three-step test, the panel started the general analysis of the third requirement by interpreting the meaning of its words. The panel said that 'first, one has to define what are the "interests" of right holders at stake and which attributes make them "legitimate". Then, it is necessary to develop an interpretation of the term "prejudice" and what amount of it reaches a level that should be considered "unreasonable"'.[45]

The panel first noted that 'interests' is not limited to actual or potential economic advantage or detriment, as the US had argued. 'Interests' may encompass a legal right or title, as well as concern about a potential detriment or advantage. In the European Communities opinion, legitimate interests of the right holder consisted of the possibility of preventing all uses of its work, including, at a minimum, all commercial uses.

The term 'legitimate' on its part connoted both lawfulness from a positive perspective and legitimacy from a more normative perspective, while 'prejudice' connoted damage, harm or injury.

With regard to 'not unreasonably', the panel stated that a certain amount of 'prejudice' to the legitimate interests of the right holder is acceptable as long as it is not unreasonable. The crucial question was which degree or level of prejudice may be considered as unreasonable. It determined that to measure this it would look at the economic value of the exclusive rights, acknowledging though that legitimate interests are not confined to this economic value. In the panel's view, 'prejudice to the legitimate interests of right holders reaches an unreasonable level if an exception or limitation causes or has the potential to cause an unreasonable loss of income to the copyright owner'.[46]

The panel determined that its analysis of whether the exceptions were of an unreasonable level would not be limited to the right holders of the

---

45 Panel report 6.222.
46 Panel report 6.229.

European Communities because nothing in TRIPS Article 13 suggested that the assessment of prejudice should be limited to right holders of the WTO Member that brought forth the complaint.

THE BUSINESS EXCEPTION

The European Communities concentrated its arguments on the potential economic effects of the exception on the legitimate interests of right holders. It reiterated that the exception had become the rule and the protection of the exclusive right the exception, due to the fact that the business exception covered 73 percent of all drinking, 70 percent of all eating, and 45 percent of all retail establishments.

The US contended that the numbers provided by the European Communities were not useful to estimate the economic impact because they did not take into account establishments that (i) did not play music at all; (ii) relied on other sources to play music, other than radio and TV, such as CDs, tapes, jukeboxes, live music and commercial music services; (iii) were not licensed before the 1998 amendment; (iv) would avail themselves of the agreements with the CMOs, whose terms were almost identical to the exception; and (v) would rather turn off the music than pay fees.

With respect to considerations (i), (ii) and (v), the panel agreed with the statement of the US that some establishments that played broadcast music would prefer to turn off the music if required to pay royalties to the CMOs. But it was also true that several establishments using recorded music could switch to using broadcast music to avoid paying royalties or those establishments which did not play music at all could start playing broadcast music with sound systems that fulfill the requirements of the business exception. Conversely, if the exception did not exist, establishments that availed themselves of the exception could perhaps switch to using recorded music or commercial music services. Therefore, the considerations of the US, although useful to reflect the realities at a given point in time, did not take into account the substitution between the various sources of music.

With respect to consideration (iii), the panel rejected the arguments of the US, which underestimated the figures of actual distributions to right holders, past licensing practices and revenue collected and forgone by CMOs, because they disregarded the potential effects of the exception. If only actual losses were taken into account, the panel reasoned, 'it might be possible to justify the introduction of a new exception to an exclusive right irrespective of its scope in situations where the right in question was newly introduced, right holders did not previously have effective or affordable means of enforcing that right, or that right was not exercised because the right holders had not yet built the necessary collective management structure required for such exercise. While under such circumstances the introduction of a new exception might not cause immediate additional loss of income to the right holder, he or she could never build up expectations to earn income from the exercise of the right in question'.[47]

As to the US's consideration (iv), the panel recalled its arguments in the analysis of the second requirement of the three-step test (*not conflict with a normal exploitation of a work*), that private agreements with the CMOs are simply a way of exercising exclusive rights, which is irrelevant to assessing the compliance of the exception with the US's international obligations.

Due to these considerations, the panel concluded that the US had not demonstrated that the business exception did not unreasonably prejudice the legitimate interests of the right holders. Therefore the business exception did not meet the third requirement of the three-step test.

THE HOMESTYLE EXCEPTION

The panel recalled that the intention of the homestyle exception was to exempt small commercial establishments which were not of sufficient size to justify, as a practical matter, a subscription to a commercial music service. For this purpose, 16 percent of all eating, 13.5 percent of all drinking and 18 percent of all retail establishments were covered by the exception, as long as they used homestyle equipment. Finally, the panel also noted that after the 1998 amendment, the exception covered only the public communication of transmissions embodying dramatic musical works.

Because these small establishments using homestyle apparatus have never been a significant source of revenue collection for CMOs and because the European Communities did not submit evidence suggesting that 'potential effects of significant economic or practical importance could occur that they would give rise to an unreasonable level of prejudice to legitimate interests of right holder',[48] the panel concluded that the homestyle exception did comply with the third requirement of the three-step test.

Findings of the panel

In June 2000, the panel circulated its report to members, finding that the homestyle exception met the requirements of TRIPS Article 13 and consequently was consistent with Articles 11*bis*(1)(iii) and 11(1)(ii) of Berne as incorporated into TRIPS by Article 9.1 of the Agreement.

It also found that the business exception did not meet the requirements

---

47 Panel report 6.247.

48 Panel report 6.271.

of TRIPS Article 13 and consequently was inconsistent with Articles 11*bis*(1)(iii) and 11(1)(ii) of Berne as incorporated into TRIPS by Article 9.1 of the Agreement.

The recommendation of the Panel was 'that the Dispute Settlement Body request the United States to bring subparagraph (B) of Section 110(5) into conformity with its obligations under the TRIPS Agreement'.[49]

The DSB adopted the Panel Report in July 2000 and neither party appealed.

Implementation of the findings

At the request of the European Communities under Article 21(c) of the DSU, in January 2001 an Arbitrator determined that a reasonable period of time for the US to implement the recommendations of the DSB was 12 months since the adoption of the panel by the DSB. In July of that same year, the DSB extended this period until December 2001.

Under Article 25.2 of the DSU, the parties sought recourse to arbitration to determine the level of nullification and impairment of benefits caused to the European Communities as a result of the business exception. In November 2001, the Arbitrators determined that 'the level of EC benefits which are being nullified or impaired as a result of the operation of Section 110(5)(B) amounts to €1.219.900 per year'.[50]

However, because the US failed to comply with the findings, in January 2002 the European Communities requested authorization from the DSB to suspend concessions to the US under Article 22.2 of the DSU. The US requested an Arbitrator under Article 22.6 of the DSU, but the parties asked the Arbitrator to suspend the proceedings in February 2002.

In June 23, 2003, the parties notified the DSB that they had reached a mutually satisfactory solution[51] by which the US committed itself to 'make a lump-sum payment in the amount of $3.3 million (the "Payment") to a fund to be set up by performing rights societies in the European Communities for the provision of general assistance to their members and the promotion of authors rights (the "Fund")'.

The agreement, covering a three-year period starting in December 2001, ended in December 2004 without the US having implemented the recommendations of the DSB. Since then, the US has continued to notify, pursuant to Article 21.6 of the DSU, that its Administration is working 'closely with the US Congress and will continue to confer with the European

---

49 Panel report 7.2.

50 See WTO document WT/DS160/ARB25/1 of November 9, 2001.

51 See WTO document WT/DS160/23 of June 23, 2003.

Communities in order to reach a mutually satisfactory resolution of this matter'.[52]

Conclusion

The issue of exceptions and limitations to copyright is of fundamental importance in the necessary balance between the rights of right holders with those of society. Since the original Act of the Berne Convention (1884), countries have placed limitations on the rights of authors,[53] and as we have seen, limitations have also played an important role in the different revision conferences. In addition to the TRIPS Agreement, other copyright and related rights treaties, such as the Rome Convention for the Protection of Performers, Producers of Phonograms and Broadcasting Organizations, as well as the WIPO (World Intellectual Property Organization) Copyright Treaty (WCT)[54] and the Performers and Phonograms Treaty (WPPT)[55] have also recognized the importance of exceptions and limitations by incorporating specific and/or general framework exceptions (for example, the three-step test).

Exceptions and limitations have become increasingly important with the advent of the information society, where digital technologies are seen not only as a threat to the rights of authors in terms of facilitating the unauthorized use of copyrighted works, but most importantly as an opportunity to increase access to knowledge, promote competition, facilitate trade and improve education.

Developed WTO Members, such as the two parties to this dispute, have made extensive use of these flexibilities by incorporating numerous exceptions and limitations in their domestic legislation.[56] Developing countries, on the contrary, have used exceptions and limitations to a much lesser

---

[52] See, for instance, WTO document WT/DS160/24/Add.51of March 9, 2009.

[53] See Ricketson, Sam, 'WIPO Study on Limitations and Exceptions for Copyright and Related Rights in the Digital Environment', WIPO document SCCR/9/7. April 2003, p. 3.

[54] See Article 10 of the WCT and the 'Agreed statement concerning Article 10: It is understood that the provisions of Article 10 permit Contracting Parties to carry forward and appropriately extend into the digital environment limitations and exceptions in their national laws which have been considered acceptable under the Berne Convention. Similarly, these provisions should be understood to permit Contracting Parties to devise new exceptions and limitations that are appropriate in the digital network environment'.

[55] See Article 16 of the WPPT.

[56] See the US Copyright Act, 17 USC 107–22 and the Directive 2001/29/EC of the European Parliament and of the Council of 22 May 2001 on the harmonization of certain aspects of copyright and related rights in the information society.

degree, but growing attention to the issue has been captured in recent developments, such as the adoption of 45 Recommendations under the WIPO Development Agenda.[57]

WIPO has increased its work on the issue of exceptions and limitations thanks to a proposal by Chile in 2004 to study the subject of exceptions and limitations to copyright and related rights for the purposes of education, libraries and disabled persons[58] and to several studies on the issue mandated by the Secretariat.[59]

The thorough analysis of TRIPS Article 13 conducted by the panel is not only important for matters related to copyright. As we have seen, TRIPS Article 13 is based on Article 9(2) of the Berne Convention, which is also the antecedent for other general exception clauses in the TRIPS Agreement, such as in the areas of trademarks (Article 17), patents (Article 30) and industrial designs (Article 26(2)). With variations in wording, all of these provisions are very similar.[60] Due to these similarities and their common origin, TRIPS Article 13 was also the subject of analysis in the WTO panel, Canada – Pharmaceutical Patents, dealing with exceptions to patent rights.

Despite the panel report not being binding on WTO Members, the fact that the panel did not stop its analysis of the business exception once it found that it did not meet the first requirement of the three-step test (that is, certain special cases), helps to shed more light as to the scope of application of the three-step test, as there is no doubt that it is a valuable supplementary aid to interpretation.

However, the panel report has received some criticism,[61] from those arguing that the three requirements of the test should not be analyzed in isolation. Instead, the three steps should be considered together as a whole and comprehensively, *vis-à-vis* the general objectives of intellectual

---

[57] See for instance, Recommendations 17 and 22 at http://www.wipo.int/ip-development/en/agenda/recommendations.html#b, last visited March, 6, 2009.

[58] See WIPO documents SCCR/12/3, SCCR/13/5 and SCCR/16/2.

[59] See Ricketson, Sam, 'WIPO Study on Limitations and Exceptions of Copyright and Related Rights in the Digital Environment', WIPO document SCCR/9/7; Garnett, Nick, 'Automated Rights Management Systems and Copyright Limitations and Exceptions', WIPO document SCCR/14/5; Sullivan, Judith, 'Study on Copyright Limitations and Exceptions for the Visually Impaired', SCCR/15/7; Crews, Kenneth, 'Study on Copyright Limitations and Exceptions for Libraries and Archives', SCCR/17/2.

[60] See Canada – Pharmaceutical Patents, Panel Report (document WT/DS114/R), p. 130.

[61] See 'The Patry Copyright Blog', at http://williampatry.blogspot.com/2008/07/declaration-on-three-step-test.html last visited March 4, 2009.

property embodied in TRIPS Article 7 and the Preamble to the WCT, and should take into account not only the interests of copyright right holders but also of the general public as is the case with other general exceptions for patents, trademarks and industrial designs in the TRIPS Agreement, which are also modeled from the three-step test of the Berne Convention.[62]

---

[62] See 'A Balanced Interpretation of the Three-step Test in Copyright Law', declaration by the Max Planck Institute for Intellectual Property, Competition and Tax Law at http://www.ip.mpg.de/ww/en/pub/news/declaration_on_the_three_step_/declaration.cfm, last visited March 4, 2009.

8 Dispute settlement under the TRIPS Agreement: the United States–Brazil (2000) and United States–Argentina (2002) patent disputes

Viviana Muñoz Tellez

The WTO dispute settlement system and the TRIPS agreement

The objective of the dispute settlement system of the World Trade Organization (WTO) is to provide security and predictability to the multilateral trading system.[1] The settlement of situations in which a member considers that any benefits accruing to it directly or indirectly under the covered agreements are being impaired by measures taken by another member is considered essential to the effective functioning of the WTO and the maintenance of a proper balance between the rights and obligations of members.[2]

In addition to finding solutions to disputes, the dispute settlement system also works to clarify and interpret the provisions of WTO agreements. The Ministerial Conference and General Council are empowered to render interpretations of the WTO agreements. However, for the most part these bodies do not exercise their authority to do so. Instead, members often rely on the rulings of the Dispute Settlement Body (DSB), the Appellate Body, panels and arbitrations to provide interpretative guidance on the agreement provisions. Decisions taken by these bodies with respect to prior specific disputes are informative for interpretation purposes in subsequent disputes, but not binding. These decisions must not change the WTO law that is applicable between the parties, that is, add to or diminish the rights and obligations provided in the WTO Agreements.[3]

The WTO dispute settlement system applies to the Agreement on Trade-related Aspects of Intellectual Property Rights (TRIPS). Consultations and the settlement of disputes under the TRIPS Agreement are bound by the general rules and procedures for the management of disputes set out in the General Agreement on Tariffs and Trade (GATT) 1994 in Articles

1 Article 2, DSU.
2 Article 3, DSU.
3 Articles 3.2 and 19.2, DSU.

XXII and XIII, as elaborated and applied by the Dispute Settlement Understanding (DSU), except as otherwise specifically provided in the TRIPS Agreement.[4]

The effectiveness and credibility of the WTO dispute settlement continues to be an ongoing subject of intense debate. This is particularly so with respect to developing countries, which face distinct challenges in accessing the system and making it work to their advantage.[5] These challenges include lack of financial and legal resources as well as political power.

The United States–Argentina patent dispute

In May 1999, the United States filed a complaint to the DSB[6] against Argentina, supplemented by another complaint in May 2000,[7] when Argentina's further TRIPS obligations had come into force. The United States alleged that Argentina's legal regimes governing patents and data protection[8] were inconsistent with its obligations under the TRIPS agreement. Various rounds of consultations were held from June 1999 to April 2002. The United States, following demands from its pharmaceutical industry, had placed the issue of trade in pharmaceuticals high on the bilateral agenda of the two countries for over a decade before the complaint was filed.[9]

The dispute was resolved when Argentina and the United States informed the DSB in May 2002 that they had reached a mutually agreed solution.[10] The DSU states that a solution mutually acceptable to the parties to a dispute and consistent with the covered agreements is clearly

---

4 Article 64.1, the TRIPS Agreement.

5 *South Centre Quarterly on Trade Disputes*, third quarter 2006, 2(3), pp. 11–13.

6 *Argentina – Patent Protection for Pharmaceuticals and Test Data Protection for Agricultural Chemicals*, WTO document, WT/DS171/1, dated 6 May 1999.

7 *Argentina – Certain Measures on the Protection of Patents and Test Data*, WTO document WT/DS196/1, dated 30 May 2000.

8 The United States made reference to the following Argentinean laws: No. 24.481 on Patents and Utility Models (as amended by Law No. 24.572), Law 24.603 and Decree 260/96; and data protection in Law 24.766 and Regulation 440/98.

9 See Jennifer Ellen Mattson, 'Timeline of US–Argentina Dispute on Pharmaceutical Patents', University of California at Berkeley/CPTech, 20 April 2005, available at http://www.cptech.org/ip/health/c/argentina/argentinatimeline.html. Last viewed 20 January 2009.

10 *Argentina – Patent Protection for Pharmaceuticals and Test data Protection for Agricultural Chemicals, Argentina – Certain Measures on the Protection of Patents and Test Data, Notification of Mutually Agreed Solution,* dated 20 June 2002, WTO documents WT/DS171/3, WT/DS171/3/Corr.1, WT/DS196/4, WT/

the preferred manner of securing a positive solution to a dispute.[11] The terms on which the parties settle their dispute must also be consistent with the WTO agreement in question and must not nullify or impair benefits accruing to any other Member under the agreement.[12]

The mutually agreed solution includes commitments by Argentina to introduce significant changes to its patent regime. Such changes include modifications to provisions concerning process patent protection, preliminary injunctions and patentability of micro-organisms.

The mutually agreed solution

One of the exceptional features of the mutually agreed solution reached by the United States and Argentina is comprised of various distinct commitments and a time frame for the implementation of the various substantive issues in question. The mutually agreed solution comprises nine different substantive issues:

(1) compulsory licences;
(2) exclusive marketing rights;
(3) import restrictions;
(4) patent by product protection;
(5) shifting of the burden of proof in patent process infringement cases;
(6) preliminary injunctions;
(7) patentability of micro-organisms and other subject matter;
(8) transitional patents;
(9) protection of test data against unfair commercial use.

The various agreements that constitute the mutually agreed solution come under four categories:[13]

1. Mutually agreed solution reached on issues 1 through 8(a) on the basis of interpretation and systematic reading of the Argentinean laws. On issues 1–3, 7 and 8(a), both parties recognized the consistency of Argentinean law with the TRIPS Agreement.

DS196/4/Corr.1, IP/D18/Add.1, IP/D/22/Add.1, IP/D/22/Add.1/Corr.1, dated 20 June 2002.

[11] Article 3.7 DSU.

[12] Article 3.5 and 3.7 DSU.

[13] Sandra Cecilia Negro, 'Organización Mundial del Comercio y Solución Mutuamente Convenida: El Caso Argentina – Patentes', in C. Correa (2006), *Medidas Cautelares en el Régimen de Patentes*, Buenos Aires, Argentina: Lexis Nexis, pp. 129–68.

2. Mutually agreed solution reached on issues 4, 5 and 6, conditioned to modifications of the Argentinean law. The United States and Argentina agreed to a future time frame for implementing these commitments, considering that the agreed modifications to the respective provisions under the Argentinean law would require the submission of a bill by the Government of Argentina to the National Congress. Both parties agreed to continue consultations to assess the progress of the legislative process of approval.
3. Agreement reached on issue 8(b) that Argentina would fulfil its WTO obligations under Article 70.7 of the TRIPS Agreement through its legal system and practices, including decisions of the Supreme Court of Justice.
4. Agreement reached on issue 9 in which both parties agreed that differences in interpretations of the provisions of Article 39.3 of TRIPS regarding test data protection should be solved under DSU rules. The United States reserved the right in future to continue consultations or request the establishment of a panel.

Compulsory Licenses

The United States and Argentina reached the mutually agreed solution that Argentina's laws were in conformity with its obligations under Article 31(k) of the TRIPS Agreement, by specifying how certain anti-competition provisions in Argentinean law were to be interpreted for the purposes of granting the compulsory licences allowed under Article 31(k) of TRIPS.

The mutually agreed solution reached establishes that Argentina will not issue compulsory licences under Article 31(k) in making use of the anti-competitive provisions in its patent law unless certain prior conditions are met, including a prior decision by the competition authority (the National Commission on the Defence of Competition or the body that might replace it in the future) determining a practice as anti-competitive.

The complaint of the United States stated that Argentina failed to provide certain safeguards for the granting of compulsory licences, including timing and justification safeguards for compulsory licences granted on the basis of inadequate working.[14] However, the mutually agreed solution focuses on a rather different issue: the use of anti-competition provisions in Argentinean patent law in relation to the issuing of compulsory licences under Article 31(k) of the TRIPS Agreement.

Article 31(k) of TRIPS exempts members from particular conditions

---

[14] *Argentina – Certain Measures on the Protection of Patents and Test Data*, WTO document WT/DS196/1, dated 30 May 2000.

that are generally required for the granting of compulsory licences, where the use is permitted to remedy a practice determined by judicial or administrative process to be anti-competitive. The TRIPS Agreement does not expressively define what constitutes an anti-competitive practice and thus members have significant flexibility on this matter.

The United States sought to ensure that if a situation listed in Article 44 of the Argentinean Law No. 24.481 as being anti-competitive were found to exist, it would not per se warrant an automatic determination that the patent owner is engaging in anti-competitive practices. Article 40.2 of the TRIPS Agreement explicitly reserves the right for members to specify and provide for legislation on the licensing practices and conditions that may in a particular case constitute an abuse of intellectual property rights, having an adverse effect of competition in the relevant market. While Article 31(k) establishes that a compulsory licence may be granted to remedy a practice 'determined after judicial or administrative process to be anti-competitive', it gives discretion to members as to what the national authority determines to be anti-competitive practice.

In this case, the United States and Argentina agreed that Article 44 of the Argentinean Law No. 24.481 would be read in conjunction with Article 44 of Decree 260/96 to the effect that as a condition of the Instituto Nacional de Propiedad Intelectual (INPI) granting a compulsory licence, a prior decision must have been handed down by the National Commission on the Defence of Competition (or a body that might replace it in the future), analysing the practice in question based on Law No. 25.156 (Law of Defence of Competition). Article 44 of Decree 260/96 establishes that a compulsory licence may be granted without the authorization of the patent holder when the competent authority has determined that the patent holder has engaged in anti-competitive practices. It does not define which is the competent authority.

The mutually agreed solution limits the flexibility available to Argentina in implementing Article 31(k) of the TRIPS Agreement to determine what situation is anti-competitive and which is the competent authority that can determine an anti-competitive practice.

Exclusive Marketing Rights

The United States alleged that Argentina had failed to establish an effective system to grant exclusive marketing rights for pharmaceutical or agricultural chemical products in accordance with Article 70.9 of the agreement.

The United States and Argentina reached the mutually agreed solution that Argentina's patent laws are in conformity with its obligations under Article 70.9 of the TRIPS Agreement. The mutually agreed solution on the issue of exclusive marketing rights only refers to pharmaceutical products.

At the time when the complaints were made by the United States, Argentina did not grant patent protection for pharmaceutical product inventions. Argentina was eligible to make use of the transition periods available under Article 65 of the TRIPS Agreement allowing for developing countries to delay granting patent protection for pharmaceutical products until 1 January 2005. Accordingly, Argentina's patent law established that patent protection for inventions related to pharmaceutical products would not be granted until October 2000.[15] Argentina abstained from extending the transition period until 2005, under pressure from the United States.

The TRIPS Agreement requires that all WTO member countries,[16] even those that benefit from transition periods that delay granting of patents for pharmaceutical and agricultural chemical products, to provide a 'mailbox' system, whereby patent applications for such products can be filed in these countries during the transition period to secure the date of priority. These patent applications remain dormant, to be considered for the grant of a patent after the expiry of the transitional period.

Article 70.9 of the TRIPS Agreement establishes that for those patent applications that are in the mailbox in a WTO member country, the patent applicant should be given exclusive marketing rights for five years after the relevant member country has approved the marketing of the product or until a patent has been granted or rejected in that member, whichever period is shorter, in the case that (a) the patent has been filed and granted for the same product in another WTO member country, (b) has been granted marketing approval in such other member country.

The precise obligation of member countries under Article 70.9 of TRIPS remains controversial. The basis for the controversy is that the term 'exclusive marketing rights' is undefined. Member countries and legal experts diverge in their interpretation of the scope of the exclusive marketing rights to be granted and thus the legal effects of exclusive marketing rights. In the interpretation of Article 70.9 advanced by the United States and the European Communities, exclusive marketing rights should be granted to the effect of giving exclusivity to the patent applicant for the

---

[15] Article 100, Law No. 24.481 on Patents and Utility Models (as amended by Law No. 24.572).

[16] The obligations under Article 70.9 of the TRIPS Agreement do not apply to least-developed country members with respect to pharmaceutical products until 1 January 2016. The obligation was waived by the WTO General Council, WTO document WT/L/478, dated 8 July 2002.

marketing of the product, in other words, the right to exclude others from marketing the product during the prescribed period, even though there is no patent. On this interpretation, the effect of exclusive marketing rights would have the equivalent legal effects as exclusive patent rights.[17]

The interpretation of the European Communities, Argentina, India, African member countries and other developing countries is that exclusive marketing rights are not the same and are not equivalent to patent rights. Accordingly, in compliance with Article 70.9, members have greater flexibility to define what constitutes exclusive marketing rights, and what rights such a right holder would be entitled to, as compared to patent rights, which are clearly defined in the TRIPS Agreement.[18]

Legal experts also suggest that it cannot be the case that exclusive marketing rights were meant to have the same effect as patent rights in the TRIPS Agreement, since this would nullify the transition periods provided in the Agreement. In any case, the granting of exclusive marketing rights should not be used to prevent production for export to third countries and may be interpreted as not providing exclusive rights, as patents do, because the patent application may be rejected.[19]

Neither the DSB, the General Council nor the TRIPS Council have ever given an interpretation of the definition of exclusive marketing rights or what rights they confer. The DSB panel report on a dispute brought about by the United States against India regarding its obligations under Article 70.9 found that 'based on customary rules of treaty interpretation, we have reached the conclusion that under Article 70.9 there must be a mechanism ready for the grant of exclusive marketing rights at any time subsequent to the date of entry into force of the WTO Agreement'.[20] The date in question was 1 January 1995 and not the end of the transition period provided by the TRIPS Agreement. The panel, however, did not address the question of the scope of exclusive marketing rights.

In its complaint against Argentina, the United States pursued its interpretation of exclusive marketing rights, arguing that even though

---

[17] See also Nuno Pires de Carvalho (2004), *The TRIPS Regime of Patent Rights*, The Hague, The Netherlands: Kluwer Law International, UK.

[18] Minutes of the TRIPS Council Meeting, WTO document IP/C/M/40, dated 22 August 2003, pp. 42–43.

[19] Carlos Correa (2000), *Intellectual Property Rights, the WTO, and Developing Countries: The TRIPS Agreement and Policy Options*, New York: Zed Books, UK, p. 96.

[20] *India – Patent Protection for Patent Protection for Pharmaceutical and Agricultural Chemical Products* (WT/DS50), Panel Report, WTO document WT/DS50/R, dated 5 September 1997, para. 7.60.

Argentina did provide for a mailbox system in its legislation and had granted exclusive marketing rights, it was failing to provide exclusive marketing rights from 1 January 1995 in accordance with its obligations under Article 70.9 because Argentina allowed third parties to market pharmaceutical and agricultural chemical products over which exclusive marketing rights had already been granted to other patent applicants for the same product. The position of Argentina remained that member countries were free to decide on the implementation of exclusive marketing rights in accordance to Article 70.9 and on Argentina's interpretation, exclusive marketing rights did not grant the right to exclude third parties from marketing the relevant product.

Given that the mutually agreed solution between the United States and Argentina found that Argentinean law as it stood at the time was consistent with its obligations under Article 70.9, the solution did not reduce the legal flexibility for Argentina to interpret the scope of exclusive marketing rights differently from the United States.

Import Restrictions

The United States claimed that Argentina denied for patents the exclusive right of importation. The mutually agreed solution finds that Argentinean law is consistent with its obligations under the TRIPS Agreement. However, it provides a more restrictive interpretation of the Argentinean law with respect to parallel imports than might generally have been made.

Article 28.1 of the TRIPS Agreement establishes that a patent for a product confers on its owner the exclusive right, among other things, to import the product for the purposes of making, using or offering for sale that product. The provision in Article 28 specifies in a footnote that the right to importation, like all other rights conferred under the TRIPS Agreement in respect of the use, sale, importation and other distribution of goods, is subject to the provisions of Article 6. Article 6 of the TRIPS Agreement allows member countries the freedom to define their regime for the exhaustion of intellectual property rights. It states that 'for the purposes of dispute settlement under this Agreement, subject to the provisions of Articles 3 and 4 nothing in this Agreement shall be used to address the issue of the exhaustion of intellectual property rights'.[21]

This flexibility is relevant for member countries to allow or curtail parallel imports, that is, when a product made legally abroad is imported without the permission of the intellectual property right holder (that is,

---

21 Article 6, the TRIPS Agreement.

patent owner). Whether or not parallel imports are allowed in a given member country depends on the doctrine of exhaustion that it decides to implement.

The Argentinean law permitted parallel imports, as it applied international exhaustion of patent rights for both products and processes. It established that the rights conferred in a patent shall have no effect against any person who acquires, uses, imports or in any way deals in the product patented or obtained by the patented process once the said product has been lawfully placed on the market in any country. It further establishes that it will be considered that the placement on the market has been lawful when it has been made in accordance with Part III, Section IV of the TRIPS Agreement.[22]

The mutually agreed solution adds an additional element that is not explicit in the Argentinean law. It notes that 'a voluntary licensee in Argentina authorized by the Argentinean patent owner to import the patented product may import the product if he proves that the product has been put on the market in a foreign country by the owner of the Argentinean patent or by a third party authorized for its commercialization'.[23]

Argentinean law made no reference to the effect that authorization by the patent owner would be required as a precondition for parallel imports. The flexibility for Argentina in making use of the provision was thus limited by the agreed mutual solution.

Product by Process Patent Protection

The United States alleged that Argentina denied exclusive rights concerning the protection of products produced by patented processes. As a result of the mutually agreed solution, Argentina agreed to submit a bill to the National Congress to amend the provisions in its patent law relating to process patent protection (otherwise known as product-by-process patent protection).

The TRIPS Agreement requires member countries to expand the scope

---

[22] Article 36(c), Law No. 24.481 on Patents and Utility Models (as amended by Law No. 24.572) (consolidated text), constitutes Decree No. 260/96 of 20 March 1996, WTO documents IP/N/1/ARG/I/2IP/N/1/ARG/I/2/Corr.1.

[23] *Argentina – Patent Protection for Pharmaceuticals and Test Data Protection for Agricultural Chemicals, Argentina – Certain Measures on the Protection of Patents and Test Data, Notification of Mutually Agreed Solution,* dated 20 June 2002, WTO documents WT/DS171/3, WT/DS171/3/Corr.1, WT/DS196/4, WT/DS196/4/Corr.1, IP/D18/Add.1, IP/D/22/Add.1, IP/D/22/Add.1/Corr.1, dated 20 June 2002.

of patent protection to cover patented products as well as patented processes. It defines the exclusive rights conferred by a patent and differentiates between patents for products and patents for processes.[24] With regard to process patents, these are to be granted to cover the process itself and also to the product obtained 'directly' by that patented process. Article 28.1 of the TRIPS Agreement establishes that: 'A patent shall confer on its owner the following exclusive rights: where the subject matter of a patent is a process, to prevent third parties not having the owner's consent from the act of using a process, and from acts of: using, offering for sale, selling or importing for these purposes at least the product obtained directly by that process'.

While at the time of the complaint Argentina provided process patent protection, the United States requested that Argentina amend its patent law to include specific wording denoting the exclusive rights that a patent shall also confer to prevent third parties not having the owner's consent from the acts of using, offering for sale, selling or importing a product obtained directly by the patented process.

The agreed amendment to the Argentinean law falls in line with Article 28.1, but adds further wording to the text of the article to specifically identify the holder of a patent process as the party with the right to prevent third parties from undertaking the acts referred to.

Shifting of the Burden of Proof in Process Patent Infringement Cases

The United States alleged that Argentina improperly limited the authority of its judiciary to shift the burden of proof in civil proceedings involving the infringements of process patent rights, as required in Article 34 of the TRIPS Agreement. As a result of the mutually agreed solution, Argentina agreed to submit a bill to the National Congress to amend the provisions in its patent law to give authority to the judiciary to shift the burden of proof in process patent infringement cases.

The TRIPS Agreement requires in Article 34.1 that member countries empower their judicial authorities to shift or reverse the burden of proof (the obligation to affirmatively prove a fact in controversy or an issue) from the plaintiff to the defendant (alleged infringer) in civil proceedings to prove that the process to obtain an identical product is different from the patented process. Member countries must apply the rule with respect to either new products obtained by the patent process (Article 34.1(a)), or more broadly to products that are not new but where there is substantial

---

24 Article 28, the TRIPS Agreement.

likelihood that the identical product was made by the process and the owner of the patent has been unable through reasonable efforts to determine the process actually used (Article 34.1(b)).

Argentina agreed to amend its patent law to comply with Article 34.1.[25] The agreed amendment applies the rule with respect to the alternative in Article 34.1(a). It establishes that the courts may reverse the burden of proof in process patent infringement cases, ordering the plaintiff to prove that the process that the defendant is using for obtaining a product infringes the process patent if the product obtained by the patented process is not new. A presumption is to be made to the effect that, in the absence of proof to the contrary, the product obtained by the patented process is not new if the defendant or if an expert appointed by the court at the request of the defendant is able to show that, at the time of the alleged infringement, there exists in the market a non-infringing product identical to the one produced by the patented process that originated from a source different from the right owner or the defendant.

The amendment also includes the exact wording of Article 34.3 which provides that in the presentation of evidence to the contrary, the legitimate interests of defendants in protecting their manufacturing and business secrets shall be taken into account.

Preliminary Injunctions

The United States alleged that Argentina failed to provide prompt and effective provisional measures, such as preliminary injunctions, for purposes of preventing infringements of patent rights from occurring. As a result of the mutually agreed solution, Argentina agreed to submit a bill to the National Congress to amend the provisions of its patent law dealing with the authority of the judiciary to order pre-trial provisional measures.

Argentina agreed to amend Article 83 and Article 87 of its patent law. Article 83 establishes, in accordance to the TRIPS Agreement obligation on provisional measures,[26] that:

> the judicial authorities shall have the authority to order provisional measures in relation to a patent granted [. . .], in order to:
> (1) prevent an infringement of the patent and, in particular, to prevent the entry

---

25 Article 88, Law No. 24.481 on Patents and Utility Models (as amended by Law No. 24.572) (consolidated text), constitutes Decree No. 260/96 of March 20, 1996, WTO documents IP/N/1/ARG/I/2IP/N/1/ARG/I/2/Corr.1.

26 Article 50, the TRIPS Agreement.

into channels of commerce of goods, including imported goods, immediately after customs clearance;
(2) preserve relevant evidence in regard to the alleged infringement.

The amended article then goes on to define certain conditions that must be met for preliminary injunctions to be ordered:

(a) there is a reasonable likelihood that the patent, if challenged by the defendant as being invalid, shall be declared valid;
(b) it is summarily proven that any delay in granting such measures will cause an irreparable harm to the patent holder;
(c) the harm that may be caused to the title holder exceeds the harm that the alleged infringer will suffer in case the measure was wrongly granted;
(d) there is a reasonable likelihood that the patent is infringed.

In Article 50, the TRIPS Agreement is silent with regard to whether member countries require that certain conditions be met before a provisional measure is ordered by the judiciary. However, Article 1.1 allows member countries to determine the appropriate method of implementing the provisions of the agreement within their own legal system and practice. The inclusion of such conditions denotes the discretion allowed to member states in implementing the provisions of the agreement.

The amended text further established that: 'if the above conditions are met, in exceptional cases such as when there is a demonstrable risk of evidence being destroyed, the judicial authorities can grant preliminary injunctions *inaudita altera parte*'. The obligation to grant preliminary injunctions *inaudita altera parte* – without the accused party being heard – is asserted in Article 50.2 of the TRIPS Agreement.

The amended text also establishes that: 'In all cases, before granting a provisional measure, the judicial authority shall request that an expert appointed ex officio examine items (a) and (d) above within a maximum period of 15 days. In the case of granting of any of the measures provided for under this article, the judicial authorities shall order the applicant to provide a security or equivalent assurance sufficient to protect the defendant and to prevent abuses.'

No mention is made in Article 50 of the role of third parties in examining conditions required prior to the grant of preliminary injunctions, but again Article 1.1 of the TRIPS Agreement allows discretion in implementation. The authority given to judicial authorities to require the applicant of a provisional measure to provide a security or equivalent assurance to protect the defendant and to prevent abuses conforms to Article 50.3 of the TRIPS Agreement.

Argentina also agreed to amend Article 87 of its patent law. Before the amendment, Article 87 established that in the case where provisional measures were not granted in accordance to Article 83, the plaintiff could request that the exploitation of the alleged infringing product or process be suspended only if the defendant failed to grant a specific security. The new amended Article 87 established that: 'In cases where provisional measures were not granted pursuant Article 83, the plaintiff may demand security from the defendant not to interrupt the defendant's exploitation of the invention where he wishes to continue with such exploitation'. In other words, under the new provision, the plaintiff can either require the suspension of the exploitation of the invention by the defendant or allow the defendant to continue to exploit the invention upon the grant of a security.

Patentability of Micro-organisms and other Subject Matter

The United States alleged that Argentina was improperly excluding certain subject matter, including micro-organisms, from patentability. The mutually agreed solution refers not only to the patentability of micro-organisms but also to various forms of composition and chemical compounds.[27] Argentina was not required to amend its Argentinean patent legislation, as it was established that it was in compliance with Article 27.3(b). However, Argentina agreed to elaborate and publish guidelines for patent examiners on the applicable criteria for the examination of patent applications that are based on, or make use of, micro-organisms.

The basic criteria for patentability established in the Argentinean patent law is that inventions related to products and processes shall be patentable provided that they are new, involve an inventive step and are susceptible of industrial application.[28] The following, among others, shall not be considered inventions:

(1) discoveries;
(2) methods of surgical, therapeutic or diagnostic treatment applicable to the human body or to animals, any kind of live material or substances;
(3) the juxtaposition of known inventions or mixtures of known products, changes in the shape, dimensions or constituent materials of, except in

---

[27] *Argentina – Patent Protection for Pharmaceuticals and Test Data Protection for Agricultural Chemicals, Argentina – Certain Measures on the Protection of Patents and Test Data, Notification of Mutually Agreed Solution,* dated 20 June 2002, WTO documents WT/DS171/3, WT/DS171/3/Corr.1, WT/DS196/4, WT/DS196/4/Corr.1, IP/D18/Add.1, IP/D/22/Add.1, IP/D/22/Add.1/Corr.1, dated 20 June 2002.

[28] Article 1, Law No. 24.481 on Patents and Utility Models (as amended by Law No. 24.572).

the case of combination or merging in such a way that the elements are unable to function separately or where the characteristic qualities or functions thereof are so altered as to produce an industrial result that is not obvious to a person skilled in the field concerned;
(4) any kind of live material or substances already existing in nature.[29]

The following is specifically excluded from patentability:

(1) certain inventions whose exploitation is to be prevented in the interests of the public good or morality, the health or life of persons or animals, the conservation of plants or the avoidance of serious damage to the environment;
(2) all biological and genetic materials existing in nature or derived therefrom in biological processes associated with animal, plant and human reproduction, including genetic processes applied to the said material that are capable of bringing about the normal, free duplication thereof in the same way as in nature.[30]

With specific reference to the case of applications relating to micro-organisms, the law notes that the product obtainable by means of a claimed process must be described as well as the process itself in the relevant application, and a strain of the micro-organism must be deposited with an institution authorized for the purpose.[31] The public shall have access to the micro-organism culture at the depositary institution, as from the day of publication of the patent application.

Article 27 of the TRIPS Agreement establishes the criteria for patentability, which allow for considerable leeway for member countries to mould their patent laws according to their needs and interests. The exceptions from patentability criteria that are made in the Argentinean law are in accordance with Article 27.2 and 27.3 of the TRIPS Agreement. The first sentence of Article 27.3(b) notes that member countries can exclude from patentability: 'plants and animals other than micro-organisms, and essentially biological processes for the production of plants or animals other than non-biological and microbiological processes'. The

---

[29] Article 6, Law No. 24.481 on Patents and Utility Models (as amended by Law No. 24.572).

[30] Article 7, Law No. 24.481 on Patents and Utility Models (as amended by Law No. 24.572).

[31] Article 20, Law No. 24.481 on Patents and Utility Models (as amended by Law No. 24.572).

TRIPS Agreement does not define the terms micro-organism, essentially biological processes or non-biological and microbiological processes.

As a result of the consultations with the United States, Argentina elaborated further the provisions of its patent law with explanatory guidelines for the patentability of micro-organisms, as well as for compounds, microbiological processes and products derived from microbiological processes. The effect of the guidelines is that it has reduced the flexibility previously available for Argentina in this area.

The guidelines specify that all micro-organisms that comply with the patentability criteria are patentable, as in the case of modified micro-organisms. Micro-organisms pre-existing in nature, whether isolated or purified, would not be patentable. Compounds that include micro-organisms and microbiological processes are patentable if they comply with the patentability criteria. The term 'microbiological process' is defined as covering not only industrial processes but also processes to produce new micro-organisms, for example in the case of genetic engineering. Products derived from microbiological processes, including a micro-organism, are also patentable if they comply with the patentability criteria.

Transitional Patents

The United States alleged that Argentina places impermissible limitations on certain transitional patents so as to limit the exclusive rights conferred by these patents, and to deny the opportunity for patentees to amend pending applications in order to claim certain enhanced protection provided by the TRIPS Agreement. The United States put into question the compliance of Argentinean patent law and practice in respect of Article 70.4 and 70.7 of the TRIPS Agreement.

The mutually agreed solution finds that the Argentinean patent law is in compliance with Article 70.4 of the TRIPS Agreement. In relation to Argentina's obligations under Article 70.7 of TRIPS, it was agreed that Argentina would fulfil its obligations on this matter through its own legal system and practices, including decisions of the Supreme Court of Justice.

Article 70.4 establishes a prior user's right rule. If a third party was making use of a subject matter before such subject matter became subject to protection, the third party user, while infringing the patent, can be allowed to continue to perform such an act, on condition that the third party provides for payment of equitable remuneration to the right holder.

Article 70.7 concerns intellectual property rights that require registration as a condition for protection. It establishes that applications that are pending on the date of application of the TRIPS Agreement for the member country in question can be amended to claim enhanced protection. Given that the requirement of registration and the scope of protection can vary among national legislations, it is logical that the mutually agreed solution between the United States and Argentina on Article 70.7 recognizes that such determinations should be made in accordance with the national legal system and practice of each member country.

Protection of Test Data against Unfair Commercial Use

In its first request for consultations with Argentina, the United States contended that Argentina failed to ensure that changes in its laws, regulations and practice during the transition period provided under Article 65.2 of the TRIPS Agreement do not result in a lesser degree of consistency with the provisions of TRIPS. The United States argued that the issuance of Regulation 440/98, which the United States perceived as not providing effective protection for test data against commercial use, made Argentina's legal regime inconsistent with Article 65.2 of the TRIPS Agreement. The United States claimed that Regulation 440/98 revoked an earlier regulation under which Argentina had provided until August 1998 a ten-year term of protection against unfair commercial use for 'undisclosed' test data or other data submitted in support of applications for marketing approval for agricultural chemical products. Connectedly, in the complaint filed in 2000, the United States alleged that Argentina fails to protect against unfair commercial use of undisclosed test or other data submitted as a requirement for market approval of pharmaceutical or agricultural chemical products.

The United States and Argentina did not agree on a common interpretation of the provisions of Article 39.3 of the TRIPS Agreement regarding protection for undisclosed test data. Instead, they agreed that the issue should be solved under DSU rules. In light of the assessment of the progress of the legislative changes to be undertaken by Argentina on other issues as a result of the mutually agreed solution (product by process patent protection, shifting of burden of proof in process patent infringement cases and preliminary injunctions), the United States reserved the right to continue consultations or request the establishment of a panel related to Article 39.3 of TRIPS. If in future the DSB were to adopt recommendations and rulings clarifying the content of the rights related to undisclosed test data submitted for marketing approval according to Article 39.3 of TRIPS, and if Argentinean law was found to be inconsistent with Article 39.3 as clarified in such recommendations and rulings, Argentina agreed that it would submit to the National Congress within one year an amendment to Argentinean law with the effect of putting its legislation in conformity with its obligations under Article 39.3.

The thrust of the complaint by the United States was that Argentina failed to provide data exclusivity. The United States provides a sui generis system of data protection whereby the first applicant submitting data for the registration of pharmaceutical and agricultural chemical products is granted a temporary exclusive right to use the data after marketing approval. This means that subsequent applicants, such as applicants for generic versions of the product, cannot rely on the data submitted by the first for the purpose of registering a similar product for commercial use. Some experts point out that data protection has become a substitute for patent protection over pharmaceutical and agricultural chemical products in countries that provided such protection until the end of the allowed transitional periods of the TRIPS Agreement, and has also become a strategic tool to compensate for the declining rate of industry's success in developing new products.[32]

Argentina, on the other hand, did not provide for data exclusivity as per the system applied by the United States, nor did it agree to amend its law to such effect, on the basis that Article 39.3 does oblige member countries to grant data exclusivity. Argentina held that the practice of relying upon the data the regulatory authority receives from a first applicant to approve the marketing of a similar (that is, generic) product was not in violation of Article 39.3.

There is no mention of data exclusivity in Article 39.3. The obligation is to protect the related undisclosed test or other data against unfair commercial use, recognizing that producing such data requires considerable effort on the part of the applicant. The term 'unfair commercial use' is undefined in Article 39.3. The United States interprets the term as encompassing any use of the data submitted for registration by the first applicant, without the applicant's authorization. Argentina, on the other hand, held that Article 39.3 does not create exclusive rights. Rather, test data should be protected under the 'unfair commercial use' framework, as established in the Paris Convention Article 10 bis and Article 39.1 of the TRIPS Agreement.

The agreement between the United States and Argentina to solve their differences in interpretations of Article 39.3 also stemmed from the fact that no prior WTO law existed on the matter to provide member countries with interpretative guidance. To date, the DSB has not adopted recommendations or rulings concerning Article 39.3, nor has the United States requested further consultations.

32 See Carlos M. Correa (2004), 'Protecting Test Data for Pharmaceutical and Agrochemical Products under Free Trade Agreements', UNCTAD – ICTSD Dialogue on Moving the Pro-development IP Agenda Forward, Bellagio.

The United States–Brazil patent dispute

In May 2000, the United States requested consultations with Brazil concerning the provisions of its 1996 industrial property law which introduced a local working requirement for patented inventions and established that a patent may be subject to a compulsory licence if the subject matter of the patent is not worked (manufactured) in the territory of Brazil within three years of the issuance of the patent. The United States considered that such a requirement was inconsistent with Articles 27 and 28 of the TRIPS Agreement and Article III of the GATT 1994.[33] The parties held two rounds of consultations on 29 June 2000 and 1 December 2000 but failed to reach a mutually satisfactory solution. Subsequently, on 9 January 2001, the United States launched a formal challenge against Brazil, requesting the establishment of a panel specifically concerning Article 68.I of the 1996 Brazilian industrial property law concerning the granting of compulsory licences in cases when patents are not worked locally.[34] On 31 January 2001, Brazil requested consultations with the United States concerning certain provisions of the United States Patents Code that limit the right to use or sell any federally owned invention only to a licensee that agrees that any products embodying the invention or produced through the use of the invention will be manufactured substantially in the United States. Brazil claimed that such provisions infringe the TRIPS Agreement, as well as the Agreement on Trade-related Investment Measures (TRIMS) Agreement and Articles III and XI of GATT 1994.[35] In July 2001, the United States and Brazil announced that they reached a mutually agreed solution on the challenge brought by the United States against Brazil.[36] The mutually agreed solution also led Brazil not to pursue further consultations with the United States in relation to the United States Code.

The mutually agreed solution

The mutually agreed solution took the form of an exchange of letters. The United States and Brazil maintained their positions regarding the

---

33 *Brazil – Measures Affecting Patent Protection,* WTO document WT/DSS199/1, dated 8 June 2000.

34 *Brazil – Measures Affecting Patent Protection,* Request for the Establishment of a Panel by the United States, WTO document WT/DS199/3, dated 9 January 2001.

35 *United States – US Patents Code,* WTO document WT/DS224/1, dated 7 February 2001.

36 *Brazil – Measures Affecting Patent Protection,* Notification of Mutually Agreed Solution, WTO document WT/DSI199/4, dated 19 July 2001.

compatibility of Article 68 of the Brazilian law with the TRIPS Agreement, but agreed that prior talks would be held in the context of the United States–Brazil consultative mechanism, before the granting by Brazil as per Article 68 of a compulsory licence on patents held by US companies. The United States and Brazil also agreed that Brazil would pursue the challenge against the United States regarding sections 204 and 209 of the United States Patent Code.

Given that the complaints were withdrawn in both Brazil – Measures Affecting Patent Protection and the United States – US Patents Code cases before the establishment of a panel and the submission of written pleadings, uncertainty thus remains as to whether the provisions of the Brazilian patent law and the US patent law are compliant with the TRIPS Agreement. However, the WTO General Council has provided new guidance to member countries on the use of the flexibilities contained in the TRIPS Agreement to protect public health, including compulsory licences and parallel imports through the 2001 Doha declaration on the TRIPS Agreement and Public Health.[37]

Background to the dispute

Brazil is widely regarded as a regional and global leader in the fight against HIV/AIDS on the basis of its effective national HIV/AIDS programme established in 1986 covering prevention, care and treatment. One of the cornerstones of the programme is to ensure that medical products are available at affordable prices or at no cost to people living with HIV/AIDS. The use of the flexibilities provided by the TRIPS Agreement for public health is one means by which Brazil seeks to ensure the availability and affordability of medical products. Accordingly, in the view of Brazil, the measure under Article 68 of its law is not only compatible with the TRIPS Agreement but 'an important instrument available to the Government, in particular in its efforts to increase access of the population to medicines and to combat diseases such as AIDS'.[38]

The United States' pharmaceutical industry played a central role, leading to the decision by the United States to launch a legal challenge against Brazil in relation to the working requirement in its patent law.[39] Prior to

---

[37] Declaration on the TRIPS Agreement and Public Health, Adopted on 14 November 2001, WTO document WT/MIN(01)/DEC/2, dated 20 November 2001.

[38] See Press Statement by the Government of Brazil, 25 June 2001, at http://www.cptech.org/ip/health/c/brazil/brazilstatement06252001.html. Last viewed 20 January 2009.

[39] See Jennryn Wetzler, 'Timeline on Brazil's Compulsory Licensing, Program

the WTO launching of the challenge, the United States included Brazil in the 2000 '"Special 301" Priority Watch List', following a request by the Pharmaceutical Research and Manufacturers of America (PhRMA). The PhRMA alleged that: 'Article 68 of the Brazilian Industrial property law requires domestic exploitation of the subject matter of a patent. Importation may only satisfy this requirement if local manufacture is not feasible, a requirement that is inconsistent with the terms of TRIPS Article 27.1. Our industry is very concerned about this provision, and hopes that it could be resolved quickly at the local level have faded. Brazil stubbornly refuses to address this violation, and has invited a WTO case to resolve the issue. The adverse impact of this provision looms closer for company patents, and has begun to affect the "sitting" decisions of PhRMA member companies. Based on the seriousness of this issue for research-based pharmaceutical companies operating in Brazil, PhRMA requests that Brazil be included in the 2000.'[40]

The claims

There were no formal position papers or submission of pleadings by the United States and Brazil, given that the dispute was not further pursued by the United States.

United States

In the request for the establishment of a panel, the United States challenged the compliance of Article 68 of the 1996 Brazilian industrial property law with Articles 27 and 28 of the TRIPS Agreement and Article III of the GATT 1994. The main claim by the United States was that Article 27.1 of the TRIPS Agreement prohibits WTO member countries from adopting local working requirements in relation to patented inventions as a condition for enjoying exclusive patent rights. The basis for the claim is that Article 27.1 requires that 'patents shall be available and patent rights enjoyable without discrimination as to the place of invention, the field of technology and whether products are imported or locally produced'.[41] To date this 'anti-discrimination' provision has not been interpreted by the WTO. In the interpretation of the United States, the obligation that a member country may impose on patent holders to 'work' the patent can be satisfied through the importation of the patented products or

---

Footnote 39 (*cont.*)
on Information Justice and Intellectual Property', American University – Washington College of Law, 15 June 2007.

[40] See http://www.cptech.org/ip/health/phrma/301-00/brazil.html. Last viewed 20 January 2009.

[41] Last sentence, Article 27.1, the TRIPS Agreement.

the importation of the product obtained from the patented process. Consequently, the United States asserted that the local working requirement in Brazilian patent law discriminates against patent holders who import patented products but do not produce them locally in the territory of Brazil.

The United States also claimed that the Brazilian local working requirement restricts the exclusive rights conferred on the patent holders by their patents, in violation of Article 28.1 of the TRIPS Agreement.

BRAZIL

Throughout the consultations and as reasserted in the exchange of letters on the mutually agreed solution, Brazil asserted that Article 68 of its industrial property law is entirely consistent with Article 27.1 and 28.1 of the TRIPS Agreement. Article 68 sets out the grounds under which a patent shall be subject to compulsory licensing. In numeral I it establishes that as a ground for compulsory licence, the: 'failure to work the subject matter of a patent on the territory of Brazil, failure to manufacture or incomplete manufacture of the product or failure to completely use a patented process, except for failure to work due to lack of economic viability, in which case importing shall be admitted'.[42] Brazil had never made use of the provision. However, by signalling its intention to do so, that is, to issue compulsory licenses by implementing the local working provision with respect to certain pharmaceutical products in 2001, it was able to negotiate substantial price discounts with foreign pharmaceutical companies.[43]

In the view of Brazil and other WTO member countries, granting a compulsory licence, including enforcing a local working requirement, would not be in violation of the anti-discrimination provision in Article 27.1 of the TRIPS Agreement. The main argument is that the provision cannot be read in isolation, but rather, should be taken together with Articles 7, 8, 31 and 40 of the Agreement and Article 5 of the Paris Convention.[44] Article 5(c) of the Paris Convention establishes that each party: '(2) shall

[42] Law No. 9.279, of 14 May 1996 to Regulate Rights and Obligations Relating to Industrial Property.

[43] 'Ministry of Health Announces Compulsory Licensing of Nelfinavir Patent', Press Office, National STD/Aids Program, Brazilian Ministry of Health, dated 22 August 2001. Available at http://www.cptech.org/ip/health/c/brazil/nelf08222001.html. Last viewed 20 January 2008.

[44] Submission by the African Group, Barbados, Bolivia, Brazil, Cuba, Dominican Republic, Ecuador, Honduras, India, Indonesia, Jamaica, Pakistan, Paraguay, Philippines, Peru, Sri Lanka, Thailand and Venezuela to the TRIPS Council, WTO document IP/C/W/296, 29 June 2001.

have the right to take legislative measures providing for the grant of compulsory licenses to prevent the abuses which might result from the exercise of the exclusive rights conferred by the patent, for example, failure to work'. In the view of Brazil, the TRIPS Agreement did not supersede the Paris Convention provision nor include an express prohibition of local working.

Legal experts have also noted that the patent laws of numerous countries contain local working requirements, and that the negotiating history of the TRIPS Agreement indicates that member countries held strong opposing views on the issue.[45]

[45] C. Correa (2003), 'Can the TRIPS Agreement Foster Technology Transfer to Developing Countries?', in Markus, K., Reichman J. (eds), *International Public Goods and Transfer of Technology under a Globalized Intellectual Property Regime*, Cambridge University Press, Cambridge, UK. p. 241.

9 Canada – patent protection of pharmaceutical products

Pedro Roffe and Christoph Spennemann

Introduction

This chapter analyses the *Canada – Patent Protection of Pharmaceuticals* case decided by a WTO panel chaired by Professor Robert Hudec that had the European Communities as the main complainant and Canada as respondent. The issues under discussion were in the main the compatibility of the Canadian Patent Law regarding the protection of inventions in the area of pharmaceuticals with Articles 27, 28 and 30 of the Agreement on Trade-related Aspects of Intellectual Property Rights (TRIPS). The European Communities and their Member States requested the Dispute Settlement Body (DSB), in November 1998, to establish a panel to examine these matters. The Panel was established in February 1999 and its final decision was adopted on 7 April 2000.[1] The decision was not submitted to the Appellate Body for reconsideration.

The decision has been characterized by commentators as being 'the most important analysis of the TRIPS Agreement to date',[2] having 'tremendously important consequences for public health'.[3] As to the regulatory review exception – one of the main issues before the Panel – it has been highlighted that the case confirmed as 'TRIPS-compliant' a patent exception which is still relatively new, as compared to patent exceptions traditionally known under WTO Members' domestic laws.[4] The Panel

---

[1] The report of the Panel is to be found in WTO document WT/DS114/R of 17 March 2000, hereinafter referred to as the Panel Report.

[2] See Frederick M. Abbott (2003), 'Bob Hudec as Chair of the Canada-Generic Pharmaceuticals Panel – The WTO Gets Something Right', 6 *Journal of International Economic Law*, 733, 734 (hereinafter Abbott, 2003).

[3] UNCTAD-ICTSD (2006), 'Exceptions to Patent Rights in Developing Countries', Issue Paper No. 17, Geneva, by Christopher Garrison (hereinafter Garrison), p. 41 (available at http://www.iprsonline.org/resources/docs/Garrison%20-%20Patent%20Exceptions%20DC%20-%20Blue%2017.pdf).

[4] Garrison, p. 40; the same author provides a detailed overview of long-established examples of exceptions to patent rights under domestic legislation. A regulatory review exception was first introduced into US patent law, after the Court of Appeals for the Federal Circuit (CAFC) considered that the US experimental use exception was not wide enough to cover the use by generic producers

considered also the compatibility of the stockpiling exception – recognized in the Canadian Patent Law as part of the regulatory review exception – with the TRIPS Agreement. On this score, the Panel came to the conclusion that this exception was not TRIPS-compliant.

From a public health policy perspective, it is important to underline the wide scope of the Canadian regulatory review exception as considered by the Panel. First, Members may introduce such an exception without the need to compensate the patent holder with an extended term of protection for the affected patent.[5] Second, the Panel made clear that the exception may also be invoked to justify uses of the patented substance that are reasonably related to the development and submission of information to foreign drug regulatory authorities.[6] These are important clarifications, because they deviate from the first-ever adopted regulatory review exception, that is, the United States regulatory review exception as introduced by the 1984 Drug Price Competition and Patent Term Restoration ('Hatch-Waxman') Act.[7]

The Panel observed also that there was an important difference between the notion of 'discrimination' under Article 27.1 of the TRIPS Agreement and differential treatment of different areas of technology for bona-fide purposes.[8] This approach may have important implications for domestic public health policies, as discussed particularly in the second section of this chapter.

The decision is also significant, as pointed out, for its comprehensive analysis of the TRIPS Agreement and how its different provisions interrelate, not only with provisions of the Agreement itself, but also with related international treaties on intellectual property. The case is also remarkable

---

Footnote 4 (*cont.*)
of patented pharmaceutical substances for the purpose of gaining marketing approval from a drug regulatory authority (DRA). See *Roche Products Inc. v. Bolar Pharmaceuticals Co.*, 733 F.2d 858, 863 (Fed. Cir. 1984), and the discussion by Garrison, pp. 13–15.

[5] Panel Report, para. 7.82, p. 168.

[6] Panel Report, para. 7.46, p. 159.

[7] In its third party submission to the Panel, the United States, while supporting, in general, the Canadian position, emphasized the need for a regulatory review exception to be limited to domestic marketing approvals and to be accompanied by an extension of the patent term. See Panel Report, para. 5.36 (with respect to the 'limited exceptions' and the 'legitimate interests of third parties' tests). In this context, it has been pointed out in the literature that some of the US-sponsored Free Trade Agreements have made the narrower US model mandatory for some developing country trading partners. See Garrison, pp. 59–60.

[8] Panel Report, pp. 171–4.

from the point of view of the analysis made of the pharmaceutical industry and how it operates in a determined regulatory framework.

To consider all the above questions, the chapter is divided into two main sections. The first deals extensively with the decision of the Panel, the issues under consideration and summarizes, drawing on the decision itself, its main findings and conclusions. The second section looks at the implications and relevance of the case, with emphasis on the effects for generic producers and for national law making on issues such as the scope of the regulatory review exception and on the implications of Article 27.1, TRIPS, regarding the question that 'patents shall be available and patent rights enjoyable without discrimination as to the place of invention, the field of technology and whether products are imported or locally produced'.

1. The issues before the Panel and its main conclusions

Section 55.2 of the Canadian Patent Law,[9] stipulating an exception to the exclusive rights of the patent holder, was at the centre of the dispute. Section 55.2 deals mainly with the regulatory review exception or 'Bolar'[10] exception and with the related stockpiling exception. The main issue raised by the European Communities and their Member States was that Section 55.2 of the Patent Act, together with the Manufacturing and Storage of Patented Medicines Regulations, were inconsistent with the TRIPS Agreement, particularly the provisions contained in Articles 27.1 (patents shall be available and patent rights enjoyable without discrimination as to the place of invention, the field of technology and whether products

---

[9] The pertinent provisions of the Patent Act Section 55.2 are:

(1). It is not an infringement of a patent for any person to make, construct, use or sell the patented invention solely for uses reasonably related to the development and submission of information required under any law of Canada, a province or a country other than Canada that regulates the manufacture, construction, use or sale of any product.
(2). It is not an infringement of a patent for any person who makes, constructs, uses or sells a patented invention in accordance with subsection (1) to make, construct or use the invention, during the applicable period provided for by the regulations, for the manufacture and storage of articles intended for sale after the date on which the term of the patent expires.
(3). The Governor in Council may make regulations for the purposes of subsection (2), but any period provided for by the regulations must terminate immediately preceding the date on which the term of the patent expires.

[10] Named after the first court case on this exception in the United States (*Roche Products Inc. v. Bolar Pharmaceutical Co.*; 733 F.2d. 858, Fed. Cir., cert. denied, 469 US 856, 1984).

are imported or locally produced); 28.1 (exclusive rights conferred by patents); and 33 (term of protection). The exception established by Section 55.2(2) regarding stockpiling did not become effective until implementing regulations were issued and according to information provided during the case, the only regulations issued under the stockpiling exception were regulations making the exception operative with regard to pharmaceutical products. The period during which pharmaceutical products could be made and stockpiled was six months immediately prior to the expiration of the patent.

Further, according to the European Communities, Canada treated patent holders in the field of pharmaceutical inventions less favourably than inventors in all other fields of technology, in violation of its obligations under Article 27.1 of the TRIPS Agreement, requiring patents to be available and patent rights enjoyable without discrimination as to the field of technology. And, that 'Canada, by allowing manufacturing and stockpiling of pharmaceutical products without the consent of the patent holder during the six months immediately prior to the expiration of the 20-year patent term by virtue . . . of the Patent Act together with the Manufacturing and Storage of Patented Medicines Regulations, violated its obligations under Article 28.1 together with Article 33 of the TRIPS Agreement'.

The European Communities argued also that 'Canada was the only country in the world – industrialized or developing – which allowed manufacturing and stockpiling of products covered by a patent during the term of such a patent. Canada itself recognized that, at least in the United States and the member States of the European Communities, such a possibility did not exist.'

The text of Section 55.2(2) gives permission only to 'make, construct or use' the patented product for purposes of stockpiling. Canada explained in the deliberations of the case that the exception will be construed also to allow the 'sale' of patented ingredients that have been ordered by a producer who is stockpiling the final patented product – for example, with regard to pharmaceuticals, sales by fine chemical producers of active ingredients ordered by the generic producer.

The stockpiling exception was available only to persons who invoked the regulatory review exception in Section 55.2(1) and, as clarified during the proceedings, only persons who actually obtained regulatory permission to market such regulated products would be able to benefit from the stockpiling exception, because there would be no commercial advantage in having a stock of goods on hand when the patent expires unless one also has regulatory permission to sell those goods as of that date.

Canada argued further that neither Section 55.2(1) nor Section 55.2(2) violated any of the three TRIPS provisions cited. With regard to the claimed violation of Article 28.1 of the TRIPS Agreement, Canada acknowledged that Sections 55.2(1) and 55.2(2) permitted conduct that conflicted with the patent rights granted in accordance with Article 28.1, but Canada claimed that each of these two provisions was an exception authorized by Article 30 of the Agreement. With regard to the claimed violation of Article 27.1, Canada presented two defences: first, that Article 27.1 did not apply to measures authorized by Article 30 of the Agreement and second, that, even if Article 27.1 did apply to measures authorized by Article 30, the two provisions of the Patent Act in question would not discriminate in violation of Article 27.1.

Faced with the above issues, the Panel, finally, concluded[11]

(i) The regulatory review exception (Section 55.2(1) of Canada's Patent Act) was not inconsistent with Canada's obligations under Article 27.1 and Article 28.1 of the TRIPS Agreement.
(ii) The stockpiling exception (Section 55.2(2) of Canada's Patent Act) was not consistent with the requirements of Article 28.1 of the TRIPS Agreement. The Panel thus recommended that the Dispute Settlement Body request that Canada bring its law into conformity with Canada's obligations under the TRIPS Agreement.

The main findings

Rules of interpretation and issues on the burden of proof[12]
The Panel in its main findings recalled that the legal issues in the dispute primarily involved differences over interpretation of the key TRIPS provisions invoked by the parties and that for these purposes the rules that govern the interpretation of WTO agreements were the rules of treaty interpretation stated in Articles 31 and 32 of the Vienna Convention.[13]

An important question addressed by the Panel was the extent to which a WTO panel may have recourse to certain provisions of the major pre-existing international instruments on intellectual property, for purposes of interpretation of specific TRIPS provisions. In this regard, the Panel concluded that the context to which a panel may have recourse is not restricted to the text, Preamble and Annexes of the TRIPS Agreement itself, but also includes the provisions of the international instruments

---

11 Panel Report, 8.1.

12 See Panel Report, paras 7.13–7.16.

13 Vienna Convention on the Law of Treaties 1969, entered into force on 27 January 1980.

on intellectual property incorporated into the TRIPS Agreement, as well as any agreement between the parties relating to these agreements within the meaning of Article 31(2) of the Vienna Convention on the Law of Treaties. Thus, as the Panel elaborated further, Article 9(2) of the Berne Convention for the Protection of Literary and Artistic Works (1971) is an important contextual element for the interpretation of Article 30 of the TRIPS Agreement.

The legal issues in the dispute dealt primarily with questions of legal interpretation – the meaning of the TRIPS provisions under which the two provisions of Canada's Patent Act were challenged. However, the Panel noted that a small number of factual issues have been raised with regard to the meaning of certain aspects of the Canadian law, and about the actual impact of that law in practice. Application of legal standards frequently involves mixed questions of law and fact, and disagreements over the application of such standards sometimes therefore involve disagreement over factual premises. To the extent that such factual disagreements do exist, rules pertaining to burden of proof are potentially relevant whenever the weight of the evidence does not permit conclusive judgements. The Panel recalled the Appellate Body decision in *United States – Measure Affecting Imports of Woven Wool Shirts and Blouses from India*.[14]

Accordingly, in the present case, the EC bore the burden to present evidence and argument sufficient to establish a prima-facie case that Canada had violated provisions of the TRIPS Agreement and it would be up to Canada to advance sufficient argument and evidence to rebut such a prima-facie case. Canada, in the opinion of the Panel, had, for all practical purposes, conceded the violation of Article 28, because it had resorted to the exception of Article 30 of the TRIPS Agreement in this case. 'Since Article 30 is an exception to the obligations of the TRIPS Agreement, it would be up to Canada to demonstrate that the provisions of Sections 55.2(1) and 55.2(2) comply with the criteria laid down in Article 30.'

Application of Article 28.1 and Article 30 of the TRIPS Agreement in the case of the stockpiling exception[15]

The Panel began by considering the claims of violation concerning Section 55.2(2), the so-called stockpiling provision. It began with the EC claim that this measure was in violation of Article 28.1 of the TRIPS Agreement,

[14] Document WT/DS33/AB/R, pp. 13–16 (adopted 23 May 1997).

[15] See Panel Report, 7.17–7.38.

and Canada's defence that the measure was an exception authorized by Article 30 of the Agreement.

For the Panel, there was no dispute as to the meaning of Article 28.1 on exclusive rights as they pertain to Section 55.2(2) of Canada's Patent Act. Canada acknowledged that the provisions of Section 55.2(2) permitting third parties to 'make', 'construct' or 'use' the patented product during the term of the patent, without the patent owner's permission, would be a violation of Article 28.1 if not excused under Article 30 of the Agreement. The dispute on the claim of violation of Article 28.1 involved whether Section 55.2.(2) of the Patent Act complied with the conditions of Article 30.

The Panel also added that the TRIPS Agreement contains two provisions authorizing exceptions to the exclusionary patent rights laid down in Article 28 – Articles 30 and 31 (Other Use without Authorization of the Right Holder). Of these two, Article 30 – the so-called limited exceptions provision – was invoked by Canada in the case. Article 30 establishes three criteria that must be met in order to qualify for an exception (the so-called 'Three-step Test'): (1) the exception must be 'limited'; (2) the exception must not 'unreasonably conflict with normal exploitation of the patent'; (3) the exception must not 'unreasonably prejudice the legitimate interests of the patent owner, taking account of the legitimate interests of third parties'. The Panel concluded that the three conditions are cumulative, each being a separate and independent requirement that must be satisfied. Failure to comply with any one of the three conditions results in the Article 30 exception being disallowed. The three conditions, in the opinion of the Panel, must be interpreted in relation to each other. Each of the three must be presumed to mean something different from the other two, or else there would be redundancy. Normally, the order of listing can be read to suggest that an exception that complies with the first condition can nevertheless violate the second or third, and that one which complies with the first and second can still violate the third. Further, the syntax of Article 30 supports the conclusion that an exception may be 'limited' and yet fail to satisfy one or both of the other two conditions. The ordering further suggests that an exception that does not 'unreasonably conflict with normal exploitation' could nonetheless 'unreasonably prejudice the legitimate interests of the patent owner'.

Object and purpose[16]

With respect to the argument raised by Canada on a number of other provisions of the TRIPS Agreement being relevant to the purpose and

[16] See Panel Report, 7.23–7.26.

objective of Article 30, namely, Articles 7 and 8.1 dealing with the objectives and principles of the Agreement, the Panel's view was that Article 30's very existence amounts to a recognition that the definition of patent rights contained in Article 28 would need certain adjustments. On the other hand, the three limiting conditions attached to Article 30 testify strongly that the negotiators of the Agreement did not intend Article 30 to bring about what would be equivalent to a renegotiation of the basic balance of the Agreement. The exact scope of Article 30's authority will depend on the specific meaning given to its limiting conditions. The words of those conditions must be examined with particular care on this point. Both the goals and the limitations stated in Articles 7 and 8.1 must obviously be borne in mind when doing so, as well as those of other provisions of the TRIPS Agreement which indicate its object and purposes.

Limited exceptions: the first condition of Article 30[17]

In considering how to approach the parties' conflicting positions regarding the meaning of the term 'limited exceptions', the Panel recalled that the text of Article 30 had antecedents in the text of Article 9(2) of the Berne Convention. However, the words 'limited exceptions' in Article 30 of the TRIPS Agreement are different from the corresponding words in the Berne Convention, which reads 'in certain special cases'.[18] The Panel examined the documented negotiating history of TRIPS Article 30 with respect to the reasons why negotiators may have chosen to use the term 'limited exceptions' in place of 'in special circumstances'. The negotiating records show only that the term 'limited exceptions' was employed very early in the drafting process, well before the decision to adopt a text modelled on the Berne Convention.

In this context, the Panel agreed with the EC that the word 'limited' has a narrower connotation than the rather broad definitions advocated by Canada. The word 'exception' by itself connotes a limited derogation, one that does not undercut the body of rules from which it is made. When a treaty uses the term 'limited exception', the word 'limited' must be given a meaning separate from the limitation implicit in the word 'exception' itself. The term 'limited exception' must therefore be read to connote a

---

17 See Panel Report, 7.27–7.38.

18 Article 9(2) of the Berne Convention reads: 'It shall be a matter for legislation in the countries of the Union to permit the reproduction of [literary and artistic] works in certain special cases, provided that such reproduction does not conflict with a normal exploitation of the work and does not unreasonably prejudice the legitimate interests of the author'.

narrow exception – one which makes only a small diminution of the rights in question.

The Panel agreed with the EC interpretation that 'limited' is to be measured by the extent to which the exclusive rights of the patent owner have been curtailed. The full text of Article 30 refers to 'limited exceptions to the exclusive rights conferred by a patent'. In the absence of other indications, the Panel concluded that it would be justified in reading the text literally, focusing on the extent to which legal rights have been curtailed, rather than the size or extent of the economic impact. In support of this conclusion, the Panel noted that the following two conditions of Article 30 ask more particularly about the economic impact of the exception, and provide two sets of standards by which such impact may be judged. The term 'limited exceptions' is the only one of the three conditions in Article 30 under which the extent of the curtailment of rights as such is dealt with.

However, the Panel did not agree with the EC's position that the curtailment of legal rights can be measured by simply counting the number of legal rights impaired by an exception. A very small act could well violate all five rights provided by Article 28.1 and yet leave each of the patent owner's rights intact for all useful purposes. To determine whether a particular exception constitutes a limited exception, the extent to which the patent owner's rights have been curtailed must be measured.

The Panel could not accept Canada's argument that the curtailment of the patent owner's legal rights is 'limited' just so long as the exception preserves the exclusive right to sell to the ultimate consumer during the patent term. The Panel did not find any support for creating such a hierarchy of patent rights within the TRIPS Agreement.

In the Panel's view, the question of whether the stockpiling exception is a 'limited' exception turns on the extent to which the patent owner's rights to exclude 'making' and 'using' the patented product have been curtailed. The right to exclude 'making' and 'using' provides protection, additional to that provided by the right to exclude sale, during the entire term of the patent by cutting off the supply of competing goods at the source and by preventing use of such products however obtained. With no limitations at all upon the quantity of production, the stockpiling exception removes that protection entirely during the last six months of the patent term, without regard to what other, subsequent, consequences it might have.

The Panel also considered whether the market advantage gained by the patent owner in the months after expiration of the patent could also be considered a purpose of the patent owner's rights to exclude 'making' and 'using' during the term of the patent. In both theory and practice, the Panel concluded that such additional market benefits were within the purpose of these rights. In theory, the rights of the patent owner are generally viewed as a right to prevent competitive commercial activity by others, and manufacturing for commercial sale is a quintessential competitive commercial activity, whose character is not altered by a mere delay in the commercial reward.

For the above reasons, the Panel concluded that the stockpiling exception of Section 55.2(2) constituted a substantial curtailment of the exclusionary rights required to be granted to patent owners under Article 28.1 of the TRIPS Agreement. Without seeking to define exactly what level of curtailment would be disqualifying, it was clear to the Panel that an exception which results in a substantial curtailment of this dimension cannot be considered a 'limited exception' within the meaning of Article 30 of the Agreement. Having concluded that the exception in Section 55.2(2) of the Canadian Patent Act did not satisfy the first condition of Article 30 of the TRIPS Agreement, the Panel therefore concluded that Section 55.2(2) was inconsistent with Canada's obligations under Article 28.1 of the Agreement.

Application of Article 28.1 and Article 30 of the TRIPS Agreement in the case of the regulatory review exception[19]

Limited exceptions: the first condition of Article 30[20]

In the Panel's view, Canada's regulatory review exception is a 'limited exception' within the meaning of TRIPS Article 30. It is 'limited' because of the narrow scope of its curtailment of Article 28.1 rights. As long as the exception is confined to conduct needed to comply with the requirements of the regulatory approval process, the extent of the acts unauthorized by the right holder that are permitted by it will be small and narrowly bounded. Even though regulatory approval processes may require substantial amounts of test production to demonstrate reliable manufacturing, the patent owner's rights themselves are not impaired any further by the size of such production, as long as they are solely for regulatory purposes and no commercial use is made of resulting final products.

The Panel found further that there was no basis for believing that activities seeking product approvals under foreign regulatory procedures would be any less subject to these limitations. There was no a priori basis to assume that the requirements of foreign regulatory procedures would

---

19 See Panel Report, 7.39–7.105.
20 See Panel Report, 7.39–7.50.

require activities unrelated to legitimate objectives of product quality and safety, nor did the EC provide any evidence to that effect. Nor was there any reason to assume that Canadian law would apply the exception in cases where foreign requirements clearly had no regulatory purpose. Nor, finally, was there any reason to assume that it would be any more difficult to enforce the requirements of Canadian law when Canadian producers claimed exceptions under foreign procedures. With regard to the latter issue, the Panel concurred with Canada's point that the government is not normally expected to regulate the actual conduct of third parties in such cases. The enforcement of these conditions, as with other enforcement of patent rights, occurs by means of private infringement actions brought by the patent owner.

In reaching this conclusion, the Panel also considered Canada's additional arguments that both the negotiating history of Article 30 of the TRIPS Agreement and the subsequent practices of certain WTO Member governments supported the view that Article 30 was understood to permit regulatory review exceptions similar to Section 55.2(1). The Panel did not accord any weight to either of those arguments, however, because there was no documented evidence of the claimed negotiating understanding, and because the subsequent acts by individual countries did not constitute 'practice in the application of the treaty which establishes the agreement of the parties regarding its interpretation' within the meaning of Article 31.3(b) of the Vienna Convention.

After analysing all three conditions stated in Article 30 of the TRIPS Agreement, the Panel was satisfied that Article 30 does in fact address the issue of economic impact, but only in the other two conditions contained in that Article. Viewing all three conditions as a whole, it is apparent that the first condition ('limited exception') is neither designed nor intended to address the issue of economic impact directly.

In sum, the Panel found that the regulatory review exception of Section 55.2(1) is a 'limited exception' within the meaning of Article 30 of the TRIPS Agreement.

Normal exploitation: the second condition of Article 30[21]

The Panel considered that 'exploitation' refers to the commercial activity by which patent owners employ their exclusive patent rights to extract economic value from their patent. The term 'normal' defines the kind of commercial activity Article 30 seeks to protect. The ordinary meaning of the word 'normal' is found in the dictionary definition: 'regular, usual, typical,

21 See Panel Report, 7.51–7.59.

ordinary, conventional'.[22] As so defined, the term can be understood to refer either to an empirical conclusion about what is common within a relevant community, or to a normative standard of entitlement. The Panel concluded that the word 'normal' was being used in Article 30 in a sense that combined the two meanings.

In the view of the Panel, normal practice of exploitation by patent owners, as with owners of any other intellectual property right, is to exclude all forms of competition that could detract significantly from the economic returns anticipated from a patent's grant of market exclusivity. The specific forms of patent exploitation are not static, for to be effective, exploitation must adapt to changing forms of competition due to technological development and the evolution of marketing practices. Protection of all normal exploitation practices is a key element of the policy reflected in all patent laws. Patent laws establish a carefully defined period of market exclusivity as an inducement to innovation, and the policy of those laws cannot be achieved unless patent owners are permitted to take effective advantage of that inducement once it has been defined.

With respect to the argument raised by Canada that market exclusivity occurring after the 20-year patent term expires should not be regarded as 'normal', the Panel was unable to accept that as a categorical proposition. According to the Panel, some of the basic rights granted to all patent owners, and routinely exercised by all patent owners, will produce a certain period of market exclusivity after the expiration of a patent. For example, the separate right to prevent 'making' the patented product during the term of the patent often prevents competitors from building an inventory needed to enter the market immediately upon expiration of a patent.

The Panel considered that Canada was on firmer ground, however, in arguing that the additional period of de facto market exclusivity created by using patent rights to preclude submissions for regulatory authorization should not be considered 'normal'. The additional period of market exclusivity in this situation is not a natural or normal consequence of enforcing patent rights. It is an unintended consequence of the conjunction of the patent laws with product regulatory laws, where the combination of patent rights with the time demands of the regulatory process gives a greater than normal period of market exclusivity to the enforcement of certain patent rights. For the vast majority of patented products, there is no marketing regulation of the kind covered by Section 55.2(1), and thus there is no possibility to extend patent exclusivity by delaying the marketing approval process for competitors.

---

22 *The New Shorter Oxford English Dictionary*, p. 1940.

On this count, the Panel found that the regulatory review exception of Section 55.2(1) does not conflict with a normal exploitation of patents, within the meaning of the second condition of Article 30 of the TRIPS Agreement. The fact that no conflict was found made it unnecessary to consider the question of whether, if a conflict were found, the conflict would be 'unreasonable'. Accordingly, it was also unnecessary to determine whether or not the final phrase of Article 30, calling for consideration of the legitimate interests of third parties, does or does not apply to the determination of 'unreasonable conflict' under the second condition of Article 30.

LEGITIMATE INTERESTS: THE THIRD CONDITION OF ARTICLE 30[23]
The ultimate issue with regard to the regulatory review exception's compliance with the third condition of Article 30 involved similar considerations to those arising under the second condition ('normal exploitation') – the fact that the exception would remove the additional period of de facto market exclusivity that patent owners could achieve if they were permitted to employ their rights to exclude 'making' and 'using' (and 'selling') the patented product during the term of the patent to prevent potential competitors from preparing and/or applying for regulatory approval during the term of the patent. The issue was whether patent owners could claim a 'legitimate interest' in the economic benefits that could be derived from such an additional period of de facto market exclusivity and, if so, whether the regulatory review exception 'unreasonably prejudiced' that interest.

Based on how the term 'legitimate' is commonly defined, that term must be defined, in the opinion of the Panel, in the way that it is often used in legal discourse – as a normative claim calling for protection of interests that are 'justifiable' in the sense that they are supported by relevant public policies or other social norms. The Panel took as illustration one of the most widely adopted Article 30-type exceptions in national patent laws – the exception under which use of the patented product for scientific experimentation, during the term of the patent and without consent, is not an infringement.

The negotiating history of Article 30 The negotiating history of the TRIPS Agreement itself casts no further illumination on the meaning of the term 'legitimate interests', but the negotiating history of Article 9(2) of the Berne Convention, in the view of the Panel, supported that interpretation. With regard to the TRIPS negotiations themselves, the meaning of

23 See Panel Report, 7.60–7.83.

several important drafting changes turns out to be equivocal upon closer examination. The negotiating records of the TRIPS Agreement itself show that the first drafts of the provision that was to become Article 30 contemplated authorizing 'limited exceptions' that would be defined by an illustrative list of exceptions – private use, scientific use, prior use, a traditional exception for pharmacists, and the like.[24] Eventually, this illustrative list approach was abandoned in favour of a more general authorization following the outlines of the present Article 30. The negotiating records of the TRIPS Agreement give no explanation of the reason for this decision.

The Panel concluded in this respect that the text of the present more general version of Article 30 of the TRIPS Agreement was based on the text of Article 9(2) of the Berne Convention. The Panel added that the text of Berne Article 9(2) was not adopted into Article 30 of the TRIPS Agreement without change. Whereas the final condition in Berne Article 9(2) ('legitimate interests') simply refers to the legitimate interests of the author, the TRIPS negotiators added in Article 30 that account must be taken of 'the legitimate interests of third parties'. Absent further explanation in the records of the TRIPS negotiations, however, the Panel was not able to attach a substantive meaning to this change other than what is already apparent in the text itself, namely that the reference to the 'legitimate interests of third parties' makes sense only if the term 'legitimate interests' is construed as a concept broader than legal interests. In doing so, the Panel examined the legislative history of Article 9(2) of the Berne Convention.

Addressing the ECs arguments In sum, after consideration of the ordinary meaning of the term 'legitimate interests', as it is used in Article 30, the Panel was unable to accept the EC's interpretation of that term as referring to legal interests pursuant to Article 28.1. Accordingly, the Panel was unable to accept the primary EC argument with regard to the third condition of Article 30. It found that the argument based solely on the patent owner's legal rights pursuant to Article 28.1, without reference to any more particular normative claims of interest, did not raise a relevant claim of non-compliance with the third condition of Article 30.

After reaching the previous conclusion concerning the EC's primary argument under the 'legitimate interests' condition of Article 30, the Panel then directed its attention to another line of argument raised in statements

---

[24] See document MTN.GNG/NG11/W/76 of 23 July 1990 – Status of Work in the Negotiating Group: Chairman's Report to the Group of Negotiations on Goods, Part III, Section 5, para. 2.2.

made by the EC. This second line of argument called attention to the fact that patent owners whose innovative products are subject to marketing approval requirements suffer a loss of economic benefits to the extent that delays in obtaining government approval prevent them from marketing their product during a substantial part of the patent term. The EC argued that patent owners who suffer a reduction of effective market exclusivity from regulatory approval should be entitled to impose the same type of delay in connection with corresponding regulatory requirements upon the market entry of competing products.

This kind of argument rested on a claim of equal treatment for all patent owners. One of the policy rationales behind patent laws is to give innovative producers the advantage of market exclusivity during the 20-year term of the patent. Although patent laws do not guarantee that patent owners will obtain economic benefits from this opportunity, most patent owners have at least the legal opportunity to market the patented product during all or virtually all this 20-year period of market exclusivity. Producers whose products are subject to regulatory approval requirements may be deprived of this opportunity for a substantial part of the 20-year period.

Under the Panel's interpretation of Article 30, this argument could be characterized as a claim of 'legitimate interest' under the third condition of Article 30. It was distinct from the claim made under the second condition of Article 30 ('normal exploitation'), because it did not rest on a claim of interest in the 'normal' means of extracting commercial benefits from a patent. Instead, it was a distinctive claim of interest, resting on a distinctive situation applicable only to patent owners affected by marketing approval requirements, asking for an additional means of exploitation, above and beyond 'normal exploitation', to compensate for the distinctive disadvantage claimed to be suffered by this particular group of claimants.

The Panel therefore examined whether the claimed interest should be considered a 'legitimate interest' within the meaning of Article 30. The primary issue was whether the normative basis of that claim rested on a widely recognized policy norm. The type of normative claim put forward by the EC has been affirmed by a number of governments that have enacted de jure extensions of the patent term, primarily in the case of pharmaceutical products, to compensate for the de facto diminution of the normal period of market exclusivity due to delays in obtaining marketing approval. This positive response to the claim for compensatory adjustment has not been universal, however. In addition to Canada, several countries have adopted, or were in the process of adopting, regulatory review exceptions similar to Section 55.2(1) of the Canadian Patent Act, thereby removing the de facto extension of market exclusivity, but these countries have not enacted, and were not planning to enact, any de jure extensions of the patent term for producers adversely affected by delayed marketing approval.

On balance, the Panel concluded that the interest claimed on behalf of patent owners whose effective period of market exclusivity had been reduced by delays in marketing approval was neither so compelling nor so widely recognized that it could be regarded as a 'legitimate interest' within the meaning of Article 30 of the TRIPS Agreement. Notwithstanding the number of governments that had responded positively to that claimed interest by granting compensatory patent term extensions, the issue itself was of relatively recent standing, and governments were still divided over the merits of such claims. Moreover, the Panel believed that it was significant that concerns about regulatory review exceptions in general, although well-known at the time of the TRIPS negotiations, were apparently not clear enough, or compelling enough, to make their way explicitly into the recorded agenda of the TRIPS negotiations. The Panel believed that Article 30's 'legitimate interests' concept should not be used to decide, through adjudication, a normative policy issue that was still obviously a matter of unresolved political debate.

Consequently, having considered the two claims of 'legitimate interest' put forward by the EC, and having found that neither of these claimed interests can be considered 'legitimate interests' within the meaning of the third condition of Article 30 of the TRIPS Agreement, the Panel concluded that Canada had demonstrated to the Panel's satisfaction that Section 55.2(1) of Canada's Patent Act did not prejudice 'legitimate interests' of affected patent owners within the meaning of Article 30.

The Panel concluded, thus, that Section 55.2(1) did satisfy all three conditions of Article 30, and was not inconsistent with Canada's obligations under Article 28.1 of the TRIPS Agreement.

Application of Article 27.1 of the TRIPS Agreement[25]

The EC claimed that Section 55.2(1) of the Canada Patent Act was also in conflict with the obligations under Article 27.1 of the TRIPS Agreement, particularly with respect to the obligation that 'patents shall be available and patent rights enjoyable without discrimination as to the place of invention, the field of technology and whether products are imported or locally produced'. The EC argued that the anti-discrimination rule stated in the text of Article 27.1 not only requires that the core patent rights made available under Article 28 be non-discriminatory, but also requires that any exceptions to those basic rights made under Articles 30 and 31 must be

25 See Panel Report, 7.85–7.105.

non-discriminatory as well. The EC contended that Section 55.2(1) of the Canadian Patent Act did not comply with the obligations of Article 27.1, because it is limited, both de jure and de facto, to pharmaceutical products alone, and thus discriminates by field of technology.

Canada advanced two defences to the EC's claim of an Article 27.1 violation. First, Canada argued that the non-discrimination rule of Article 27.1 did not apply to exceptions taken under Article 30. Second, Canada argued that Section 55.2(1) did not discriminate against pharmaceutical products. The Panel examined these two defences in order.

Applicability of Article 27.1 to Article 30 Exceptions[26]

Canada's position Canada took the position that the reference in Article 27.1 to 'patent rights' that must be enjoyable without discrimination as to field of technology refers to the basic rights enumerated in Article 28.1 subject to any exceptions that might be made under Article 30. In other words, governments may discriminate when making the 'limited' exceptions allowed under Article 30, but they may not discriminate as to patent rights as modified by such exceptions.

In support of this position, Canada argued that the scope of Article 30 would be irrelevant if governments were required to treat all fields of technology the same, for if all exceptions had to apply to every product, it would be far more difficult to meet the requirement that Article 30 exceptions be 'limited'. It would also be more difficult to target particular social problems, as are anticipated, according to Canada, by Articles 7 and 8 of the TRIPS Agreement. Conversely, Canada argued, requiring that exceptions be applied to all products would cause needless deprivation of patent rights for those products as to which full enforcement of patent rights causes no problem.

Canada acknowledged that there are certain textual difficulties with this position. It acknowledged that two of the primary purposes of Article 27.1 were to eliminate two types of discrimination that had been practised against pharmaceuticals and certain other products – either a denial of patentability for such products, or, if patents were granted, automatic compulsory licences permitting others to manufacture such products for a fee. Canada acknowledged that, in order to preclude discrimination as to compulsory licences, the non-discrimination rule of Article 27 was made applicable to Article 31 of the TRIPS Agreement, which grants a limited exception for compulsory licences under specified conditions. To defend

---

26 See Panel Report, 7.88–7.93.

its position, therefore, Canada was required to explain how Article 27.1 could apply to exceptions made under Article 31, but not to exceptions made under its neighbouring exception provision in Article 30. Canada argued that Article 31 was 'mandatory' in character while Article 30 was 'permissive', and that this distinction made it appropriate to apply the non-discrimination provision to the former but not the latter.

The Panel's view The Panel was unable to agree with Canada's contention that Article 27.1 did not apply to exceptions granted under Article 30. The text of the TRIPS Agreement offers no support for such an interpretation. Article 27.1 prohibits discrimination as to enjoyment of 'patent rights' without qualifying that term. Article 30 exceptions are explicitly described as 'exceptions to the exclusive rights conferred by a patent' and contain no indication that any exemption from non-discrimination rules is intended. A discriminatory exception that takes away enjoyment of a patent right is discrimination as much as is discrimination in the basic rights themselves. The acknowledged fact that the Article 31 exception for compulsory licences and government use is understood to be subject to the non-discrimination rule of Article 27.1, without the need for any textual provision so providing, further strengthens the case for treating the non-discrimination rules as applicable to Article 30. Articles 30 and 31 are linked together by the opening words of Article 31 that define the scope of Article 31 in terms of exceptions not covered by Article 30.[27] Finally, the Panel could not agree with Canada's attempt to distinguish between Articles 30 and 31 on the basis of their mandatory/permissive character; both provisions permit exceptions to patent rights subject to certain mandatory conditions. Nor could the Panel understand how such a 'mandatory/permissive' distinction, even if present, would logically support making the kind of distinction Canada was arguing. In the Panel's view, what was important was that in the rights available under national law, the forms of discrimination referred to in Article 27.1 should not be present.

Nor was the Panel able to agree with the policy arguments in support of Canada's interpretation of Article 27. To begin with, it is not true, according to the Panel, that being able to discriminate against particular patents will make it possible to meet the requirement under Article 30 that the exception be 'limited'. An Article 30 exception cannot be made 'limited' by limiting it to one field of technology, because the effects of each exception

[27] Article 31 is titled 'Other Use without Authorization of the Rights Holder', and footnote 7 to Article 31 defines 'other use' as 'use' (derogations from exclusive patent rights) other than that allowed by Article 30.

must be found to be 'limited' when measured against each affected patent. Beyond that, it was not true in the view of the Panel that Article 27 requires all Article 30 exceptions to be applied to all products. Article 27 prohibits only discrimination as to the place of invention, the field of technology, and whether products are imported or produced locally. 'Article 27 does not prohibit bona fide exceptions to deal with problems that may exist only in certain product areas.' Moreover, to the extent the prohibition of discrimination does limit the ability to target certain products in dealing with certain of the important national policies referred to in Articles 7 and 8.1, that fact may well constitute a deliberate limitation rather than a frustration of purpose.

The Panel concluded, therefore, that the anti-discrimination rule of Article 27.1 does apply to exceptions of the kind authorized by Article 30.

Discrimination as to the Field of Technology[28]

The meaning of 'discrimination' The Panel then turned to the question of whether Section 55.2(1) of the Canadian Patent Act discriminated as to fields of technology. In undertaking this task, the Panel considered that the primary TRIPS provisions that deal with discrimination, such as the national treatment and most-favoured-nation provisions of Articles 3 and 4, do not use the term 'discrimination'. They speak in more precise terms. The ordinary meaning of the word 'discriminate' is potentially broader than these more specific definitions. It certainly extends beyond the concept of differential treatment. It is a normative term, pejorative in connotation, referring to results of the unjustified imposition of differentially disadvantageous treatment. Discrimination may arise from explicitly different treatment, sometimes called 'de jure discrimination', but it may also arise from ostensibly identical treatment that due to differences in circumstances, produces differentially disadvantageous effects, sometimes called 'de facto discrimination'. The standards by which the justification for differential treatment is measured are a subject of infinite complexity. 'Discrimination' is a term to be avoided whenever more precise standards are available, and, when employed, it is a term to be interpreted with caution, and with care to add no more precision than the concept contains.

The EC pointed out that de jure and de facto, the Canadian Patent Act in the challenged provisions were targeting only pharmaceutical products.

---

[28] See Panel Report, 7.94–7.105.

Conversely, Canada argued that this was not the case and that the relevant provisions of its law applied and were available to any product for which marketing approval was needed.

In considering how to address these conflicting claims of discrimination, the Panel recalled that various claims of discrimination, de jure and de facto, have been the subject of legal rulings under GATT or the WTO. These rulings have addressed the question whether measures were in conflict with various GATT or WTO provisions prohibiting variously defined forms of discrimination. Given the very broad range of issues that might be involved in defining the word 'discrimination' in Article 27.1 of the TRIPS Agreement, the Panel decided that it would be better to defer attempting to define that term at the outset, but instead to determine which issues were raised by the record before the Panel, and to define the concept of discrimination to the extent necessary to resolve those issues.

De jure discrimination With regard to the issue of de jure discrimination, the Panel concluded that the European Communities had not presented sufficient evidence to raise the issue in the face of Canada's formal declaration that the exception of Section 55.2(1) was not limited to pharmaceutical products. Absent other evidence, the words of the statute compelled the Panel to accept Canada's assurance that the exception was legally available to every product that was subject to marketing approval requirements. In reaching this conclusion, the Panel took note that its legal finding was based on the meaning of the Canadian law that was in turn based on Canada's representations as to the meaning of that law, and that this finding of conformity would no longer be warranted if, and to the extent that, Canada's representations as to the meaning of that law were to prove wrong.

De facto discrimination The Panel then turned to the question of de facto discrimination. Although the EC's response to the Panel's questions indicated that it did intend to raise the issue of de facto discrimination, the EC did not propose a formal definition of de facto discrimination, nor did it submit a systematic exposition of the evidence satisfying the elements of such a concept. Notwithstanding the limited development of the arguments on the issue of de facto discrimination, the Panel concluded that its terms of reference required it to pursue that issue once raised, and accordingly the Panel proceeded to examine the claim of a de facto discrimination violation on the basis of its own examination of the record in the light of the concepts usually associated with claims of de facto discrimination.

De facto discrimination is a general term describing the legal conclusion that an ostensibly neutral measure transgresses a non-discrimination norm because its actual effect is to impose differentially disadvantageous consequences on certain parties, and because those differential effects are found to be wrong or unjustifiable. Two main issues figure in the application of that general concept in most legal systems. One is the question of de facto discriminatory effect – whether the actual effect of the measure is to impose differentially disadvantageous consequences on certain parties. The other, related to the justification for the disadvantageous effects, is the issue of purpose – not an inquiry into the subjective purposes of the officials responsible for the measure, but an inquiry into the objective characteristics of the measure from which one can infer the existence or non-existence of discriminatory objectives.

With regard to the first issue – the actual effects of the measure – the Panel was not convinced on the arguments advanced on this matter and concluded that the EC had not demonstrated that the provisions of the Canadian Patent Act had a discriminatory effect limited to pharmaceutical products.

On the issue of discriminatory purpose, the Panel did not find evidence from the legislative history of Section 55.2(1) of the Canadian law to be persuasive evidence of a discriminatory purpose. To be sure, such evidence makes it clear that the primary reason for passing the measure was its effect on promoting competition in the pharmaceutical sector. This was also evident from Canada's justification for the measure presented in the proceedings. But preoccupation with the effects of a statute in one area does not necessarily mean that the provisions applicable to other areas are a sham, or of no actual or potential importance. Individual problems are frequently the driving force behind legislative actions of broader scope. The broader scope of the measure usually reflects an important legal principle that rules being applied in the area of primary interest should also be applied to other areas where the same problem occurs. Indeed, it is a common desideratum in many legal systems that legislation applies its underlying principles as broadly as possible.

In sum, the Panel found that the evidence on record before it did not raise a plausible claim of discrimination under Article 27.1 of the TRIPS Agreement. It was not proved that the legal scope of Section 55.2(1) was limited to pharmaceutical products, as would normally be required to raise a claim of de jure discrimination. Likewise, it was not proved that the adverse effects of Section 55.2(1) were limited to the pharmaceutical industry, or that the objective indications of purpose demonstrated a purpose to impose disadvantages on pharmaceutical patents in particular, as is often required to raise a claim of de facto discrimination. Having found that the record did not raise any of these basic elements of a discrimination claim, the Panel was able to find that Section 55.2(1) was not inconsistent with Canada's obligations under Article 27.1 of the TRIPS Agreement.

2. Implications

After the detailed consideration of the main findings of the *Canada – Patent Protection of Pharmaceuticals* case, we turn now to some of the broad implications of the Panel decision. We begin with the consequences for generic producers and competition aspects in the pharmaceutical sector in general.

Implications for generic producers

The scope of the regulatory review exception

The confirmation by the Panel of the Canadian regulatory review exception as TRIPS-compliant has resulted in the introduction of comparable legislation in a considerable number of other WTO Members, including the complainant in this case, that is, the EC,[29] but also many developing countries and LDCs. Garrison, in his review of state practice on patent exceptions, emphasizes the fact that a number of advanced developing countries, such as Brazil, Egypt and India have followed this approach, authorizing the use of patented substances for purposes of requesting marketing approval abroad.[30]

Recent research by UNCTAD on the patent legislation in Burundi, Kenya, Rwanda, Uganda, and the United Republic of Tanzania found that a majority of these countries were about to pass legislation containing regulatory review exceptions covering activities by generic producers regarding foreign approvals of pharmaceutical products.[31] Three of these

---

[29] See Directive 2001/83/EC as amended by Directive 2004/27/EC.

[30] Garrison, pp. 58–9.

[31] See UNCTAD (2008), 'Comparative Study of Provisions of EAC Partner States' Patent Laws Reflecting TRIPS Flexibilities Relevant for the Access to Medicines', Geneva. The study was prepared upon request from the EAC Secretariat and is not publicly available, but on file with the authors. The review was based on the following legislation: Burundi: Draft Patents Act of 2007 (to replace the current Patents Act No. 9 of 1964); Kenya: Industrial Property Act 2001, enacted 3 August 2001, in force since 1 May 2002 (Kenyan Patents Act; in this context, see review by the TRIPS Council, 2001–04: IP/Q/KEN/1, IP/Q2/KEN/1, IP/Q3/KEN/1, IP/Q4/KEN/1 of 7 May 2004) and Regulation 37 of the Industrial Property Regulations, 12 April 2002; Rwanda: draft Law on the Protection of Intellectual Property (as adopted by the Chamber of Deputies on 31 March 2008) to replace Loi Brevets of 25 February 1963; Uganda: the Industrial Property Draft Bill (as of 28 November 2007), to replace the Patents Statute No. 10 of December 1991; United Republic of Tanzania: (1) Tanzania – mainland: Patents Act of 1987 (at the time of finalizing the study, the new draft law was not yet available), (2) Tanzania–Zanzibar: Draft Bill for an Act on Industrial Property Rights for Zanzibar (as of March 2008), to replace a decree of 1932. The countries

jurisdictions have chosen express language to cover under this exception not only clinical, but also pre-clinical trials, as previously done under the Canadian and US legislation.[32] This is an important new aspect, which cannot directly be inferred from the *Canada – Patent Protection of Pharmaceuticals* case, but which follows from the 2005 US Supreme Court Decision in *Merck v. Integra Lifesciences*.[33] In this decision, the Supreme Court interpreted the US regulatory review exception as authorizing the use of patented inventions for the purpose of conducting research with respect to drugs as to which there is some reasonable prospect that an application for marketing approval may be submitted, regardless of whether an application is, in fact, eventually submitted or successful.[34] This option has important implications for competitors of a company holding a pharmaceutical patent. These competitors may depend on the availability of patented materials not only for the purpose of the actual submission of the approval request, but also during the early phases of their own pharmaceutical research and development (R&D), to the extent this is necessary for the development of generic drugs. This may be of particular importance where generic producers or other competitors seek to engage in follow-on innovation on the patented substance, for example by identifying the potential of a patented compound for new medical indications.[35]

---

following the broad Canadian approach (encompassing submissions for approvals abroad) are Burundi, Rwanda, Uganda and Tanzania–Zanzibar.

32 The jurisdictions following this approach are Burundi, Uganda and Tanzania–Zanzibar.

33 125 S. Ct. 2372 of 13 June 2005.

34 See the discussion of this decision in UNCTAD–ICTSD (2006), 'Intellectual Property Provisions of Bilateral and Regional Trade Agreements in Light of U.S. Federal Law', Issue Paper No. 12, by Frederick M. Abbott, p. 8 (available at http://www.iprsonline.org/resources/docs/Abbott%20-%20US%20bilateral%20 and%20regional%20trade%20agreements%20-%20Blue%2012.pdf). The Supreme Court based its reasoning on the express language of the US regulatory review exception, which refers to uses 'reasonably related to' the development and submission of information required for marketing approvals of drugs or veterinary or biological products. Legislation in many of the above-mentioned developing countries contains comparable language.

35 In the *Merck v. Integra Lifesciences* case, Merck used compounds patented by Integra Lifesciences in order to find out more about potential new medical indications, but abandoned these activities as the patented substance proved unpromising in this regard. Integra sued Merck for patent infringement. See Garrison, p. 58. A more narrow reading of the US regulatory review exception would have found Merck liable for patent infringement, as its use of the patented substance never actually contributed to a request for regulatory approval.

In that case, however, it is not only the design of a country's regulatory review exception that will have a bearing on the extent to which competitors engage in follow-on R&D on incremental medical innovation. The scope of pharmaceutical patents plays a considerable role in determining the degree in which competitors will have recourse to an existing regulatory review exception in this particular context. The incentives for competitors to discover new medical indications seem quite limited where the scope of the original patent is wide enough to encompass all medical uses of the patented substance, even those unknown at the time of filing the original patent application.[36] Competitors would seem to be more inclined to engage in follow-on R&D where they stand a chance of obtaining a separate exclusive right on the new use themselves, either in the form of a (product or process) patent, or in the form of a utility model. Alternatively, R&D into incremental medical innovation could be spurred by providing the follow-on innovator with a right to claim compensation for the use of his discovery, possibly after a short period of exclusivity to establish his brand in the market.[37]

---

[36] Patents of comparable width exist in the Member States of the European Patent Convention (EPC); see case T128/82, OJ EPO 1984, p. 164, as cited by South Centre, 'A Guide to Pharmaceutical Patents', Vol. I, Carlos M. Correa (ed.) (hereinafter South Centre Guide), p. 140. However, through a legal fiction, Article 54(5) of the revised European Patent Convention (2007) clarifies that second, third and subsequent pharmaceutical uses of known pharmaceutical substances still qualify for use-bound product claims, despite the fact that the patent on the first medical use originally covered all possible medical uses. The broad first use patent may be considered as retroactively limited by the grant of a subsequent product patent on a specific, later discovered medical use. See South Centre Guide, p. 139, in respect of the relationship between an original, non-pharmaceutical product patent and a subsequent product patent on a first medical use. The same legal fiction may be applied to the relationship between a broad first-use pharmaceutical product claim and product claims for subsequent pharmaceutical uses.

[37] First proposals of such non-exclusive, 'compensatory liability' regimes have been developed by J.H. Reichman (2000), 'Of Green Tulips and Legal Kudzu: Repackaging Rights in Subpatentable Innovation', *Vanderbilt Law Review* 53, 1743–98; J.H. Reichman and T. Lewis (2005), 'Using Liability Rules to Stimulate Local Innovation in Developing Countries: Application to Traditional Knowledge', in *International Public Goods and Transfer of Technology Under a Globalized Intellectual Property Regime*, K.E. Maskus and J.H. Reichman (eds) (Cambridge University Press, Cambridge), pp. 337–66. For a concrete example, see the International Treaty on Plant Genetic Resources for Food and Agriculture (ITPGRFA), establishing a compensatory liability (or 'use and pay') regime for plant breeders who breed new varieties from exemplars deposited in a repository managed by the Consultative Group on International Agricultural Research (CGIAR). The compensatory liability approach may be more appropriate for

Legislation comparable to the WTO-approved Canadian law provides generic producers with a considerably increased level of legal certainty and predictability in their activities. Under a regulatory review exception, a generic producer may use the patented substance for any activity required for the preparation of a request for marketing approval from a national drug regulatory authority (DRA). This includes in any case the manufacturing of the generic copy of the patented drug and its submission to the DRA to establish a showing of bioequivalence between the generic copy and the patented original.[38] Authorized activities also include the importation of ingredients needed by the generic competitor, as well as the possibility to export generic copies to foreign DRAs for their approval. As noticed by Garrison, this may be an essential tool for producers in countries lacking an important domestic pharmaceutical market to benefit from economies of scale.[39] Finally, authorized activities include, as expressly provided under the Canadian legislation, the right to 'sell the patented invention solely for uses reasonably related to' the preparation and submission of a request for regulatory approval.[40] As noted by the EC in its arguments, this right concerns not the generic producer himself, but fine chemical producers who 'often supply generic drug manufacturers with the ingredients needed to make test products'.[41]

In the US Supreme Court's *Merck v. Integra Lifesciences* decision, the question arose as to whether the regulatory review exemption would not only cover uses of a patented medical substance that a generic producer

---

many poor and middle income developing countries, where local pharmaceutical producers do not as yet have the capacity to compete with foreign firms. The latter would most likely draw the main benefits from exclusive rights on new medical uses. A non-exclusive compensatory liability regime would avoid the blocking effects on local producers arising under the patent system. See also South Centre Guide, p. 133.

38 Generic producers obligated to demonstrate bioequivalence may do so by measuring 'the time it takes the generic drug to reach the bloodstream in 24 to 36 healthy volunteers. This gives them the rate of absorption, or bioavailability, of the generic drug, which they can then compare to that of the innovator drug. The generic version must deliver the same amount of active ingredients into a patient's bloodstream in the same amount of time as the innovator drug.' See Meir P. Pugatch (2006), 'Intellectual Property, Data Exclusivity, Innovation and Market Access', in *Negotiating Health. Intellectual Property and Access to Medicines*, P. Roffe, G. Tansey and D. Vivas-Eugui (eds) (Earthscan London); (hereinafter Pugatch, 2006), p. 102, referring to FDA-CDER.

39 Garrison, p. 20.

40 See Section 55.2(1) of the Canadian Patent Act, as quoted in para. 2.1 of the Panel Report.

41 See para. 7.43 of the Panel Report.

intends to copy, but also uses of other patented materials, such as research tools needed for the manufacture of the patented drug.[42] The Supreme Court declined to pronounce itself on this matter.

In order to answer this question, it could first be argued that language comparable to the Canadian and US statutes ('[. . .] uses reasonably related to the development and submission of information [. . .]') is sufficiently wide to encompass the use of research tools, to the extent these are necessary to generate the information needed for regulatory approval requests. For the regulatory research exemption to be useful, it would seem that its scope should extend to all patents that could prevent the generic producer from effectively preparing a request for regulatory approval.

This being said, the answer to the above question would in the final analysis depend on the nature and purpose of the particular research tool at issue. In order to meet the 'limited' exception requirement under the three-step test as interpreted by the Panel, use of the patented research tool by an unauthorized competitor must not 'abrogate such rights entirely' during the time the regulatory review exemption is in effect, as phrased by the Panel with respect to Canada's stockpiling exemption.[43] In case a research tool by its nature may serve only one particular purpose, that is, to enable the development of one particular end product, extending the regulatory review exception to this research tool would effectively remove patent protection entirely from the protected product, which could be compared in its impact on the patent to the Canadian stockpiling exception. It is maybe for this reason that with respect to the experimental use exemption, which is closely related to the regulatory research exemption, the new Swiss Patents Act excludes research tools from the very broad scope of this exception. The experimental use exception could potentially comprise the totality of activities undertaken with research tools, that is, the undertaking of any kind of research. Instead, the Swiss Patents Act subjects patented research tools to a licence of right available for any interested party against the payment of appropriate licensing fees.[44] This could also be a model for countries that intend to exclude research tools from the scope of their regulatory review exception.

---

42 See Garrison, p. 58.

43 See para. 7.34 of the Panel Report. But see below for suggestions in the literature regarding a modified, more holistic approach to the interpretation of the three-step test.

44 See Article 40b of the Swiss Patent Act, as entered into force on 1 July 2008 (French-language version available at http://www.admin.ch/ch/f/rs/232_14/; German language version available at http://www.admin.ch/ch/d/sr/232_14/index.html). The experimental use exception is contained in Article 9(b).

The situation would differ if a particular research tool could be used for various research purposes, for example, for the development of a variety of different products. In that case, the generic competitor, to the extent he is only interested in one particular product, would not claim the entirety of activities that the patented research tool may be used for; such recourse to the regulatory review exception would likely meet the 'limited exception' requirement as interpreted by the *Canada – Patent Protection of Pharmaceuticals* Panel. This being said, it should be noted that many WTO Members' patent laws, for example in the Member States of the European Patent Convention or in the United States, deny patents on research tools that are claimed for an undefined variety of different uses, in order to preserve researchers' freedom to operate.[45]

THE IMPACT OF LEGISLATION ON CLINICAL TEST DATA

While the decision of the Panel recognizes an important tool for generic manufacturers to support their early entry into the market after patent expiry, it is important to note that laws protecting the use of clinical test data (both in the domestic OECD context and as spread among developing nations through bilateral and regional free trade agreements)[46] can interfere with the generic producer's ability to reap the full benefits of an existing regulatory review exception.[47] While this exception authorizes a

---

45 In EPO practice, such exclusions are based on the understanding that the industrial application standard requires the existence of an industrial product, as opposed to purely experimental research tools; see, for example, EPO Boards of Appeal, Decision of 11 May 2005, case no. T 0870/04 – 3.3.8, p. 20, para. 21: 'In the board's judgment, although the present application describes a product (a polypeptide), means and methods for making it, and its prospective use thereof for basic science activities, it identifies no practical way of exploiting it in at least one field of industrial activity. In this respect, it is considered that a vague and speculative indication of possible objectives that might or might not be achievable by carrying out further research with the tool as described is not sufficient for fulfilment of the requirement of industrial applicability. The purpose of granting a patent is not to reserve an unexplored field of research for an applicant.'

In USPTO practice, a research tool claimed for various undefined purposes would lack 'substantial utility', according to USPTO Utility Examination Guidelines. See J.R. Thomas (2005), *Pharmaceutical Patent Law* (BNA Books, Washington, DC), pp. 68–9.

46 See, for example, the free trade agreements between the United States and Chile; as well as Morocco, and the United States – Dominican Republic/Central American Free Trade Agreement (DR/CAFTA). All agreements are available at <http://www.ustr.gov/Trade_Agreements/Section_Index.html>.

47 For further details, see Carsten Fink and Patrick Reichenmiller (2005), 'Tightening TRIPS: The Intellectual Property Provisions of Recent US Free Trade Agreements', *World Bank Trade Note* 20, 7 February; see also Pedro Roffe and

generic producer to carry out the necessary steps to submit a request for regulatory approval to a DRA, some countries' laws on clinical test data limit the DRAs' possibilities of granting such approval, thereby reducing the policy space for generic producers under the regulatory review exemption.

In essence, these laws provide originator companies with exclusive rights in clinical test data and thereby prevent a DRA from granting marketing approval to generic competitors based on the original test data results before the expiry of a period of exclusivity (often five years). In addition, many of these laws link the independent areas of medicines regulation and patent law, making the approval by a DRA of generic copies of on-patent products dependent on the consent or acquiescence of the holder of the pharmaceutical patent. Under the minimum standards of the TRIPS Agreement (Article 39.3), nothing prevents a DRA from granting marketing approval during the term of a pharmaceutical patent, leaving rights enforcement up to the patent holder. This point was also stressed by the *Canada – Patent Protection of Pharmaceuticals* Panel, which stated that

> [. . .] the Panel concurred with Canada's point that the government is not normally expected to regulate the actual conduct of third parties in such cases [i.e. the use by a generic competitor of patented materials under a regulatory review exception]. The enforcement of these conditions, as with other enforcement of patent rights, occurs by means of private infringement actions brought by the patent owner. The patent owner merely has to prove that the challenged conduct is inconsistent with the basic patent rights created by national law. Once that initial case is made, the burden will be on the party accused of infringement to prove its defence by establishing that its conduct with respect to foreign regulatory procedures was in compliance with the conditions of Section 55.2(1).[48]

Footnote 47 (*cont.*)
Christoph Spennemann (2006), 'The Impact of Free Trade Agreements on Public Health Policies and TRIPS Flexibilities', *International Journal of Intellectual Property Management*, 1(1–2); Karin Timmermans (2007), 'Monopolizing Clinical Trial Data: Implications and Trends', *PLoS Medicine Journal*, 13 February (hereinafter Timmermans; available at http://medicine.plosjournals.org/perlserv/?request=get-document&doi=10.1371/journal.pmed.0040002#journal-pmed-0040002-b011); Jerome H. Reichman (2009), 'Rethinking the Role of Clinical Trial Data in International Intellectual Property Law: The Case for a Public Goods Approach', 13 *Marquette Intellectual Property Law Review* 3 (forthcoming). With respect to US–DR/CAFTA, see C.M. Correa (2006), 'Implementación de la Proteccion de Datos de Prueba de Productos Farmacéuticos y Agroquímicos en DR-CAFTA-ley Modelo', UNCTAD-ICTSD Regional Research Agenda (http://www.iprsonline.org/unctadictsd/regional_research.htm).

48 See para. 7.46 of the Panel Report.

Generic producers who consider an existing patent to be weak may under these circumstances decide to challenge the patent and to enter the market immediately.[49] Under a 'linkage' provision, generic producers can no longer do so, due to the lack of regulatory approval.[50]

Thus, despite the existence of regulatory review exceptions, data exclusivity and patent linkage provisions delay the date on which a DRA may grant regulatory approval. Before receiving such a grant, a generic producer lacks legal security and may not be ready to invest in the establishment or enlargement of manufacturing facilities to ensure timely commencement of production immediately after expiry of the patent on the originator drug.

The difference between regulatory approval and stockpiling

As discussed in the above analysis of the *Canada – Patent Protection of Pharmaceuticals* case, the Panel dealt with two interrelated exceptions – the regulatory review exception and the stockpiling exception – to the exclusive rights of the patent holder. Garrison has noted in this respect that 'in terms of the public policy aim of the two disputed exceptions, it

---

[49] In this context, it should be noted that as of June 2002, 73 per cent of patent invalidation claims initiated by generic producers in the United States had been successful; see US Federal Trade Commission, 'Generic Drug Entry Prior to Patent Expiration: An FTC Study', Washington, DC, July 2002, p. 16. Between 2000 and 2007, generic competitors prevailed in 75 per cent of the final opposition and appeals decisions rendered by the European Patent Office, and in 62 per cent of patent litigation cases in EU Member States; see European Commission, 'Pharmaceutical Sector Inquiry', Preliminary Report, DG Competition, 28 November 2008, pp. 10–11; (available at http://ec.europa.eu/competition/sectors/pharmaceuticals/inquiry/preliminary_report.pdf).

[50] In this context, it should be noted that due to a May 2007 bipartisan agreement between the US Congress and the Administration, the most recent US free trade agreements with Colombia, Panama and Peru do not include a mandatory linkage provision (see, for example, Article 16.10.3 and 4 of the US–Peru FTA). Note that at the time of writing, only the US–Peru FTA has been approved by the US Congress, see http://www.ustr.gov/Trade_Agreements/Bilateral/Section_Index.html). Instead, these agreements require parties to provide for procedures and remedies to adjudicate expeditiously the validity of any patent infringement claim concerning an approved pharmaceutical product or its approved method of use (Article 16.10.3 of the US–Peru FTA). According to Article 16.10.4, parties are free (but not obliged) to implement this obligation through a linkage provision under domestic law. In that case, however, parties have to provide for remedies by which the party requesting marketing approval may challenge the validity of the identified patent, as well as effective rewards for the successful challenge of the validity or applicability of the identified patent, such as periods of marketing exclusivity (Article 16.10.4(c)).

was much more important that the Regulatory Review exception would survive than the Stockpiling exception'.[51] This is because the regulatory review exception enables a generic producer to avoid undergoing the marketing approval process after patent expiry, which will usually save him several years.[52] On the other hand, in case the stockpiling exception had been approved, generic producers in the Canadian context would have been awarded six months before patent expiry to initiate production of the amounts required for immediate market entry after patent expiry. Compared to several years gained under the regulatory review exception, these six months appear to confer a very limited benefit in terms of availability of competing generic products. Despite these differences in impact on the economic situation of the patent holder, the Panel found that it was the stockpiling exception that was not 'limited' within the meaning of Article 30, TRIPS Agreement, as opposed to the regulatory review exception. Garrison criticizes the reasoning of the Panel as 'far from clear',[53] pointing to the fact that in case of the stockpiling exception, the Panel relied on the view that 'six months was a commercially significant period of time'[54] in order to support its denial to qualify this exception as 'limited' within the first step under Article 30, TRIPS Agreement. By contrast, in respect of the regulatory review exception, the Panel acknowledged that an acceleration of generic market entry by three to six-and-a-half years could potentially have a considerable economic impact,[55] but expressly rejected considering any issue of economic impact under the first step ('limited exception') of Article 30, TRIPS Agreement.[56]

In response to Garrison, it may be observed that the Panel did not rely on the commercial significance of the six-month period as a major argument to reject the 'limited' character of the stockpiling exception. Before turning to the commercial significance of the six-month period, the Panel had already established its view that the stockpiling exception 'cannot be

---

[51] See p. 41.

[52] See para. 7.48 of the Panel Report, where the Panel states that '[. . .] approximately three to six-and-a-half years are required for generic drug producers to develop and obtain regulatory approval for their products. If there were no regulatory review exception allowing competitors to apply for regulatory approval during the term of the patent, therefore, the patent owner would be able to extend its period of market exclusivity, de facto, for some part of that three to six-and-a-half year period, [. . .]'

[53] Garrison, p. 33.

[54] Panel Report, para. 7.37.

[55] Ibid., para. 7.48.

[56] Ibid., para. 7.49, noting that economic impact issues would exclusively be dealt with under the second and third steps in Article 30, TRIPS Agreement.

considered a "limited exception" within the meaning of Article 30 of the TRIPS Agreement'.[57] It had reached this conclusion through an analysis focused exclusively on the assessment of the extent to which the patent holders' legal rights were curtailed under the stockpiling exception, which 'removes that protection [i.e. the exclusive right to make and use a protected product] entirely during the last six months of the patent term'.[58] Thus, the Panel kept faithful to its own prior decision to limit the analysis under the first step ('limited exception') to 'the extent to which legal rights have been curtailed, rather than the size or extent of the economic impact'.[59] The Panel merely addressed the economic issue in response to the Canadian argument that the stockpiling exception only applied during the last six months of the patent term. In doing so, the Panel did not focus on the economic impact alone, but again stressed the degree of curtailment of the patentee's legal rights. The Panel considered the commercial impact of the exception as being significant, 'especially since there were no limits at all on the volume of production allowed, or the market destination of such production'.[60]

Implications for domestic legislators

As noted in the first part of this chapter, after concluding that at least the regulatory review exception was exonerated from a finding of infringement of Article 28 of the TRIPS Agreement, the Panel had to decide whether the same exception was in line with the non-discrimination requirement under Article 27.1 of the TRIPS Agreement.[61] The EC claimed that this was not the case, based on its understanding that the regulatory review exception applied, de jure and de facto, exclusively to pharmaceutical products and thereby discriminated by field of technology.[62] The Panel, after expressly confirming that Article 30-based exceptions are subject to the non-discrimination requirement under Article 27,[63] found no evidence to support the EC claims, in respect of either de jure or de facto discrimination.[64]

---

57 Ibid., para. 7.36.

58 Ibid., para. 7.34.

59 Ibid., para. 7.31.

60 Ibid., para. 7.37 *in fine*.

61 Article 27.1 of the TRIPS Agreement reads in relevant part: '[. . .] patents shall be available and patent rights enjoyable without discrimination as to the place of invention, the field of technology and whether products are imported or locally produced'.

62 See para. 7.86 of the Panel Report.

63 Ibid., para. 7.91.

64 Ibid., para. 7.105.

The Panel expressly stated that the above finding did not provide any response to the question raised by certain third parties of whether measures that are in fact limited to one particular area of technology

> are necessarily 'discriminatory' by virtue of that fact alone, or whether under certain circumstances they may be justified as certain special measures needed to restore equality of treatment to the area of technology in question.[65]

This raises an important issue for domestic legislators, which goes beyond the scope of the case under analysis, namely whether patent legislation may, under certain circumstances, treat the area of pharmaceuticals – or any other sector for this purpose – differently than other areas of technology. Such an approach has been taken in the past in an attempt to promote a country's domestic generic industry as well as to promote the availability of affordable generic medicines.[66] They remain relevant at present, as illustrated by claims that India's current patent regime, by introducing as a patentability requirement the criterion of 'enhanced efficacy of pharmaceutical substances', as compared to existing products, makes it more difficult to obtain a patent in India in the area of pharmaceuticals than in other areas of technology, thereby violating Article 27.1, TRIPS Agreement.[67]

In response to this issue, it may be questioned whether patentability requirements that are specifically tailored to pharmaceutical substances discriminate to the detriment of pharmaceuticals as compared to other areas of technology. A requirement like the enhanced efficacy criterion, even where it applies to pharmaceutical substances only, does not

---

[65] Ibid., footnote 439, accompanying text in para. 7.105 of the Panel Report.

[66] An example is Canada's pre-1993 patent legislation, which facilitated the availability of compulsory licences specifically in the area of pharmaceutical products, and which was modified due to Canada's accession to the newly created WTO as well as the North American Free Trade Agreement (NAFTA). See EC submission to the *Canada – Generics* Panel, para. 4.6 of the Panel Report. See also UNCTAD–ICTSD (2003), 'Non-voluntary Licensing of Patented Inventions: Historical Perspective, Legal Framework under TRIPS, and an Overview of the Practice in Canada and the United States of America', Issue Paper No. 5, by Jerome H. Reichman and Catherine Hasenzahl (available at http://www.iprsonline.org/resources/docs/Reichman%20-%20Non-voluntary%20Licensing%20-%20Blue%205.pdf).

[67] For more details on this case see, for example, Janice M. Mueller, 'Taking TRIPS to India – Novartis, Patent Law and Access to Medicines', *New England Journal of Medicine*, 8 February 2007, pp. 541–543; IP Watch Newsletter of 7 August 2007, available at http://www.ip-watch.org/weblog/index.php?p=712&res=1280&print=0.

constitute an additional requirement of patentability, but a necessary element of the invention, novelty or inventive step test. It can be based on the specific purpose of pharmaceuticals to cure diseases. Other fields of technology serve other purposes and will therefore rely on different criteria to determine the meaning of novelty and inventive step. Using such criteria is arguably no discrimination between different fields of technology, but a necessary tool to ensure that patent grants take account of the particularities of a given technological area and are limited to those products that bring an extraordinary benefit to society.

In addition, and beyond the specific issue of patentability requirements, it is important to note the Panel's description of 'discrimination' under Article 27.1 of the TRIPS Agreement:

> The ordinary meaning of the word 'discriminate' is potentially broader than these more specific definitions. [i.e. the definitions employed under Articles 3 (national treatment) and 4 (most-favored nation treatment) of the TRIPS Agreement] It certainly extends beyond the concept of differential treatment. It is a normative term, pejorative in connotation, referring to results of the unjustified imposition of differentially disadvantageous treatment. [. . .] The standards by which the justification for differential treatment is measured are a subject of infinite complexity.[68]

It has been suggested in the literature that this statement could be interpreted as permitting governments to adopt different rules for particular product areas or locations of production, as long as the differences are adopted for bona-fide purposes.[69] Differential treatment of pharmaceutical patents vis-à-vis other patents could therefore be justified to the extent that this is conducive to the promotion of public health (that is, through an increased availability of affordable drugs). This being said, it is acknowledged that one measure could serve two different purposes. While promoting the bona-fide purpose of access to medicines, a measure could at the same time seek to confer an economic advantage upon local producers. While the local production of pharmaceuticals has been recognized as bearing some important potential to address the public health crisis in many developing countries,[70] a country would need to ensure that the

---

68 See para. 7.94 of the Panel Report.

69 See UNCTAD–ICTSD Resource Book, p. 481.

70 See, for example, OECD, 'Noordwijk Medicines Agenda' of 21 June 2007, para. 3 (p. 4) (www.oecd.org/dataoecd/62/11/38845838.pdf); see also Resolution by the European Parliament of 12 July 2007 on the TRIPS Agreement and access to medicines (http://www.europarl.europa.eu/sides/getDoc.do?pubRef=-//EP//TEXT+TA+P6-TA-2007-0353+0+DOC+XML+V0//EN).

benefits of such legislation are not limited to local producers but effectively passed on to patients, in terms of more reasonable prices for medicines.

As long as the WTO dispute settlement organs have not expressly pronounced themselves on this issue, the TRIPS-compatibility of pharmaceuticals-specific legislation will remain contested. In this respect, it is interesting to note that the European Patent Office (EPO) in its 2007 'Scenarios for the Future' presents a fictitious scenario for the future development of the patent system.[71] Under one of these scenarios, the basic question discussed by the EPO is whether the 'one-size-fits-all' approach to patenting is still appropriate, against the background of new developments in certain technological sectors, which lend themselves to patent misuse, such as the blocking of downstream innovation through upstream patent thickets.[72] According to one proposal advanced under this scenario, 'strong patent protection would remain in areas such as pharmaceuticals, but weaker rights in areas such as the information and communication technology'.

While this solution may correspond to the situation in OECD countries, the particular health and access to medicines problems in many developing countries would require a different approach. This being said, the basic idea of tailoring patent rules to specific technological developments, including differential treatment of technological sectors, seeks to accommodate emerging technological trends and merits further deliberation.

The Canada – Patent Protection of Pharmaceuticals *case and the three-step test: a tool to design patent policy?*

The *Canada – Patent Protection of Pharmaceuticals* decision played a decisive role in acknowledging the regulatory review exception in patent law, with all the implications discussed in this chapter. The question arises to what extent and how the main object of the Panel's decision, that is, the three-step test under Article 30, TRIPS Agreement, may be employed to promote a balanced implementation of the TRIPS Agreement in domestic laws, taking into account the specific needs and priorities of the implementing country.

Despite the positive assessment by commentators of the public health impact of the regulatory review exception, the same academics have also

---

71 See EPO, 'Scenarios for the Future – How might IP regimes evolve by 2025? What global legitimacy might such regimes have?', Munich 2007 (in particular the 'Blue Skies' Scenario, pp. 85 et seq. (see also http://www.epo.org/topics/patent-system/scenarios-for-the-future.html).

72 Ibid., p. 95, discussing, inter alia, proposals to introduce licences of right to enable interoperability of software products.

criticized the decision to interpret Article 30 of the TRIPS Agreement in a manner that erects too many unnecessary barriers for WTO Members' freedom to design appropriate public health policies. Professor Abbott has noted that the Panel's definition of 'limited' is 'narrower than the dictionary requires',[73] and has himself advanced a somewhat wider definition.[74] In addition, Abbott has expressed disagreement with the Panel's view that exceptions under Article 30, TRIPS Agreement, should be subject to the non-discrimination requirement under Article 27.1, TRIPS Agreement.[75] The main criticism raised, for example, by Garrison relates to the Panel's arguable failure to take into account, in its interpretation of Article 30, TRIPS Agreement, all pre-existing exceptions to patent rights as established in WTO Members prior to the entry into force of the Agreement.[76] Both authors note that in light of the Doha Declaration on the TRIPS Agreement and Public Health, which was adopted more than a year after the *Canada – Patent Protection of Pharmaceuticals* decision, a panel would nowadays interpret Article 30, TRIPS Agreement, differently than in *Canada – Generics*.[77]

The *Canada – Patent Protection of Pharmaceuticals* case has so far been the only decision by a WTO adjudicatory body regarding the interpretation of Article 30 of the TRIPS Agreement. From the perspective of public health and public policies in general, it is important to reflect upon the manner in which the Panel approached the three-step test under this provision. The interpretation of Article 30 has some major implications for WTO Members' policy space to design domestic health and other policies. In this context, it is important to note that voices in the literature, albeit in different tones, commented on the surprising result of the Panel's

---

73 See Abbott, 2003, p. 736.

74 See Frederick M. Abbott (2002), 'Compulsory Licensing for Public Health Needs: The TRIPS Agenda at the WTO after the Doha Declaration on Public Health', Quaker United Nations Office Geneva, p. 35 (expressing the view that the term 'limited' does not necessarily suggest 'that the established boundaries should be narrow').

75 See Abbott, 2003, p. 736. Developing countries have expressed the same view as regards the relationship between Article 31, TRIPS Agreement (compulsory licensing) and the non-discrimination requirement. See 'TRIPS and Public Health', Submission by the African Group of WTO Members and other countries, WTO document IP/C/W/296 of 29 June 2001.

76 See Garrison, p. 42.

77 See Abbott, 2003, p. 736; Garrison, pp. 41–42. Both authors express the view that the heightened sensitivity for public health issues as brought about by events leading to the Doha Declaration should be accommodated by WTO jurisprudence, having recourse to an 'evolutionary' interpretation of Article 30, TRIPS Agreement.

reasoning, that is, to invalidate the exception (stockpiling) that is economically less significant to the patent holder, while upholding the exception (regulatory review) that bears a more important economic impact.[78] In order to guide future policy making and to avoid seemingly contradictory results, attempts have been made in the literature to devise means, drawing on the case, for the creation of new exceptions to granted patent rights that are in line with Article 30 of the TRIPS Agreement.

Garrison, on the one hand, lays much emphasis on the need to take account of various patent exceptions that are widely recognized and practised under domestic laws and criticizes the Panel for not having done so.[79]

Senftleben, on the other hand, seeks to identify common principles for broader intellectual property rights limitations arising from the *Canada – Patent Protection of Pharmaceuticals* case, as well as two parallel WTO Panel decisions in the areas of copyright and trademark law.[80]

Finally, in a recent 'Declaration' on 'A Balanced Interpretation of the "Three-step Test" in Copyright Law',[81] a number of eminent intellectual property scholars have proposed a new approach to the interpretation of the three-step test at least under copyright law and have in this context criticized the Panel for its rigid step-by-step approach to Article 30, especially the Panel's understanding that failure to meet one of the three steps will necessarily result in a violation of Article 30 of the TRIPS Agreement.[82]

In the following, we shall seek to briefly analyze these approaches in terms of their possible contributions to a balanced interpretation of Article 30, TRIPS Agreement, and possibly other TRIPS exceptions clauses, in light of the Doha Declaration and other important developments at the World Intellectual Property Organization (WIPO) and the World Health Organization (WHO).

---

[78] Abbott (2002), p. 45, *supra* note 74; Garrison, p. 41.

[79] Garrison, p. 42: '[. . .] it is arguable that the *Canada – Generics* Panel erred in their interpretation of "limited" in not systematically taking account of all the pre-existing exceptions which were known to be valid, including, for example, the broad Foreign Vehicles and Chicago exceptions'.

[80] Martin Senftleben (2006), 'Towards a Horizontal Standard for Limiting Intellectual Property Rights? – WTO Panel Reports Shed Light on the Three-step Test in Copyright Law and Related Tests in Patent and Trademark Law', *IIC* 37(4) (2006) (hereinafter Senftleben).

[81] See http://www.ip.mpg.de/shared/data/pdf/declaration_three_steps.pdf. Initiators and coordinators of the Declaration include the Director of the Max-Planck Institute for Intellectual Property in Munich.

[82] See footnote 1 to the Declaration.

According to Garrison,

> The central point is that it is perhaps hard to understand how a sensible definition of the term 'limited' in Art. 30 TRIPS can be reached without a reasonable consideration, in some way or another, of all the exceptions which are certainly regarded as valid by Members. Unless and until a systematic analysis of all these exceptions is carried out, including either all the exceptions whose scope is agreed upon and/or a common core in terms of the more contentious ones, it would seem that a definition of 'limited' cannot be reached which embraces them all.[83]
> [. . .]
> The central problem raised in this part of the paper is, bluntly stated, that the interpretation of 'limited' adopted by the Panel seems to exclude a number of these exceptions to patent rights which must surely be regarded as valid and properly 'limited' for the purposes of Art. 30 TRIPS.[84]

He then refers to the 'Foreign Vessels exception'[85] and the 'International Civil Aviation (Chicago) exception'[86] to show that the Panel in the

---

83 Garrison, p. 34.

84 Ibid., p. 35.

85 For the Foreign Vessels exception, see Article 5*ter* of the Paris Convention: 'In any country of the Union the following shall not be considered as infringements of the rights of a patentee: (i) the use on board vessels of other countries of the Union of devices forming the subject of his patent in the body of the vessel, in the machinery, tackle, gear and other accessories, when such vessels temporarily or accidentally enter the waters of the said country, provided that such devices are used there exclusively for the needs of the vessel; (ii) the use of devices forming the subject of the patent in the construction or operation of aircraft or land vehicles of other countries of the Union, or of accessories of such aircraft or land vehicles, when those aircraft or land vehicles temporarily or accidentally enter the said country'.

86 See Article 27 of the Chicago Convention on International Civil Aviation (1944): '(a) While engaged in international air navigation, any authorized entry of aircraft of a contracting State into the territory of another contracting State or authorized transit across the territory of such State with or without landings shall not entail any seizure or detention of the aircraft or any claim against the owner or operator thereof or any other interference therewith by or on behalf of such State or any person therein, on the ground that the construction, mechanism, parts, accessories or operation of the aircraft is an infringement of any patent, design, or model duly granted or registered in the State whose territory is entered by the aircraft, it being agreed that no deposit of security in connection with the foregoing exemption from seizure or detention of the aircraft shall in any case be required in the State entered by such aircraft. b) The provisions of paragraph a) of this Article shall also be applicable to the storage of spare parts and spare equipment for the aircraft and the right to use and install the same in the repair of an aircraft of a contracting State in the territory of any other contracting State, provided that any patented part or equipment so stored shall not be sold or distributed internally in or exported commercially from the contracting State entered by the aircraft. [. . .]'

Canada – Patent Protection of Pharmaceuticals case erred in finding that the Canadian stockpiling exception was not 'limited' in terms of Article 30, TRIPS Agreement.[87]

Garrison expresses the view that both the Foreign Vessels and the Chicago exception are comparable to the Canadian stockpiling exception as regards their adverse impact on the patentee's legal rights:

> Under the Foreign Vessels exception, with regard to vessels that are engaged in international travel and only visit the territory in question, a patent holder's right to prevent unauthorised third parties from 'using' (and arguably 'importing' for that purpose) the patented invention is entirely removed. [. . .] It is difficult to see how this exception can meet the Panel's *legal* test as to 'limited'.
>
> The situation is similar, if not more compelling, for the Chicago exception. Not only is the right of a patent holder to prevent unauthorised third parties from 'using' (and, again, arguably 'importing' for that purpose) their invention entirely removed in respect of the international movement of aircraft flying into and out of the territory in question, but spare parts for those aircraft, which could otherwise also be infringing items, are permitted to be imported and *stockpiled* for use at any time during the lifetime of a relevant patent. [. . .] It is again difficult to see how this exception can meet the Panel's *legal* test as to 'limited'.[88] (emphasis in original)

In the literature, others have also voiced doubts about the compatibility of well-established patent exceptions with the interpretation of the term 'limited' as employed by the *Canada – Patent Protection of Pharmaceuticals* Panel. Pires de Carvalho in this respect refers to the pharmacy and the prior user exceptions:

> Many WTO Members have established an exception concerning the manual preparation of medicines by pharmacists and medical doctors, in accordance with a medical prescription. Following the reasoning of the Panel in *Canada – Patent Protection of Pharmaceutical Products*, it is difficult to accept that such exclusion could be a 'limited' one, because it gives third parties the unqualified and unlimited right to 'make' and 'sell' the patented medicine. [. . .] The same can be said of the 'prior user' exception [. . .]. The prior user exception, like the pharmacist exception is not 'limited' because the prior user will be allowed to make, use and sell the product [. . .].[89]

Thus, albeit drawing opposite conclusions, both authors agree that a number of traditional patent exceptions cannot be considered as 'limited'

---

[87] Garrison, pp. 35-7.
[88] Ibid., p. 36.
[89] Nuno Pires de Carvalho (2002), *The TRIPS Regime of Patent Rights*, The Hague, The Netherlands (Kluwer Law International), p. 227.

within the meaning of Article 30, TRIPS Agreement, as interpreted by the *Canada – Patent Protection of Pharmaceuticals* Panel.[90] Following this view could have wide-ranging implications on WTO Members' use of patent exceptions. On the one hand, it could generate a chilling effect on the actual use of traditionally established exceptions, while on the other hand, Members might be encouraged to establish new domestic stockpiling exemptions, relying on a more permissive interpretation of the 'limited exceptions' criterion by future WTO panels.

Contrary to the opinions expressed by Garrison and Pires de Carvalho, the view in this chapter is that all of the above-mentioned exceptions (that is, Foreign Vessels; Chicago; pharmacy; and prior user exception) may be considered as meeting the requirements of the term 'limited' as interpreted by the *Canada – Patent Protection of Pharmaceuticals* Panel. All of these exceptions only concern a very limited range of activities covered under a patent, and do not reach beyond very specific situations. Under the Chicago exception, the patentee's rights are not entirely removed, because the exception concerns only the narrow context of an aircraft engaged in international air navigation. Spare parts may only be used without the patent holder's authorization to the extent required to repair an aircraft engaged in international air navigation. The same applies to the Foreign Vessels exception, which only authorizes uses of patented products in connection with temporary or accidental entries by a vessel (or aircraft or vehicle) into a foreign territory. A patent confers rights not only in respect of uses during air or sea travel, but exclusive rights in general. The patent holder may prevent all unauthorized uses that do not occur during a plane's or vessel's transit through foreign territories, including the separate use, sale or production of patented elements of the aircraft or vessel. Under the prior user exception, the patent holder may prevent all uses occurring outside the very specific context of good faith uses carried out in good faith prior to the filing of the patent application. Finally, the pharmacy exception does not authorize any broad use of pharmaceutical substances, but only in the narrow context where the product is made on the pharmacy premises, in a 'sporadic, improvised and medically prompted' manner.[91]

By contrast, the Canadian stockpiling exemption concerned the very core of a pharmaceutical producer's activity, that is, production of the drug for

---

90 While Pires de Carvalho seems to indicate that a number of patent exceptions as traditionally established under domestic laws are incompatible with Article 30, TRIPS Agreement, Garrison arrives at the opposite conclusion, that is, that the *Canada – Patent Protection of Pharmaceuticals* Panel applied Article 30, TRIPS Agreement, incorrectly, disregarding these well-established exceptions.

91 See Garrison, p. 7.

marketing purposes. While unauthorized uses of patented aircraft parts during international air navigation do not cover the entire gamut of economically relevant uses, unauthorized production of pharmaceuticals arguably take up most of the economically relevant activity reserved to the patent holder, because it concerns the principal use of the product, which the patent holder typically wants to have covered by the patent. As put by the *Canada – Patent Protection of Pharmaceuticals* Panel: '[. . .] and manufacturing for commercial sale is a quintessential competitive commercial activity, whose character is not altered by a mere delay in the commercial reward'.[92]

For these reasons, it is argued that even if the *Canada – Patent Protection of Pharmaceuticals* Panel had expressly considered the above-mentioned exceptions, it would still have considered the stockpiling exemption as failing to meet the 'limited' exception test under Article 30, TRIPS Agreement. For the same reasons, it is also clear that the above-mentioned exceptions, which are well established under Members' domestic patent laws, cannot be considered as failing the 'limited exceptions' test.

In a somewhat broader attempt to develop guidelines for future policy making on the interface between IPRs and their limitations, Senftleben in a detailed analysis has compared the interpretation of the three-step test under Article 30, TRIPS Agreement, as employed by the Panel, with the approaches taken by two other panels[93] on the TRIPS exception clauses in copyright (that is, Article 13, TRIPS Agreement) and trademark law (that is, Article 17, TRIPS Agreement). These provisions contain similar, albeit not identical, language as provided under Article 30.

Senftleben reaches a contradictory result. On the one hand, he is able to distil common principles in the interpretation of the three-step test under all of the above provisions. In particular, all three panels decided to limit the first step examination ('limited exceptions/certain special cases') to an assessment of the extent to which the IP right holder's legal rights had been curtailed by the claimed exception at issue, but refused to engage in a normative assessment of whether the exceptions in question would seem legitimate in terms of overall IP policy goals.[94] On the second step ('normal

---

92 See para. 7.35 of the Panel Report.

93 On copyright: *United States – Section 110(5) of the US Copyright Act* (hereinafter *US – Copyright*), Report of the Panel of 15 June 2000, WTO document WT/DS160/R; on trademarks: *European Communities – Protection of Trademarks and Geographical Indications for Agricultural Products and Foodstuffs*, WT/DS174/R of 15 March 2005 (US complaint) and WT/DS290/R of 15 March 2005 (Australian complaint). Both complaints were essentially based on the same claims.

94 Senftleben, pp. 420, 421, referring also to other points of coherence and incoherence in the decisions of the three panels.

exploitation'), all panels agreed that 'exploitation' referred to commercial activities by which the right holder extracts economic value from his creations, and that such exploitation would be 'normal' where, according to empirical evidence, most right holders would expect to extract value from the IP right.[95]

On the other hand, Senftleben concluded that

> [. . .] it can hardly be overlooked that the panels did not base their interpretative analyses on the same theoretical approach. Whereas the patent panel and the trademark panel sought to open gateways for normative policy considerations, particularly in the context of the normal exploitation test and the identification of legitimate interests, the copyright panel pursued a legal positivist approach throughout the interpretative analysis. The question of an emerging international standard for limiting intellectual property rights can therefore be answered either way – in the affirmative as well as in the negative.[96]

The 'normative policy considerations' that the *Canada – Patent Protection of Pharmaceuticals* Panel applied in the context of the normal exploitation test consisted of its interpretation of the term 'normal'. In the view of the Panel, this term not only refers to empirical evidence, but also to an exploitation of a patent that is 'essential to the achievement of the goals of patent policy'.[97] As to the identification of legitimate interests, the Panel rejected the EC's view that the latter are identical with the patent holder's legal interests as examined under the first step.[98] Rather, it considered 'legitimate interests' of the patent holder as well as of third parties as

---

[95] Ibid., p. 428. In the context of defining 'normal', the *Canada – Patent Protection of Pharmaceuticals* Panel expressed the view that: 'Patent laws establish a carefully defined period of market exclusivity as an inducement to innovation, and the policy of those laws cannot be achieved unless patent owners are permitted to take advantage of that inducement once it has been defined' (para. 7.55). According to Professor Correa, 'This statement hints at the panel's conception on the role of the objectives of the patent system. The panel seems to have ignored the fact that there is no *universal* patent system, and that the national patent laws have historically reflected different philosophies and objectives largely correlated to different levels of economic and technological development. Moreover, while emphasizing the stimulation to innovation, the panel's view failed to consider other essential objectives of the patent system, such as the diffusion of knowledge and its continuous improvement. In the last instance, patents were instituted to serve the public interest and not to benefit individual inventors.' See Carlos M. Correa (2007), *Trade Related Aspects of Intellectual Property Rights: A Commentary on the TRIPS Agreement*, Oxford: Oxford University Press, p. 309.

[96] Ibid., p. 435.

[97] See *Canada – Patent Protection of Pharmaceuticals* Panel, at para. 7.58.

[98] Ibid., para. 7.68.

'a normative claim calling for protection of interests that are "justifiable" in the sense that they are supported by relevant public policies or other social norms'.[99]

This analysis may provide some important guidance for the future design of exceptions in patent law. Under the normal exploitation test, there appears to be some room for the consideration of the crucial policy objectives listed under Article 7 of the TRIPS Agreement (that is, the promotion of technological innovation and the transfer of technology), which focus not only on economic benefits by the right holders, but especially and above all on the overall advancement of society at large. Against this background, the examination of what constitutes a 'normal' exploitation would have to take into account to what extent the exercise of the rights conferred by a patent contributes to technological innovation and – in the context of technology transfer – technological learning. Depending on the circumstances, overly broad patents that are mainly used as strategic weapons to block competitors from developing new products could be considered as blocking, rather than promoting, innovation and would thus not constitute a 'normal' exploitation of the patent.[100]

The interpretation of 'legitimate interests' (that is, the third prong of the three-step test) as applied by the Panel also lends support to the consideration of public policy interests beyond the legal rights of the patent holder. Rather than referring back to the legal rights attributed to the patent holder, the examination of the third step has to strike a balance between competing (economic, societal and other public policy-related) interests of the right holder and the users of the protected invention, in a way that seeks to avoid excessive damage to any of the involved parties.[101]

By contrast, the approach taken by the *US – Copyright* Panel in its interpretation of the three-step test under Article 13 of the TRIPS

---

[99] Ibid., at para. 7.69.

[100] The use of patents as strategic tools to block competition is frequent practice among certain sectors of the industry; see, for example, 'The Arms Race: Companies are Preparing for the Intellectual Property Battle', *The Economist*, 22 October 2005, Special Issue 'A Market for Ideas: A Survey of Patents and Technology', pp. 8–9. This practice has raised serious concerns about the ability of the patent system to stimulate innovation; see, for example, 'To Promote Innovation: The Proper Balance of Competition and Patent Law and Policy', *A Report by the Federal Trade Commission*, October 2003 (http://www.ftc.gov/os/2003/10/innovationrpt.pdf); and Adam B. Jaffe and Joshua Lerner (2004), *Innovation and its Discontents: How Our Broken Patent System is Endangering Innovation and Progress, and what to Do about it* (Princeton, NJ: Princeton University Press).

[101] See Senftleben, p. 438, referring to the principle of proportionality.

Agreement appears to put less emphasis on public policy goals, but rather focuses on the rights and interests of the copyright owner.[102] While the *Canada – Patent Protection of Pharmaceuticals* Panel under the 'normal exploitation' test referred, inter alia, to the goals of patent policy, the *US – Copyright* Panel interpreted the term 'normal' as follows:

> Thus it appears that one way of measuring the normative connotation of normal exploitation is to consider, in addition to those forms of exploitation that currently generate significant or tangible revenue, those forms of exploitation which, with a certain degree of likelihood and plausibility, could acquire considerable economic or practical importance.
> [. . .] In contrast, exceptions or limitations would be presumed not to conflict with a normal exploitation of works if they are confined to a scope or degree that does not enter into economic competition with non-exempted uses. [. . .][103]

This interpretation appears to leave much less room for considering the goals of intellectual property protection, as provided under Article 7 of the TRIPS Agreement. The focus on the economic importance of the uses in question arguably neglects other important considerations, such as the legitimacy of the way the IP right is used, especially in respect of the extent to which follow-on creativity may be hindered, or the extent to which use of the copyright has a bearing on the effective dissemination of knowledge. It is therefore difficult to see how the *US – Copyright* Panel Report could be relied upon for attempts to design IP exceptions that take account of the importance for creativity of an appropriate balance between exclusive rights and the public domain.

This being said, even the *Canada – Patent Protection of Pharmaceuticals* Panel's more flexible approach toward integrating public policy considerations into the application of the second and third prong of the three-step test cannot unfold its full potential under the premise that, as the Panel put it: 'The three conditions are cumulative, each being a separate and independent requirement that must be satisfied. *Failure to comply with any one of the three conditions results in the Article 30 exception being disallowed*'[104] (emphasis added).

As illustrated by the case of the Canadian stockpiling exemption, a piece of contested legislation may never be submitted for testing against the second and the third step in case it fails to meet the first. This approach

---

[102] Senftleben in this regard refers to a 'legal positivist approach'; see ibid., p. 429.

[103] *US – Copyright*, at paras. 6.180, 6.181.

[104] *US – Copyright,* para. 7.20.

may thereby limit the analysis of patent exceptions to an examination of the curtailment of legal rights suffered by the patent holder. This fails to take into account the societal considerations that support the protection of IP, such as the promotion of innovation and technology dissemination and transfer, as enunciated under Article 7 of the TRIPS Agreement. It also fails to take account of the impact IPRs may have on various areas of public policy, such as health, as illustrated in the WTO Doha Declaration on the TRIPS Agreement and Public Health, as well as the World Health Assembly (WHA) Resolution on a 'Global strategy and plan of action on public health, innovation and intellectual property'.[105] These objectives cannot be promoted through the protection of exclusive rights alone, but through an appropriate mix of exclusive rights and unrestricted access to essential building blocks of knowledge as part of the public domain.[106]

While it is important to uphold the legal rights afforded to inventors and creators under the TRIPS Agreement, such analysis will remain incomplete without considering the public policy reasons for possible curtailments of these rights, even in cases where the rights in question have been curtailed beyond what would normally be considered a 'limited' exception. A final assessment can only be made after taking account of the public policy and economic considerations implied in the examination of the second and third steps. Only a complete analysis of all competing interests in a particular case will reveal to what extent innovation and creativity are best promoted through exclusive rights and to what degree the public domain plays a role in this respect. A rigid step-by-step analysis as advanced by the *Canada – Patent Protection of Pharmaceuticals* Panel accords inappropriate priority to the exclusive legal rights under step one, while artificially eliminating all considerations regarding the importance of the public domain for innovation and creativity (in case the step one test is not met). Such an approach carries a certain risk of imbalance of competing interests and arguably neglects the cross-cutting nature of intellectual property and its potential impact on society at large. It was the perception of these exclusive rights-centred approaches to IP which, inter alia, contributed to the formulation of a number of policy recommendations under the 2007

---

105 See WHA61.21 of 24 May 2008.

106 On the importance for creativity and innovation of an appropriate mix between exclusive rights and public domain elements, see, for example, Nikolaus Thumm, 'Reasonable Patent Protection with a Statutory Research Exemption', in IPR Helpdesk Bulletin, No 29, September–October 2006 (www.ipr-helpdesk.org) (on the particular situation in Switzerland and corresponding legislative changes). See also most recently James Boyle (2008), *The Public Domain: Enclosing the Commons of the Mind* (New York, Conn.: Yale University Press).

WIPO Development Agenda, emphasizing, inter alia, the importance of promoting 'norm-setting activities related to IP that support a robust public domain in WIPO's Member States'.[107]

As noted above, the rigid and exclusionary step-by-step application of the three-step test has also been criticized in an important 'Declaration' issued by a number of prominent officials and researchers at the Munich-based Max-Planck-Institute for Intellectual Property on 'A Balanced Interpretation of the "Three-step Test" in Copyright Law'.[108] The Declaration expresses, inter alia, the following consideration in respect of the three-step test in copyright law:

> When correctly applied, the Three-Step Test requires a comprehensive overall assessment, rather than the step-by-step application that its usual, but misleading, description implies. No single step is to be prioritized. As a result, the Test does not undermine the necessary balancing of interests between different classes of rightholders or between rightholders and the larger general public. Any contradictory results arising from the application of the individual steps of the test in a particular case must be accommodated within this comprehensive, overall assessment. The present formulation of the Three-Step Test does not preclude this understanding. However, this approach has often been overlooked in decided cases. [. . .][109]

It goes on to declare, inter alia, that:

> [. . .]
> 2. The Three-Step Test does not require limitations and exceptions to be interpreted narrowly. They are to be interpreted according to their objectives and purposes. [. . .][110]

The Declaration is limited to the area of copyright law. While it is understood that creative activity in copyright-relevant areas may be subject to other considerations and dynamics than in patent-related areas,[111] it is

---

107 See at http://www.wipo.int/ip-development/en/agenda/recommendations.html (recommendation no. 20).

108 See http://www.ip.mpg.de/ww/en/pub/news/declaration_on_the_three_step_/declaration.cfm.

109 See third consideration of the Declaration, p. 2.

110 Ibid., p. 4,

111 In this respect, it is interesting to note the dividing line in the United States between information and communication (ICT) companies and the pharmaceutical industry as regards the reform of the US patent system. See Helen Disney and Meir P. Pugatch, 'Commentary – The Patent Reform Act – Divided We Are, United We Stand', in *Know IP – The Stockholm Network's Monthly IPR Journal*, 3(6), August 2007, pp. 1–4 (referring to the *Coalition of Patent Fairness,* mainly

nevertheless submitted that the overall purposes of copyright and patent protection are alike, that is, the promotion of creative and/or innovative endeavor to the benefit of society at large. A comprehensive assessment of all competing interests and an equal treatment of all three prongs under the three-step test would offer a sufficient degree of flexibility under both copyright and patent law to take account of the varying extents to which the public domain contributes to innovation and creativity. This approach should therefore not be limited to copyright law, but also be considered for the area of patent law and policy.

Footnote 111 (*cont.*)
made up of ICT-oriented companies, as the most fervent criticizers of the current US patent system, while the *Coalition for 21st Century Patent Reform*, which counts among its members several big pharmaceutical companies, has cautioned against drastic modifications of the current patent system).

10 Mandatory regulation versus discretionary regulation, unilateralism, and national treatment: an analysis of the *United States – Section 211 Omnibus Appropriations Act of 1998* dispute

Christophe Charlier

The *US – Section 211 Appropriations Act* dispute[1] arbitrated by the Dispute Settlement Body (DSB) of the World Trade Organization (WTO) was raised by Section 211 of the United States Omnibus Appropriations Act of 1998 (Section 211). It opposed the European Communities (EC) as complainant to the United States (US) as defendant. Section 211 deals with trademarks and commercial names that are identical or similar to trademarks and commercial names that were used in connection with a business or assets that were confiscated by the Cuban Government on or after 1 January 1959. The EC alleges that Section 211 is incompatible with certain dispositions of the Agreement on Trade-related Aspects of Intellectual Property Rights (the TRIPS Agreement), as read in conjunction with the relevant provisions of the Paris Convention for the Protection of Industrial Property (the Paris Convention (1967)).

All transactions, involving goods under US jurisdiction in which a Cuban national has an interest, require a licence from the Office of Foreign Assets Control (OFAC). OFAC is an agency of the US Department of the Treasury in charge of the Cuban Assets Control Regulations (CACR). This specific regulation on the control of Cuban assets was set out in the Code of Federal Regulations (CFR) in 1963 under the Trading with the Enemy Act of 1917.

Section 211 has the effect of modifying dispositions of the CACR (Section 515 of Title 31 CFR). Before it came into force, a general licence was available under the CACR for the registration and renewal of trademarks previously owned by Cuban nationals irrespective of whether such

[1] *United States – Section 211 Omnibus Appropriations Act of 1998*, DS 176.

trademarks had been confiscated by the Cuban Government. This was no longer possible after Section 211 came into force.[2]

The effect of Section 211, read with the relevant provisions of the CACR, is to withdraw certain aspects of protection actually guaranteed in the US to a defined category of trademarks and trade names.[3] For this reason, the EC requested consultation with the US in July 1999 and asked the DSB to establish a Panel in September 2000.

In its complaint, the EC outlines what, from its point of view, are the aspects of intellectual property protection nullified by Section 211. The object of protection is at stake in the first two of the EC's claims. The EC argued that Section 211(a)(1) is incompatible with Article 2.1 of the TRIPS Agreement read in conjunction with Article 6quinquies A(1)

---

[2] Section 211 states that:

(a)(1) Notwithstanding any other provision of law, no transaction or payment shall be authorized or approved pursuant to section 515.527 of title 31, Code of Federal Regulations, as in effect on September 9, 1998, with respect to a mark, trade name, or commercial name that is the same as or substantially similar to a mark, trade name, or commercial name that was used in connection with a business or assets that were confiscated unless the original owner of the mark, trade name, or commercial name, or the bona fide successor-in-interest has expressly consented.
(a)(2) No U.S. court shall recognize, enforce or otherwise validate any assertion of rights by a designated national based on common law rights or registration obtained under such section 515.527 of such a confiscated mark, trade name, or commercial name.
(b) No U.S. court shall recognize, enforce or otherwise validate any assertion of treaty rights by a designated national or its successor-in-interest under sections 44 (b) or (e) of the Trademark Act of 1946 (15 U.S.C. 1126 (b) or (e)) for a mark, trade name, or commercial name that is the same as or substantially similar to a mark, trade name, or commercial name that was used in connection with a business or assets that were confiscated unless the original owner of such mark, trade name, or commercial name, or the bona fide successor-in-interest has expressly consented.
(c) The Secretary of the Treasury shall promulgate such rules and regulations as are necessary to carry out the provisions of this section.
(d) In this section:
(1) The term 'designated national' has the meaning given such term in section 515.305 of title 31, Code of Federal Regulations, as in effect on September 9, 1998, and includes a national of any foreign country who is a successor-in-interest to a designated national.
(2) The term 'confiscated' has the meaning given such term in section 515.336 of title 31, Code of Federal Regulations, as in effect on September 9, 1998.

[3] Appellate Body (AB) Report, para. 8.

of the Paris Convention (1967) obliging WTO Member States (Member States) to accept for filing and to protect 'as is' in its country of origin, every trademark duly registered in other Paris Convention (1967) countries. The EC also maintained that WTO Members should register trademarks that are 'protectable' in the sense of Article 15:1 of the TRIPS Agreement and that Section 211(a)(1) does not fall within the exception which permits denial of registration. The third claim of the EC considers the right conferred on the owners of a registered trademark. The EC argues that Sections 211(a)(2) and (b), having the effect of refusing access to US Courts for certain kinds of nationals, are incompatible with Article 16:1 of the TRIPS Agreement, which states that the owner of a trademark shall have the exclusive right to defend his trademark. The fourth claim of the EC focuses on fair and equitable civil and administrative procedures. Using the preceding idea of barring access to US courts impeding certain trademark owners from enforcing their rights, the EC alleges that Sections 211(a)(2) and (b) are incompatible with Article 42 of the TRIPS Agreement. According to this article, Member States 'shall make available to right holders civil judicial procedures concerning the enforcement of any intellectual property right' covered by the TRIPS Agreement. The final claim of the EC focuses on the issues of national treatment and most-favoured-nation treatment. The national treatment obligation in Article 2(1) of the Paris Convention (1967) and Article 3:1 of the TRIPS Agreement requires a Member State to accord no less favourable treatment to non-nationals than nationals. The EC claims that Sections 211(a)(2) and (b) violate this obligation by treating non US nationals less favourably than US nationals in two different situations (that of successors-in-interest to original owners, and that of original owners) and in different ways. The EC claims that, in relation to the same two situations, Sections 211(a)(2) and (b) are inconsistent with the most-favoured-nation obligation set out in Article 4 of the *TRIPS Agreement*. This obligation requires a Member State to accord immediately and unconditionally to the nationals of all Member States any advantage granted to the nationals of another country.

The Panel report of August 2001 outlines three kinds of conclusions. First, it concludes that Section 211(a)(2) is inconsistent with Article 42 of the TRIPS Agreement. Second, it concludes that the EC failed to prove that Section 211(b) was inconsistent with Article 2:1 of the TRIPS Agreement in conjunction with Article 6bis of the Paris Convention (1967) and with Article 16:1 of the TRIPS Agreement. Third, the Panel rejected all other EC allegations.

Both the EC and the US appealed. The US appealed the Panel's finding concerning Article 42 of the TRIPS Agreement and the EC appealed the other findings. In addition, the EC asked the Appellate Body (AB) to reverse the Panel's finding that trade names are not covered by the TRIPS Agreement.[4] In January 2002, the AB issued its report and reversed the Panel's findings on Article 42 of the TRIPS Agreement and its conclusions on national treatment and most-favoured-nation treatment. It upheld the other findings of the Panel against which the EC appealed. Finally, it reversed the Panel's conclusion that trade names are not covered in the TRIPS Agreement and ruled that trade names be treated the same as trademarks.

This dispute raises many issues.[5] Some are specific to the subject under scrutiny, while others, such as consideration of trade names within the TRIPS Agreement,[6] are more general.[7] We choose to focus on the national treatment claims since it is the first time this cornerstone principle has been challenged in the field of intellectual property governed by the TRIPS Agreement. Also, there was disagreement between the Panel and the AB, as described above, over national treatment claims. We can therefore, expect, there to be some general lessons on national treatment that can be drawn from this dispute.

1. The principle of national treatment in the AB report

Before directly tackling the question of national treatment, the AB underlined that it was an important issue. The principle is seen as 'a cornerstone of the world trading system that is served by the WTO'.[8] Furthermore, the AB recalls that national treatment appears in Article 2(1) of the Paris Convention (1967) and in Article 3:1 of the TRIPS Agreement. Thus, that 'in drafting the TRIPS Agreement, the framers of the *WTO Agreement* saw fit to include an additional provision on national treatment'[9] which is

---

4 The US agreed with the EC on this point. See AB Report, para. 325.

5 For an analysis of this dispute, see R.L. Howse and D.J. Neven, 'United-States – Section 211 Omnibus Appropriation Act of 1998 (WT/DS176/AR/R; DSR 2002:11, 589, DSR 2002:II, 683): A comment', in H. Horn and P. C. Mavroidis (eds) *WTO Case Law: Legal and Economic Analysis*, Cambridge, Cambridge University Press, 2007, pp. 482–521.

6 For a presentation of the TRIPS Agreement, see T. Cottier, 'The Agreement on Trade-related Aspects of Intellectual Property Rights', in P.F.J. Macrory, A.E. Appleton and M.G. Plummer (eds) *The World Trade Organization: Legal, Economic and Political Analysis*, Vol. I, New York: Springer, 2005, pp. 1041–120.

7 For an overview of the TRIPS dispute, see C.M. Correa, 'The TRIPS Agreement and Developing Countries', in P.F.J. Macrory, A.E. Appleton and M.G. Plummer (eds), *The World Trade Organization: Legal, Economic and Political Analysis*, Vol. II, New York: Springer, 2005, pp. 417–55.

8 AB Report, para. 241.

9 AB Report, para. 240.

already taken into account within this text *via* the consideration of the Paris Convention (1967), is a clear indication of 'the fundamental significance of the obligation of national treatment . . . in the TRIPS Agreement'.[10]

National treatment as established in Article 3.1 of the TRIPS Agreement states that:

> Each Member shall accord to the nationals of other Members treatment no less favourable than that it accords to its own nationals with regard to the protection of intellectual property, subject to the exceptions already provided in, respectively, the Paris Convention (1967), the Berne Convention (1971), the Rome Convention or the Treaty on Intellectual Property in Respect of Integrated Circuits.

As noted by the AB, national treatment in the context of this dispute means that US regulation should afford to a foreign owner of intellectual property rights treatment no less favourable than that afforded to a US national. The obligations implied by national treatment can be presented both negatively and positively. The negative view sees national treatment as a non-discrimination norm.[11] Regulations that discriminate on the grounds of nationality are prohibited. The positive view of the principle is that compliance with national treatment allows a Member to develop internal regulations that are not protectionist.[12] National treatment, in particular, ensures that access to a given domestic market afforded to a foreign producer is not conditional on the internal regulation choice of his government.[13] These interpretations clearly show that national treatment does not require countries to adopt any particular regulatory regime.[14] It shall not be seen as a consequence as a vehicle for international harmonization of rules.[15] However, in applying national treatment, for

---

10 *Ibid.*

11 See M.J. Trebilcock and R. Howse, (2005) *The Regulation of International Trade*, 3rd edition, London and New York, Routledge.

12 See F. Roessler (1997), 'Diverging Domestic Policies and Multilateral Trade Integration', in J.N. Bhagwati and R.E. Hudec (eds), *Fair Trade and Harmonization: Prerequisites for free trade? Vol. 2: Legal Analysis*, Cambridge, MA, MIT Press, pp. 21–56.

13 This was very important in the dispute *European Communities – Protection of trademarks and geographical indications for agricultural products and foodstuffs*, opposing the EC with the US and Australia. See C. Charlier and M.A. Ngo (2007), 'An Analysis of the European Communities – Protection of Trademarks and Geographical Indications for Agricultural Products and Foodstuffs Dispute', *Journal of World Intellectual Property*, 10(3/4), 171–86.

14 This idea is underlined by the AB Report, para. 243.

15 See J. Bhagwati (1997), 'The Demands to Reduce Domestic Diversity among Trading Nations', in J.N. Bhagwati and R.E. Hudec (eds), *Fair Trade*

example, with respect to the intellectual property of other countries' nationals, a country will expect some reciprocity. Unilateral implementation of national treatment by any country could be seen as altruistic[16] since it affords foreign nationals the advantages of intellectual property rights protection in its territory, although its nationals do not receive similar advantages abroad. Reciprocal respect for national treatment therefore will be sought. As a result, the inscription of national treatment in Article 3:1 of the TRIPS Agreement shows that some kind of international harmonization of the rules (reciprocal respect for national treatment) is necessary for intellectual property protection. This reciprocity in national treatment should prevent situations where a country's regulation has a positive, but not reciprocal, externality for others.

To conclude, in national treatment there are two requisites. First, differences in the treatment given to national producers and that given to foreign producers have to be established. This is not sufficient, however, to conclude that national treatment has been infringed. The main problem then is to determine whether the delineated difference on treatment implies some discrimination incompatible with national treatment. As Trebilcock and Howse (2005)[17] note, this has the potential to raise significant interpretation issues, as illustrated by *US – Section 211 Appropriations Act*, where the Panel and the AB reached different conclusions in national treatment claims.

The issue of national treatment within the dispute *US – Section 211 Appropriations Act* is complicated from the outset. The AB report notes that the EC

> claims that Sections 211(a)(2) and (b) violate the national treatment obligation in both Article 2(1) of the Paris Convention (1967) and Article 3.1 of the TRIPS Agreement by treating non-United States nationals less favourably than United States nationals in *two different situations* to which the measure applies . . . . The EC contends that this discrimination occurs in *different ways in these two different situations*, but, in each situation, they see a violation of the fundamental obligation of national treatment.[18]

These two situations correspond to the cases of successors-in-interest to original owners and of original owners. These two cases are examined

---

Footnote 15 (*cont.*)
and Harmonization: Prerequisites for Free Trade? Vol. 1: Economic Analysis, Cambridge, MA, MIT Press, pp. 9–40.

[16] See S. Scotchmer (2004) 'The Political Economy of Intellectual Property Treaties', *Journal of Law, Economics, & Organization*, 20(2), 415–37.

[17] Op. cit. note 11.

[18] AB Report, para. 244. Emphasis added.

below, considering the claims of the parties, the ruling of the Panel and how the AB dealt with them.

1.1 The case of successors-in-interest to original owners

In order to reach the conclusion that Section 211 violates the national treatment obligation the EC had first to establish differences in the treatment given to nationals and that given to foreigners, and second, to show that this difference in treatment implies some discrimination incompatible with national treatment. It claimed first that Section 211(a)(2) is only relevant to Cuban nationals and other foreigners. Section 211(a)(2) impedes US courts' recognition of any rights based on registration of trademarks obtained through a licence from OFAC for a Cuban national or a foreign national who is a successor-in-interest to a designated national, whereas this limit would not apply to a US national successor-in-interest to a designated national in the same situation. The EC then claimed that this situation imposes burdens on Cubans and other foreign nationals that US nationals do not bear.

The US acknowledged the first part of the EC's claim, but claimed that such differential treatment in respect of intellectual property right protection is of little if any consequences for two reasons. First, the US pointed out that CACR prohibits US nationals from becoming successors-in-interest without a specific licence from OFAC. Second, it claimed that 'OFAC has never issued a specific licence to a US national for the purpose of becoming a successor-in-interest to trademarks that were used in connection with confiscated assets'.[19] In other words, the US acknowledges that OFAC has discretionary power to allow 'the national authority to act in a manner consistent with the WTO Agreement'[20] but that this power has never been used and there is no reason to believe that it would be used 'in a manner contrary to its international obligations'.[21] As a consequence, the US argued that Section 211 does not contradict national treatment.

The Panel considered that 'Such differential treatment in respect of intellectual property right protection could be considered to provide a less favourable treatment to nationals of other Members as it denies effective equality of opportunities to non-US nationals in the United States'.[22] Relying on two other disputes,[23] the Panel focused on the 'actual application' of this discretionary power by the US executive authority, and reached the same conclusion as the US. In so doing, the Panel distinguished

---

19 Panel Report, para. 8.134.
20 *Ibid.*
21 *Ibid.*
22 Panel Report, para. 8.133.
23 Panel Report, para. 8.136.

between two kinds of regulation: those that directly contradict WTO principles and those that give discretionary power to the executive authority of a Member, which, if exercised, would violate the Member's WTO obligations. It stated that only the former was contestable, since, as noted by the AB, 'it cannot be assumed that the WTO Member will fail to implement its obligations under the *WTO Agreement* in good faith'.[24] As a consequence of this analysis, the Panel concluded that Section 211(a)(2) was not inconsistent with national treatment, given that OFAC has never delivered a specific licence to allow any US national to become a successor-in-interest to a 'designated national'.

The AB reversed this conclusion. It agreed with the Panel's approach so far, but went further. For the AB, the opposition between legislation that is WTO-inconsistent and legislation giving discretionary power to the executive authority of a Member, does not exhaust the question of national treatment. When national treatment is at stake, the AB ruled that proof is needed that the discretionary authority given to the executive authority will not be exercised in any case. In reaching its conclusion, the AB pointed out that the US might be right to claim that the likelihood of a US national having a licence from OFAC to become successor-in-interest to a 'designated national' is minimal. But, the AB asserted that the US did not show that 'in every individual case the courts of the United States would not validate the assertion of rights by a successor-in-interest'.[25] As a consequence, whereas a US national faces possibly only one administrative hurdle to defend its rights (the limitation imposed by Section 515.201 of the CACR), a non-national of the US faces two (the former plus the limitation imposed by Section 211(a)(2)). The AB then relied on the Panel's finding in *US – Section 337*, according to which 'while the likelihood of having to defend imported products in two fora is small, the existence of the possibility is inherently less favourable than being faced with having to conduct a defence in only one of those fora'.[26] The AB consequently concluded that Section 211(a)(2) imposing an 'extra hurdle' only for non-US successors-in-interest violates national treatment.

1.2 The case of original owners

The EC argued that the original owner of US trademarks similar to a trademark used in connection with a business or assets that were confiscated

---

24 AB Report, para. 259.
25 AB Report, para. 267.
26 Panel Report, *US – Section 337*, para. 5.19.

in Cuba, who is a Cuban national, is subject to Sections 211(a)(2) and (b), whereas the original owner, who is a non-Cuban foreign national, is not. For the EC, this situation introduces discrimination in favour of US nationals against Cuban nationals, when both are original owners. In order to illustrate its claim, the EC took the following example:

> There are two separate owners who acquired rights, either at common law or based on registration, in two separate United States trademarks, before the Cuban confiscation occurred. Each of these two United States trademarks is the same, or substantially similar to, the signs or combination of signs of which a trademark registered in Cuba is composed. That same or similar Cuban trademark was used in connection with a business or assets that were confiscated in Cuba. Neither of the two original owners of the two United States trademarks was the owner of that same or similar trademark that was registered in Cuba. Those two original owners each seek to assert rights in the United States in their two respective United States trademarks. The situation of these two original owners of these two United States trademarks is identical in every relevant respect, but one. That one difference is this: one original owner is a national of Cuba, and the other original owner is a national of the United States.[27]

The AB observed that the discrimination pointed out by the EC exists because the limitations of Sections 211(a)(2) and (b) apply to the original owners, who are 'designated nationals' (here, Cuba and Cuban nationals for instance) and not to US national original owners. In order to contest this idea, the US produced a series of arguments aimed at demonstrating that Sections 211(a)(2) and (b) do not apply to a Cuban national who is an original owner of a US trademark. Every argument was refuted by the AB.[28]

The US alleged that Sections 211(a)(2) and (b) do not apply to Cuban nationals that are original owners because they have their own consent. The AB showed this situation might emerge, but does not encompass the entire range of possible situations. A Cuban original owner of a trademark in the US is not necessarily the same person as the original owner of the same Cuban trademark.[29] The US then claimed that because the Cuban original owners, in the situation depicted by the EC, registered

27 AB Report, para. 276.

28 The EC claimed before the Panel that Section 211 contradicts most-favoured-nation treatment. The Panel disagreed and the EC appealed against that finding. The allegations of the EC on most-favoured-nation treatment of original owners are the same as those on national treatment (AB Report, para. 305). The AB therefore developed a similar analysis and reached the conclusion that Section 211 contradicts most-favoured-nation treatment of the original owner.

29 AB Report, para. 282.

their trademark in the US before Section 515.527 of Title 31 CFR became effective, Section 211(a)(2) does not apply to them.[30] The AB pointed out that Section 211(a)(2) would, however, apply to them when they renewed the trademark registration. Furthermore, the AB remarked that this argument did not address the case where Cuban nationals are original owners of trademark rights in the US, based on common law rather than registration.[31]

The US then argued that the illustration given by the EC was not pertinent because the Cuban original owner would not in any case have been able to import the trademarked goods from Cuba. The AB retorted that it could import the goods from another country than Cuba under its trademark so that the ability to maintain its trademark is relevant.[32]

The US further argued that OFAC, under Section 515.505, automatically allows the Cuban original owner to be 'unblocked' and therefore to be treated as a US national. The AB stated that this argument was only valid for a Cuban owner living in the US. Cuban owners residing in an 'authorized trade territory' can apply to OFAC to be unblocked, but would face an additional administrative constraint incompatible with national treatment. Finally, Cuban owners living in Cuba cannot apply to be 'unblocked', a situation judged once again by the AB as violating national treatment obligation.

The US alleged that '*any* discrimination implicit in Sections 211(a)(2) and (b)' is offset by Section 515.201 of the CACR,[33] which sets out a list of prohibited transactions for a US original owner. This Section, as a consequence, would offset the less favourable treatment of the Cuban national original owner under Sections 211. Comparing the semantics of Sections 211 and Section 515.201 of the CACR, the AB disagreed with the US.

The last of the US claims referred to 'its longstanding doctrine of non-recognition of foreign confiscations'. The AB concluded that 'this policy could not possibly apply to trademarks that existed *in the United States* when a business or assets connected with a trademark composed of the same or substantially similar signs were confiscated *in Cuba*'.[34]

2. Analysis

The issue of national treatment in this dispute is interesting for several reasons. The first is that the conclusions of the Panel and the AB diverged

---

30 AB Report, para. 284.
31 AB Report, para. 283.
32 AB Report, para. 285.
33 AB Report, para. 291 (emphasis in original).
34 AB Report, para. 295.

on the issue, within a dispute where almost every other of the Panel's conclusions was upheld by the AB. The second is the fact that within the most-favoured-nation obligation, national treatment is one of the cornerstones of the multilateral trading system. Another reason can be found in the impressive list of arguments developed by the US in order to defend its stand. This shows the importance that the US assigns to a request from the DSB to bring US regulation into conformity with the obligations of that country under the TRIPS Agreement, even though neither the CACR nor the Trading with the Enemy Act were being challenged. Finally, we can derive some interesting conclusions concerning the issue of international harmonization of national regulations from the AB's analysis of national treatment in this dispute. We focus on these in the rest of this chapter.

The issue of international harmonization was not directly raised by the parties in *US – Section 211 Appropriations Act,* but was included in the rulings of the Panel and the AB at two different points in the national treatment judgment. The AB referred to it implicitly in its consideration of one of the arguments of the US in the case of original owners. Both the Panel and the AB referred to it indirectly in the case of successors-in-interest to original owners.

2.1 National treatment and unilateralism

One of the stakes in dispute in *US – Section 211 Appropriations Act* was perhaps US unilateralism,[35] where legislation imposing economic sanctions for foreign policy reasons would have come under scrutiny. However, the EC did not make any claims in that area and therefore neither the Panel nor the AB was asked to rule directly, for example, on the legality of the Trading with the Enemy Act.

The issue is implicitly considered in the ruling of the AB over the arguments proposed by the US in defending its legislation in the national treatment claim in the case of the trademark original owners. As we saw above, the US allegation used to defend its legislation in that case was that OFAC under Section 515.05 automatically allows Cuban original owners of trademarks to be 'unblocked' and treated as US nationals. The AB disagreed with this allegation and showed that Cuban owners residing in Cuba are not covered by this disposition and cannot apply to OFAC to be unblocked since they do not reside in an 'authorized trade territory'. The isolation policy within this legislation impeding Cuban original owners living in Cuba to register their trademarks and to defend

[35] See B.E. Carter (2008), *International Economic Sanction: Improving the Haphazard U.S. Legal Regime*, Cambridge, Cambridge University Press.

their intellectual property rights is considered by the AB, therefore, as contradicting national treatment even though this policy was not considered directly by the AB.

2.2 The distinction between mandatory and discretionary legislations

The ruling on national treatment in the case of successors-in-interest to original owners does not question unilateralism, but rather the degree of freedom of a Member State when choosing a legislation that potentially discriminates on the basis of nationality. In order to reject the EC's claim about national treatment in that case, the Panel relied on the Report of the Panel in *US Measures Affecting the Importation, Internal Sale and Use of Tobacco* and on the AB Report in *US – Anti-dumping Act of 1916*. Both these reports tackle the question of determining factors in the contestability of a national regulation under the GATT/WTO framework. They distinguish the case where a legislation *as such* is inconsistent with GATT (1947) and WTO obligations, from the case where a *specific application* of the concerned legislation is inconsistent with GATT (1947) and WTO obligations. Within this distinction, legislations that 'mandate' action inconsistent with GATT and WTO obligations (called *mandatory legislation* as a consequence) can be challenged, whereas legislations which give 'discretion' to the executive authority of a Member State to act in contradiction of its GATT/WTO obligations (called *discretionary legislation* as a consequence) cannot be challenged. In the latter case, only a specific application of the legislation by the executive authority contradicting a GATT/WTO obligation can be contested.

The 'logic' of this distinction is straightforward: the effective contradiction of a GATT/WTO obligation is the only trigger for a challenge to national regulation under the GATT/WTO framework. In the *mandatory legislation* case, the legislation is in direct contradiction to WTO principles and therefore is contestable. In the *discretionary legislation* case, the legislation is not directly in contradiction with GATT/WTO obligations and cannot therefore be deemed contestable.

This distinction between *mandatory legislation* and *discretionary legislation* may seem odd, since it could be seen as inviting Member States to play 'cat and mouse'.[36] What is the interest to an executive authority of a legislation that allows a certain type of behaviour which if exercised, can be

[36] This distinction between mandatory and discretionary legislations was made under GATT and continues to be relevant under the WTO. See S. Bhuiyan (2002), 'Mandatory and Discretionary Legislation: The Continued Relevance of the Distinction under the WTO', *Journal of International Economic Law*, 5(3), 571–604.

challenged under the WTO? We can give an answer based on international harmonization of rules. From this perspective, the main advantage for a Member State in distinguishing between mandatory and discretionary legislation is to push, as far as possible, the idea of a discretionary choice of a national legislation without questioning WTO obligations.

Interestingly, national treatment can also be considered by making reference to the international harmonization of national regulations. Positively interpreted, it allows a national regulation to depart from an international standard as long as this introduces no less favourable treatment of foreign nationals. National treatment therefore allows the idea of a discretionary choice of national regulation compatible with the non-discrimination WTO obligation, to be pushed to the limits. This 'fundamental principle of the world trading system', as the AB calls it in *US – Section 211 Appropriations Act*, is a real safeguard against behaviour discriminating on the grounds of nationality. As a consequence, applying the distinction between *mandatory* and *discretionary* legislations to situations relevant to national treatment creates the risk of jeopardizing this fundamental safeguard. The contradictory conclusions of the Panel and the AB in *US – Section 211 Appropriations Act* clearly demonstrate this result when intellectual property is considered.

The Panel in *US – Section 211 Appropriations Act* used the distinction between *mandatory* and *discretionary* legislation to refute the EC's claim that Section 211(a)(2) was incompatible with the WTO principle of national treatment when the case of successors-in-interest to original owners is considered. Section 211(a)(2) impedes US courts from recognizing any rights based on registration of trademarks obtained through a licence from OFAC for a foreign national who is a successor-in-interest to a designated national, whereas this limit does not apply to a US national successor-in-interest in a similar situation. The US argued that the CACR prohibits US nationals from becoming successors-in-interest without obtaining a specific licence from OFAC. The practice of OFAC refusing to issue specific licences to US nationals in this case would therefore counter the discrimination introduced. Here lies the *discretionary legislation*, since there is nothing to oblige OFAC to behave in this way. According to the Panel, the distinction between mandatory and discretionary legislation is relevant here in order that the practice of OFAC can be seen as a counterforce to the discrimination introduced by Section 211(a)(2).

The AB agreed with the approach developed by the Panel, but pointed out that it did not exhaust the subject of national treatment. For the AB, the procedures implemented by the US legislation place foreign nationals in a less favourable position than US nationals. Where US nationals face only one administrative constraint to defence of their intellectual property rights, foreign nationals face two. The AB concluded, therefore, that Section 211(a)(2) contradicts national treatment.

Comparison of the approaches of the Panel and of the AB reveals two conceptions of what should be the 'matter for' national treatment. Relying on the distinction between mandatory and discretionary legislations, the Panel linked national treatment with what we previously termed the 'logic of this distinction', that is to say, with the '*effective* contradiction' of the WTO standard of non-discrimination. Because this contradiction had never appeared in US practice and there was no reason to believe that it would ever appear, national treatment was not contradicted for the Panel. In going further, and considering procedural matters, the AB departed from this view and considered not only the effective but also the *potential* contradiction of the norm of non-discrimination. What is important for the AB is that both US and foreign nationals would face the same administrative hurdle if they wanted to defend their intellectual property rights in the situation depicted. In embracing both *effective* and *potential* contradiction of the norm of non-discrimination, national treatment, in the field of international harmonization of regulations, appears more constraining than the distinction between *mandatory* and *discretionary* legislations.

3. Conclusion

In its concluding remarks, the AB expressed the view that 'the validity of the expropriation of intellectual or any other property rights without compensation by a WTO Member within its own territory is not before us',[37] but at the same time underlined that

> where a WTO Member chooses not to recognize intellectual property rights in its own territory relating to a confiscation of rights in another territory, a measure resulting from and implementing that choice must, if it affects other WTO Members, comply with the *TRIPS Agreement*, by which all WTO Members are voluntarily bound. In such a measure, that WTO Member must accord 'no less favourable treatment' to the nationals of all other WTO Members than it accords to its own nationals, and must grant to the nationals of all other WTO Members 'any advantage, favour, privilege or immunity' granted to any other WTO Member.[38]

The US policy of unilateralism, therefore, was not judged in substance. Tackling national treatment using a procedural argument (the extra administrative hurdle claim), the AB indirectly contradicted this policy. Not surprisingly, therefore, the US could not change its legislation. The

[37] AB Report, para. 362.
[38] AB Report, para. 363.

DSB adopted the Report of the AB on February 2002, requesting the US to bring its legislation into conformity with its obligations regarding the protection of intellectual property. The reasonable period of time for implementing the required legislative changes has been deferred several times and the US still has to adopt implementing measures.

Index